Passages from the Life
of a Philosopher

CHARLES BABBAGE

Passages from the Life
of a Philosopher

EDITED, WITH A NEW INTRODUCTION, BY

MARTIN CAMPBELL-KELLY

RUTGERS

RUTGERS UNIVERSITY PRESS
NEW BRUNSWICK, NEW JERSEY

IEEE PRESS
PISCATAWAY, NEW JERSEY

First published in the United States of America by

Rutgers University Press and IEEE Press, 1994

This edition first published in the United Kingdom and Europe by

Pickering & Chatto (Publishers) Limited, 1994

Library of Congress Cataloging-in-Publication Data
Babbage, Charles, 1791–1871.
   [Passages from the life of a philosopher]
   Charles Babbage : passages from the life of a philosopher / edited by
Martin Campbell-Kelly.
     p.   c.m.
   Originally published: Passages from the life of a philosopher.
1864.
   Includes bibliographical references.
   ISBN 0–8135–2066–5 (pbk.)
   1. Babbage, Charles, 1791–1871.   2. Mathematicians—England—
Biography.   I. Campbell-Kelly, Martin.   II. Title.
QA29.B2A3   1994
510′.92—dc20
[B]   93–43903
                                                CIP

Printed and bound in Great Britain by
Redwood Books
Trowbridge

CONTENTS

INTRODUCTION

Mr. Babbage
Lived entirely on cabbage.
He used his head, rather than his thumbs
In inventing his machine for doing sums.

E. Clerihew Bentley and
Maurice Solomon, *c.* 1893[a]

CHARLES BABBAGE (1791–1871) was a man of contradictions, both in terms of his character and his intellectual achievements. This makes it difficult – especially for the twentieth-century reader – to grasp the dimensions of his elusive personality and wide-ranging intellect. Babbage was notorious for his irascibility; but he was also a sociable and charming man who 'brought brilliance and radiance to every gathering'.[b] On occasions, he showed an almost brutal disregard for the sensibilities of his peers; and yet his correspondence reveals many instances of his gracious treatment and kindnesses to private individuals. In his intellectual life Babbage displayed an enormous capacity for taking pains and often demonstrated real genius; yet these high points have to be contrasted with much pedestrian work of no real importance.

Today, Babbage is celebrated as the 'pioneer of the computer'. Indeed, were it not for the enormous importance of computing in the second half of the twentieth century, he would today be regarded as little more than the footnote in history he was until recent times. But the perception of Babbage as primarily an inventor of computers is misleading, for he was a considerable polymath, even by the standards of his day. Modern Babbage scholarship has thrown much light on his calculating engines, but only in the last decade or two has it begun to illuminate his full intellectual range.

---

[a] E. Clerihew Bentley *et al, The first clerihews* (Oxford, 1982).
[b] E. Healy, *Lady unknown: the life of Angela Burdett-Coutts* (London, 1978), p. 60.

It is impossible to separate Babbage's personality from his intellectual life. If hc had been less obsessive, less radical, and more open to suggestion then his work would have been more readily accepted; but it would also have been less original, and much less interesting. Although there have been several biographies of Babbage, none of them have been wholly successful in capturing his multi-faceted persona. Thus, for all its idiosyncrasies – indeed *because* of its idiosyncrasies – there is no more revealing guide to Babbage than his own *Passages from the life of a philosopher*.

Passages is a long, rambling, entertaining, and only occasionally chronological, account of his life and work. Although never a sparkling writer, Babbage had a vigorous prose style which ensures that, well over a century after its original publication, *Passages* will carry the reader along on a stream of vivid anecdotes and miscellanea. Babbage declined to call *Passages* an autobiography, stating that he had 'no desire to write my own biography, as long as I have strength and means to do better work'. But in fact, when Babbage wrote this in the Preface to *Passages*, he was in his early seventies; his best work lay long in the past and throughout the book the latent frustration and disappointment of a man who had failed to realize his full potential is never far below the surface.

During his life Babbage published six full-length monographs and 86 papers. He was happy to be judged by his printed works which he considered 'formed the best life of an author' and on several occasions he published a list of his writings. The last of these lists appeared as an appendix to *Passages*, and is reproduced in this edition in facsimile (on pp. 372–5). In 1989, the complete *Works of Babbage* was published in eleven volumes under my editorship.[a] Shortly after publication of the *Works* I was asked if there was any single passage in the *œuvres* which captured the essential Babbage. I had never given the question any thought before, but I had no hesitation in singling out Babbage's description of a visit to a knacker's yard at Montfaucon, near Paris, which he recorded in the last edition of his most famous book, the *Economy of machinery and manufactures*, in 1835. In this account Babbage described in gruesome detail the disembodiment of a worn-out horse into its dozen or so by-products. These included hair from the mane used by upholsterers,

---

[a] M. Campbell-Kelly, ed., *The Works of Charles Babbage*, 11 vols (London and New York, 1989).

the skin made into leather by tanners, flesh used by the animal-meat trade, fat used by soap-makers, bones used by glue-makers and cutlers, and so on. But Babbage did not stop there; he continued:

> Even the maggots, which are produced in great numbers in the refuse, are not lost. Small pieces of the horse flesh are piled up, about half a foot high; and being covered slightly with straw to protect them from the sun, soon allure the flies, which deposit their eggs in them. In a few days the putrid flesh is converted into a living mass of maggots. These are sold by measure; some are used for bait in fishing, but the greater part as food for fowls, and especially for pheasants. One horse yields maggots which sell for about 1s. 5d.
>
> The rats which frequent these establishments are innumerable, and they have been turned to profit by the proprietors. The fresh carcass of a horse is placed at night in a room, which has a number of openings near the floor. The rats are attracted into it, and the openings then closed. 16,000 rats were killed in one room in four weeks, without any perceptible diminution of their number. The furriers puchase the rat skins at about 3s. the hundred.[a]

As a result, the dead horse 'which can be purchased at from 8s. 6d. to 12s., produces from £2 9s. to £4 14s'.

What does this passage tell us about Babbage? First, it reveals a passion for field research that set Babbage apart from most of his peers. While industrial observation was a common pursuit for journalists and practical engineers of the period, Babbage's observations were always at a much higher level than mere fact-gathering; he provided an insight that came from an extensive reading of the scientific and economic literature of the day. It took a rare talent to marry the practical observation of a slaughter-house with economic theory in order to wring out one further by-product from a dead horse: namely an unforgettable 'illustration of the profitable conversion of substances apparently of little value'.

Secondly, Babbage's decomposition of the dead horse into its components illustrates a view of the structure of knowledge that was common in his time, and which was typified by the 'dissections' practised in hospitals, botanic gardens etc., and by the classifications of objects from the natural and man-made worlds in museums. In effect, Babbage gives us an analytical, economic deconstruction of

---

[a] C. Babbage, *Economy of machinery and manufactures*, *Works of Babbage*, Vol. 8, pp. 10–11.

the carcass. Such analytical approaches were the mainstay of British science until after mid-century, when experimentalism came to dominate the ideology of science.[a] While Babbage was a capable experimentalist, analysis was his accustomed mode – whether studying machines or economics, or pursuing mathematics. Thus, while Babbage was undoubtedly a considerable polymath, one must temper admiration for his range by the fact that he tended to choose problems that yielded to systematic analysis. And while Babbage may *seem* a man ahead of his time because of his computers, this is misleading – his way of thinking was fundamentally rooted in the early decades of the nineteenth century, and much of his later work has an old-fashioned tone.

Thirdly, it is revealing that the description of the slaughter-house was actually inserted into the fourth edition of the *Economy* as an addition at the end of the book when it had already been typeset. It was typical of Babbage that he could not resist gilding the lily by piling one more anecdote into a book already teeming with pithy examples. He had much the same problem with *Passages* 'adding story after story until friends feared it would never be finished'.[b] And of course the same tendency affected Babbage's engines, whose design he was temperamentally incapable of freezing and committing to brass-work.

Finally, the slaughter-house visit illustrates Babbage's lack of pretension and condescension. He had an ability – quite literally – to deal on equal terms with people from the lowest ranks of the social scale up to the most elevated. In the Preface to *Passages* he wrote 'I thought it might be rendered less unpalatable by relating some of my experience amongst various classes of society, widely differing from each other, in which I have occasionally mixed'. Thus, above all, *Passages* is a collection of anecdotes about Babbage's friendships and enmities, furnished with many 'illustrations of human character'. But the character most clearly illustrated is Babbage's own.

CHARLES BABBAGE was born in London on Boxing Day, 26 December 1791. He was the eldest child of Benjamin Babbage, a wealthy banker, and his wife Elizabeth. The Babbages were from old

---

[a] J. V. Pickstone, 'Ways of knowing: towards a historical sociology of science, technology and medicine', *British journal for the history of science*, Vol. 26 (1993), pp. 433–58.
[b] A. Hyman, *Charles Babbage: pioneer of the computer* (Oxford, 1982), p. 248.

Devonshire families, and Charles spent his childhood in Totnes, Devon, where today he is celebrated as one of the town's most famous sons, and is commemorated in the Totnes Museum.

Babbage's early education was haphazard. He was taught first at a small school near Exeter, Devon, and then at another near Enfield, Middlesex (where he came to know, as a boy, the novelist Captain Frederick Marryat, 1792–1848). He was then sent to a clergyman-tutor in Cambridge – from whom he learned very little – before returning to the West Country to be educated at Totnes Grammar School. Finally, he studied classics under an Oxford tutor before going up to Trinity College, Cambridge University.

Although Babbage's formal education was chequered, he was self-taught in mathematics to a remarkable degree, having read widely from both British and Continental authors. In 1810, when Babbage entered Cambridge University, mathematics was not perceived foremost as a research topic, but rather as a 'training of the mind' for future clergymen, lawyers, and gentlemen of learning. Mathematics dominated the curriculum, but the emphasis was on intensive coaching to solve standard problems in the end-of-year examinations.[a] Although these problems were often extremely difficult, they had no intrinsic value other than to hone mental agility. This activity was not to Babbage's taste, so that he withdrew from the formal curriculum and pursued his own mathematical agenda. This included the formation of the Analytical Society with his friends John F. W. Herschel (1792–1871) and George Peacock (1791–1858).[b]

The Analytical Society was established for the advancement of mathematics at Cambridge, and one of the prime objectives was to liberate the study of the calculus at the University from the archaic notation of Newton to the more productive notation of Leibniz used in Continental Europe. (In Britain at this time, the first differential of x with respect to t, for example, was represented by $\dot{x}$ in Newton's notation, instead of dx/dt in the now almost universal Leibniz notation.) This campaign Babbage called 'The Principles of pure D-ism in opposition to the Dot-age of the University' (p. 21). Here, he demonstrated a not

---

[a] J. M. Dubbey, *The mathematical work of Charles Babbage* (Cambridge, 1978). T. W. Heyck, *The transformation of intellectual life in Victorian England* (London, 1982), chapter 3.

[b] M. V. Wilkes, 'Herschel, Peacock, Babbage and the development of the Cambridge curriculum', *Notes and records*, Vol. 44 (1990), pp. 205–19.

11

always fastidious taste for puns which regularly punctuate the pages of *Passages*.

Babbage had an intuitive understanding of the importance of notation and rightly perceived that mathematical analysis at Cambridge would never take off until a satisfactory notation was employed.[a] This aim was eventually achieved, partly through translating the French mathematician Lacroix' *Differential and integral calculus* into English in 1816, followed by a textbook of examples in 1820; and partly by converts rising to positions in Cambridge where they were able to set the examinations (and hence prescribe the notation). But it is also fair to say that the Analytical Society came into existence at a moment when Cambridge was 'ripe for change', and to some extent the Society was pushing at an open door.[b] But victory was not achieved until long after Babbage had gone down from Cambridge, which he did in 1814, receiving his M.A. in 1817. This early lesson on the importance of notation was never far from Babbage's mind, and it underpinned much of his work on mathematics and the calculating engines.

In his last year at Cambridge, Babbage became engaged to Georgiana Whitmore, the daughter of another Devonshire family. They were married in summer 1814, and after a short period in the West Country, made their permanent home in London. With a modest allowance from his father, and his wife's own small income, Babbage settled down to the comfortable life of a gentleman philosopher in Regency London. He quickly made his mark on the scientific scene, giving a series of popular lectures on astronomy to the Royal Institution during 1815. In spring 1816 he was elected a member of the Royal Society. For the next several years, Babbage's researches were almost exclusively mathematical. He published more than a dozen mathematical papers, several of which were technically first-rate, but none of them were of permanent importance. After the early 1820s he made few further mathematical contributions as his interests became ever widening, and the calculating engines consumed more of his time.

Passages is completely silent on Babbage's domestic life, for which we must turn to his modern biographers. Georgiana bore him his first

---

[a] I. Grattan-Guinness, 'Charles Babbage as an algorithmic thinker', *Annals of the history of computing*, Vol. 14 (1992), pp. 34–48.

[b] Wilkes, op. cit., p. 207.

son in 1815, the first of at least eight children, of whom only three survived to maturity. The Babbages led the gregarious social life of a leisured upper-class family. There were regular visits to friends in the country and family visits to Devonshire. And in the season, their home was the venue for some of London's more sought-after soirées. But there was a darker side to Babbage, and it was at about this time that his character began to harden: Carlyle, perhaps the greatest literary portrait painter of his age, wrote in a private letter in 1820 'Babbage continues eminently unpleasant to me, with his frog mouth and viper eyes, with his hide-bound, wooden irony, and the acridest egotism looking through it'.[a]

In 1819 Babbage made the first of several visits to France, on this occasion accompanied by his friend John Herschel. In France they met several of the senior French academicians including Fourier, Laplace, Arago and Biot – of whom Babbage relates many anecdotes in chapter 14 of *Passages*.

It was probably during this visit to France that Babbage first learned of the great French table-making project, the *Tables du Cadastre* (the tables for the French ordnance survey), which had been supervised in the 1790s by the eminent civil engineer Baron Gaspard Clair François Marie Riche de Prony (1755–1839). De Prony had been commissioned to produce a definitive set of logarithmic and trigonometrical tables for the newly introduced metric system. The operation was organized by de Prony according to Adam Smith's principles of the division of labour set forth in his *Wealth of nations* (1776). The project made use of two small élite planning and executive staffs, which oversaw the work of between 60 and 80 human 'computers', who used the standard table-making technique known as the method of differences. The human computers needed to be capable only of the elementary operations of addition and subtraction, and generally had only a minimal education. Many of the workers were redeployed hairdressers, who had been made redundant in the new republic – the hair styles of the aristocracy being 'one of the most hated symbols of the ancien régime'.[b]

Babbage was very struck by the tables project, and he later used it

---

[a] C. R. Saunders, *Carlyle's friendships and other studies* (Durham, N.C., 1977), p. 14.

[b] I. Grattan-Guinness, 'Work for the hairdressers: the production of de Prony's logarithmic and trigonometric tables', *Annals of the history of computing*, Vol. 12 (1990), pp. 177–85.

as the prime example of 'the division of mental labour' in the *Economy of manufactures*. More importantly, it planted a seed in his mind that would shortly flower as the Difference Engine – a machine that would effectively mechanize what de Prony had achieved using people. Babbage is inconsistent in his explanations of the invention of the Difference Engine. As he tells the story in *Passages*:

> One evening I was sitting in the rooms of the Analytical Society, at Cambridge, my head leaning forward on the table in a kind of dreamy mood, with a table of logarithms lying open before me. Another member, coming into the room, and seeing me half asleep, called out, 'Well, Babbage, what are you dreaming about?' to which I replied, 'I am thinking that all these tables (pointing to the logarithms) might be calculated by machinery.' (pp. 30–1)

Although this is a charming anecdote, very likely it was the figment of the imagination; nowhere in *Passages* should one place too much credence on precise historical veracity. Writing in 1822, much closer to the event, Babbage attributed the idea of the Difference Engine to working on a set of astronomical tables with John Herschel in 1820 when:

> In the course of our conversations on this subject it was suggested by one of us, in a manner which certainly at the time was not altogether serious, that it would be extremely convenient if a steam-engine could be contrived to execute calculations for us; to which it was replied that such a thing was quite possible, a sentiment in which we both entirely concurred and here the conversation terminated.[a]

Shortly after this incident, Babbage evolved the concept of the Difference Engine. This machine would use the method of differences to produce, automatically, completely accurate mathematical tables. Of course, the idea of a mechanical calculator was not new at this time: there were antecedents from the times of Pascal and Leibniz, and indeed 1820 saw the invention of the Thomas de Colmar Arithmometer that would (much later) become a commercially available device manufactured by the thousand.[b] However, Babbage proposed something quite different to an ordinary calculating machine. First,

---

[a] C. Babbage, 'The science of number reduced to mechanism' (1822), *Works of Babbage*, Vol. 2, pp. 15–32.

[b] M. R. Williams, *A history of computing technology* (Englewood Cliffs, N.J., 1985).

the Difference Engine would be *autonomous*: once set up, the machine would continue to churn out results as long as the operator turned the handle. Second, the results would be *printed*: this would obviate one of the main sources of error in table making – namely type-setting errors.

The method of differences and the operation of the Difference Engine are too detailed to attempt a didactic explanation here. In any case, we have in *Passages* Babbage's own diverting explanation (pp. 35–42), where he simultaneously elucidates and obscures his description by appealing to analogies such as the tariff of a butcher's shop, and 'a boy playing with his marbles, or a young lady with the balls of her solitaire board'.

In its autonomous action and printing capability, it is difficult to overstate how far the Difference Engine was ahead of the contemporary art in calculating machinery. In 1822, Babbage announced his invention in an open letter to Sir Humphrey Davy, President of the Royal Society.[a] In the letter Babbage argued that the real utility of his engine would lie in producing error free nautical tables for the Board of Longitude and other tables normally produced with 'intolerable labour and fatiguing monotony'. The letter was to be instrumental in gaining government support for the project. In early 1824 he was awarded, for the invention of the Difference Engine, the gold medal of the Astronomical Society, an organization he had helped found in 1820.

Although Babbage never published a contemporary account of the Difference Engine, he did encourage others to do so – notably his friend and mentor, the stockbroker and scientist Francis Baily FRS (1774–1844), and the science popularizer Dionysius Lardner (1793–1859).[b] Babbage's only published account of the Difference Engine appeared as chapter 5 of *Passages*; although it adds almost nothing to the much earlier accounts written by others, it is important as Babbage's first-hand description.

For the next decade the construction of the Difference Engine was central to Babbage's scientific life. However, the engine by no means

---

[a] C. Babbage, 'A letter to Sir Humphrey Davy . . .' (1822), *Works of Babbage*, Vol. 2, pp. 5–14.

[b] F. Baily, 'On Mr Babbage's new machine for calculating and printing mathematical and astronomical tables' (1823), *Works of Babbage*, Vol. 2, pp. 44–56. D. Lardner, 'Babbage's calculating engine' (1834), *Works of Babbage*, Vol. 2, pp. 118–86.

consumed all of his energies and this decade was comfortably the most productive period of his life. It culminated in the publication of the *Economy of manufactures* in 1832, and the invention of the Analytical Engine the following year – the two works on which his modern reputation stands.

One of Babbage's more intriguing endeavours during this period was his one attempt at forging a career in commerce – in the life assurance business – during 1824–5.[a] In 1824 Babbage was asked to become actuary of a newly promoted joint-stock company, the Protector Life Assurance Company of London. Babbage was tempted: now in his early thirties, he had increasing family commitments which were beginning to put a strain on his income. He was encouraged by his friend Francis Baily – himself a former actuary – to accept the offer. It was a lucrative opportunity that promised a total income in excess of £2500 – several times the allowance grudgingly given him by his father. To set the Protector in context, the period 1823–5 was one of wild financial speculation in which many life assurance companies were organized, more than doubling the total number of British life offices to over fifty. Established actuaries for the newly promoted life assurance companies were in short supply and besides Babbage, a number of his contemporaries were drawn into the business – including Benjamin Gompertz FRS, Griffith Davis, and Thomas Young FRS.

Characteristically, Babbage began his insurance career by first making an analysis of the existing insurance companies and devising a new set of life tables, which he considered reflected the mortality of the insured population better than the existing tables. The Protector was due to open in the summer of 1824, but never did – probably due to a dispute over policy between Babbage and some of his directors. The whole episode only occupied three months of Babbage's life, but he put his newly acquired knowledge to good use by publishing a slim volume, the *Assurance of lives*, in 1826. It was not a very good book, but it had the fortune to be translated into German at a time when the German life assurance industry was virtually non-existent, and Babbage's mortality table (which was also not very good) was adopted by the Life Assurance Bank of Gotha. Babbage never appreciated the degree that luck had played in giving his book such an influence over

---

[a] M. Campbell-Kelly, 'Charles Babbage and the assurance of lives', *Annals of the history of computing*, forthcoming.

the German life assurance industry, and *Passages* (pp. 356–8) reveals his inflated sense of his own importance in the affair. This account has been taken at face value by some of Babbage's less critical obituarists and biographers, and given him an undeserved reputation as a pioneer of life assurance.

Babbage's father was well pleased by the *Assurance of lives*, but if he had hoped that it would lead to a remunerative commercial career for his son instead of his scientific dabbling, then he was doomed to disappointment. Apart from a brief appearance at a Parliamentary Select Committee on Friendly Societies in 1827, at which Babbage failed to distinguish himself, he had no further contact either with commerce or life assurance.

The life assurance episode illustrates Babbage's ability to bring his analytical technique to bear on a new field quite effortlessly. But it was only one of a wide range of activities that occupied him in the 1820s. He was an active experimentalist, conducting experiments in magnetism and making barometric observations. He investigated inventions such as micrometers and diving bells. He made statistical enquiries, wrote on mathematical notation, and did much more that was never published. These were mostly dilettantish efforts, but he did publish in 1827 what was for at least half a century widely regarded as the definitive *Table of logarithms*.[a] He also made extensive tours of industrial Britain, and in 1826 and 1828 made further Continental tours. On these tours he was always on the look-out for examples to serve as illustrations for his *Economy of manufactures*; and he was always seeking out mechanical inventions that he could put to use in the Difference Engine.

Babbage's father died in early 1827, leaving him the bulk of his estate which made him a moderately wealthy man and financially independent. Later the same year tragedy struck with the death of his wife Georgiana, which left him desolate. Babbage filled the void in his life with a year of travel in which he toured the Continent.

During the 1820s Babbage's scientific reputation steadily rose, and in 1826 he put himself forward for the Lucasian Chair at Cambridge which had just become vacant. At that time, there were more favoured candidates than Babbage competing for the Chair, but the best of them withdrew for different reasons, and in 1828 – while he

---

[a] M. Campbell-Kelly, 'Charles Babbage's table of logarithms (1827)', *Annals of the history of computing*, Vol. 10 (1988), pp. 159–69.

was away on his Continental tour – Babbage learned that he had been elected.[a] Although the emolument of the position was small (Babbage says £80–90 a year in *Passages*, p. 24), it made up for this in prestige. The Chair, once held by Newton, was the most desirable in England for a mathematician, and it confirmed Babbage's place in the front rank of British science. It was the only paid position he ever accepted, although he treated it as a sinecure, and never took up residence in Cambridge; nor had he given a single lecture by the time he resigned in 1839.

While on his trip to the Continent, Babbage attended the Great Congress of Philosophers in Berlin, September 1828. He was deeply impressed by the professional organization of and high public interest in science on the Continent compared with the amateurism of the Royal Society in England, and he warmly recounted the details of his visit in *Passages* (pp. 148–9). It was partly as a result of his attendance at the Congress that in 1830 he published his most famous polemic, the *Decline of science in England*. This book was a trenchant attack on the organization of British science in general and the Royal Society in particular. Described as a 'growling, complaining, but wide-ranging book', the *Decline of science* was a milepost in the reform of science in England.[b] Unfortunately the book was marred by a critical tone that often descended to personal attacks. For example, he was highly disparaging of Sir Humphrey Davy and other leading lights of the Royal Society (and he could not resist raking over the embers in *Passages*, chapter 13). Babbage's complaints against the Royal Society were partly about its institutional failings, which were fully justified, but he also had personal grievances. The deepest of these was that the Society had failed to confer its Royal Medal on him in 1826 for his invention of the Mechanical Notation.

The Mechanical Notation, which was a direct outgrowth of his earlier absorption with mathematical notation, was a means of describing any mechanical apparatus. It used a lettering convention to label the fixed and moving parts of a machine, and a system of notations to describe the relative motions and timings of the parts. The Mechanical Notation was very useful to Babbage in the complex

[a] Wilkes, op. cit., pp. 210-12.
[b] J. Morrell and A. Thackray, *Gentlemen of science* (Oxford, 1981), p. 47.

design of the Difference Engine. Yet despite his personal conviction of the importance of the Mechanical Notation, it had almost no impact on contemporary mechanical engineering. In *Passages* he even took to task the author of a textbook written in 1860 stating:

> I have not been able to find in it a single word concerning 'Mechanical Notation', not even the very simplest portion of that science, namely, the art of lettering drawings. It would seem impossible that any *Professor* of so limited a subject could be ignorant of the existence of such an important addition to its powers. (p. 112)

Even at this late date, Babbage could not accept that the Mechanical Notation had been largely without influence, and his failure to win the Royal Medal still rankled.

Babbage's reforming spirit was not confined to the world of science. He was caught up in the Reform Movement and became active in liberal politics from 1829. After the passing of the Reform Bill in 1832 and the subsequent dissolution of Parliament, Babbage was invited to contest the newly created constituency of Finsbury in London. He was not elected, but the experience left him with a fund of anecdotes that were the basis of chapter 21 of *Passages*, 'Electioneering experience' – and the following chapter, which is a rather clumsy parody of how Babbage (alias Mr Turnstile MP) imagined life might have been had he been elected. Babbage scholarship has a long way to go towards getting a complete picture of his political activity; although Babbage states in the Turnstile parody that 'the dramatis personae ... are living characters not unknown in the fashionable and political circles' (p. 218), no one has yet succeeded in putting a name to all of them. However, as it stands the 'squib' is very revealing of Babbage's liberal leanings and his deep cynicism at the outcome of the Reform Bill. In 1833, Babbage's reformist aspirations met more tangible success when he was one of the founders of the British Association for the Advancement of Science, which was to prove a major instrument for scientific reform in England.

On quite a different plane to the polemical *Decline of Science* and his electioneering manifestos, Babbage's *Economy of manufactures* was an acknowledged masterpiece of his own time. A 'brilliant and utterly original foray into political economy', the *Economy of manufactures* was published in four editions and translated into six different languages between 1832 and 1835.[a] Although in the late twentieth century, Babbage is celebrated as the pioneer of the computer, for his contemporaries, his reputation rested as least as much on the *Economy of manufactures*.

The book was in large part the outcome of Babbage's observations of manufacturing industry and practical mechanics during the 1820s. In his tours of England and on the Continent he always took the opportunity to seek out local workshops and factories, and to interview both owners and hands. His knowledge of the myriad details of arts and manufactures soon became encyclopaedic, and his initial aim was to consolidate this knowledge into a work that would be accessible to both manufacturers and artisans. His earliest treatment of the topic appeared as a lengthy article in the *Encyclopaedia metropolitana* – a popular encyclopaedia of arts and manufactures – in 1829. This article was then developed into a full-length book in 1832. Babbage's *Economy of machinery and manufactures* fitted well into the rapidly growing contemporary popular literature on manufacturing and machinery. This genre included the numerous mechanics' magazines, as well as books such as Andrew Ure's *Philosophy of manufactures* (1835), Peter Gaskell's *Artisans and machinery* (1836), or the more journalistic George Dodd's *Days at the factories* (1843). But Babbage's *Economy of manufactures* went far beyond popular industrial observation in that it was founded on economic principles – particularly the division of labour expounded by Adam Smith in the *Wealth of nations*. Babbage analysed what he called 'the domestic economy of the factory' and evolved his most important economic concept, which was later known as the 'Babbage principle':

> That the master manufacturer, by dividing the work to be executed into different processes, each requiring different degrees of skill or of force, can purchase exactly that precise quantity of both which is necessary for each process; whereas, if the whole work were executed by one workman, that person must possess sufficient skill to perform the most difficult, and sufficient strength to execute the most laborious, of the operations into which the art is divided.[b]

By making this refinement of Smith's principle of the division of

---

[a] 'General introduction', *Works of Babbage*, Vol. 1, p. 27. M. Berg, *The machinery question and the making of political economy, 1815–1848* (Cambridge, 1980).

[b] C. Babbage, *Economy of manufactures, Works of Babbage*, Vol. 8, p. 125.

labour, the *Economy of manufactures* can be seen as being in the direct line of descent from Smith's *Wealth of nations* to Frederick Winslow Taylor's classic *Principles of scientific management* (1911).[a]

The Difference Engine, however, was always the activity closest to Babbage's heart. Unfortunately, the project was constantly blighted by difficulties over funding and his fraught relationship with his engineer, Joseph Clement. As early as 1822, Babbage had constructed a small prototype Difference Engine (no longer extant), which, although too small to do useful work, successfully demonstrated the principle of his conception. Thanks to the support of the Royal Society, he was successful in mid-1823 in reaching an agreement with the Chancellor of the Exchequer, F. J. Robinson (later Lord Goderich), that resulted in a grant of £1500 to begin the construction of a full-scale engine. Babbage also reached the understanding that further funds would be forthcoming as necessary; unfortunately no official minute was made of this agreement nor anything that would have constituted a contract in law.

On the recommendation of Marc Brunel, Babbage employed the engineer Joseph Clement (1779–1844) to build the engine.[b] Clement came from a humble background, but had learned his trade under the famous engineers Joseph Bramah and Henry Maudslay, and had become one of the outstanding draughtsmen and mechanics in England. The Difference Engine project was perhaps the most challenging and prestigious mechanical engineering project of its day. Babbage and Clement needed one another, but their relationship was not a happy one. At the personal level, Babbage made the mistake of treating Joseph Clement as a minion; while it was true that Clement had humble origins, he had risen in his career to a point where he had the right to be treated by Babbage as an equal, if not socially, then certainly as a practical engineer and inventor. On the other hand, Clement was completely insensitive to the financial implications of the Difference Engine project for Babbage and made no discernible attempt to contain costs. In 1828, while Babbage was on his Continental tour, Clement ran up vast expenses. On his return to England

---

[a] Many works on scientific management make this point. See for example: A. Marshall, *Industry and trade* (London, 1919); H. F. Merrill, ed., *Classics in management* (New York, 1960).

[b] M. R. Williams, 'Joseph Clement: the first computer engineer', *Annals of the history of computing*, Vol. 14 (1992), pp. 69–76.

at the end of 1828, Babbage urgently needed more funds, the original £1500 granted by the government in 1823 having long since been spent. Babbage approached the government a second time, and Lord Goderich sought the opinion of the Royal Society before advancing further funds. The Royal Society formed a Babbage Engine Committee, which reported enthusiastically in February 1829 that 'in the present state of Mr Babbage's engine, they do regard it as likely to fulfil the expectations entertained of it by its inventor'.[a] Following this favourable report, Babbage was granted further funding of several thousand pounds which sustained the project for another two or three years. Some of the money was used to construct a workshop and living accommodation near his home in Dorset Street, Portland Place, so that the engines and Clement would be under his more direct control. Unfortunately, Clement was unwilling to move to the new workshops, and relations between him and Babbage deteriorated further. Clement's charges became ever more extravagant, and Babbage refused to pay him anything further out of his own pocket until the expenditure had been sanctioned by the Treasury. As a result Clement withdrew his services, and retained all the drawings of the engine and the machine tools he had created for its construction – as he was by law entitled to do – and work on the engine came to a stop.

By early 1833, however, a functioning portion of the Difference Engine (without its printing unit) had been assembled. Babbage displayed the machine proudly in his Dorset Street home, where it served as a conversation piece at his soirées. Babbage recalled in *Passages* that the Duke of Wellington was particularly intrigued by the machine. Another admirer of the Difference Engine was Ada, the daughter of the poet Byron, of whom more later. (The 1833 Difference Engine – of which a woodcut was reproduced as a frontispiece to *Passages* – is now a permanent exhibit in the Science Museum, London.)

It was while the Difference Engine project was suspended in 1833 that Babbage conceived of the Analytical Engine. The Analytical Engine was a general purpose digital computer, as we now understand the term. Important as the earlier Difference Engine had been,

---

[a] J. F. W. Herschel, *Report of the Babbage engine committee* (1829), *Works of Babbage*, Vol. 2, pp. 108–14.

it was fundamentally a limited conception in that its scope was restricted to that of producing mathematical tables. By contrast, the Analytical Engine would be a universal machine capable of any mathematical computation. The idea of the Analytical Engine originated when Babbage was considering how to further eliminate human intervention in the Difference Engine by feeding back the results of a computation – which he referred to as the engine 'eating its own tail'. Babbage took this simple refinement of the Difference Engine, and from it evolved the design of the Analytical Engine, which embodies almost all of the important functions of the modern digital computer. The most significant concept in the Analytical Engine was the separation of arithmetic computation from the storage of numbers. In the original Difference Engine, these two functions had been intimately connected: in effect numbers were stored in the adding mechanisms, as in an ordinary calculating machine. Originally, Babbage had been concerned at the slow speed of his adding mechanisms, which he attempted to speed up by the invention of the 'anticipatory carriage' – a method of rapid adding that has its analogue in the modern computer in the so-called carry-look-ahead adder. The extreme complexity of the anticipating carriage was such that it would have been prohibitively expensive to replicate the mechanisms unnecessarily, so he separated the arithmetic and number-storage functions. Babbage named these two functional parts of the engine the mill and the store respectively. This terminology was an elegant metaphor from the textile industry where yarns were brought from the store to the mill where they were woven into fabric, which was then sent back to the store. In the Analytical Engine, numbers would be brought from the store to the arithmetic mill for processing, and the results of the computation returned to the store.

For about two years Babbage wrestled with the problem of organizing the calculation – the process we now call programming, but for which Babbage had no vocabulary.[a] After toying with various mechanisms, such as the pegged cylinders of barrel organs, he lighted upon the Jacquard loom. The Jacquard loom, invented in 1802, had started to come into use in the English weaving and ribbon-making industries in the 1820s. The Jacquard loom was a general purpose

---

[a] M. V. Wilkes, 'Babbage as a computer pioneer', *Historia mathematica*, Vol. 4 (1977), pp. 415–40.

device, which, once loaded with a set of specially punched cards, could weave infinite varieties of pattern. Babbage envisaged just such an arrangement with his Analytical Engine. Today, the idea of programming a computer is so commonplace that no further elaboration is necessary here. As soon as Babbage came up with the idea of the Analytical Engine, he decided that its powers were so much greater than the Difference Engine that it was pointless to proceed with the latter.

Meanwhile, the funding difficulties of the original Difference Engine were still not resolved, and Babbage was asked by the Duke of Wellington – then Prime Minister – to prepare a written statement. It was in this statement, dated 23 December 1834, that Babbage first alluded to the Analytical Engine – 'a totally new engine possessing much more extensive powers'.[a] It may be that Babbage was aware that raising the subject of the Analytical Engine would weaken his case, but he claimed in his statement that he was merely doing the honourable thing by mentioning the new engine, so that 'you may have fairly before you all the circumstances of the case'. Nonetheless, the clear messages the government read into the statement were, first, that it should abandon the Difference Engine – and the £17,470 that it had already spent on it – in favour of Babbage's new vision; and, second, that Babbage was more interested in building the engine than in making the tables that were its *raison d'être*. As a result, Babbage fatally undermined the government's confidence in the project and no decision on the engines was to be forthcoming for several years.

Between 1834 and 1846, without any financial support, Babbage elaborated the design of the Analytical Engine.[b] During this period he produced a vast outpouring of machine drawings and notebooks – which have only recently been studied and catalogued.[c] There was no question at this time of Babbage attempting construction of the machine without government finance, although he did make a number of trial pieces.

During this period of preoccupation with the Analytical Engine, his other scientific and economic activities fell off considerably. He

---

[a] C. Babbage, *Statement addressed to the Duke of Wellington respecting the calculating engine* (1834), *Works of Babbage*, Vol. 3, pp. 2–8.

[b] A. G. Bromley, 'Charles Babbage's Analytical Engine, 1838', *Annals of the history of computing*, Vol. 4 (1980), pp. 196–217.

[c] A. G. Bromley, *The Babbage papers in the Science Museum Library* (London, 1991).

dabbled a little in geology, he played with cryptography, and he undertook a study of railway dynamics for Brunel's Great Western Railway (described in chapter 25 of *Passages*). His only major publication during this period was the *Ninth Bridgewater treatise* (1837), an idiosyncratic essay on natural theology which he boasted in *Passages* 'has now stood the test of more than a quarter of a century, during which time it has been examined by some of the deepest thinkers in many countries' (p. 331). The original eight Bridgewater treatises had been sponsored by the will of the Reverend Francis Henry Egerton FRS (1756–1829) to produce works 'on the Power, Wisdom and Goodness of God, as manifested in the Creation'. Eight treatises were published under the terms of the will. In these works – which pre-dated Darwinism – the authors marshalled the arguments of science in defence of natural theology, at a time when developments in geology had begun to undermine orthodox religious dogma.[a] Babbage was not invited to be an author of one of the treatises, and was particularly stung by the remarks of William Whewell FRS (1794–1866) – the author of the first and most influential of the treatises – who argued that 'deductive' mathematicians (like Babbage) were incapable of even participating in the Creation debate since they were without 'any authority with regard to their views of the administration of the universe; we have no reason whatever to expect from their speculations any help, when we ascend to the first cause and supreme ruler of the universe'.[b]

It was evidently to answer this statement by Whewell that Babbage wrote his unofficial and unremunerated *Ninth Bridgewater treatise*. It was a short, fragmentary work, and stylistically unpolished even by Babbage's standards. Easily the most interesting idea in the book, and the one which has particularly appealed to computer-literate readers in the late twentieth century, is Babbage's explanation of miracles. Babbage did not see miracles as *post hoc* interventions by God in the running of the world, but rather that they were the workings of God's higher laws that humankind simply could not perceive. In modern terms, Babbage saw God as the programmer of a divine algorithm. In this context, a miracle was merely an interesting

---

[a] W. H. Brock, 'The selection of the authors of the Bridgewater treatises', *Notes and records*, Vol. 21 (1966), pp. 162–79.

[b] W. Whewell, *Astronomy and general physics considered with reference to natural theology* (London, 1833).

– but anticipated – variation in the Godly algorithm. In *Passages* (pp. 290–2) Babbage rehashed these ideas, although they were starting to become passé with the publication of Darwin's *Origin of species* in 1859.

In 1840, when he was approaching fifty, Babbage was invited by the Italian mathematician Giovanni Plana (1781–1864) to make a presentation on the Analytical Engine to a scientific meeting in Turin. Babbage was more than a little encouraged by Plana's elegant encapsulation of the underlying principles of the Analytical Engine. Plana's words clung to Babbage's mind and he quoted them in *Passages*:

> Hitherto the *legislative* department of our analysis has been all-powerful – the *executive* all feeble.
>
> Your engine seems to give us the same control over the executive which we have hitherto only possessed over the legislative department.
> (p. 97)

For once, Babbage would not be in the position of a missionary talking to cannibals. The Turin meeting was to be one of the few wholly agreeable episodes of Babbage's life, and it was the only occasion he gave a detailed public presentation of the Analytical Engine to his scientific peers. Babbage never forgot the pleasure of his acclaim in Italy and while he ostentatiously declined English honours, he accepted the Italian Order of Saint Maurice and Saint Lazarus. During his trip to Turin he also had an extensive audience with King Charles Albert, which again Babbage lovingly recounted in *Passages* (chapter 24). He dedicated *Passages* to his son King Victor Emmanuel II.

At the Turin meeting, a young military mathematician, Lieutenant Luigi Frederico Menabrea (1809–96), made notes on Babbage's presentation, with the aim of publishing a memoir. He and Babbage corresponded during the next year to clarify the exposition, and Menabrea (who was later to rise meteorically to become Prime Minister of Italy), published the memoir as a twenty-four page paper in French in the *Bibliothèque universelle de Genève* in 1842.[a]

It was in connection with having Menabrea's paper translated into English that Babbage was to develop a close working relationship

---

[a] L. F. Menebrea, 'Notions sur la machine analytique de M. Charles Babbage' (1842), *Works of Babbage*, Vol. 3, pp. 62–82.

with Ada Augusta, Countess of Lovelace (1815–52). Ada had become Countess by her marriage to William King, Earl of Lovelace, in 1835. Babbage was a regular guest at Ockham Park, their country seat in Surrey, and at their smaller home, Ashley Combe, on the Somerset coast. Ada was an enigmatic young woman who had set about learning mathematics in her early twenties with the avuncular help of Babbage and Augustus de Morgan among others.[a] At Babbage's suggestion, in 1842 she set about translating the Menabrea article into English. With Babbage's encouragement, she added extensive notes of her own. By the time Lovelace's *Sketch of the Analytical Engine* appeared in Taylor's *Scientific memoirs* in 1843, Menabrea's original article had almost quadrupled in length.[b] The *Sketch* was the only detailed account of the Analytical Engine ever published in Babbage's lifetime – and indeed until the 1980s. Although Babbage devoted a full chapter to the Analytical Engine in *Passages*, it had nothing like the detail or intellectual weight of the *Sketch*. Moreover, Ada had a wonderful turn-of-phrase, which Babbage never had. Who, for example, could resist Lovelace's statement that:

> The distinctive characteristic of the Analytical Engine, and that which has rendered it possible to endow mechanism with such extensive faculties as bid fair to make this engine the executive right hand of abstract algebra, is the introduction into it of the principle which Jacquard devised for regulating, by means of punched cards, the most complicated patterns in the fabrication of brocaded stuffs. . . . We may say most aptly that the Analytical Engine *weaves algebraical patterns* just as the Jacquard loom weaves flowers and leaves.[c]

The extent of Lovelace's intellectual contribution to the *Sketch* has been much exaggerated in recent years. She has been pronounced the world's first programmer, and even had a programming language (ADA) named in her honour. However, scholarship of the last decade has shown that most of the technical content and all of the programs in the *Sketch* were Babbage's work. But even if the *Sketch*

---

[a] B. A. Toole, *Ada, the enchantress of numbers* (Mill Valley, Ca., 1992). D. L. Moore, *Ada, Countess of Lovelace* (London, 1977). D. Stein, *Ada: a life and a legacy* (Cambridge, Ma., 1985).

[b] A. A. Lovelace, 'Sketch of the Analytical Engine' (1843), *Works of Babbage*, Vol. 3, pp. 89–170.

[c] Ibid., p. 121.

was based solely on Babbage's ideas, there is no question that Lovelacc providcd its soul. Lovelace's role as the prime expositor of the Analytical Engine was of enormous importance to Babbage, and he described her as his 'dear and much admired interpreter' without any trace of condescension.[a]

In 1841, Robert Peel became Prime Minister and Babbage once again revived his efforts to obtain a decision from the government about the future of his calculating engine. Peel sought the advice of Babbage's peers in the Royal Society, including the Astronomer Royal George Biddell Airy who expressed the opinion of the engine that 'it was worthless'.[b] As a result, Babbage was informed in writing of the government's decision to abandon the calculating engine project. Babbage would not be satisfied with a written rejection, and secured a personal interview with Robert Peel on 11 November 1842. It was an 'entirely unsatisfactory' encounter, and Babbage failed to get the decision reversed.

Babbage never accepted the demise of his engines with good grace, and could never see that he had handled the negotiations incompetently. Moreover he had personally invested a large sum of money in the project. By his own account (*Passages*, p. 79) he had spent upwards of £20,000 on the engines and 'other works of science' – a sum that represented a significant fraction of his net worth, and the equivalent of at least £½ million at today's prices. For the rest of his life he saw himself as the victim of government ineptitude and short-sightedness, and grumbled about his misfortunes to those who would listen. One such was Charles Dickens, a long-time member of Babbage's circle, who parodied Babbage's dealings with the government as the 'Circumlocution Office' in *Little Dorrit* (1855–57). Babbage also encouraged a number of writers to take up his case. The most important pamphlet was written by his political ally, the reformist antiquary Sir Harris Nicholas (1799–1848), who wrote a *Statement of the circumstances respecting Mr Babbage's calculating engines* in 1843, which Babbage reprinted in full as chapter 6 of *Passages*. A little later, he made all his materials available to Charles R. Weld (1813–69), who related the story of the engines in his two-volume *History of the Royal Society* (1849). He was also taken up by an obscure

---

[a] Letter from Babbage to Ada Lovelace, 9 September 1843. Reproduced in Toole, op. cit., pp. 236–9.

[b] G. B. Airy, *Autobiography* (Cambridge, 1896), p. 152.

lawyer, James Jerwood, who wrote what amounted to a short biography, *On the calculation and printing of mathematical tables by machinery* (1861).[a] None of these publications had the slightest effect in changing Babbage's fortune.

Babbage stopped work on the Analytical Engine in 1846. For the next two years he devoted himself to producing complete plans for what he called Difference Engine Number 2 – the machine he had originally proposed making for the government. Although the government had at this time written off the expenditure on the calculating engines, and wanted nothing more to do with them or Babbage, he stubbornly insisted on fulfilling his original obligation in order to secure the moral high-ground. When the plans were offered to the government, it refused to accept them; they were eventually given by Babbage's son, Major Henry P. B. Babbage, to the Science Museum, Kensington, where they lay neglected for over a century. (In 1986, however, the Science Museum resurrected Babbage's plans and successfully constructed the arithmetic part of the Difference Engine in time to celebrate Babbage's bi-centenary in 1991.)[b]

The government's complete lack of interest in the plans for Difference Engine Number 2 finally brought home to Babbage that all prospects of funding his engines were gone forever. The demise of his cherished project was the 'central trauma in Babbage's scientific life', and he never fully recovered his *joie de vivre*.[c] He did not have the heart to take up the calculating engines again for nearly ten years.

As Babbage reached his mid-fifties, his intellectual powers were a shadow of those he had had twenty years previously. He occupied himself with numerous projects of no real importance. He wrote a mildly reformist tract on the *Principles of taxation* in 1848, which appeared in three editions. He also amused himself with semi-recreational excursions into cryptography,[d] and miscellaneous inventions, some of which bordered on the eccentric. For example, he

---

[a] C. R. Weld, 'The eleventh chapter of the history of the Royal Society' (1849), *Works of Babbage*, Vol. 10, pp. 149–63. J. Jerwood, *On the calculation and printing of mathematical tables by machinery* (1861), *Works of Babbage*, Vol. 1, pp. 1–36.

[b] D. Swade, 'Redeeming Charles Babbage's mechanical computer', *Scientific American*, February 1993, pp. 86–91.

[c] D. Swade, *Charles Babbage and his calculating engines* (London, 1991), p. 18.

[d] O. I. Franksen, *Mr Babbage's secret: the tale of a cypher – and APL* (Strandberg, 1984). O. I. Franksen, 'Babbage and cryptography. Or, the mystery of Admiral Beaufort's cipher', *Mathematics and computers in simulation*, Vol. 35 (1993), pp. 327–67.

flirted with the idea of building a tic-tac-toe playing machine in order to raise funds for building the Analytical Engine (*Passages*, pp. 349–53). Not everything was dross, however; he made a significant contribution to lighthouse signalling (*Passages*, pp. 340–5) which influenced lighthouse-keeping practice, particularly in the United States, and he contributed to the invention of the ophthalmoscope. Generally, however, Babbage was an increasingly spent and irrelevant force in the scientific world and in the societies that he had helped establish in his prime. Whereas in his early days he had been a scientific gadfly, he was now little more than a thorn in the flesh.

One of the great disappointments of Babbage's later years was his exclusion from Lyon Playfair's Commission for the Great Exhibition of 1851, the first of the great international exhibitions. The exhibition was an undertaking that was very much in Babbage's line, and his exclusion from the Commission did not prevent him putting forward suggestions. But he was studiously ignored, and as a result he wrote a vitriolic book *The Exposition of 1851* which appeared shortly after the exhibition opened. This book, described as the 'diatribe of a disappointed man', frequently boils over with Babbage's impotent rage.[a] But even more than his exclusion from the planning of the exhibition, he was affronted by the fact that the Commission had not seen fit to exhibit his 1833 Difference Engine. Babbage's anger was still simmering years later when he wrote in *Passages*:

> In 1851, the Commissioners of the International Exhibition did not think proper to exhibit the Difference Engine, although it was the property of the nation. They were as insensible to the greatest mechanical as to, what has been regarded by some, the greatest intellectual triumph of their country. (p. 112)

There was no false modesty in *Passages*.

One of the few bright spots that cheered Babbage's existence in the last twenty years of his life was the successful development of the Scheutz Difference Engine. It had happened that Dionysius Lardner's 1834 article describing the Difference Engine had been read by a Swedish printer and his son, Georg and Edvard Scheutz.[b] After an

---

[a] 'Charles Babbage (1792–1871)', *Dictionary of national biography*, Vol. 2 (Oxford, 1885–1900), pp. 776–8.
[b] M. Lindgren, *Glory and failure: the difference engines, of Johann Müller, Charles Babbage and Georg and Edvard Scheutz* (Cambridge, Ma., 1990).

heroic engineering effort of nearly twenty years that rivalled Babbage's own, the father and son completed a full-scale engine of which Babbage learned in 1852. The engine was subsequently exhibited at the Paris Exposition in 1855. Babbage personally visited the Exposition and was gratified to see the engine win the gold medal in its class. In 1856 the engine was purchased by the Dudley Observatory in the United States for $5000. And in Britain, William Farr FRS (1807–83), the statistical superintendent of the General Register Office, succeeded in obtaining funds to have a copy of the machine made at a cost of £1200 to compute a new set of life tables. In the Great Exhibition of 1861, Babbage had hoped to see his 1833 Difference Engine and the British-made Scheutz engine exhibited side-by-side. But alas, the Scheutz engine was busily employed at Somerset House grinding out the new English life table. The 1833 Difference Engine was exhibited, but Babbage noted caustically in *Passages* 'The only place offered for its reception was a small hole, 4 feet 4 inches in front by 5 feet deep' (p. 115). Babbage was very hard to please at this stage of his life.

If Babbage's reputation for cantankerousness was in the ascendant prior to the publication of *Passages*, it certainly reached its zenith with the *Chapter on street nuisances*, his celebrated vendetta against street musicians. Originally written as chapter 23 of *Passages, Street nuisances* was published as a separate pamphlet ahead of the book and ran into three editions.

Street nuisances shows Babbage simultaneously the indefatigable reformer and a gift to parodists. He opens, typically, with a catalogue of the nuisances – there are elaborate lists of 'instruments of torture' (i.e. musical instruments), he gives the provenance of musicians, and their nationalities. In its way *Street nuisances* is a good example of Babbage's analytical style, seen at its best in the *Economy of manufactures*, but now turned to somewhat ludicrous subject matter.

There is no question that Babbage, like many other well-to-do Londoners, suffered from the nuisance of street musicians from the 1850s, but Babbage claimed with characteristic precision that 'one-fourth part of my working power has been destroyed by the nuisance'. When driven to the limit by performers in the vicinity of his house who refused to move on when requested, Babbage would on occasion fetch a policeman to have the offender arrested, but this rarely resulted in a successful prosecution and merely aggravated the situation. Babbage was verbally abused, followed by marching bands in the street, not to mention 'the smaller evils of dead cats, and other offensive materials, thrown down my area; of windows from time to time purposely broken, or from occasional blows from stones projected by unseen hands' (p. 264). While Babbage's *Street nuisances* undoubtedly helped raise public awareness of the problem, effective legislation was largely the work of an unsung member of parliament, Michael Bass (1799–1884), the liberal member for Derby, and heir to the brewery fortune.[a] In the same year that Babbage's *Street nuisances* appeared, Bass published a small volume *Street music in the Metropolis* in which he quoted letters written to him on the subject by the literati – including Carlyle, Tennyson, Thackeray, Dickens and Millais – as well as ordinary householders. In the House of Commons, Bass sought leave to bring the Street Music (Metropolis) Bill on 3 May 1864. There was a lively debate between members for and against. Sir Robert Peel – for once siding with Babbage – urged the House to 'put down the abominable nuisance'. Those against the Bill included William Gladstone who thought that it was 'an unwarrantable interference with the amenities of the people', while others saw it as a kill-joy measure 'brought forward at the insistence of such as Mr. Babbage, who was now commencing a crusade against the popular game of tip-cat and the trundling of hoops'.[b] As a result, the more draconian measures of the bill were diluted by the time the Bill received the Royal Assent on 25 July 1864.

Typically, Babbage's obituarists and less discerning biographers have exaggerated his role in the passing of the Bill, completely overlooking Bass's painstaking parliamentary foot-soldiering.

CHARLES BABBAGE was never quite able to give up on his calculating engines. In 1856, after a gap of approximately ten years, he started work on the Analytical Engine again. He was now in his mid-sixties, and he understood that there was no serious prospect that it would ever be built. Right up to the end of his life he would

---

[a] 'Michael Bass (1799–1884)', *Dictionary of national biography*, Vol. 2 (Oxford, 1885–1900), pp. 1291–2.
[b] *Hansard* (Session, 1864), Vol. 174, pp. 2115–19; Vol. 175, pp. 467–77, pp. 1529–33; Vol. 176, pp. 679–83, p. 1367.

continue to refine the designs of the engine, working almost entirely in isolation, filling notebook after notebook with closely-written notations but publishing nothing. When he died there was several thousand pages of material, but its bulk was so daunting and the details so impenetrable, that his intellectual legacy was effectively untouched until the 1970s.

In 1864, the same year that *Passages* was published, William Farr published the definitive *English life table*.[a] Of the 764 pages of tables, just 28 pages had been entirely produced by the Scheutz Difference Engine and 216 pages partly so – and as Farr himself explained, they had to be coaxed with some difficulty from the temperamental engine which required 'incessant attention'.[b] Even Babbage realized the tables were 'not of any pressing necessity', but they were the only tangible result of his work on the calculating engines he was to see in his lifetime. There were other attempts to build difference engines in the nineteenth century, but only one of them was technically success-ful – in the sense of producing useful mathematical tables. It also has to be said that despite its remarkable foreshadowing of the modern computer, the Analytical Engine had no influence whatever on its invention – which occurred quite independently in the United States during the Second World War.[c]

In the last few years of his life, Babbage was an increasingly isolated and frustrated man. We know very little of him during this period. One glimpse of the ageing Babbage was recorded by the American Joseph Henry, the Secretary of the Smithsonian Institu-tion, who visited Babbage towards the end of his life in 1870. He found him 'in the same house, still interested in the calculating-machine, with apparently but little diminution of mental activity'. Babbage's only complaint was of 'the loss of memory, since with it was the loss of personal identity'.[d] Another vignette was given by Lord Moulton (1844–1921), the liberal statesman and scientific ad-ministrator. Giving the inaugural address to a mathematical confer-ence in July 1914, on the eve of the First World War, Moulton recalled a visit he had paid on Babbage many years previously:

[a] W. Farr, *English life table* (London, 1864).
[b] Ibid., p. cxl.
[c] N. Metropolis and W. J. Worlton, 'A trilogy of errors in the history of computing', *Annals of the history of computing*, Vol. 2 (1980), pp. 49–59.
[d] N. S. Dodge, 'Charles Babbage', *Annual report of the Smithsonian Institution for 1873* (Washington, 1874), pp. 162–97.

One of the sad memories of my life is a visit to the celebrated mathematician and inventor, Mr Babbage. He was far advanced in age, but his mind was still as vigorous as ever. He took me through his workrooms. In the first room I saw the parts of the original Calculating Machine, which had been shown in an incomplete state many years before and had even been put to some use. I asked him about its present form. 'I have not finished it because in working at it I came on the idea of my Analytical Machine, which would do all that it was capable of doing and much more. Indeed, the idea was so much simpler that it would have taken more work to complete the Calculating Machine than to design and construct the other in its entirety, so I turned my attention to the Analytical Machine.' After a few minutes' talk we went into the next work-room, where he showed and explained to me the working of the elements of the Analytical Machine. I asked if I could see it. 'I have never completed it,' he said, 'because I hit upon an idea of doing the same thing by a different and far more effective method, and this rendered it useless to proceed on the old lines.' Then we went into the third room. There lay scattered bits of mechanism, but I saw no trace of any working machine. Very cautiously I approached the subject, and received the dreaded answer, 'It is not constructed yet, but I am working at it, and it will take less time to construct it altogether than it would have taken to complete the Analytical Machine from the stage in which I left it.' I took leave of the old man with a heavy heart. When he died a few years later, not only had he constructed no machine, but the verdict of a jury of kind and sympathetic scientific men who were deputed to pronounce upon what he had left behind him, either in papers or mechanism, was that everything was too incomplete to be capable of being put to any useful purpose.[a]

No doubt Moulton had embellished the anecdote over the years, but this does not diminish the allegorical power of this final picture of Babbage that reaches us across the decades. For Babbage the best was ever the enemy of the good. He died 18 October 1871, in his eightieth year.

---

[a] Lord Moulton, 'The invention of logarithms, its genesis and growth', in G. C. Knott, ed., *Napier tercentenary memorial volume* (London, 1915), pp. 1–24.

Acknowledgement

I am most grateful to William F. Aspray, Richard Coopey, John V. Pickstone, C. J. D. Roberts and Doron Swade who commented on a draft version of the Introduction.

Further reading

There is now a substantial literature on Charles Babbage, which includes biographies, monographs on different aspects of his work, and a great many papers in academic periodicals. It would be very easy to overwhelm the aspiring Babbage scholar with several dozen citations; here I confine myself to a handful of the best and most accessible books currently in print or widely available in libraries.

The standard biography is Anthony Hyman's *Charles Babbage: pioneer of the computer* (Oxford and Princeton, 1982). An excellent general history of Babbage's engines – though going well beyond them – is Bruce Collier's *The little engines that could've: the calculating machines of Charles Babbage* (Harvard 1970 and New York, 1991). The leading scholar of Babbage's calculating engines is Allan Bromley whose most accessible account appears as chapter 2 'Difference Engines and Analytical Engines' in William F. Aspray, ed., *Computing before computers* (Iowa, 1990). John Dubbey's *The mathematical work of Charles Babbage* (London, 1976) is the best description of Babbage's mathematical work. By far the most authoritative account of Babbage's economic writings appears in Maxine Berg's *The machinery question and the making of political economy, 1815–1848* (Oxford, 1980). The latest book about Ada Lovelace is Betty Toole's *Ada, the enchantress of numbers* (Mill Valley, Ca., 1992); this exquisitely printed and illustrated book includes a selection from Lovelace's correspondence and an account of her *Sketch* of the Analytical Engine. In addition to these full-length works, there are many journal articles (some examples of which have been cited in the footnotes to the Introduction). This literature is quite widely scattered, and is best located through the secondary literature and the review columns of the *Annals of the history of computing*.

The major primary source for the Babbage scholar is the Pickering Masters edition of *The Works of Charles Babbage*, ed. Martin Campbell-Kelly, 11 vols (London and New York, 1989). A single volume pot-pourri of Babbage's miscellaneous writings is *Science and reform: selected works of Charles Babbage*, ed. A. Hyman (Cambridge, 1989). A selection of papers on the calculating engines was assembled by Babbage's son Henry P. B. Babbage and published as *Babbage's calculating engines* in 1889; this has recently been reprinted in facsimile with an introduction by Allan Bromley (Los Angeles, 1984). Another useful selection of contemporary writings on the calculating engines is published by Dover as *Charles Babbage and his calculating engines*, ed. Philip and Emily Morrison (New York, 1961).

Note on the text

This text was first prepared for the Pickering Masters edition of *The Works of Charles Babbage*. So that scholars can follow up citations in the secondary literature, the original pagination is given at the top of each page, and in the text page-turns are indicated by a solidus (/). Editorial notes appear at the foot of each page under a short line and are marked in the text with superscript letters. Typographical errors and misprints in the original have been silently corrected, although all substantive corrections have been made either by a footnote or by an editorial interpolation in angle brackets. The remaining editorial conventions – which will not materially affect the reading of this edition – are fully explained in the *Works of Babbage*, Vol. 1, pp. *48–50*.

MARTIN CAMPBELL-KELLY
University of Warwick

PASSAGES

FROM

THE LIFE OF A PHILOSOPHER.

BY

CHARLES BABBAGE, ESQ., M.A.,

F.R.S., F.R.S.E., F.R.A.S., F. STAT. S., HON. M.R.I.A., M.C.P.S.,

COMMANDER OF THE ITALIAN ORDER OF ST. MAURICE AND ST. LAZARUS,

INST. IMP. (ACAD. MORAL.) PARIS CORR., ACAD. AMER. ART. ET SC. BOSTON, REG. OECON. BORUSS.,

PHYS. HIST. NAT. GENEV., ACAD. REG. MONAC., HAFN., MASSIL., ET DIVION., SOCIUS.

ACAD. IMP. ET REG. PETROP., NEAP., BRUX., PATAV., GEORG. FLOREN, LYNCEI ROM., MUT., PHILOMATH.

PARIS, SOC. CORR., ETC.

" I'm a philosopher. Confound them all—
Birds, beasts, and men; but no, not womankind."—*Don Juan.*

" I now gave my mind to philosophy: the great object of my ambition was to make out a complete system of the universe, including and comprehending the origin, causes, consequences, and termination of all things. Instead of countenance, encouragement, and applause, which I should have received from every one who has the true dignity of an oyster at heart, I was exposed to calumny and misrepresentation. While engaged in my great work on the universe, some even went so far as to accuse me of infidelity;—such is the malignity of oysters."—" *Autobiography of an Oyster*" *deciphered by the aid of photography in the shell of a philosopher of that race,—recently scolloped.*

LONDON:

LONGMAN, GREEN, LONGMAN, ROBERTS, & GREEN.

1864.

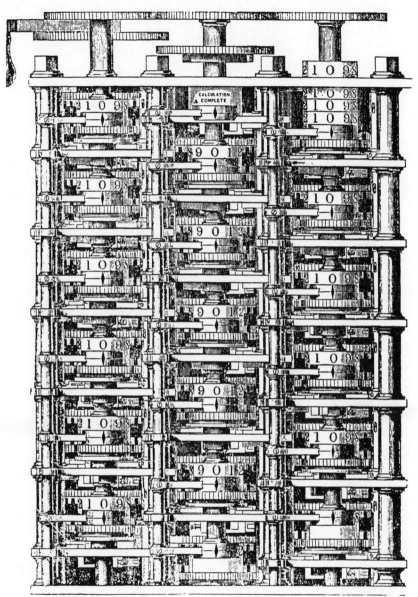

CALCULATION
& COMPLETE

B. H. Babbage, del.

Impression from a woodcut of a small portion of Mr. Babbage's Difference Engine No. 1, the property of Government, at present deposited in the Museum at South Kensington.

It was commenced 1823.
This portion put together 1833.
The construction abandoned 1842.
This plate was printed June, 1853.
This portion was in the Exhibition 1862.

DEDICATION

TO VICTOR EMMANUEL II, KING OF ITALY

Sire,

In dedicating this volume to your Majesty, I am also doing an act of justice to the memory of your illustrious father.

In 1840, the King, Charles Albert, invited the learned of Italy to assemble in his capital. At the request of her most gifted analyst, I brought with me the drawings and explanations of the Analytical Engine. These were thoroughly examined and their truth acknowledged by Italy's choicest sons.

To the King, your father, I am indebted for the first public and official acknowledgement of this invention.

I am happy in thus expressing my deep sense of that obligation to his son, the Sovereign of united Italy, the country of Archimedes and of Galileo.

I am, Sire,
With the highest respect,
Your Majesty's faithful servant,

CHARLES BABBAGE /

PREFACE

Some men write their lives to save themselves from *ennui*, careless of the amount they inflict on their readers.

Others write their personal history, lest some kind friend should survive them, and, in showing off his own talent, unwittingly show them up.

Others, again, write their own life from a different motive – from fear that the vampires of literature might make it their prey.

I have frequently had applications to write my life, both from my countrymen and from foreigners. Some caterers for the public offered to pay me for it. Others required that I should pay them for its insertion; others offered to insert it without charge. One proposed to give me a quarter of a column gratis, and as many additional lines of eloge as I chose to write and pay for at tenpence per line. To many of these I sent a list of my works, with the remark that they formed the best life of an author; but nobody cared to insert them.

I have no desire to write my own biography, as long as I have strength and means to do better work.

The remarkable circumstances attending those calculating machines, on which I have spent so large a portion of my / life, make me wish to place on record some account of their past history. As, however, such a work would be utterly uninteresting to the greater part of my countrymen, I thought it might be rendered less unpalatable by relating some of my experience amongst various classes of society, widely differing from each other, in which I have occasionally mixed.

This volume does not aspire to the name of an autobiography. It relates a variety of isolated circumstances in which I have taken part – some of them arranged in the order of time, and others grouped together in separate chapters, from similarity of subject.

The selection has been made in some cases from the importance of the matter. In others, from the celebrity of the persons concerned; whilst several of them furnish interesting illustrations of human character. /

CHAPTER I

MY ANCESTORS

Traced his descent, through ages dark,
From cats that caterwauled in Noah's ark.

Value of a celebrated name – My ancestors – Their ante-mosaic origin –
Flint-workers – Tool-makers – Not descended from Cain – Ought a
philosopher to avow it if he were? – Probability of descent from Tubal Cain
– Argument in favour, he worked in iron – on the other side, he invented
organs – Possible origin of my name – Family history in very recent times.

What is there in a name? It is merely an empty basket, until you put
something into it. My earliest visit to the Continent taught me the
value of such a basket, filled with the name of my venerable friend
the first Herschel, ere yet my younger friend his son, had adorned his
distinguished patronymic with the additional laurels of his own well-
earned fame.

The inheritance of a celebrated name is not, however, without its
disadvantages. This truth I never found more fully appreciated, nor
more admirably expressed, than in a conversation with the son of
Filangieri, the author of the / celebrated treatise on legislation, with
whom I became acquainted at Naples, and in whose company I
visited several of the most interesting institutions of that capital.

In the course of one of our drives, I alluded to the advantages of
inheriting a distinguished name, as in the case of the second
Herschel. His remark was, 'For my own part, I think it a great
disadvantage. Such a man must feel in the position of one inheriting a
vast estate, so deeply mortgaged that he can never hope, by any
efforts of his own, to redeem it.'

Without reverting to the philosophic, but unromantic, views of our
origin taken by Darwin, I shall pass over the long history of our
progress from a monad up to man, and commence tracing my
ancestry as the world generally do: namely, as soon as there is the
slightest ground for conjecture. Although I have contended for the

1

mosaic date of the creation of man as long as I decently could, and have even endeavoured to explain away* some of the facts relied upon to prove man's long anterior origin; yet I must admit that the continual accumulation of evidence probably will, at last, compel me to acknowledge that, in this single instance, the writings of Moses may have been misapprehended.

Let us, therefore, take for granted that man and certain extinct races of animals lived together, thousands of years before Adam. We find, at that period, a race who formed knives, and hammers, and arrow-heads out of flint. Now, considering my own inveterate habit of contriving *tools*, it is more probable that I should derive my passion by hereditary transmission from these original tool-makers, than from any other inferior race existing at that period. /

Many years ago I met a very agreeable party at Mr Rogers' table. Somebody introduced the subject of ancestry. I remarked that most people are reluctant to acknowledge as their father or grandfather, any person who had committed a dishonest action or a crime. But that no one ever scrupled to be proud of a remote ancestor, even though he might have been a thief or a murderer. Various remarks were made, and reasons assigned, for this tendency of the educated mind. I then turned to my next neighbour, Sir Robert H. Inglis, and asked him what he would do, supposing he possessed undoubted documents, that he was lineally descended from Cain.

Sir Robert, said he was at that moment proposing to himself the very same question. After some consideration, he said he should burn them; and then enquired what I should do in the same circumstances. My reply was, that I should preserve them: but simply because I thought the preservation of any *fact* might ultimately be useful.

I possess no evidence that I am descended from Cain. If any herald suppose that there may be such a presumption, I think it must arise from his confounding Cain with Tubal Cain, who was a great worker in iron. Still, however he might argue that, the probabilities are in favour of his opinion: for I, too, work in iron. But a friend of mine, to whose kind criticisms I am much indebted, suggests that as Tubal Cain invented the *Organ*, this probability is opposed to the former one.

* On the remains of human art, mixed with the bones of extinct races of animals. 'Proceedings of the Royal Society', 26 May, 1859. <*Works of Babbage*, Vol. 5.>

The next step in my pedigree is to determine whence the origin of my modern family name.

Some have supposed it to be derived from the cry of sheep. If so, that would point to a descent from the Shepherd Kings. Others have supposed it is derived from the name of a place called Bab or Babb, as we have, in the West of England, Bab / Tor, Babbacombe, etc. But this is evidently erroneous; for, when a people took possession of a desert country, its various localities could possess no names; consequently, the colonists could not take names from the country to which they migrated, but would very naturally give their own names to the several lands they appropriated: '*mais revenons à nos moutons*'.

How my blood was transmitted to me through more modern races, is quite immaterial, seeing the admitted antiquity of the flint-workers.

In recent times, that is, since the Conquest, my knowledge of the history of my family is limited by the unfortunate omission of my name from the roll of William's followers. Those who are curious about the subject, and are idlers, may, if they think it worth while, search all the parish registers in the West of England and elsewhere.

The light I can throw upon it is not great, and rests on a few documents, and on family tradition. During the past four generations I have no surviving collateral relatives of my own name.

The name of Babbage is not uncommon in the West of England. One day during my boyhood, I observed it over a small grocer's door, whilst riding through the town of Chudley. I dismounted, went into the shop, purchased some figs, and found a very old man of whom I made enquiry as to his family. He had not a good memory himself, but his wife told me that his name was Babb when she married him, and that it was only during the last twenty years he had adopted the name of Babbage, which, the old man thought, sounded better. Of course I told his wife that I entirely agreed with her husband, and thought him a very sensible fellow.

The craft most frequently practised by my ancestors seems / to have been that of a goldsmith, although several are believed to have practised less dignified trades.

In the time of Henry the Eighth one of my ancestors, together with a hundred men, were taken prisoners at the siege of Calais.

When William the Third landed in Torbay, another ancestor of mine, a yeoman possessing some small estate, undertook to distribute his proclamations. For this bit of high treason he was rewarded with a silver medal, which I well remember seeing, when I was a boy. It had descended to a very venerable and truthful old lady, an unmarried aunt, the historian of our family, on whose authority the identity of the medal I saw with that given by King William must rest.

Another ancestor married one of two daughters, the only children of a wealthy physician, Dr Burthogge, an intimate friend and correspondent of John Locke.[a]

Somewhere about 1700 a member of my family, one Richard Babbage, who appears to have been a very wild fellow, having tried his hand at various trades, and given them all up, offended a wealthy relative.

To punish this idleness, his relative entailed all his large estates upon eleven different people, after whom he gave it to this Richard Babbage, who, had there been no entail, would have taken them as heir-at-law.

Ten of these lives had dropped, and the eleventh was in a consumption, when Richard Babbage took it into his head to go off to America with Bamfylde Moore Carew, the King of the Beggars.

The last only of the eleven lives existed when he embarked, and that life expired within twelve months after Richard Babbage sailed. The estates remained in possession of the representatives of the eleventh in the entail. /

If it could have been proved that Richard Babbage had survived twelve months after his voyage to America, these estates would have remained in my own branch of the family.

I possess a letter from Richard Babbage, dated on board the ship in which he sailed for America.

In the year 1773 it became necessary to sell a portion of this property, for the purpose of building a church at Ashbrenton. A private Act of Parliament was passed for that purpose, in which the rights of the true heir were reserved. /

---

[a] Buxton MSS 7, Museum of the History of Science, Oxford, contains copies of letters from Richard Burthogge to John Locke, 1694–1703.

CHAPTER II

CHILDHOOD

The Prince of Darkness is a gentleman. *Hamlet*

Early passion for enquiry and inquisition into toys – Lost on London Bridge – Supposed value of the young philosopher – Found again – Strange coincidence in after-years – Poisoned – Frightened a schoolfellow by a ghost – Frightened himself by trying to raise the devil – Effect of want of occupation for the mind – Treasure-trove – Death and non-appearance of a schoolfellow.

From my earliest years I had a great desire to enquire into the causes of all those little things and events which astonish the childish mind. At a later period I commenced the still more important enquiry into those laws of thought and those aids which assist the human mind in passing from received knowledge to that other knowledge then unknown to our race. I now think it fit to record some of those views to which, at various periods of my life, my reasoning has led me. Truth only has been the object of my search, and I am not conscious of ever having turned aside in my enquiries from any fear of the conclusions to which they might lead.

As it may be interesting to some of those who will hereafter read these lines, I shall briefly mention a few events of my earliest, and even of my childish years. My parents being born at a certain period of history, and in a certain latitude and longitude, of course followed the religion / of their country. They brought me up in the Protestant form of the Christian faith. My excellent mother taught me the usual forms of my daily and nightly prayer; and neither in my father nor my mother was there any mixture of bigotry and intolerance on the one hand, nor on the other of that unbecoming and familiar mode of addressing the Almighty which afterwards so much disgusted me in my youthful years.

My invariable question on receiving any new toy, was 'Mamma, what is inside of it?' Until this information was obtained those around me had no repose, and the toy itself, I have been told, was generally

5

broken open if the answer did not satisfy my own little ideas of the 'fitness of things'.

Earliest recollections

Two events which impressed themselves forcibly on my memory happened, I think, previously to my eighth year.

When about five years old, I was walking with my nurse, who had in her arms an infant brother of mine, across London Bridge, holding, as I thought, by her apron. I was looking at the ships in the river. On turning round to speak to her, I found that my nurse was not there, and that I was alone upon London Bridge. My mother had always impressed upon me the necessity of great caution in passing any street-crossing: I went on, therefore, quietly until I reached Tooley Street, where I remained watching the passing vehicles, in order to find a safe opportunity of crossing that very busy street.

In the meantime the nurse, having lost one of her charges, had gone to the crier, who proceeded immediately to call, by the ringing of his bell, the attention of the public to the fact that a young philosopher was lost, and to the still more important fact that five shillings would be the reward of his fortunate discoverer. I well remember sitting on the steps of / the door of the linendraper's shop on the opposite corner of Tooley Street, when the gold-laced crier was making proclamation of my loss; but I was too much occupied with eating some pears to attend to what he was saying.

The fact was, that one of the men in the linendraper's shop, observing a little child by itself, went over to it, and asked what it wanted. Finding that it had lost its nurse, he brought it across the street, gave it some pears, and placed it on the steps at the door: having asked my name, the shopkeepers found it to be that of one of his own customers. He accordingly sent off a messenger, who announced to my mother the finding of young Pickle before she was aware of his loss.

Those who delight in observing coincidences may perhaps account for the following singular one. Several years ago when the houses in Tooley Street were being pulled down, I believe to make room for the new railway terminus, I happened to pass along the very spot on which I had been lost in my infancy. A slate of the

6

largest size, called a Duchess,* was thrown from the roof of one of the houses, and penetrated into the earth close to my feet.

The other event, which I believe happened some time after the one just related, is as follows. I give it from memory, as I have always repeated it.

I was walking with my nurse and my brother in a public garden, called Montpelier Gardens, in Walworth. On returning through the private road leading to the gardens, I gathered and swallowed some dark berries very like blackcurrants – these were poisonous. /

On my return home, I recollect being placed between my father's knees, and his giving me a glass of castor-oil, which I took from his hand.

My father at that time possessed a collection of pictures. He sat on a chair on the right-hand side of the chimney-piece in the breakfast room, under a fine picture of our Saviour taken down from the cross. On the opposite wall was a still-celebrated 'Interior of Antwerp Cathedral'.

In after-life I several times mentioned the subject both to my father and to my mother; but neither of them had the slightest recollection of the matter.

Having suffered in health at the age of five years, and again at that of ten by violent fevers, from which I was with difficulty saved, I was sent into Devonshire and placed under the care of a clergyman (who kept a school at Alphington, near Exeter), with instructions to attend to my health; but, not to press too much knowledge upon me: a mission which he faithfully accomplished. Perhaps great idleness may have led to some of my childish reasonings.

Relations of ghost stories often circulate amongst children, and also of visitations from the devil in a *personal* form. Of course I shared the belief of my comrades, but still had some doubts of the existence of these personages, although I greatly feared their appearance. Once, in conjunction with a companion, I frightened another boy, bigger than myself, with some pretended ghost; how prepared or how represented by natural objects I do not now remember: I believe it was by the accidental passing shadows of some external objects upon the walls of our common bedroom.

The effect of this on my playfellow was painful; he was much

* There exists an aristocracy even amongst slates, perhaps from their occupying the most *elevated* position in every house. Small ones are called Ladies, a larger size Countesses, and the biggest of all are Duchesses.

7

frightened for several days; and it naturally occurred to me, after some time, that as I had deluded him with ghosts, / I might myself have been deluded by older persons, and that, after all, it might be a doubtful point whether ghost or devil ever really existed. I gathered all the information I could on the subject from the other boys, and was soon informed that there was a peculiar process by which the devil might be raised and become personally visible. I carefully collected from the traditions of different boys the visible forms in which the Prince of Darkness had been recorded to have appeared. Amongst them were –

> A rabbit
> An owl
> A black cat, very frequently
> A raven
> A man with a cloven foot, also frequent.

After long thinking over the subject, although checked by a belief that the enquiry was wicked, my curiosity at length overbalanced my fears, and I resolved to attempt to raise the devil. Naughty people, I was told, had made written compacts with the devil, and had signed them with their names written in their own blood. These had become very rich and great men during their life, a fact which might be well known. But, after death, they were described as having suffered and continuing to suffer physical torments throughout eternity, another fact which, to my uninstructed mind, it seemed difficult to prove.

As I only desired an interview with the gentleman in black simply to convince my senses of his existence, I declined adopting the legal forms of a bond, and preferred one more resembling that of leaving a visiting card, when, if not at home, I might expect the satisfaction of a return of the visit by the devil in person. /

Accordingly, having selected a promising locality, I went one evening towards dusk up into a deserted garret. Having closed the door, and I believe opened the window, I proceeded to cut my finger and draw a circle on the floor with the blood which flowed from the incision.

I then placed myself in the centre of the circle, and either said or read the Lord's Prayer backwards. This I accomplished at first with some trepidation and in great fear towards the close of the scene. I then stood still in the centre of that magic and superstitious circle, looking with intense anxiety in all directions, especially at the window

8

and at the chimney. Fortunately for myself, and for the reader also, if he is interested in this narrative, no owl or black cat or unlucky raven came into the room.

In either case my then weakened frame might have expiated this foolish experiment by its own extinction, or by the alienation of that too curious spirit which controlled its feeble powers.

After waiting some time for my expected but dreaded visitor, I, in some degree, recovered my self-possession, and leaving the circle of my incantation, I gradually opened the door and gently closing it, descended the stairs, at first slowly, and by degrees much more quickly. I then rejoined my companions, but said nothing whatever of my recent attempt. After supper the boys retired to bed. When we were in bed and the candle removed, I proceeded as usual to repeat my prayers silently to myself. After the few first sentences of the Lord's Prayer, I found that I had forgotten a sentence, and could not go on to the conclusion. This alarmed me very much, and having repeated another prayer or hymn, I remained long awake, and very unhappy. I thought that this forgetfulness was a punishment inflicted / upon me by the Almighty, and that I was a wicked little boy for having attempted to satisfy myself about the existence of a devil. The next night my memory was more faithful, and my prayers went on as usual. Still, however, I was unhappy, and continued to brood over the enquiry. My uninstructed faculties led me from doubts of the existence of a devil to doubts of the book and the religion which asserted him to be a living being. My sense of justice (whether it be innate or acquired) led me to believe that it was impossible that an almighty and all-merciful God could punish me, a poor little boy, with eternal torments because I had anxiously taken the only means I knew of to verify the truth or falsehood of the religion I had been taught. I thought over these things for a long time, and, in my own childish mind, wished and prayed that God would tell me what was true. After long meditation, I resolved to make an experiment to settle the question. I thought, if it was really of such immense importance to me here and hereafter to believe rightly, that the Almighty would not consign me to eternal misery because, after trying all means that I could devise, I was unable to know the truth. I took an odd mode of making the experiment; I resolved that at a certain hour of a certain day I would go to a certain room in the house, and that if I found the door open, I would believe the Bible; but that if it were closed, I should conclude that it was not true. I

9

remember well that the observation was made, but I have no recollection as to the state of the door. I presume it was found open from the circumstances that, for many years after, I was no longer troubled by doubts, and indeed went through the usual religious forms with very little thought about their origin.

At length, as time went on, my bodily health was restored / by my native air: my mind, however, receiving but little instruction, began, I imagine, to prey upon itself – such at least I infer to have been the case from the following circumstance. One day, when uninterested in the sports of my little companions, I had retired into the shrubbery and was leaning my head, supported by my left arm, upon the lower branch of a thorn-tree. Listless and unoccupied, I *imagined* I had a headache. After a time I perceived, lying on the ground just under me, a small bright bit of metal. I instantly seized the precious discovery, and turning it over, examined both sides. I immediately concluded that I had discovered some valuable treasure, and running away to my deserted companions, showed them my golden coin. The little company became greatly excited, and declared that it must be gold, and that it was a piece of money of great value. We ran off to get the opinion of the usher; but whether he partook of the delusion, or we acquired our knowledge from the higher authority of the master, I know not. I only recollect the entire dissipation of my headache, and then my ultimate great disappointment when it was pronounced, upon the undoubted authority of the village doctor, that the square piece of brass I had found was a half-dram weight which had escaped from the box of a pair of medical scales. This little incident had an important effect upon my after-life. I reflected upon the extraordinary fact, that my headache had been entirely cured by the discovery of the piece of brass. Although I may not have put into words the principle, *that occupation of the mind is such a source of pleasure that it can relieve even the pain of a headache*; yet I am sure it practically gave an additional stimulus to me in many a difficult enquiry. Some few years after, when suffering under a form of tooth-ache, not acute though tediously / wearing, I often had recourse to a volume of Don Quixote, and still more frequently to one of Robinson Crusoe. Although at first it required a painful effort of attention, yet it almost always happened, after a time, that I had forgotten the moderate pain in the overpowering interest of the novel.

My most intimate companion and friend was a boy named Dacres, the son of Admiral Richard Dacres. We had often talked over such questions as those I have mentioned in this chapter, and we had made an agreement that whichever died first should, if possible, appear to the other after death, in order to satisfy the survivor about their solution.

After a year or two my young friend entered the Navy, but we kept up our friendship, and when he was ashore I saw him frequently. He was in a ship of eighty guns at the passage of the Dardanelles, under the command of Sir Thomas Duckworth. Ultimately he was sent home in charge of a prize-ship, in which he suffered the severest hardships during a long and tempestuous voyage, and then died of consumption.

I saw him a few days before his death, at the age of about eighteen. We talked of former times, but neither of us mentioned the compact. I believe it occurred to his mind: it was certainly strongly present to my own.

He died a few days after. On the evening of that day I retired to my own room, which was partially detached from the house by an intervening conservatory. I sat up until after midnight, endeavouring to read, but found it impossible to fix my attention on any subject, except the overpowering feeling of curiosity, which absorbed my mind. I then undressed and went into bed; but sleep was entirely banished. I had previously carefully examined whether any cat, bird, or living animal might be accidentally concealed in my room, / and I had studied the forms of the furniture lest they should in the darkness mislead me.

I passed a night of perfect sleeplessness. The distant clock and a faithful dog, just outside my own door, produced the only sounds which disturbed the intense silence of that anxious night. /

CHAPTER III

BOYHOOD

Taken to an exhibition of mechanism – Silver ladies – School near London –
Unjustly punished – Injurious effect – Ward's young mathematician's guide ,
– Got up in the night to study – Frederick Marryat interrupts – Treaty of
peace – Found out – Strange effect of treacle and cognac on boys – Taught to
write sermons under the Rev. Charles Simeon.

During my boyhood my mother took me to several exhibitions of
machinery. I well remember one of them in Hanover Square, by a
man who called himself Merlin. I was so greatly interested in it, that
the exhibitor remarked the circumstance, and after explaining some
of the objects to which the public had access, proposed to my mother
to take me up to his workshop, where I should see still more
wonderful automata. We accordingly ascended to the attic. There
were two uncovered female figures of silver, about twelve inches
high.

One of these walked or rather glided along a space of about four
feet, when she turned round and went back to her original place. She
used an eye-glass occasionally, and bowed frequently, as if
recognizing her acquaintances. The motions of her limbs were
singularly graceful.

The other silver figure was an admirable *danseuse*, with a bird on
the forefinger of her right hand, which wagged its tail, flapped its
wings, and opened its beak. This lady attitudinized in a most
fascinating manner. Her eyes were full of imagination, and
irresistible. /

These silver figures were the chef-d'oeuvres of the artist: they had
cost him years of unwearied labour, and were not even then finished.

After I left Devonshire I was placed at a school in the
neighbourhood of London, in which there were about thirty boys.

My first experience was unfortunate, and probably gave an
unfavourable turn to my whole career during my residence of three
years.

12

After I had been at school a few weeks, I went with one of my companions into the playground in the dusk of the evening. We heard a noise, as of people talking in an orchard at some distance, which belonged to our master. As the orchard had recently been robbed, we thought that thieves were again at work. We accordingly climbed over the boundary wall, ran across the field, and saw in the orchard beyond a couple of fellows evidently running away. We pursued as fast as our legs could carry us, and just got up to the supposed thieves at the ditch on the opposite side of the orchard.

A roar of laughter then greeted us from two of our own companions who had entered the orchard for the purpose of getting some manure for their flowers out of a rotten mulberry-tree. These boys were aware of our mistake, and had humoured it.

We now returned all together towards the playground, when we met our master, who immediately pronounced that we were each fined one shilling for being out of bounds. We two boys who had gone out of bounds to protect our master's property, and who if thieves had really been there would probably have been half-killed by them, attempted to remonstrate and explain the case; but all / remonstrance was vain, and we were accordingly fined. I never forgot that injustice.

The school-room adjoined the house, but was not directly connected with it. It contained a library of about three hundred volumes on various subjects, generally very well selected; it also contained one or two works on subjects which do not usually attract at that period of life. I derived much advantage from this library; and I now mention it because I think it of great importance that a library should exist in every school-room.

Among the books was a treatise on algebra, called 'Ward's Young Mathematician's Guide'.[a] I was always partial to my arithmetical lessons, but this book attracted my particular attention. After I had been at this school for about a twelvemonth, I proposed to one of my school-fellows, who was of a studious habit, that we should get up every morning at three oclock, light a fire in the school-room, and work until five or half-past five. We accomplished this pretty regularly for several months. Our plan had, however, become partially known to a few of our companions. One of these, a tall boy, bigger than ourselves, having heard of it, asked me to allow him to

---

[a] John Ward, *The young mathematician's guide* (London, 1707, etc.).

13

get up with us, urging that his sole object was to study, and that it would be of great importance to him in after-life. I had the cruelty to refuse this very reasonable request. The subject has often recurred to my memory, but never without regret.

Another of my young companions, Frederick Marryat,* made the same request, but not with the same motive. I told him we got up in order to work; that he would only play, and that we should then be found out. After some time, having exhausted all his arguments, Marryat told me he was / determined to get up, and would do it whether I liked it or not.

Marryat slept in the same room as myself: it contained five beds. Our room opened upon a landing, and its door was exactly opposite that of the master. A flight of stairs led up to a passage just over the room in which the master and mistress slept. Passing along this passage, another flight of stairs led down, on the other side of the master's bedroom, to another landing, from which another flight of stairs led down to the external door of the house, leading by a long passage to the school-room.

Through this devious course I had cautiously threaded my way, calling up my companion in his room at the top of the last flight of stairs almost every night for several months.

One night on trying to open the door of my own bedroom, I found Marryat's bed projecting a little before the door, so that I could not open it. I perceived that this was done purposely, in order that I might awaken him. I therefore cautiously, and by degrees, pushed his bed back without awaking him, and went as usual to my work. This occurred two or three nights successively.

One night, however, I found a piece of pack-thread tied to the door lock, which I traced to Marryat's bed, and concluded it was tied to his arm or hand. I merely untied the cord from the lock, and passed on.

A few nights later I found it impossible to untie the cord, so I cut it with my pocket-knife. The cord then became thicker and thicker for several nights, but still my pen-knife did its work.

One night I found a small chain fixed to the lock, and passing thence into Marryat's bed. This defeated my efforts for that night, and I retired to my own bed. The next night / I was provided with a pair of pliers, and unbent one of the links, leaving the two portions attached to Marryat's arm and to the lock of the door. This occurred

* Afterwards Captain Marryat.

14

several times, varying by stouter chains, and by having a padlock which I could not pick in the dark.

At last one morning I found a chain too strong for the tools I possessed; so I retired to my own bed, defeated. The next night, however, I provided myself with a ball of pack-thread. As soon as I heard by his breathing that Marryat was asleep, I crept over to the door, drew one end of my ball of pack-thread through a link of the too-powerful chain, and bringing it back with me to bed, gave it a sudden jerk by pulling both ends of the pack-thread passing through the link of the chain.

Marryat jumped up, put out his hand to the door, found his chain all right, and then lay down. As soon as he was asleep again, I repeated the operation. Having awakened him for the third time, I let go one end of the string, and drew it back by the other, so that he was unable at daylight to detect the cause.

At last, however, I found it expedient to enter into a treaty of peace, the basis of which was that I should allow Marryat to join the night party; but that nobody else should be admitted. This continued for a short time; but, one by one, three or four other boys, friends of Marryat, joined our party, and, as I had anticipated, no work was done. We all got to play; we let off fireworks in the playground, and were of course discovered.

Our master read us a very grave lecture at breakfast upon the impropriety of this irregular system of turning night into day, and pointed out its injurious effects upon the health. This, he said, was so remarkable that he could distinguish by / their pallid countenances those who had taken part in it. Now he certainly did point out every boy who had been up on the night we were detected. But it appeared to me very odd that the same means of judging had not enabled him long before to discover the two boys who had for several months habitually practised this system of turning night into day.

Another of our pranks never received its solution in our master's mind; indeed I myself scarcely knew its early history. Somehow or other, a Russian young gentleman, who was a parlour-boarder, had I believe, expatiated to Marryat on the virtues of cognac.

One evening my friend came to me with a quart bottle of what he called excellent stuff. A council was held amongst a few of us boys to decide how we should dispose of this treasure. I did not myself much admire the liquid, but suggested that it might be very good when mixed up with a lot of treacle. This thought was unanimously adopted, and a subscription made to purchase the treacle. Having no vessel sufficiently large to hold the intended mixture, I proposed to take one of our garden-pots, stopping up the hole in its bottom with a cork.

A good big earthen vessel, thus extemporised, was then filled with this wonderful mixture. A spoon or two, an oyster-shell, and various other contrivances delivered it to its numerous consumers, and all the boys got a greater or less share, according to their taste for this extraordinary liqueur.

The feast was over, the garden-pot was restored to its owner, and the treacled lips of the boys had been wiped with their handkerchiefs or on their coat-sleeves, when the bell announced that it was prayer-time. We all knelt in silence at our respective desks. As soon as the prayers were over, one of the oddest scenes occurred. /

Many boys rose up from their knees – but some fell down again. Some turned round several times, and then fell. Some turned round so often that they resembled spinning dervishes. Others were only more stupid than usual; some complained of being sick; many were very sleepy; others were sound asleep, and had to be carried to bed; some talked fast and heroically, two attempted psalmody, but none listened.

All investigation at the time was useless: we were sent off to bed as quickly as possible. It was only known that Count Cognac had married the sweet Miss Treacle, whom all the boys knew and loved, and who lodged at the grocer's, in the neighbouring village. But I believe neither the pedigree of the bridegroom nor his domicile were ever discovered. It is probable that he was of French origin, and dwelt in a cellar.

After I left this school I was for a few years under the care of an excellent clergyman in the neighbourhood of Cambridge. There were only six boys; but I fear I did not derive from it all the advantage that I might have done. I came into frequent contact with the Rev. Charles Simeon, and with many of his enthusiastic disciples. Every Sunday I had to write from memory an abstract of the sermon he preached in our village. Even at that period of my life I had a taste for generalization. Accordingly, having generalized some of Mr Simeon's sermons up to a kind of skeleton form, I tried, by way of experiment, to fill up such a form in a sermon of my own composing from the text of 'Alexander the coppersmith hath done us much harm'. As well as I remember, there were in my sermon some queer deductions from this text; but then they fulfilled all the usual conditions of our sermons: so thought also two of my companions to whom I communicated *in confidence* this new manufacture. /

By some unexplained circumstance my sermon relating to copper being isomorphous with Simeon's own productions, got by substitution into the hands of our master as the recollections of one of the other boys. Thereupon arose an awful explosion which I decline to paint.

I did, however, learn something at this school, for I observed a striking illustration of the economy of manufactures. Mr Simeon had the cure of a very wicked parish in Cambridge, whilst my instructor held that of a tolerably decent country village. If each minister had stuck to the instruction of his own parish, it would have necessitated the manufacture of four sermons per week, whilst, by this beneficial interchange of duties, only two were required.

Each congregation enjoyed also another advantage from this arrangement – the advantage of variety, which, when moderately indulged in, excites the appetite. /

CHAPTER IV

CAMBRIDGE

Universal language – Purchase Lacroix's quarto work on the integral calculus – Disappointment on getting no explanation of my mathematical difficulties – Origin of the Analytical Society – The Ghost Club – Chess – Sixpenny whist and guinea whist – Boating – Chemistry – Elected Lucasian Professor of Mathematics in 1828.

My father, with a view of acquiring some information which might be of use to me at Cambridge, had consulted a tutor of one of the colleges, who was passing his long vacation at the neighbouring watering-place, Teignmouth. He dined with us frequently. The advice of the Rev. Doctor was quite sound, but very limited. It might be summed up in one short sentence: 'Advise your son not to purchase his wine in Cambridge.'

Previously to my entrance at Trinity College, Cambridge, I resided for a time at Totnes, under the guidance of an Oxford tutor, who undertook to superintend my classical studies only.

During my residence at this place I accidentally heard, for the first time, of an idea of forming a universal language. I was much fascinated by it, and, soon after, proceeded to write a kind of grammar, and then to devise a dictionary. Some trace of the former, I think, I still possess: but I was stopped in my idea of making a universal dictionary by the apparent impossibility of arranging signs in any consecutive / order, so as to find, as in a dictionary, the meaning of each when wanted. It was only after I had been some time at Cambridge that I became acquainted with the work of 'Bishop Wilkins on Universal Language'.[a]

Being passionately fond of algebra, I had instructed myself by means of Ward's 'Young Mathematician's Guide', which had casually fallen into my hands at school. I now employed all my leisure in studying such mathematical works as accident brought to my knowledge. Amongst

---

[a] John Wilkins, *The mathematical and philosophical works* . . . (London, 1802) is listed in [R. Tucker], *Mathematical and scientific library of the late Charles Babbage* (London, 1872).

these were Humphrey Ditton's 'Fluxions', of which I could make nothing; Madame Agnesi's 'Analytical Institutions', from which I acquired some knowledge; Woodhouse's 'Principles of Analytical Calculation', from which I learned the notation of Leibnitz; and Lagrange's 'Théorie des Fonctions'. I possessed also the Fluxions of Maclaurin and of Simpson.[a]

Thus it happened that when I went to Cambridge I could work out such questions as the very moderate amount of mathematics which I then possessed admitted, with equal facility, in the dots of Newton, the d's of Leibnitz, or the dashes of Lagrange. I had, however, met with many difficulties, and looked forward with intense delight to the certainty of having them all removed on my arrival at Cambridge. I had in my imagination formed a plan for the institution amongst my future friends of a chess club, and also of another club for the discussion of mathematical subjects.

In 1811, during the war, it was very difficult to procure foreign books. I had heard of the great work of Lacroix, on the 'Differential and Integral Calculus',[b] which I longed to possess, and being misinformed that its price was two guineas, I resolved to purchase it in London on my passage to Cambridge. As soon as I arrived I went to the French / bookseller, Dulau, and to my great surprise found that the price of the book was seven guineas. After much thought I made the costly purchase, went on immediately to Cambridge, saw my tutor Hudson, got lodgings, and then spent the greater part of the night in turning over the pages of my newly acquired purchase. After a few days, I went to my public tutor Hudson, to ask the explanation of one of my mathematical difficulties. He listened to my question, said it would not be asked in the Senate House, and was of no sort of consequence, and advised me to get up the earlier subjects of the university studies.

After some little while I went to ask the explanation of another difficulty from one of the lecturers. He treated the question just in the same way. I made a third effort to be enlightened about what was really

---

[a] H. Ditton, *An institution of fluxions . . .* (London, 1706, etc.); M. G. A. M. Agnesi *Analytical institutions . . .* (London, 1801); R. Woodhouse, *The principles of analytical calculation* (Cambridge, 1803); J. L. Lagrange, *Théorie des fonctions analytiques* (Paris, 1797); C. Maclaurin, *A treatise on fluxions* (London, 1801); T. Simpson, *The doctrine and application of fluxions . . .* (London, 1805). (The works by Agnesi, Woodhouse, Maclaurin and Simpson are listed in [R. Tucker], *Mathematical and scientific library of the late Charles Babbage* (London, 1872).)

[b] S. F. Lacroix, *Traité du calcul differential et du calcul intégral* (Paris, 1797, etc.).

a doubtful question, and felt satisfied that the person I addressed knew nothing of the matter, although he took some pains to disguise his ignorance.

I thus acquired a distaste for the routine of the studies of the place, and devoured the papers of Euler and other mathematicians, scattered through innumerable volumes of the academies of Petersburgh, Berlin, and Paris, which the libraries I had recourse to contained.

Under these circumstances it was not surprising that I should perceive and be penetrated with the superior power of the notation of Leibnitz.

At an early period, probably at the commencement of the second year of my residence at Cambridge, a friend of mine, Michael Slegg, of Trinity, was taking wine with me, discussing mathematical subjects, to which he also was enthusiastically attached. Hearing the chapel bell ring, he took leave of me, promising to return for a cup of coffee. /

At this period Cambridge was agitated by a fierce controversy. Societies had been formed for printing and circulating the Bible. One party proposed to circulate it with notes, in order to make it intelligible; whilst the other scornfully rejected all explanations of the word of God as profane attempts to mend that which was perfect.

The walls of the town were placarded with broadsides, and posters were sent from house to house. One of the latter form of advertisement was lying upon my table when Slegg left me. Taking up the paper, and looking through it, I thought it, from its exaggerated tone, a good subject for a parody.

I then drew up the sketch of a society to be instituted for translating the small work of Lacroix on the Differential and Integral <Calculus>.[a] It proposed that we should have periodical meetings for the propagation of D's; and consigned to perdition all who supported the heresy of dots. It maintained that the work of Lacroix was so perfect that any comment was unnecessary.

On Slegg's return from chapel I put the parody into his hands. My friend enjoyed the joke heartily, and at parting asked my permission to show the parody to a mathematical friend of his, Mr Bromhead.[*]

The next day Slegg called on me, and said that he had put the joke into the hand of his friend, who, after laughing heartily, remarked that

---

[*] Afterwards Sir Edward Ffrench Bromhead, Bart., the author of an interesting paper in the Transactions of the Royal Society.

[a] S. F. Lacroix, *Traité elementaire de calcul différential et de calcul integral* . . . (Paris, 1802).

it was too good a joke to be lost, and proposed seriously that we should form a society for the cultivation of mathematics.

The next day Bromhead called on me. We talked the subject over, and agreed to hold a meeting at his lodgings / for the purpose of forming a society for the promotion of analysis.

At that meeting, besides the projectors, there were present Herschel, Peacock, D'Arblay,* Ryan,†, Robinson,‡ Frederick Maule,§ and several others. We constituted ourselves 'The Analytical Society'; hired a meeting-room, open daily; held meetings, read papers, and discussed them. Of course we were much ridiculed by the dons; and, not being put down, it was darkly hinted that we were young infidels, and that no good would come of us.

In the meantime we quietly pursued our course, and at last resolved to publish a volume of our transactions. Owing to the illness of one of the number, and to various other circumstances, the volume which was published was entirely contributed by Herschel and myself.

At last our work was printed, and it became necessary to decide upon a title. Recalling the slight imputation which had been made upon our faith, I suggested that the most appropriate title would be –

The Principles of pure D-ism in opposition to the Dot-age of the University.‖

In thus reviving this wicked pun, I ought at the same time to record an instance of forgiveness unparalleled in history. Fourteen years after, being then at Rome, I accidentally read in Galignani's newspaper the following paragraph, dated Cambridge: 'Yesterday the bells of St Mary rang on the election of Mr Babbage as Lucasian Professor of Mathematics.' /

If this event had happened during the lifetime of my father, it would have been most gratifying to myself, because, whilst it would have given him much pleasure, it would then also have afforded intense delight to my mother.

I concluded that the next post would bring me the official confirmation of this report, and after some consideration I sketched the draft of a letter, in which I proposed to thank the University sincerely for the honour they had done me, but to decline it.

* The only son of Madame D'Arblay.
† Now the Right Honourable Sir Edward Ryan.
‡ The Rev. Dr Robinson, Master of the Temple.
§ A younger brother of the late Mr Justice Maule.
‖ Leibnitz indicated fluxions by a d, Newton by a dot.

21

This sketch of a letter was hardly dry when two of my intimate friends, the Rev. Mr Lunn and Mr Beilby Thompson,* who resided close to me in the Piazza del Populo, came over to congratulate me on the appointment. I showed them my proposed reply, against which they earnestly protested. Their first, and as they believed their strongest, reason was that it would give so much pleasure to my mother. To this I answered that my mother's opinion of her son had been confirmed by the reception he had met with in every foreign country he had visited, and that this, in her estimation, would add but little to it. To their next argument I had no satisfactory answer. It was that this election could not have occurred unless some friends of mine in England had taken active measures to promote it; that some of these might have been personal friends, but that many others might have exerted themselves entirely upon principle, and that it would be harsh to disappoint such friends, and reject such a compliment.

My own feelings were of a mixed nature. I saw the vast field that the Difference Engine had opened out; for, before I left England in the previous year, I had extended its mechanism to the tabulation of functions having no constant / difference, and more particularly I had arrived at the knowledge of the entire command it would have over the computation of the most important classes of tables, those of astronomy and of navigation. I was also most anxious to give my whole time to the completion of the mechanism of the Difference Engine No. 1 which I had then in hand. Small as the admitted duties of the Lucasian Chair were, I felt that they would absorb time which I thought better devoted to the completion of the Difference Engine. If I had then been aware that the lapse of a few years would have thrown upon me the enormous labour which the Analytical Engine absorbed, no motive short of absolute necessity would have induced me to accept any office which might, in the slightest degree, withdraw my attention from its contrivance.

The result of this consultation with my two friends was, that I determined to accept the Chair of Newton, and to hold it for a few years. In 1839 the demands of the Analytical Engine upon my attention had become so incessant and so exhausting, that even the few duties of the Lucasian Chair had a sensible effect in impairing my bodily strength. I therefore sent in my resignation.

* Afterwards Lord Wenlock.

In January, 1829, I visited Cambridge, to fulfil one of the first duties of my new office, the examination for Dr Smith's prizes.

These two prizes, of twenty-five pounds each, exercise a very curious and important influence. Usually three or four hundred young men are examined previously to taking their degree. The University officers examine and place them in the order of their mathematical merit. The class called Wranglers is the highest; of these the first is called the senior wrangler, the others the second and third, etc., wranglers. /

All the young men who have just taken their degree, whether with or without honours, are qualified to compete for the Smith's prizes by sending in notice to the electors, who consist of the three Professors of Geometry, Astronomy, and Physics, assisted occasionally by two official electors, the Vice-Chancellor and the Master of Trinity College. However, in point of fact, generally three, and rarely above six young men compete.

It is manifest that the University officers, who examine several hundred young men, cannot bestow the same minute attention upon each as those who, at the utmost, only examine six. Nor is this of any importance, except to the few first wranglers, who usually are candidates for these prizes. The consequence is that the examiners of the Smith's prizes constitute, as it were, a court of appeal from the decision of the University officers. The decision of the latter is thus therefore, necessarily appealed against upon every occasion. Perhaps in one out of five or six cases the second or third wrangler obtains the first Smith's prize. I may add that in the few cases known to me previously to my becoming an examiner, the public opinion of the University always approved those decisions, without implying any censure on the officers of the University.

In forming my set of questions, I consulted the late Dean of Ely[a] and another friend, in order that I might not suddenly deviate too much from the usual style of examinations.

After having examined the young men, I sat up the whole night, carefully weighing the relative merits of their answers. I found, with some mortification, that, according to my marks, the second wrangler ought to have the first prize. I therefore put aside the papers until the day before the decision. I then took an unmarked copy of my questions, and put new / numbers for their respective values. After

---

[a] George Peacock (1791–1858).

very carefully going over the whole of the examination papers again, I arrived almost exactly at my former conclusion.

On our meeting at the Vice-Chancellor's, that functionary asked me, as the senior professor, what was my decision as to the two prizes. I stated that the result of my examination obliged me to award the first prize to the second wrangler. Professor Airy was then asked the same question. He made the same reply. Professor Lax being then asked, said he had arrived at the same conclusion as his two colleagues.

The Vice-Chancellor remarked that when we altered the arrangement of the University Examiners, it was very satisfactory that we should be unanimous. Professor Airy observed that this satisfaction was enhanced by the fact of the remarkable difference in the tastes of the three examiners.

The Vice-Chancellor, turning to me, asked whether it might be permitted to enquire the numbers we had respectively assigned to each candidate.

I and my colleagues immediately mentioned our numbers, which Professor Airy at once reduced to a common scale. On this it appeared that the number of marks assigned to each by Professor Airy and myself very nearly agreed, whilst that of Professor Lax differed but little.

On this occasion the first Smith's prize was assigned to the second wrangler, Mr Cavendish, now Duke of Devonshire, the present Chancellor of the University.

The result of the whole of my after experience showed that amongst the highest men the peculiar tastes of the examiners had no effect in disturbing the proper decision.

I held the Chair of Newton for some few years, and still feel deeply grateful for the honour the University conferred / upon me – the only honour I ever received in my own country.*

I must now return to my pursuits during my residence at Cambridge, the account of which has been partially interrupted by the history of my appointment to the Chair of Newton.

Whilst I was an undergraduate, I lived probably in a greater variety

---

* This professorship is not in the gift of the Government. The electors are the masters of the various colleges. It was founded in 1663 by Henry Lucas, M.P. for the University, and was endowed by him with a small estate in Bedfordshire. During my tenure of that office my net receipts were between £80 and £90 a year. I am glad to find that the estate is now improved, and that the University have added an annual salary to the Chair of Newton.

of sets than any of my young companions. But my chief and choicest consisted of some ten or a dozen friends who usually breakfasted with me every Sunday after chapel; arriving at about nine, and remaining to between twelve and one o'clock. We discussed all knowable and many unknowable things.

At one time we resolved ourselves into a Ghost Club, and proceeded to collect evidence, and entered into a considerable correspondence upon the subject. Some of this was both interesting and instructive.

At another time we resolved ourselves into a club which we called The Extractors. Its rules were as follows:

1. Every member shall communicate his address to the Secretary once in six months.

2. If this communication is delayed beyond twelve months, it shall be taken for granted that his relatives had shut him up as insane.

3. Every effort legal and illegal shall be made to get him out of the madhouse. Hence the name of the club – The Extractors. /

4. Every candidate for admission as a member shall produce six certificates. Three that he is sane and three others that he is insane.

It has often occurred to me to enquire of my legal friends whether, if the sanity of any member of the club had been questioned in after-life, he would have adduced the fact of membership of the Club of Extractors as an indication of sanity or of insanity.

During the first part of my residence at Cambridge, I played at chess very frequently, often with D'Arblay and with several other good players. There was at that period a fellow-commoner at Trinity named Brande, who devoted almost his whole time to the study of chess. I was invited to meet him one evening at the rooms of a common friend for the purpose of trying our strength.

On arriving at my friend's rooms, I found a note informing me that he had gone to Newmarket, and had left coffee and the chessmen for us. I was myself tormented by great shyness, and my yet unseen adversary was, I understood, equally diffident. I was sitting before the chess-board when Brande entered. I rose, he advanced, sat down, and took a white and a black pawn from the board, which he held, one in either hand. I pointed with my finger to the left hand and won the move.

The game then commenced; it was rather a long one, and I won it: but not a word was exchanged until the end: when Brande uttered the first word. 'Another?' To this I nodded assent.

How that game was decided I do not now remember; but the first sentence pronounced by either of us, was a remark by Brande, that he had lost the first game by a certain move of his white bishop. To this I replied, that I thought he was / mistaken, and that the real cause of his losing the game arose from the use I had made of my knight two moves previously to his white bishop's move.

We then immediately began to replace the men on the board in the positions they occupied at that particular point of the game when the white bishop's move was made. Each took up any piece indiscriminately, and placed it without hesitation on the exact square on which it had stood. It then became apparent that the effective move to which I had referred was that of my knight.

Brande, during his residence at Cambridge, studied chess regularly several hours each day, and read almost every treatise on the subject. After he left college he travelled abroad, took lessons from every celebrated teacher, and played with all the most eminent players on the Continent.

At intervals of three or four years I occasionally met him in London. After the usual greeting he always proposed that we should play a game of chess.

I found on these occasions, that if I played any of the ordinary openings, such as are found in the books, I was sure to be beaten. The only way in which I had a chance of winning, was by making early in the game a move so bad that it had not been mentioned in any treatise. Brande possessed, and had read, almost every book upon the subject.

Another set which I frequently joined were addicted to sixpenny whist. It consisted of Higman, afterwards Tutor of Trinity; Follet, afterward Attorney-General; of a learned and accomplished Dean still living, and I have no doubt still playing an excellent rubber, and myself. We not unfrequently sat from chapel-time in the evening until the sound / of the morning chapel bell again called us to our religious duties.

I mixed occasionally with a different set of whist players at Jesus College. They played high: guinea points, and five guineas on the rubber. I was always a most welcome visitor, not from my skill at the game; but because I never played more than shilling points and five shillings on the rubber. Consequently my partner had what they considered an advantage: namely, that of playing guinea points with one of our adversaries and pounds points with the other.

Totally different in character was another set in which I mixed. I was very fond of boating, not of the manual labour of rowing, but the more intellectual art of sailing. I kept a beautiful light, London-built boat, and occasionally took long voyages down the river, beyond Ely into the fens. To accomplish these trips, it was necessary to have two or three strong fellows to row when the wind failed or was contrary. These were useful friends upon my aquatic expeditions, but not being of exactly the same calibre as my friends of the Ghost Club, were very cruelly and disrespectfully called by them 'my Tom fools'.

The plan of our voyage was thus: I sent my servant to the apothecary for a thing called an aegrotat, which I understood, for I never saw one, meant a certificate that I was indisposed, and that it would be injurious to my health to attend chapel, or hall, or lectures. This was forwarded to the college authorities.

I also directed my servant to order the cook to send me a large well-seasoned meat pie, a couple of fowls, etc. These were packed in a hamper with three or four bottles of wine and one of noyeau. We sailed when the wind was fair, and rowed when there was none. Whittlesea Mere was a very / favourite resort for sailing, fishing, and shooting. Sometimes we reached Lynn. After various adventures and five or six days of hard exercise in the open air, we returned with our health and more renovated than if the best physician had prescribed for us.

During my residence at Cambridge, Smithson Tennant was the Professor of Chemistry, and I attended his lectures. Having a spare room, I turned it into a kind of laboratory, in which Herschel worked with me, until he set up a rival one of his own. We both occasionally assisted the Professor in preparing his experiments. The science of chemistry had not then assumed the vast development it has now attained. I gave up its practical pursuit soon after I resided in London, but I have never regretted the time I bestowed upon it at the commencement of my career. I had hoped to have long continued to enjoy the friendship of my entertaining and valued instructor, and to have profited by his introducing me to the science of the metropolis, but his tragical fate deprived me of that advantage. Whilst riding with General Bulow across a drawbridge at Boulogne, the bolt having been displaced, Smithson Tennant was precipitated to the bottom, and killed on the spot. The General, having an earlier warning, set spurs to his horse, and just escaped a similar fate.

My views respecting the notation of Leibnitz now (1812) received confirmation from an extensive course of reading. I became convinced that the notation of fluxions must ultimately prove a strong impediment to the progress of English science. But I knew, also, that it was hopeless for any young and unknown author to attempt to introduce the notation of Leibnitz into an elementary work. This opinion naturally / suggested to me the idea of translating the smaller work of Lacroix. It is possible, although I have no recollection of it, that the same idea may have occurred to several of my colleagues of the Analytical Society, but most of them were so occupied, first with their degree, and then with their examination for fellowships, that no steps were at that time taken by any of them on that subject.

Unencumbered by these distractions, I commenced the task, but at what period of time I do not exactly recollect, I had finished a portion of the translation, and laid it aside, when, some years afterwards, Peacock called on me in Devonshire Street, and stated that both Herschel and himself were convinced that the change from the dots to the D's would not be accomplished until some foreign work of eminence should be translated into English. Peacock then proposed that I should either finish the translation which I had commenced, or that Herschel and himself should complete the remainder of my translation. I suggested that we should toss up which alternative to take. It was determined by lot that we should make a joint translation. Some months after, the translation of the small work of Lacroix was published.

For several years after, the progress of the notation of Leibnitz at Cambridge was slow. It is true that the tutors of the two largest colleges had adopted it, but it was taught at none of the other colleges.

It is always difficult to think and reason in a new language, and this difficulty discouraged all but men of energetic minds. I saw, however, that, by making it their interest to do so, the change might be accomplished. I therefore proposed to make a large collection of examples of the differential and integral calculus, consisting merely of the statement of each problem and its final solution. I foresaw that if such a publication / existed, all those tutors who did not approve of the change of the Newtonian notation would yet, in order to save their own time and trouble, go to this collection of examples to find problems to set to their pupils. After a short time the use of the new signs would become familiar, and I anticipated their general adoption at Cambridge as a matter of course.

I commenced by copying out a large portion of the work of Hirsch.[a] I then communicated to Peacock and Herschel my view, and proposed that they should each contribute a portion.

Peacock considerably modified my plan by giving the process of solution to a large number of the questions. Herschel prepared the questions in finite differences, and I supplied the examples to the calculus of functions. In a very few years the change was completely established; and thus at last the English cultivators of mathematical science, untrammelled by a limited and imperfect system of signs, entered on equal terms into competition with their continental rivals. /

---

[a] M. Hirsch, *Integraltafeln, oder sammlung von integralformeln* (Berlin, 1810).

29

CHAPTER V

DIFFERENCE ENGINE NO. 1

Oh no! we never mention it,
Its name is never heard.

Difference Engine No. 1 – First idea at Cambridge, 1812 – Plan for dividing
astronomical instruments – Idea of a machine to calculate tables by
differences – Illustrations by piles of cannonballs.

Calculating machines comprise various pieces of mechanism for assisting the human mind in executing the operations of arithmetic. Some few of these perform the whole operation without any mental attention when once the given numbers have been put into the machine.

Others require a moderate portion of mental attention: these latter are generally of much simpler construction than the former, and it may also be added, are less useful.

The simplest way of deciding to which of these two classes any calculating machine belongs is to ask its maker – Whether, when the numbers on which it is to operate are placed in the instrument, it is capable of arriving at its result by the mere motion of a spring, a descending weight, or any other constant force? If the answer be in the affirmative, the machine is really automatic; if otherwise, it is not self-acting.

Of the various machines I have had occasion to examine, many of those for addition and subtraction have been found / to be automatic. Of machines for multiplication and division, which have fully come under my examination, I cannot at present recall one to my memory as absolutely fulfilling this condition.

The earliest idea that I can trace in my own mind of calculating arithmetical tables by machinery arose in this manner:

One evening I was sitting in the rooms of the Analytical Society, at Cambridge, my head leaning forward on the table in a kind of dreamy mood, with a table of logarithms lying open before me. Another

30

member, coming into the room, and seeing me half asleep, called out, 'Well, Babbage, what are you dreaming about?' to which I replied, 'I am thinking that all these tables (pointing to the logarithms) might be calculated by machinery.'

I am indebted to my friend, the Rev. Dr Robinson, the Master of the Temple, for this anecdote. The event must have happened either in 1812 or 1813.

About 1819 I was occupied with devising means for accurately dividing astronomical instruments, and had arrived at a plan which I thought was likely to succeed perfectly. I had also at that time been speculating about making machinery to compute arithmetical tables.

One morning I called upon the late Dr Wollaston, to consult him about my plan for dividing instruments. On talking over the matter, it turned out that my system was exactly that which had been described by the Duke de Chaulnes, in the Memoirs of the French Academy of Sciences, about fifty or sixty years before. I then mentioned my other idea of computing tables by machinery, which Dr Wollaston thought a more promising subject.

I considered that a machine to execute the mere isolated / operations of arithmetic, would be comparatively of little value, unless it were very easily set to do its work, and unless it executed not only accurately, but with great rapidity, whatever it was required to do.

On the other hand, the method of differences supplied a general principle by which *all* tables might be computed through limited intervals, by one uniform process. Again, the method of differences required the use of mechanism for addition only. In order, however, to ensure accuracy in the printed tables, it was necessary that the machine which computed tables should also set them up in type, or else supply a mould in which stereotype plates of those tables could be cast.

I now began to sketch out arrangements for accomplishing the several partial processes which were required. The arithmetical part must consist of two distinct processes – the power of adding one digit to another, and also of carrying the tens to the next digit, if it should be necessary.

The first idea was, naturally, to add each digit successively. This, however, would occupy much time if the numbers added together consisted of many places of figures.

The next step was to add all the digits of the two numbers each to

31

each at the same instant, but reserving a certain mechanical memorandum, wherever a carriage became due. These carriages were then to be executed successively.

Having made various drawings, I now began to make models of some portions of the machine, to see how they would act. Each number was to be expressed upon wheels placed upon an axis; there being one wheel for each figure in the number operated upon.

Having arrived at a certain point in my progress, it became necessary to have teeth of a peculiar form cut upon these / wheels. As my own lathe was not fit for this job, I took the wheels to a wheel-cutter at Lambeth, to whom I carefully conveyed my instructions, leaving with him a drawing as his guide.

These wheels arrived late one night, and the next morning I began putting them in action with my other mechanism, when, to my utter astonishment, I found they were quite unfit for their task. I examined the shape of their teeth, compared them with those in the drawings, and found they agreed perfectly; yet they could not perform their intended work. I had been so certain of the truth of my previous reasoning, that I now began to be somewhat uneasy. I reflected that, if the reasoning about which I had been so certain should prove to have been really fallacious, I could then no longer trust the power of my own reason. I therefore went over with my wheels to the artist who had formed the teeth, in order that I might arrive at some explanation of this extraordinary contradiction.

On conferring with him, it turned out that, when he had understood fully the peculiar form of the teeth of wheels, he discovered that his wheel-cutting engine had not got amongst its divisions that precise number which I had required. He therefore had asked me whether another number, which his machine possessed, would not equally answer my object. I had inadvertently replied in the affirmative. He then made arrangements for the precise number of teeth I required; and the new wheels performed their expected duty perfectly.

The next step was to devise means for printing the tables to be computed by this machine. My first plan was to make it put together movable type. I proposed to make metal boxes, each containing 3,000 types of one of the ten digits. These types were to be made to pass out one by one from the / bottom of their boxes, when required by the computing part of the machine.

But here a new difficulty arose. The attendant who put the types into the boxes might, by mistake, put a wrong type in one or more of them. This cause of error I removed in the following manner: There are usually certain notches in the side of the type. I caused these notches to be so placed that all the type of any given digit possessed the same characteristic notches, which no other type had. Thus, when the boxes were filled, by passing a small wire down these peculiar notches, it would be impeded in its passage, if there were included in the row a single wrong figure. Also, if any digit were accidentally turned upside down, it would be indicated by the stoppage of the testing wire.

One notch was reserved as common to every species of type. The object of this was that, before the types which the Difference Engine had used for its computation were removed from the iron platform on which they were placed, a steel wire should be passed through this common notch, and remain there. The tables, composed of movable types, thus interlocked, could never have any of their figures drawn out by adhesion to the inking-roller, and then by possibility be restored in an inverted order. A small block of such figures tied together by a bit of string, remained unbroken for several years, although it was rather roughly used as a plaything by my children. One such box was finished, and delivered its type satisfactorily.

Another plan for printing the tables, was to place the ordinary printing type round the edges of the wheels. Then, as each successive number was produced by the arithmetical part, the type-wheels would move down upon a plate of soft composition, upon which the tabular number would be impressed. / This mould was formed of a mixture of plaster of Paris with other materials, so as to become hard in the course of a few hours.

The first difficulty arose from the impression of one tabular number on the mould being distorted by the succeeding one.

I was not then aware that a very slight depth of impression from the type would be quite sufficient. I surmounted the difficulty by previously passing a roller, having longitudinal wedge-shaped projections, over the plastic material. This formed a series of small depressions in the matrix between each line. Thus the expansion arising from the impression of one line partially filled up the small depression or ditch which occurred between each successive line.

The various minute difficulties of this kind were successively overcome; but subsequent experience has proved that the depth necessary for stereotype moulds is very small, and that even thick

33

paper, prepared in a peculiar manner, is quite sufficient for the purpose.

Another series of experiments were, however, made for the purpose of punching the computed numbers upon copperplate. A special machine was contrived and constructed, which might be called a co-ordinate machine, because it moved the copperplate and steel punches in the direction of three rectangular co-ordinates. This machine was afterwards found very useful for many other purposes. It was, in fact, a general shaping machine, upon which many parts of the Difference Engine were formed.[a]

Several specimens of surface and copperplate printing, as well as of the copperplates, produced by these means, were exhibited at the Exhibition of 1862.

I have proposed and drawn various machines for the purpose of calculating a series of numbers forming tables / by means of a certain system called 'The Method of Differences', which it is the object of this sketch to explain.

The first Difference Engine with which I am acquainted comprised a few figures, and was made by myself, between 1820 and June 1822. It consisted of from six to eight figures. A much larger and more perfect engine was subsequently commenced in 1823 for the Government.

It was proposed that this latter Difference Engine should have six orders of differences, each consisting of about twenty places of figures, and also that it should print the tables it computed.

The small portion of it which was placed in the International Exhibition of 1862 was put together nearly thirty years ago. It was accompanied by various parts intended to enable it to print the results it calculated, either as a single copy on paper – or by putting together movable types – or by stereotype plates taken from moulds punched by the machine – or from copperplates impressed by it. The parts necessary for the execution of each of these processes were made, but these were not at that time attached to the calculating part of the machine.

A considerable number of the parts by which the printing was to be accomplished, as also several specimens of portions of tables punched on copper, and of stereotype moulds, were exhibited in a glass case adjacent to the engine.

---

[a] The proofs of *Passages from the life of a philosopher* (MSS Buxton 10–12, Museum of the History of Science, Oxford) include the following autograph addition: 'In an improved form it is still found one of the most serviceable machine tools in my own workshop, being of a size which can be worked by the foot although it is more frequently driven by the steam-engine.'

In 1834 Dr Lardner published, in the *Edinburgh Review*,* a very elaborate description of this portion of the machine, in which he explained clearly the method of differences.

It is very singular that two persons, one resident in London, the other in Sweden, should both have been struck, on reading this review, with the simplicity of the mathematical principle / of differences as applied to the calculation of tables, and should have been so fascinated with it as to have undertaken to construct a machine of the kind.

Mr Deacon, of Beaufort House, Strand, whose mechanical skill is well known, made, for his own satisfaction, a small model of the calculating part of such a machine, which was shown only to a few friends, and of the existence of which I was not aware until the Swedish machine was brought to London.

Mr Scheutz, an eminent printer at Stockholm, had far greater difficulties to encounter. The construction of mechanism, as well as the mathematical part of the question, was entirely new to him. He, however, undertook to make a machine having four differences, and fourteen places of figures, and capable of printing its own tables.

After many years' indefatigable labour, and an almost ruinous expense, aided by grants from his government, by the constant assistance of his son, and by the support of many enlightened members of the Swedish Academy, he completed his Difference Engine. It was brought to London, and some time afterwards exhibited at the great Exhibition at Paris. It was then purchased for the Dudley Observatory at Albany by an enlightened and public-spirited merchant of that city, John F. Rathbone, Esq.

An exact copy of this machine was made by Messrs Donkin and Co., for the English Government, and is now in use in the Registrar-General's Department at Somerset House. It is very much to be regretted that this specimen of English workmanship was not exhibited in the International Exhibition. /

Explanation of the Difference Engine

Those who are only familiar with ordinary arithmetic may, by following out with the pen some of the examples which will be given, easily make themselves acquainted with the simple principles on which the Difference Engine acts.

It is necessary to state distinctly at the outset, that the Difference

---

* 'Edinburgh Review', No. cxx, July, 1834. <Reprinted in *Works of Babbage*, Vol. 2.>

Engine is not intended to answer special questions. Its object is to calculate and print a *series* of results formed according to given laws. These are called tables – many such are in use in various trades. For example there are collections of tables of the amount of any number of pounds from 1 to 100 lb. of butchers' meat at various prices per lb. Let us examine one of these tables: viz. – the price of meat 5*d*. per lb., we find

Number Lbs	Table Price s. d.
1	0 5
2	0 10
3	1 3
4	1 8
5	2 1

There are two ways of computing this table:

1. We might have multiplied the number of pounds in each line by 5, the price per lb., and have put down the result in £. *s. d.*, as in the 2nd column: or,

2. We might have put down the price of 1 lb., which is 5*d*., and have added five pence for each succeeding lb.

Let us now examine the relative advantages of each plan. We shall find that if we had multiplied each number of pounds in / the table by 5, and put down the resulting amount, then every number in the table would have been computed independently. If, therefore, an error had been committed, it would not have affected any but the single tabular number at which it had been made. On the other hand, if a single error had occurred in the system of computing by adding five at each step, any such error would have rendered the whole of the rest of the table untrue.

Thus the system of calculating by differences, which is the easiest, is much more liable to error. It has, on the other hand, this great advantage: viz., that when the table has been so computed, if we calculate its last term directly, and if it agree with the last term found by the continual addition of 5, we shall then be quite certain that every term throughout is correct. In the system of computing each term directly, we possess no such check upon our accuracy.

Now the table we have been considering is, in fact, merely a table whose first difference is constant and equal to five. If we express it in pence it becomes –

36

	Table	1st difference
1	5	5
2	10	5
3	15	5
4	20	5
5	25	

Any machine, therefore, which could add one number to another, and at the same time retain the original number called the first difference for the next operation, would be able to compute all such tables.

Let us now consider another form of table which might readily occur to a boy playing with his marbles, or to a young lady with the balls of her solitaire board. /

The boy may place a row of his marbles on the sand, at equal distances from each other, thus –

He might then, beginning with the second, place two other marbles under each, thus –

He might then, beginning with the third, place three other marbles under each group, and so on; commencing always one group later, and making the addition one marble more each time. The several groups would stand thus arranged –

He will not fail to observe that he has thus formed a series of triangular groups, every group having an equal number of marbles in each of its three sides. Also that the side of each successive group contains one more marble than that of its preceding group.

Now an inquisitive boy would naturally count the numbers in each group and he would find them thus –

1   3   6   10   15   21

37

He might also want to know how many marbles the thirtieth or any other distant group might contain. Perhaps he might go to papa to obtain this information; but I much fear papa would snub him, and would tell him that it was nonsense – that it was useless – that nobody knew the number, and so forth. If the boy is told by papa, that he is not able to answer the question, then I recommend him to pay careful attention to whatever that father may at any time say, for he has overcome two of the greatest obstacles to the acquisition / of knowledge – inasmuch as he possesses the consciousness that he does not know – and he has the moral courage to avow it.*

If papa fail to inform him, let him go to mamma, who will not fail to find means to satisfy her darling's curiosity. In the meantime the author of this sketch will endeavour to lead his young friend to make use of his own common sense for the purpose of becoming better acquainted with the triangular figures he has formed with his marbles.

In the case of the table of the price of butcher's meat, it was obvious that it could be formed by adding the same *constant* difference continually to the first term. Now suppose we place the numbers of our groups of marbles in a column, as we did our prices of various weights of meat. Instead of adding a certain difference, as we did in the former case, let us subtract the figures representing each group of marbles from the figures of the succeeding group in the table. The process will stand thus:

Number of the group	Table Number of marbles in each group	1st difference Difference between the number of marbles in each group and that in the next	2nd difference
1	1	1	1
2	3	2	1
3	6	3	1
4	10	4	1
5	15	5	1
6	21	6	
7	28	7	

It is usual to call the third column thus formed *the column of / first differences*. It is evident in the present instance that that column

* The most remarkable instance I ever met with of the distinctness with which any individual perceived the exact boundary of his own knowledge, was that of the late Dr Wollaston.

38

represents the natural numbers. But we already know that the first difference of the natural numbers is constant and equal to unity. It appears, therefore, that a table of these numbers, representing the group of marbles, might be constructed to any extent by mere addition – using the number 1 as the first number of the table, the number 1 as the first difference, and also the number 1 as the second difference, which last always remains constant.

Now as we could find the value of any given number of pounds of meat directly, without going through all the previous part of the table, so by a somewhat different rule we can find at once the value of any group whose number is given.

Thus, if we require the number of marbles in the fifth group, proceed thus:

Take the number of the group	5
Add 1 to this number, it becomes	6
Multiply these numbers together	2)30
Divide the product by 2	15

This gives 15, the number of marbles in the fifth group.

If the reader will take the trouble to calculate with his pencil the five groups given above, he will soon perceive the general truth of this rule.

We have now arrived at the fact that this table – like that of the price of butchers' meat – can be calculated by two different methods. By the first, each number of the table is calculated independently: by the second, the truth of each number depends upon the truth of all the previous numbers.

Perhaps my young friend may now ask me, What is the use of such tables? Until he has advanced further in his / arithmetical studies, he must take for granted that they are of some use. The very table about which he has been reasoning possesses a special name – it is called a Table of Triangular Numbers. Almost every general collection of tables hitherto published contains portions of it of more or less extent.

Above a century ago, a volume in small quarto, containing the first 20,000 triangular numbers, was published at the Hague by E. De Joncourt, A.M., and Professor of Philosophy.* I cannot resist

---

* 'On the Nature and Notable Use of the most Simple Trigonal Numbers', by E. De Joncourt, at the Hague, 1762.

quoting the author's enthusiastic expression of the happiness he enjoyed in composing his celebrated work:

The Trigonals here to be found, and nowhere else, are exactly elaborate. Let the candid reader make the best of these numbers, and feel (if possible) in perusing my work the pleasure I had in composing it.

That sweet joy may arise from such contemplations cannot be denied. Numbers and lines have many charms, unseen by vulgar eyes, and only discovered to the unwearied and respectful sons of art. In features the serpentine line (who starts not at the name) produces beauty and love; and in numbers, high powers, and humble roots, give soft delight.

Lo! the raptured arithmetician! Easily satisfied, he asks no Brussels lace, nor a coach and six. To calculate, contents his liveliest desires, and obedient numbers are within his reach.

I hope my young friend is acquainted with the fact – that the product of any number multiplied by itself is called the square of that number. Thus 36 is the product of 6 multiplied by 6, and 36 is called the square of 6. I would now recommend him to examine the series of square numbers

$$1, 4, 9, 16, 25, 36, 49, 64, \ldots /$$

and to make, for his own instruction, the series of their first and second differences, and then to apply to it the same reasoning which has been already applied to the Table of Triangular Numbers.

When he feels that he has mastered that table, I shall be happy to accompany mamma's darling to Woolwich or to Portsmouth, where he will find some practical illustrations of the use of his newly acquired numbers. He will find scattered about in the arsenal various heaps of cannonballs, some of them triangular, others square or oblong pyramids.

Looking on the simplest form – the triangular pyramid – he will observe that it exactly represents his own heaps of marbles placed each successively above one another until the top of the pyramid contains only a single ball.

The new series thus formed by the addition of his own triangular numbers is:

Number	Table	1st difference	2nd difference	3rd difference
1	1	3	3	1
2	4	6	4	1
3	10	10	5	1
4	20	15	6	
5	35	21		
6	56			

40

He will at once perceive that this table of the number of cannon-balls contained in a triangular pyramid can be carried to any extent by simply adding successive differences, the third of which is constant.

The next step will naturally be to enquire how any number in this table can be calculated by itself. A little consideration will lead him to a fair guess; a little industry will enable him to confirm his conjecture.

It will be observed at p. 36 that in order to find independently / any number of the table of the price of butchers' meat, the following rule was observed:

Take the number whose tabular number is required.
Multiply it by the first difference.
This product is equal to the required tabular number.

Again, at p. 39, the rule for finding any triangular number was:

Take the number of the group	5
Add 1 to this number, it becomes	6
Multiply these numbers together	2)30
Divide the product by 2	15

This is the number of marbles in the 5th group.

Now let us make a bold conjecture respecting the table of cannon-balls, and try this rule:

Take the number whose tabular number is required, say	5
Add 1 to that number	6
Add 1 more to that number	7
Multiply all three numbers together	2)210
Divide by 2	105

The real number in the 5th pyramid is 35. But the number 105 at which we have arrived is exactly three times as great. If, therefore, instead of dividing by 2 we had divided by 2 and also by 3, we should have arrived at a true result in this distance.

The amended rule is therefore – /

41

Take the number whose tabular number is required, say	n
Add 1 to it	$n + 1$
Add 1 to this	$n + 2$
Multiply these three numbers together	$n \times (n + 1) \times (n + 2)$
Divide by $1 \times 2 \times 3$	
The result is	$\dfrac{n\,(n + 1)\,(n + 2)}{6}$

This rule will, upon trial, be found to give correctly every tabular number.

By similar reasoning we might arrive at the knowledge of the number of cannonballs in square and rectangular pyramids. But it is presumed that enough has been stated to enable the reader to form some general notion of the method of calculating arithmetical tables by differences which are constant.

It may now be stated that mathematicians have discovered that all the tables most important for practical purposes, such as those relating to astronomy and navigation, can, although they may not possess any constant differences, still be calculated in detached portions by that method.

Hence the importance of having machinery to calculate by differences, which, if well made, cannot err; and which, if carelessly set, presents in the last term it calculates the power of verification of every antecedent term.

Of the mechanical arrangements necessary for computing tables by the method of differences

From the preceding explanation it appears that all tables may be calculated, to a greater or less extent, by the method of differences. That method requires, for its successful / execution, little beyond mechanical means of performing the arithmetical operation of addition. Subtraction can, by the aid of a well-known artifice, be converted into addition.

The process of addition includes two distinct parts. The first consists of the addition of any one digit to another digit. The second consists in carrying the tens to the next digit above.

Let us take the case of the addition of the two following numbers, in which no carriages occur:

$$6023$$
$$1970$$

$$7993$$

It will be observed that, in making this addition, the mind acts by successive steps. The person adding says to himself –

> 0 and 3 make three,
> 7 and 2 make nine,
> 9 and 0 make nine,
> 1 and 6 make seven.

In the following addition there are several carriages:

$$2648$$
$$4564$$

$$7212$$

The person adding says to himself –

> 4 and 8 make 12: put down 2 and carry one.
> 1 and 6 are 7 and 4 make 11: put down 1 and carry one.
> 1 and 5 are 6 and 6 make 12: put down 2 and carry one.
> 1 and 4 are 5 and 2 make   7: put down 7.

Now, the length of time required for adding one number to another is mainly dependent upon the number of figures to / be added. If we could tell the average time required by the mind to add two figures together, the time required for adding any given number of figures to another equal number would be found by multiplying that average time by the number of digits in either number.

When we attempt to perform such additions by machinery we might follow exactly the usual process of the human mind. In that case we might take a series of wheels, each having marked on its edges the digits 0, 1, 2, 3, 4, 5, 6, 7, 8, 9. These wheels might be placed above each other upon an axis. The lowest would indicate the units' figure, the next above the tens, and so on, as in the Difference Engine at the Exhibition, a woodcut of which faces the title-page.

Several such axes, with their figure wheels, might be placed around a system of central wheels, with which the wheels of any one or more axes might at times be made to gear. Thus the figures on any one axis might, by means of those central wheels, be added to the figure wheels of any other axis.

But it may fairly be executed, and it is indeed of great importance that calculations made by machinery should not merely be exact, but that they should be done in a much shorter time than those performed by the human mind. Suppose there were no tens to carry, as in the first of the two cases; then, if we possessed mechanism capable of adding any one digit to any other in the units' place of figures, a similar mechanism might be placed above it to add the tens' figures, and so on for as many figures as might be required.

But in this case, since there are no carriageways, each digit might be added to its corresponding digit at the same time. Thus, the time of adding by means of mechanism, any two numbers, however many figures they might consist of, would / not exceed that of adding a single digit to another digit. If this could be accomplished it would render additions and subtractions with numbers having ten, twenty, fifty, or any number of figures, as rapid as those operations are with single figures.

Let us now examine the case in which there were several carriages. Its successive stages may be better explained, thus –

	2648
Stages	4584
	———
1 Add units figure = 4	2642
2 Carry	1
	———
	2652
3 Add tens figure = 8	8
	———
	2632
4 Carry	1
	———
	2732
5 Add hundreds figure = 5	5
	———
	2232
6 Carry	1
	———
	3232
7 Add thousands figure = 4	4
	———
	7232
8 Carry 0. There is no carriage.	

44

Now if, as in this case, all the carriages were known, it would then be possible to make all the additions of digits at the same time, provided we could also record each carriage as it became due. We might then complete the addition by adding, at the same instant, each carriage in its proper place. The process would then stand thus: /

		2648	
		4564	
Stages	⌠	6102	Add each digit to the digit above
1	⌡	111	Record the carriages
2	{	7212	Add the above carriages

Now, whatever mechanism is contrived for adding any one digit to any other must, of course, be able to add the largest digit, nine, to that other digit. Supposing, therefore, one unit of number to be passed over in one second of time, it is evident that any number of pairs of digits may be added together in nine seconds, and that, when all the consequent carriages are known, as in the above case, it will cost one second more to make those carriages. Thus, addition and carriage would be completed in ten seconds, even though the numbers consisted each of a hundred figures.

But, unfortunately, there are multitudes of cases in which the carriages that become due are only known in successive periods of time. As an example, add together the two following numbers:

	8473
Stages	1528
1 Add all the digits	9991
2 Carry on tens and warn next carriage	1
	9901
3 Carry on hundreds, and ditto	1
	9001
4 Carry on thousands, and ditto	1
	00001
5 Carry on ten thousands	1
	10001 /

45

In this case the carriages only become known successively, and they amount to the number of figures to be added; consequently, the mere addition of two numbers, each of fifty places of figures, would require only nine seconds of time, whilst the possible carriages would consume fifty seconds.

The mechanical means I employed to make these carriages bears some slight analogy to the operation of the faculty of memory. A toothed wheel had the ten digits marked upon its edge; between the nine and the zero a projecting tooth was placed. Whenever any wheel, in receiving addition, passed from nine to zero, the projecting tooth pushed over a certain lever. Thus, as soon as the nine seconds of time required for addition were ended, every carriage which had *become due* was indicated by the altered position of its lever. An arm now went round, which was so contrived that the act of replacing that lever caused the carriage which its position indicated to be made to the next figure above. But this figure might be a nine, in which case, in passing to zero, it would put over its lever, and so on. By placing the arms spirally round an axis, these successive carriages were accomplished.

Multitudes of contrivances were designed, and almost endless drawings made, for the purpose of economizing the time and simplifying the mechanism of carriage. In that portion of the Difference Engine in the Exhibition of 1862 the time of carriage has been reduced to about one-fourth part of what was at first required.

At last having exhausted, during years of labour, the principle of successive carriages, it occurred to me that it might be possible to teach mechanism to accomplish another mental process, namely – to foresee. This idea occurred to me in October, 1834. It cost me much thought, but the / principle was arrived at in a short time. As soon as that was attained, the next step was to teach the mechanism which could foresee to act upon that foresight. This was not so difficult: certain mechanical means were soon devised which, although very far from simple, were yet sufficient to demonstrate the possibility of constructing such machinery.

The process of simplifying this form of carriage occupied me, at intervals, during a long series of years. The demands of the Analytical Engine, for the mechanical execution of arithmetical operations, were of the most extensive kind. The multitude of similar parts required by the Analytical Engine, amounting in some instances to upwards of fifty thousand, rendered any, even the simplest, improvement of each part a matter of the highest importance, more especially as regarded the diminished amount of expenditure for its construction.

Description of the existing portion of Difference Engine No. 1

That portion of Difference Engine, No. 1, which during the last twenty years has been in the museum of King's College, at Somerset House, is represented in the woodcut opposite the title page.

It consists of three columns; each column contains six cages; each cage contains one figure-wheel.

The column on the right hand has its lowest figure-wheel covered by a shade which is never removed, and to which the reader's attention need not be directed.

The figure-wheel next above may be placed by hand at any one of the ten digits. In the woodcut it stands at zero.

The third, fourth, and fifth cages are exactly the same as the second.

The sixth cage contains exactly the same as the four just / described. It also contains two other figure-wheels, which with a similar one above the frame, may also be dismissed from the reader's attention. Those wheels are entirely unconnected with the moving part of the engine, and are only used for memoranda.

It appears, therefore, that there are in the first column on the right-hand five figure-wheels, each of which may be set by hand to any of the figures 0, 1, 2, 3, 4, 5, 6, 7, 8, 9.

The lowest of these figure-wheels represents the unit's figure of any number; the next above the ten's figure, and so on. The highest figure-wheel will therefore represent tens of thousands.

Now, as each of these figure-wheels may be set by hand to any digit, it is possible to place on the first column any number up to 99999. It is on these wheels that the table to be calculated by the engine is expressed. This column is called the table column, and the axis of the wheels the table axis.

The second or middle column has also six cages, in each of which a figure-wheel is placed. It will be observed that in the lowest cage, the figure on the wheel is concealed by a shade. It may therefore be dismissed from the attention. The five other figure-wheels are exactly like the figure-wheels on the table axis, and can also represent any number up to 99999.

47

This column is called the first difference column, and the axis is called the first difference axis.

The third column, which is that on the left hand, has also six cages, in each of which is a figure-wheel capable of being set by hand to any digit.

The mechanism is so contrived that whatever may be the numbers placed respectively on the figure-wheels of each of / the three columns, the following succession of operations will take place as long as the handle is moved:

1. Whatever number is found upon the column of first differences will be added to the number found upon the table column.

2. The same first difference remaining upon its own column, the number found upon the column of second differences will be added to that first difference.

It appears, therefore, that with this small portion of the engine any table may be computed by the method of differences, provided neither the table itself, nor its first and second differences, exceed five places of figures.

If the whole engine had been completed it would have had six orders of differences, each of twenty places of figures, whilst the three first columns would each have had half a dozen additional figures.

This is the simplest explanation of that portion of the Difference Engine No. 1, at the Exhibition of 1862. There are, however, certain modifications in this fragment which render its exhibition more instructive, and which even give a mechanical insight into those higher powers with which I had endowed it in its complete state.

As a matter of convenience in exhibiting it, there is an arrangement by which the *three* upper figures of the second difference are transformed into a small engine which counts the natural numbers.

By this means it can be set to compute any table whose second difference is constant and less than 1000, whilst at the same time it thus shows the position in the table of each tabular number.

In the existing portion there are three bells; they can be respectively ordered to ring when the table, its first difference / and its second difference, pass from positive to negative. Several weeks after the machine had been placed in my drawing-room, a friend came by appointment to test its power of calculating tables. After the engine had computed several tables, I remarked that it was evidently finding the root of a quadratic equation; I therefore set the bells to

48

watch it. After some time the proper bell sounded twice, indicating, and giving the two positive roots to be 28 and 30. The table thus calculated related to the barometer and really involved a quadratic equation, although its maker had not previously observed it. I afterwards set the engine to tabulate a formula containing impossible roots, and of course the other bell warned me when it had attained those roots. I had never before used these bells, simply because I did not think the power it thus possessed to be of any practical utility.

Again, the lowest cages of the table, and of the first difference, have been made use of for the purpose of illustrating three important faculties of the finished engine.

1. The portion exhibited can calculate any table whose third difference is constant and less than 10.

2. It can be used to show how much more rapidly astronomical tables can be calculated in an engine in which there is no constant difference.

3. It can be employed to illustrate those singular laws which might continue to be produced through ages, and yet after an enormous interval of time change into other different laws; each again to exist for ages, and then to be superseded by new laws. These views were first proposed in the 'Ninth Bridgewater Treatise'.

Amongst the various questions which have been asked respecting the Difference Engine, I will mention a few of the most remarkable: one gentleman addressed me thus: / 'Pray, Mr Babbage, can you explain to me in two words what is the principle of this machine?' Had the querist possessed a moderate acquaintance with mathematics I might in four words have conveyed to him the required information by answering, 'The method of differences.' The question might indeed have been answered with six characters thus –

$$\Delta^7 u_x = 0$$

but such information would have been unintelligible to such enquirers.

On two occasions I have been asked – 'Pray, Mr Babbage, if you put into the machine wrong figures, will the right answers come out?' In one case a member of the Upper, and in the other a member of the Lower, House put this question. I am not able rightly to apprehend the kind of confusion of ideas that could provoke such a question. I did, however, explain the following property, which might in some measure approach towards an answer to it.

It is possible to construct the Analytical Engine in such a manner that after the question is once communicated to the engine, it may be stopped at any turn of the handle and set on again as often as may be desired. At each stoppage every figure-wheel throughout the Engine, which is capable of being moved without breaking, may be moved on to any other digit. Yet after each of these apparent falsifications the engine will be found to make the next calculation with perfect truth.

The explanation is very simple, and the property itself useless. The whole of the mechanism ought of course to be enclosed in glass, and kept under lock and key, in which case the mechanism necessary to give it the property alluded to would be useless. /

STATEMENT

OF THE

CIRCUMSTANCES RESPECTING MR. BABBAGE'S
CALCULATING ENGINES.

1843.

CHAPTER VI[a]

Statement relative to the Difference Engine, drawn up by the late Sir H. Nicolas from the author's papers.

The following statement was drawn up by the late Sir Harris Nicolas, G.S.M. & G., from papers and documents in my possession relating to the Difference Engine. I believe every paper I possessed at all bearing on the subject was in his hands for several months.

For some time previous to 1822, Mr Babbage had been engaged in contriving machinery for the execution of extensive arithmetical operations, and in devising mechanism by which the machine that made the calculations might also print the results.

On 3 July, 1822, he published a letter to Sir Humphry Davy, President of the Royal Society, containing a statement of his views on that subject; and more particularly describing an engine for calculating astronomical, nautical, and other tables, by means of the 'method of differences'. In that letter it is stated that a small model, consisting of six figures, and capable of working two orders of differences, had been constructed; and that it performed its work in a satisfactory manner.

The concluding paragraph of that letter is as follows:

Whether I shall construct a larger engine of this kind, and bring to / perfection the others I have described, will, in a great measure, depend on the nature of the encouragement I may receive.

Induced, by a conviction of the great utility of such engines, to withdraw, for some time, my attention from a subject on which it has been engaged during several years, and which possesses charms of a higher order, I have now arrived at a point where success is no longer doubtful. It must, however,

---

[a] Sir Harris Nicolas's statement, reprinted in this chapter by Babbage, was first issued as an anonymous pamphlet in 1843 titled *Statement of the circumstances respecting Mr Babbage's Calculating Engines*. A facsimile of the title page appears on the facing page.

be attained at a very considerable expense, which would not probably be replaced, by the works it might produce, for a long period of time; and which is an undertaking I should feel unwilling to commence, as altogether foreign to my habits and pursuits.

The model alluded to had been shown to a large number of Mr Babbage's acquaintances, and to many other persons; and copies of his letter having been given to several of his friends, it is probable that one of the copies was sent to the Treasury.

On 1 April, 1823, the Lords of the Treasury referred that letter to the Royal Society, requesting –

The opinion of the Royal Society on the merits and utility of this invention.

On 1 May the Royal Society reported to the Treasury, that –

Mr Babbage has displayed great talent and ingenuity in the construction of his Machine for Computation, which the Committee think fully adequate to the attainment of the objects proposed by the inventor; and they consider Mr Babbage as highly deserving of public encouragement, in the prosecution of his arduous undertaking.*

On 21 May these papers were ordered to be printed by the House of Commons.[a]

In July, 1823, Mr Babbage had an interview with the Chancellor of the Exchequer (Mr Robinson†), to ascertain if it was the wish of the Government that he should construct a large engine of the kind, which would also print the results it calculated. /

From the conversation which took place on that occasion, Mr Babbage apprehended that such was the wish of the Government. The Chancellor of the Exchequer remarked that the Government were in general unwilling to make grants of money for any inventions, however meritorious; because, if they really possessed the merit claimed for them, the sale of the article produced would be the best, as well as largest reward of the inventor: but that the present case was an *exception*; it being apparent that the construction of such a machine could not be undertaken with a view to profit from the sale of its produce; and that, as

* Parliamentary Paper, No. 370, printed 22 May, 1823.
† Afterwards Lord Goderich, now Earl of Ripon.

[a] 'Mr Babbage's invention. Copies of the correspondence between the Lords Commissioners of His Majesty's Treasury and the President and Council of the Royal Society, relative to the invention of Mr Babbage', *Parliamentary Papers*, Vol. 15 (1823), pp. 9–14.

mathematical tables were peculiarly valuable for nautical purposes, it was deemed a fit object of encouragement by the Government.

The Chancellor of the Exchequer mentioned two modes of advancing money for the construction – either through the recommendation of a Committee of the House of Commons, or by taking a sum from the Civil Contingencies: and he observed that, as the Session of Parliament was near its termination, the latter course might, perhaps, be the most convenient.

Mr Babbage thinks the Chancellor of the Exchequer also made some observation, indicating that the amount of money taken from the Civil Contingencies would be smaller than that which might be had by means of a Committee of the House of Commons: and he then proposed to take £1000 as a commencement from the Civil Contingencies Fund. To this Mr Babbage replied, in words which he distinctly remembers, 'Would it be too much, in the first instance, to take £1500?' The Chancellor of the Exchequer immediately answered, that £1500 should be advanced.

Mr Babbage's opinion at that time was, that the engine would be completed in two, or at the most in three years; and that by having £1500 in the first instance, he would be / enabled to advance, from his own private funds, the residue of the £3000, or even £5000, which he then imagined the engine might possibly cost; so that he would not again have occasion to apply to government until it was completed. Some observations were made by the Chancellor of the Exchequer about the mode of accounting for the money received, as well as about its expenditure; but it seemed to be admitted that it was not possible to prescribe any very definite system, and that much must be left to Mr Babbage's own judgement.

Very unfortunately, no minute of that conversation was made at the time, nor was any sufficiently distinct understanding between the parties arrived at. Mr Babbage's conviction was, that whatever might be the labour and difficulty of the undertaking, the engine itself would, of course, become the property of the Government, which had paid for its construction.

Soon after this interview with the Chancellor of the Exchequer, a letter was sent from the Treasury to the Royal Society, informing that body that the Lords of the Treasury

Had directed the issue of £1500 to Mr Babbage, to enable him to bring his invention to perfection in the manner recommended.

These latter words, '*in the manner recommended*', can only refer to the previous recommendation of the Royal Society; but it does not appear, from the Report of the Royal Society, that *any plan*, *terms*, or *conditions* had been pointed out by that body.

Towards the end of July, 1823, Mr Babbage took measures for the construction of the present *Difference* Engine,* and it was regularly proceeded with for four years. /

In October, 1827, the expense incurred had amounted to £3475; and Mr Babbage having suffered severe domestic affliction, and being in a very ill state of health, was recommended by his medical advisers to travel on the Continent. He left, however, sufficient drawings to enable the work to be continued, and gave an order to his own banker to advance £1000 during his absence: he also received, from time to time, drawings and enquiries relating to the mechanism, and returned instructions to the engineer who was constructing it.

As it now appeared probable that the expense would much exceed what Mr Babbage had originally anticipated, he thought it desirable to inform the Government of that fact, and to procure a further grant. As a preliminary step, he wrote from Italy to his brother-in-law, Mr Wolryche Whitmore, to request that he would see Lord Goderich upon the subject of the interview in July, 1823; but it is probable that he did not sufficiently inform Mr Whitmore of all the circumstances of the case.

Mr Whitmore, having had some conversation with Lord Goderich on the subject, addressed a letter, dated on 29 February, 1828, to Mr Babbage, who was then at Rome, stating that

That interview was unsatisfactory; that Lord Goderich did not like to admit that there was any understanding, at the time the £1500 was advanced, that more would be given by government.

On Mr Babbage's return to England, towards the end of / 1828, he waited in person upon Lord Goderich, who admitted that the understanding of 1823 was not very definite. He then addressed a statement to the Duke of Wellington, as the head of the Government, explaining the previous steps in the affair; stating the reasons for his inferences

* It will be convenient to distinguish between –
1. The small *Model* of the original or Difference Engine.
2. The *Difference* Engine itself, belonging to the Government, a part only of which has been put together.
3. The designs for another *engine*, which in this Statement is called the Analytical Engine.

from what took place at the interview with the Chancellor of the Exchequer in July, 1823; and referring his Grace for further information to Lord Goderich, to whom also he sent a copy of that statement.

The Duke of Wellington, in consequence of this application, requested the Royal Society to enquire –

Whether the progress of the machine confirms them in their former opinion, that it will ultimately prove adequate to the important object it was intended to attain.

The Royal Society reported, in February, 1829, that –

They had not the slightest hesitation in pronouncing their decided opinion in the affirmative.

The Royal Society also expressed their hope that –

Whilst Mr Babbage's mind is intensely occupied in an undertaking likely to do so much honour to his country, he may be relieved, as much as possible, from all other sources of anxiety.

On 28 April, 1829, a Treasury Minute directed a further payment to Mr Babbage of

£1500 to enable him to complete the machine by which such important benefit to Science might be expected.

At that time the sum expended on the Engine amounted to £6697 12s., of which £3000 had been received from the Treasury; so that Mr Babbage had provided £3697 12s. from his own private funds.

Under these circumstances, by the advice of Mr Wolryche Whitmore, a meeting of Mr Babbage's personal friends was held on 12 May, 1829. It consisted of – /

> The Duke of Somerset
> Lord Ashley
> Sir John Franklin
> Mr Wolryche Whitmore
> Dr Fitton
> Mr Francis Baily
> Mr (now Sir John) Herschel

Being satisfied, upon enquiry, of the following facts, they came to the annexed resolutions:

1. That Mr Babbage was originally induced to take up the work, on its present extensive scale, by an understanding on his part that it was the wish

of government that he should do so, and by an advance of £1500, at the outset; with a full impression on his mind, that such further advances would be made as the work might require.

2. That Mr Babbage's expenditure had amounted to nearly £7000, while the whole sum advanced by Government was £3000.

3. That Mr Babbage had devoted the most assiduous and anxious attention to the progress of the engine, to the injury of his health, and the neglect and refusal of other profitable occupations.

4. That a very large expense remained to be incurred; and that his private fortune was not such as would justify his completing the engine, without further and effectual assistance from the Government.

5. That a personal application upon the subject should be made to the Duke of Wellington.

6. That if such application should be unsuccessful in procuring effectual and adequate assistance, they must regard Mr Babbage (considering the great pecuniary and personal sacrifices he will then have made; the entire expedition of all he had received from the public on the subject of its destination; and the moral certainty of completing it, to which it was, by his exertions, reduced) as no longer called on to proceed with an undertaking which might destroy his health, and injure, if not ruin, his fortune.

7. That Mr Wolryche Whitmore and Mr Herschel should request an interview with the Duke of Wellington, to state to his Grace these opinions on the subject.

Mr Whitmore and Mr Herschel accordingly had an interview with the Duke of Wellington; and some time after they were informed by the Chancellor of the Exchequer, to whom they had applied for his Grace's answer, that the Duke of / Wellington intended to see the portion of the engine which had been then made.

In November, 1829, the Duke of Wellington, accompanied by the Chancellor of the Exchequer (Mr Goulburn) and Lord Ashley, saw the *model* of the engine, the drawings, and the parts in progress. On the 23rd of that month Mr Babbage received a note from Mr Goulburn, dated on the 20th, informing him that the Duke of Wellington and himself had recommended the Treasury to make a further payment towards the completion of the machine; and that their lordships had in consequence directed a payment of £3000 to be made to him. This letter also contained a suggestion about separating the calculating from the printing part of the machine, which was repeated in the letter from the Treasury of 3 December, 1829, communicating officially the information contained in Mr Goulburn's private note, and stating that directions had been given –

To pay to you the further sum of £3000, to enable you to complete the machine which you have invented for the calculation of various tables; but I have to intimate to you that, in making this additional payment, my Lords think it extremely desirable that the machine should be so constructed, that, if any failure should take place in the attempt to print by it, the calculating part of the machine may nevertheless be perfect and available for that object.

Mr Babbage inferred from this further grant, that government had adopted his view of the arrangement entered into with the Chancellor of the Exchequer in July, 1823; but, to prevent the recurrence of difficulty from any remaining indistinctnéss, he wrote to Mr Goulburn, stating that, before he received the £3000, he wished to propose some general arrangements for expediting the completion of the engine, further notes of which he would shortly submit to him. On 25 November, 1829, he addressed a letter to Lord / Ashley, to be communicated to the Chancellor of the Exchequer, stating the grounds on which he thought the following arrangements desirable:

1. That the engine should be considered as the property of government.

2. That professional engineers should be appointed by government to examine the charges made for the work already executed, as well as for its future progress; and that such charges should be defrayed by government.

3. That under this arrangement he himself should continue to direct the construction of the engine, as he had hitherto done.

Mr Babbage also stated that he had been obliged to suspend the work for nearly nine months; and that such delay risked the final completion of the engine.

In reply to these suggestions, Mr Goulburn wrote to Lord Ashley, stating –

That we (the Government) could not adopt the course which Mr Babbage had pointed out, consistently with the principle on which we have rendered him assistance in the construction of his machine, and without considerable inconvenience. The view of the Government was, to assist an able and ingenious man of science, whose zeal had induced him to exceed the limits of prudence, in the construction of a work which would, if successful, redound to his honour, and be of great public advantage. We feel ourselves, therefore, under the necessity of adhering to our original intention, as expressed in the Minute of the Treasury, which granted Mr Babbage the last £3000, and in the letter in which I informed him of that grant.

Mr Goulburn's letter was enclosed by Lord Ashley to Mr Babbage, with a note, in which his lordship observed, with reference to Mr Goulburn's opinion, that it was /

A wrong view of the position in which Mr Babbage was placed, after his conference with Lord Goderich – which must be explained to him (Mr Goulburn).

'*The original intention*' of the Government is here stated to have been communicated to Mr Babbage, both in the letter from the Treasury of 3 December, 1829, granting the £3000, and also in Mr Goulburn's private letter of 20 November, 1829. These letters have been just given; and it certainly does not appear from either of them, that the 'original intention' was then in any degree more apparent than it was at the commencement of the undertaking in July, 1823.

On 16 December, 1829, Mr Babbage wrote to Lord Ashley, observing, that Mr Goulburn seemed to think that he [Mr Babbage] had commenced the machine on his own account; and that, pursuing it zealously, he had expended more than was prudent, and had then applied to government for aid. He remarked, that a reference to papers and dates would confirm his own positive declaration, that this was never for one moment, in *his* apprehension, the ground on which the matter rested; and that the following facts would prove that it was absolutely impossible it could have been so:

1. Mr Babbage referred to the passage* (already quoted) in his letter to Sir Humphry Davy, in which he had expressed his opinion as *decidedly adverse* to the plan of making a larger machine, on his own account.

2. Mr Babbage stated that the small model of the machine seen by the Duke of Wellington and Mr Goulburn, was completed *before* his interview with Lord Goderich in July, 1823; for it was alluded to in the report of the Royal Society, of 1 May, 1823.

3. That the interview with Lord Goderich having taken place in July, 1823; the present machine (i.e. the *Difference* / Engine) was commenced in *consequence* of that interview; and *after* Mr Babbage had received the first grant of £1500 on 7 August, 1823.

Having thus shown that the light in which Mr Goulburn viewed these transactions was founded on a misconception, Mr Babbage requested Lord Ashley to enquire whether the facts to which he had

* See page 54.

called Mr Goulburn's attention might not induce him to reconsider the subject. And in case Mr Goulburn should decline revising his opinion, then he wished Lord Ashley to ascertain the opinion of government, upon the contingent questions which he enclosed; viz. –

1. Supposing Mr Babbage received the £3000 now directed to be issued, what are the claims which government will have on the engine, or on himself?

2. Would Mr Babbage owe the £6000, or any part of that sum to the Government?

If this question be answered in the negative,

3. Is the portion of the Engine now made, as completely Mr Babbage's property as if it had been entirely paid for with his own money?

4. Is it expected by government that Mr Babbage should continue to construct the engine at his own private expense; and, if so, to what extent in money?

5. Supposing Mr Babbage should decline resuming the construction of the engine, to whom do the drawings and parts already made belong?

The following statement was also enclosed:

Expenses up to 9 May, 1829, when the work ceased		* £6628
Two grants of £1500 each, amounting to	£3000	
By Treasury Minute, Nov. 1829, but not yet received	3000	
	——	6000
		£628

In January, 1830, Mr Babbage wrote to Lord Goderich, / stating that the Chancellor of the Exchequer (Mr Goulburn) would probably apply to his Lordship respecting the interview in July, 1823. He therefore recalled some of the circumstances attending it to Lord Goderich, and concluded thus:

The matter was, as you have justly observed on another occasion, left, in a certain measure, indefinite; and I have never contended that any promise was made to me. My subsequent conduct was founded upon the impression left on my mind by that interview. I always considered that, whatever difficulties I might encounter, it could never happen that I should ultimately suffer any pecuniary loss.

* The difference between this sum and £6697 12s. mentioned in page 57 seems to have arisen from the fact of the former sum having included the estimated amount of a bill which, when received, was found to be less than had been anticipated.

I understand that Mr Goulburn wishes to ascertain from your Lordship whether, from the nature of that interview, it was reasonable that I should have such expectation.

In the meantime Mr Babbage had encountered difficulties of another kind. The engineer who had been constructing the engine under Mr Babbage's direction had delivered his bills in such a state that it was impossible to judge how far the charges were just and reasonable; and although Mr Babbage had paid several thousand pounds, yet there remained a considerable balance, which he was quite prepared and willing to pay, as soon as the accounts should be examined, and the charges approved of by professional engineers.

The delay in deciding whether the engine was the property of government, added greatly to this embarrassment. Mr Babbage, therefore, wrote to Lord Ashley on 8 February, to mention these difficulties; and to point out the serious inconvenience which would arise, in the future progress of the engine, from any dispute between the engineer and himself relative to payments.

On 24 February, 1830, Mr Babbage called on Lord Ashley, to request he would represent to the Duke of Wellington the facts of the case, and point out to his Grace / the importance of a decision. In the afternoon of the same day, he again saw Lord Ashley, who communicated to him the decision of the Government; to the following effect:

1. Although the Government would not pledge themselves to *complete* the machine, they were willing to declare it their property.

2. That professional engineers should be appointed to examine the bills.

3. That the Government were willing to advance £3000 more than the sum (£6000) already granted.

4. That, when the machine was completed, the Government would be willing to attend to any claim of Mr Babbage to remuneration, either by bringing it before the Treasury, or the House of Commons.

Thus, after considerable discussion, the doubts arising from the indefiniteness of the understanding with the Chancellor of the Exchequer, in July, 1823, were at length removed. Mr Babbage's impression of the original arrangement entered into between Lord Goderich and himself was thus formally adopted in the first three propositions: and the Government voluntarily added the expression of their disposition to attend to any claim of his for remuneration when the engine should be completed.

When the arrangements consequent upon this decision were made, the work of the engine was resumed, and continued to advance.

After some time, the increasing amount of costly drawings, and of parts of the engine already executed, remaining exposed to destruction from fire and from other casualties became a source of some anxiety.

These facts having been represented to Lord Althorp (then Chancellor of the Exchequer), an experienced surveyor / was directed to find a site adapted for a building for the reception of the engine in the neighbourhood of Mr Babbage's residence.

On 19 January the surveyor's reports were forwarded to Lord Althorp (the Chancellor of the Exchequer), who referred the case to a committee of practical engineers for their opinion. This committee reported strongly in favour of the removal, on the grounds of security, and of economy in completing the engine; and also recommended the site which had been previously selected by the surveyor. The Royal Society, also, to whom Lord Althorp had applied, examined the question, and likewise reported strongly to the same effect.

A lease of some property, adjacent to Mr Babbage's residence, was therefore subsequently granted by him to the Government; and a fireproof building, capable of containing the engine, with its drawings, and workshops necessary for its completion, were erected.

With respect to the expenses of constructing the engine, the following plan was agreed upon and carried out: The great bulk of the work was executed by the engineer under the direction of Mr Babbage. When the bills were sent in, they were immediately forwarded by him to two eminent engineers, Messrs Donkin and Field, who, at the request of government, had undertaken to examine their accuracy. On these gentlemen certifying those bills to be correct, Mr Babbage transmitted them to the Treasury; and after the usual forms, a warrant was issued directing the payment of the respective sums to Mr Babbage. This course, however, required considerable time; and the engineer having represented that he was unable to pay his workmen without more immediate advances, Mr Babbage, to prevent delay in completing / the engine, did himself, from time to time, advance from his own funds several sums of money; so that he was, in fact, usually in advance from £500 to £1000. Those sums were, of course, repaid when the Treasury warrants were issued.

Early in the year 1833, an event of great importance in the history of the engine occurred. Mr Babbage had directed a portion of it, consisting of sixteen figures, to be put together. It was capable of calculating tables having two or three orders of differences; and, to some extent, of forming other tables. The action of this portion completely justified the expectations raised, and gave a most satisfactory assurance of its final success.

The fireproof building and workshops having been completed, arrangements were made for the removal of the engine. Mr Babbage finding it no longer convenient to make payments in advance, informed the engineer that he should in future not pay him until the money was received from the Treasury. Upon receiving this intimation, the engineer immediately discontinued the construction of the engine, and dismissed the workmen employed on it; which fact Mr Babbage immediately communicated to the Treasury.

In this state of affairs it appeared, both to the Treasury and to Mr Babbage, that it would be better to complete the removal of the drawings, and all the parts of the engine to the fireproof buildings; and then make such arrangements between the Treasury and the engineer, respecting the future payments, as might prevent further discussion on that subject.

After much delay and difficulty the whole of the drawings, and parts of the engine, were at length removed to the fireproof building in East Street, Manchester Square. Mr Babbage wrote, on 16 July, 1834, to the Treasury, / informing their lordships of the fact – adding that no advance had been made in its construction for above a year and a quarter; and requesting further instructions on the subject.

Mr Babbage received a letter from the Treasury, expressing their lordships' satisfaction at learning that the drawings, and parts of the Calculating Engine were removed to the fireproof building, and stating that as soon as Mr Clement's accounts should be received and examined, they would

Take into consideration what further proceedings may be requisite with a view to its completion.

A few weeks afterwards Mr Babbage received a letter from the Treasury, conveying their lordships' authority to proceed with the construction of the engine.

During the time which had elapsed since the engineer had ceased to proceed with the construction of the engine, Mr Babbage had been deprived of the use of his own drawings. Having, in the meanwhile, naturally speculated upon the general principles on which machinery for calculation might be constructed, *a principle of an entirely new kind* occurred to him, the power of which over the most complicated arithmetical operations seemed nearly unbounded. On re-examining his drawings when returned to him by the engineer, the new principle appeared to be limited only by the extent of the mechanism it might require. The invention of simpler mechanical means for executing the elementary operations of the engine now derived a far greater importance than it had hitherto possessed; and should such simplifications be discovered, it seemed difficult to anticipate, or even to overestimate, the vast results which might be attained. In the engine for calculating by differences, such simplifications affected only about a hundred and twenty / similar parts, whilst in the new or *Analytical* Engine, they would affect a great many thousand. The *Difference* Engine might be constructed with more or less advantage by employing various mechanical modes for the operation of addition: the *Analytical* Engine could not *exist* without inventing for it a method of mechanical addition possessed of the utmost simplicity. In fact, it was not until upwards of twenty different mechanical modes for performing the operation of addition had been designed and drawn, that the necessary degree of simplicity required for the Analytical Engine was ultimately attained. Hence, therefore, the powerful motive for simplification.

These new views acquired additional importance, from their bearings upon the engine already partly executed for the Government. For, if such simplifications should be discovered, it might happen that the *Analytical* Engine would execute more rapidly the calculations for which the *Difference* Engine was intended; or, that the *Difference* Engine would itself be superseded by a far simpler mode of construction. Though these views might, perhaps, at that period have appeared visionary, both have subsequently been completely realized.

To withhold those new views from the Government, and under such circumstances to have allowed the construction of the engine to be resumed, would have been improper; yet the state of uncertainty in which those views were then necessarily involved rendered any *written* communication respecting their probable bearing on the Difference Engine a matter of very great difficulty. It appeared to Mr Babbage that the most straightforward course was to ask for an interview on the subject with the Head of the Government, and to communicate to him the exact state of the case. /

Had that interview taken place, the First Lord of the Treasury might have ascertained from his enquiries, in a manner quite impracticable by any written communications, the degree of importance which Mr Babbage attached to his new inventions, and his own opinion of their probable effect, in superseding the whole or any part of the original, or *Difference*, Engine. The First Lord of the Treasury would then have been in a position to decide, either on the immediate continuation and completion of the original design, or on its temporary suspension, until the character of the new views should be more fully developed by further drawings and examination.

There was another, although a far less material point, on which also it was desirable to obtain the opinion of the Government: the serious impediments to the progress of the engine, arising from the engineer's conduct, as well as the consequent great expense, had induced Mr Babbage to consider, whether it might not be possible to employ some other person as his agent for constructing it. His mind had gradually become convinced of the practicability of that measure; but he was also aware that however advantageous it might prove to the Government, from its greater economy, yet that it would add greatly to his own personal labour, responsibility, and anxiety.

On 26 September, 1834, Mr Babbage therefore requested an interview with Lord Melbourne, for the purpose of placing before him these views. Lord Melbourne acceded to the proposed interview, but it was then postponed; and soon after, the administration of which his lordship was the head went out of office, without the interview having taken place.

For the same purpose, Mr Babbage applied in December, / 1834, for an interview with the Duke of Wellington, who, in reply, expressed his wish to receive a written communication on the subject. He accordingly addressed a statement to his Grace, pointing out the only plans which, in his opinion, could be pursued for terminating the questions relative to the *Difference* Engine; namely,

1. The Government might desire Mr Babbage to continue the construction of the engine, in the hands of the person who has hitherto been employed in making it.

2. The Government might wish to know whether any other person could be substituted for the engineer at present employed to continue the construction – a course which was possible.

3. The Government might (although he did not presume that they would) substitute some person to superintend the completion of the engine instead of Mr Babbage himself.

4. The Government might be disposed to give up the undertaking entirely.

He also stated to the Duke of Wellington, the circumstances which had led him to the invention of a *new* engine, of far more extensive powers of calculation; which he then observed did not supersede the former one, but added greatly to its utility.

At this period, the impediments relating to the *Difference* Engine had been partially and temporarily removed. The chief difficulty would have been either the formation of new arrangements with the engineer, or the appointment of some other person to supply his place. This latter alternative, which was of great importance for economy as well as for its speedy completion, Mr Babbage had carefully examined, and was then prepared to point out means for its accomplishment. /

The duration of the Duke of Wellington's administration was short; and no decision on the subject of the *Difference* Engine was obtained.

On 15 May the *Difference* Engine was alluded to in the House of Commons; when the Chancellor of the Exchequer did Mr Babbage the justice to state distinctly, that the whole of the money voted had been expended in paying the workmen and for the materials employed in constructing it, and that not one shilling of it had ever gone into his own pocket.

About this time several communications took place between the Chancellor of the Exchequer and Mr Babbage, respecting a reference to the Royal Society for an opinion on the subject of the engine.

A new and serious impediment to the possibility of executing one of the plans which had been suggested to the Duke of Wellington for completing the *Difference* Engine arose from these delays. The draftsman whom Mr Babbage had, at his own expense, employed, both on the *Difference* and on the *Analytical* Engine, received an offer of a very liberal salary, if he would enter into an engagement abroad, which would occupy many years. His assistance was indispensable, and his services were retained only by Mr Babbage considerably increasing his salary.

On 14 January, 1836, Mr Babbage received a communication from the Chancellor of the Exchequer (Mr Spring Rice*), expressing his

---

* The present Lord Monteagle.

desire to come to some definite result on the subject of the calculating engine, in which he remarked, that the conclusion to be drawn from Mr Babbage's statement to the Duke of Wellington was, that he / (Mr Babbage) having invented a new machine, of far greater powers than the former one, wished to be informed if the Government would undertake to defray the expense of this *new* engine.

The Chancellor of the Exchequer then pointed out reasons why he should feel himself bound to look to the completion of the first machine, before he could propose to Parliament to enter on the consideration of the second: and he proposed to refer to the Royal Society for their opinion, authorizing them, if they thought fit, to employ any practical mechanist or engineer to assist them in their enquiries. The Chancellor of the Exchequer concluded with expressing his readiness to communicate with Mr Babbage respecting the best mode of attaining that result.

From these statements it is evident that Mr Babbage had failed in making his own views distinctly understood by the Chancellor of the Exchequer. His first anxiety, when applying to Lord Melbourne, had been respecting the question, whether the *discoveries* with which he was then advancing might not ultimately supersede the work already executed. His second object had been to point out a possible arrangement, by which great expense might be saved in the mechanical construction of the *Difference* Engine.

So far was Mr Babbage from having proposed to the Government to defray the expenses of the *new* or *Analytical* Engine, that though he expressly pointed out in the statement to the Duke of Wellington* four courses which it was possible for the Government to take – yet in no one of them was the construction of the *new* engine alluded to.

Those views of improved machinery for making calculations / which had appeared in but faint perspective in 1834, as likely to lead to important consequences, had, by this time, assumed a form and distinctness which fully justified the anticipations then made. By patient enquiry, aided by extensive drawings and notations, the projected *Analytical* Engine had acquired such powers, that it became necessary, for its further advancement, to simplify the elements of which it was composed. In the progress of this enquiry, Mr Babbage had gradually arrived at simpler mechanical modes of

* See page 67.

performing those arithmetical operations on which the action of the *Difference* Engine depended; and he felt it necessary to communicate these new circumstances, as well as their consequences, to the Chancellor of the Exchequer.

On 20 January, 1836, Mr Babbage wrote, in answer to the communication from the Chancellor of the Exchequer, that he did not, on re-examining the statement addressed to the Duke of Wellington, perceive that it contained *any application to take up the new or Analytical Engine*; and he accompanied this reply by a statement relative to the progress of the *Analytical* Engine, and its bearing upon the *Difference* Engine belonging to the Government. The former, it was said,

Is not only capable of accomplishing all those other complicated calculations which I had intended, but it also performs all calculations which were peculiar to the Difference Engine, both in less time, and to a greater extent: in fact, it completely supersedes the Difference Engine.

The reply then referred to the statement laid before the Duke of Wellington in July, 1834, in which it was said,

That all the elements of the Analytical were essentially different from those of the Difference Engine;

and that the mechanical simplicity to which its elements had now been reduced was such, that it would probably cost more / to finish the *old Difference* Engine on its original plan than to construct a *new* Difference Engine with the simplified elements devised for the *Analytical* Engine.

It then proceeded to state that –

The fact of a *new* superseding an *old* machine, in a very few years, is one of constant occurrence in our manufactories; and instances might be pointed out in which the advance of invention has been so rapid, and the demand for machinery so great, that half-finished machines have been thrown aside as useless before their completion.

It is now nearly fourteen years since I undertook for the Government to superintend the making of the Difference Engine. During nearly four years its construction has been absolutely stopped, and, instead of being employed in overcoming the physical impediments, I have been harassed by what may be called the moral difficulties of the question. It is painful to reflect that, in the time so employed, the first Difference Engine might, under more favourable circumstances, have been completed.

In making this Report, I wish distinctly to state, that I do not entertain the slightest doubt of the success of the Difference Engine; *nor do I intend it as any application to finish the one or to construct the other*; but I make it from a conviction that the information it contains ought to be communicated to those who must decide the question relative to the Difference Engine.

The reference to the Royal Society, proposed by the Chancellor of the Exchequer, in his letter of 14 January, 1836,* did not take place; and during more than a year and a half no further measures appear to have been adopted by the Government respecting the engine.

It was obviously of the greatest importance to Mr Babbage that a final decision should be made by the Government. When he undertook to superintend the construction of the *Difference* Engine for the Government, it was, of course, understood that he would not leave it unfinished. He had now been engaged fourteen years upon an object which he / had anticipated would not require more than two or three; and there seemed no limit to the time his engagement with the Government might thus be supposed to endure, unless some steps were taken to terminate it. Without such a decision Mr Babbage felt that he should be impeded in any plans he might form, and liable to the most serious interruption, if he should venture to enter upon the execution of them. He therefore most earnestly pressed, both by his personal applications and by those of his friends, for the settlement of the question. Mr Wolryche Whitmore, in particular, repeatedly urged upon the Chancellor of the Exchequer, personally, as well as by letter, the injustice of keeping Mr Babbage so very long in a state of suspense.

Time, however, passed on, and during nearly two years the question remained in the same state. Mr Babbage, wearied with this delay, determined upon making a last effort to obtain a decision. He wrote to the First Lord of the Treasury (Lord Melbourne) on 26 July, 1838, recalling to his lordship's attention the frequency of his applications on this subject, and urging the necessity of a final decision upon it. He observed, that if the question had become more difficult, because he had invented superior mechanism, which had superseded that which was already partly executed, this consequence had arisen from the very delay against which he had so repeatedly remonstrated. He then asked, for the last time, not for any favour, but for that which it was an injustice to withhold – a decision.

* See page 68.

On 16 August Mr Spring Rice (the Chancellor of the Exchequer) addressed a note to Mr Babbage, in reference to his application to Lord Melbourne. After recapitulating his former statement of the subject, which had been shown to be founded on a misapprehension, viz., that Mr Babbage / had made an *application* to the Government to construct for them the *Analytical* Engine, the Chancellor of the Exchequer enquired whether he was solicitous that steps should be taken for the completion of the old, or for the commencement of a new machine – and what he considered would be the cost of the one proceeding, and of the other?

Being absent on a distant journey, Mr Babbage could not reply to this note until 21 October. He then reminded the Chancellor of the Exchequer of his previous communication of 20 January, 1836 (see p. 69), in which it was expressly stated that he did *not* intend to make any application to construct a *new* machine; but that the communication to the Duke of Wellington and the one to himself were made, simply because he thought it would be unfair to conceal such important facts from those who were called upon to decide on the continuance or discontinuance of the construction of the *Difference Engine*.

With respect to the expense of either of the courses pointed out by the Chancellor of the Exchequer, Mr Babbage observed that, not being a professional engineer, and his past experience having taught him not to rely upon his own judgement on matters of that nature, he should be very reluctant to offer any opinion upon the subject.

In conclusion, Mr Babbage stated that the question he wished to have settled was –

Whether the Government required him to superintend the completion of the Difference Engine, which had been suspended during the last five years, according to the original plan and principles; or whether they intended to discontinue it altogether?

In November, 1841, Mr Babbage, on his return from the Continent, finding that Sir Robert Peel had become First / Lord of the Treasury, determined upon renewing his application for a decision of the question. With this view the previous pages of this statement were drawn up, and a copy of it was forwarded to him, accompanied by a letter from Mr Babbage, in which he observed –

Of course, when I undertook to give the invention of the calculating engine to the Government, and to superintend its construction, there must

71

have been an implied understanding that I should carry it on to its termination. I entered upon that understanding, believing that two or at the utmost that three years would complete it. The better part of my life has now been spent on that machine, and no progress whatever having been made since 1834, that understanding may possibly be considered by the Government as still subsisting: I am therefore naturally very anxious that this state of uncertainty should be put an end to as soon as possible.

Mr Babbage, in reply, received a note from Sir George Clerk (Secretary to the Treasury), stating that Sir Robert Peel feared that it would not be in his power to turn his attention to the subject for some days, but that he hoped, as soon as the great pressure of business previous to the opening of the session of Parliament was over, he might be able to determine on the best course to be pursued.

The session of Parliament closed in August, and Mr Babbage had received no further communication on the subject. Having availed himself of several private channels for recalling the question to Sir Robert Peel's attention without effect, Mr Babbage, on 8 October, 1842, again wrote to him, requesting an early decision.

On 4 November, 1842, a note from Sir Robert Peel explained to Mr Babbage that some delay had arisen, from his wish to communicate personally with the Chancellor of the Exchequer, who would shortly announce to him their joint conclusion on the subject.

On the same day Mr Babbage received a letter from Mr / Goulburn (the Chancellor of the Exchequer), who stated that he had communicated with Sir Robert Peel, and that they both regretted the necessity of abandoning the completion of a machine, on which so much scientific labour had been bestowed. He observed, that the expense necessary for rendering it either satisfactory to Mr Babbage or generally useful appeared, on the lowest calculation, so far to exceed what they should be justified in incurring, that they considered themselves as having no other alternative.

Mr Goulburn concluded by expressing their hope, that by the Government withdrawing all claim to the machine as already constructed, and placing it entirely at Mr Babbage's disposal, they might in some degree assist him in his future exertions in the cause of Science.

On 6 November, 1842, Mr Babbage wrote to Sir Robert Peel and the Chancellor of the Exchequer, acknowledging the receipt of their decision, thanking them for the offer of the machine as already constructed, but, under all the circumstances, declining to accept it.*

On 11 November Mr Babbage obtained an interview with Sir Robert Peel, and stated, that having given the original invention to the Government – having superintended for them its construction – having demonstrated the possibility of the undertaking by the completion of an important portion of it – and that the non-completion of the design arose neither from his fault nor his desire, but was the act of the Government itself, he felt that he had some claims on their consideration.

He rested those claims upon the sacrifices he had made, / both personal and pecuniary, in the advancement of the mechanical arts and of science – on the anxiety and the injury he had experienced by the delay of eight years in the decision of the Government on the subject, and on the great annoyance he had constantly been exposed to by the prevailing belief in the public mind that he had been amply remunerated by large grants of public money. Nothing, he observed, but some public act of the Government could ever fully refute that opinion, or repair the injustice with which he had been treated.

The result of this interview was entirely unsatisfactory. Mr Babbage went to it prepared, had his statement produced any effect, to have pointed out two courses, by either of which it was probable that not only a Difference Engine, but even the Analytical Engine, might in a few years have been completed. The state of Sir Robert Peel's information on the subject, and the views he took of Mr Babbage's services and position, prevented Mr Babbage from making any allusion to either of those plans.

Thus finally terminated an engagement, which had existed upwards of twenty years. During no part of the last eight of those years does there appear to have been any reason why the same decision should not have been arrived at by the Government as was at last actually pronounced.

It was during this last period that all the great principles on which the *Analytical* Engine rests were discovered, and that the mechanical contrivances in which they might be embodied were invented. The establishment which Mr Babbage had long maintained in his own

* The part of the *Difference* Engine already constructed, together with all the Drawings relating to the whole machine, were, in January, 1843 (by the direction of the Government), deposited in the Museum of King's College, London.

73

house, and at his own expense, was now directed with increased energy to the new enquiries required for its perfection.

In this statement the heavy sacrifices, both pecuniary and / personal, which the invention of these machines has entailed upon their author, have been alluded to as slightly as possible. Few can imagine, and none will every know their full extent. Some idea of those sacrifices must nevertheless have occurred to every one who has read this statement. During upwards of twenty years Mr Babbage has employed, in his own house, and at his own expense, workmen of various kinds, to assist him in making experiments necessary for attaining a knowledge of every art which could possibly tend to the perfection of those engines; and with that object he has frequently visited the manufactories of the Continent, as well as our own.

Since the discontinuance of the Difference Engine belonging to the Government, Mr Babbage has himself maintained an establishment for making drawings and descriptions demonstrating the nature and power of the *Analytical* Engine, and for its construction at some future period, when its value may be appreciated.

To these remarks it will only be added, that at an early stage of the construction of the *Difference* Engine he refused more than one highly desirable and profitable situation, in order that he might give his whole time and thoughts to the fulfilment of the engagement which he considered himself to have entered into with the Government. /

August, 1843

CHAPTER VII

DIFFERENCE ENGINE NO. 2

Difference Engine No. 2 – The Earl of Rosse, President of the Royal Society, proposed to the Government a plan by which the Difference Engine No. 2 might have been executed – It was addressed to the Earl of Derby, and rejected by his Chancellor of the Exchequer.

It was not until 1848, when I had mastered the subject of the Analytical Engine, that I resolved on making a complete set of drawings of the Difference Engine No. 2. In this I proposed to take advantage of all the improvements and simplifications which years of unwearied study had produced for the Analytical Engine.

In 1852, the Earl of Rosse, who, from its commencement, had looked forward with the greatest interest to the application of mechanism to purposes of calculation, and who was well acquainted with the drawings and notations of the Difference Engine No. 2, enquired of me whether I was willing to give them to the Government, provided they would have the engine constructed. My feeling was, after the sad experience of the past, that I ought not to think of sacrificing any further portion of my life upon the subject. If, however, they chose to have the Difference Engine made, I was ready to give them the whole of the drawings, and also the notations by which it was demonstrated that such a machine could be constructed, and that when made it would necessarily do the work prescribed for it. /

My much-valued friend, the late Sir Benjamin Hawes, had also been consulted, and it was agreed that the draft of a letter to Lord Derby, who was then Prime Minister, should be prepared; in which I should make this offer. Lord Rosse proposed to place my letter in Lord Derby's hands, with his own statement of a plan by which the whole question might be determined.

Lord Rosse's suggestion was, that the Government should apply to the President of the Institution of Civil Engineers to ascertain,

75

1. Whether it was possible, from the drawings and notations, to make an estimate of the cost of constructing the machine?

2. In case this question was answered in the affirmative – then, could a mechanical engineer be found who would undertake to construct it, and at what expense?

The Institution of Civil Engineers was undoubtedly the highest authority upon the first question. That being decided in the affirmative, no other body had equal power to find out those mechanical engineers who might be willing to undertake the contract.

Supposing both these questions, or even the latter only, answered in the negative, the proposition, of course, fell to the ground. But if they were both answered in the affirmative, then there would have arisen a further question for the consideration of the Government: namely, Whether the object to be obtained was worthy of the expenditure?

The final result of this eminently *practical* plan was communicated to the Royal Society by their President, in his address at their anniversary on 30 November, 1854.[a] The following is an extract: /

The progress of the work was suspended: there was a change of Government. Science was weighed against gold by a new standard, and it was resolved to proceed no further. No enterprise could have had its beginning under more auspicious circumstances: the Government had taken the initiative – they had called for advice, and the adviser was the highest scientific authority in this country; – your Council; guided by such men as Davy, Wollaston, and Herschel. By your Council the undertaking was inaugurated – by your Council it was watched over in its progress. That the first great effort to employ the powers of calculating mechanism, in aid of the human intellect, should have been suffered in this great country to expire fruitless, because there was no tangible evidence of immediate profit, as a British subject I deeply regret, and as a Fellow my regret is accompanied with feelings of bitter diasppointment. Where a question has once been disposed of, succeeding Governments rarely reopen it, still I thought I should not be doing my duty if I did not take some opportunity of bringing the facts once more before Government. Circumstances had changed, mechanical engineering had made much progress; the tools required and trained workmen were to be found in the workshops of the leading mechanists, the founder's art was so advanced that casting had been substituted for cutting, in making the change wheels, even of screw-cutting engines, and therefore it was very probable that persons would be found willing to undertake to complete the Difference Engine for a specific sum.

---

[a] Earl of Rosse PRS, 'Address of the President', *Proceedings of the Royal Society*, Vol. 7 (1855), pp. 248–63.

76

That finished, the question would then have arisen, how far it was advisable to endeavour, by the same means, to turn to account the great labour which had been expended under the guidance of inventive powers the most original, / controlled by mathematics of a very high order; and which had been wholly devoted for so many years to the great task of carrying the powers of calculating machinery to its utmost limits. Before I took any step I wrote to several very eminent men of science, enquiring whether, in their opinion, any great scientific object would be gained if Mr Babbage's views, as explained in Mènabrèa's little essay, were completely realized. The answers I received were strongly in the affirmative. As it was necessary the subject should be laid before Government in a form as practical as possible, I wrote to one of our most eminent mechanical engineers to enquire whether I should be safe in stating to Government that the expense of the Calculating Engine had been more than repaid in the improvements in mechanism directly referable to it; he replied, – unquestionably. Fortified by these opinions, I submitted this proposition to Government:- that they should call upon the President of the Society of Civil Engineers to report whether it would be practicable to make a contract for the completion of Mr Babbage's Difference Engine, and if so, for what sum. This was in 1852, during the short administration of Lord Derby, and it led to no result. The time was unfortunate; a great political contest was impending, and before there was a lull in politics, so that the voice of Science could be heard, Lord Derby's government was at an end.

The following letter[a] was then drawn up, and placed in Lord Derby's hands by Lord Rosse:

My Lord,   8 June, 1852
I take the liberty of drawing your Lordship's attention to the subject of the construction of a Difference Engine, for / calculating and printing Astronomical and Nautical Tables, which was brought under the notice of the Government so far back as the year 1823, and upon which the Government of that day desired the opinion of the Royal Society.

I annex a copy of the correspondence which took place at that time, and which your Lordship will observe was laid before Parliament.

The Committee of the Royal Society, to which the subject was referred, reported generally that the invention was one 'fully adequate to the attainment of the objects proposed by the inventor, and that they considered Mr Babbage as highly deserving of public encouragement in the prosecution of his arduous undertaking'. (*Report of Royal Society*, 1 May, 1823. *Parliamentary Paper*, 370, 22 May, 1823)

---

[a] Printed copies of the letter are in Buxton MSS 7, Museum of the History of Science, Oxford, and in the British Library, Add. MSS 37195 f82 and 37188 f525.

And in a subsequent and more detailed report, which I annex also, they state:

'The Committee have no intention of entering into any consideration of the abstract mathematical principle on which the practicability of such a machine as Mr Babbage's relies, nor of its public utility when completed. They consider the former as not only sufficiently clear in itself, but as already admitted and acted on by the Council in their former proceedings. The latter they regard as obvious to everyone who considers the immense advantage of accurate numerical tables in all matters of calculation, especially in those which relate to astronomy and navigation, and the great variety and extent of those which it is the object and within the compass of Mr Babbage's Engine to calculate and print with perfect accuracy.' (*Report of Committee of Royal Society*, 12 February, 1829[a])

Upon the first of these reports, the Government determined to construct the machine, under my personal superintendence / and direction. The Engine was accordingly commenced and partially completed. Tables of figures were calculated, limited in extent only by the number of wheels put together.

Delays, from various causes arose in the progress of the work, and great expenses were incurred. The machine was altogether new in design and construction, and required the utmost mechanical skill which could be obtained for its execution. 'It involved,' to quote again from the Report of the Committee of the Royal Society, 'the necessity of constructing, and in many instances inventing, tools and machinery of great expense and complexity (and in many instances of ingenious contrivances likely to prove useful for other purposes hereafter), for forming with the requisite precision parts of the apparatus dissimilar to any used in ordinary mechanical works; that of making many previous trials to ascertain the validity of proposed movements; and that of altering, improving, and simplifying those already contrived and reduced to drawings. Your Committee are so far from being surprised at the time it has occupied to bring it to its present state, that they fell more disposed to wonder it has been possible to accomplish so much.' The true explanation both of the slow progress and of the cost of the work is clearly stated in this passage; and I may remark in passing, that the tools which were invented for the construction of the machine were afterwards found of utility, and that this anticipation of the Committee has been realized, as some of our most eminent mechanical engineers will readily testify.

Similar circumstances will, I apprehend, always attend and prolong the period of bringing to perfection inventions which have no parallel in the previous history of mechanical / construction. The necessary science and skill specially acquired in executing such works must also, as experience is gained, suggest deviations from, and improvements in, the original plan of those

---

[a]J. F. W. Herschel, *Report of the Royal Society Babbage Engine Committee* (1829), *Works of Babbage*, Vol. 2.

works; and the adoption or rejection of such changes, especially under circumstances similar to those in which I was placed, often involves questions of the greatest difficulty and anxiety.

From whatever cause, however, the delays and expenses arose, the result was that the Government was discouraged, and declined to proceed further with the work.

Mr Goulburn's letter, intimating this decision to me, in 1842, will be found in the accompanying printed Statement. And that the impediments to the completion of the engine, described by the Royal Society, were those which influenced the Government in the determination they came to, I infer from the reason assigned by Mr Goulburn for its discontinuance, viz., 'the expense which would be necessary in order to render it either satisfactory to yourself or generally useful'. I readily admit that the work could not have been rendered satisfactory to myself unless I was free to introduce every improvement which experience and thought could suggest. But that even with this additional source of expense its general usefulness would have been impaired, I cannot assent to, for I believe, in the words of the report I have already quoted, the 'immense advantage of accurate numerical tables in all matters of calculation, especially in those which relate to astronomy and navigation, cannot, within any reasonable limits, be over-estimated.' As to the expense actually incurred upon the first Difference Engine, that of the Government was about £17,000. On my own part, and out of my own private resources, I have sacrificed upon this and other works of science upwards of £20,000. /

From the date of Mr Goulburn's letter, nothing has been done towards the further completion of the Difference Engine by the Government or myself. So much of it as was completed was deposited in the Museum of King's College, where it now remains.

Three consequences have, however, resulted from my subsequent labours, to which I attach great importance.

First, I have been led to conceive the most important elements of another engine upon a new principle (the details of which are reduced accurately to paper), the power of which over the most complicated analytical operations appears nearly unlimited; but no portion of which is yet commenced. I have called this engine, in contradistinction to the other, the Analytical Engine.

Secondly, I have invented and brought to maturity a system of signs for the explanation of machinery, which I have called Mechanical Notation, by means of which the drawings, the times of action, and the trains for the transmission of force, are expressed in a language at once simple and concise. Without the aid of this language I could not have invented the Analytical Engine; nor do I believe that any machinery of equal complexity can ever be contrived without the assistance of that or of some other equivalent language. The Difference Engine No. 2, to which I shall presently refer, is entirely described by its aid.

Thirdly, in labouring to perfect this Analytical Machine of greater power and wider range of computation, I have discovered the means of simplifying and expediting the mechanical processes of the first or Difference Engine.

After what has passed, I cannot expect the Government to undertake the construction of the Analytical Engine, and I do not offer it for that purpose. It is not so matured as to / enable any other person, without long previous training and application, even to attempt its execution; and on my own part, to superintend its construction would demand an amount of labour, anxiety, and time which could not, after the treatment I have received, be expected from me. I therefore make no such offer.

But that I may fulfil to the utmost of my power the original expectation that I should be able to complete, for the Government, an engine capable of calculating astronomical and nautical tables with perfect accuracy, such as that which is described in the Reports of the Royal Society, I am willing to place at the disposal of Government (if they will undertake to execute a new Difference Engine) all those improvements which I have invented and have applied to the Analytical Engine. These comprise a complete series of drawings and explanatory notations, finished in 1849, of the Difference Engine No. 2 – an instrument of greater power as well as of greater simplicity than that formerly commenced, and now in the possession of the Government.

I have sacrified time, health, and fortune, in the desire to complete these Calculating Engines. I have also declined several offers of great personal advantage to myself. But, notwithstanding the sacrifice of these advantages for the purpose of maturing an engine of almost intellectual power, and after expending from my own private fortune a larger sum than the Government of England has spent on that machine, the execution of which it only commenced, I have received neither an acknowledgement of my labours, nor even the offer of those honours or rewards which are allowed to fall within the reach of men who devote themselves to purely scientific investigations. I might, perhaps, advance some claims to consideration, founded on my works and contributions / in aid of various departments of industrial and physical science – but it is for others to estimate those services.

I now, however, simply ask your Lordship to do me the honour to consider this statement and the offer I make. I prefer no claim to the distinctions or the advantages which it is in the power of the Crown or the Government to bestow. I desire only to discharge whatever *imagined* obligation may be supposed to rest upon me, in connection with the original undertaking of the Difference Engine; though I cannot but feel that whilst the public has already derived advantage from my labours, I have myself experienced only loss and neglect.

If the work upon which I have bestowed so much time and thought were a mere triumph over mechanical difficulties, or simply curious, or if the execution of such engines were of doubtful practicability or utility, some justification might be found for the course which has been taken; but I venture to assert that no mathematician who has a reputation to lose will ever *publicly* express an opinion that such a machine would be useless if made, and that no man distinguished as a Civil Engineer will venture to declare the construction of such machinery impracticable. The names appended to the Report of the Committee of the Royal Society fully justify my expressing this opinion, which I apprehend will not be disputed.

And at a period when the progress of physical science is obstructed by that exhausting intellectual and manual labour, indispensable for its advancement, which it is the object of the Analytical Engine to relieve, I think the application of machinery in aid of the most complicated and abstruse calculations can no longer be deemed unworthy of the attention of the country. In fact, there is no reason why mental as / well as bodily labour should not be economized by the aid of machinery.

With these views I have addressed your lordship, as the head of the Government; and whatever may be my sense of the injustice that has hitherto been done me, I feel, in laying this representation before your lordship, and in making the offer I now make, that I have discharged to the utmost limit every implied obligation I originally contracted with the country.

I have the honour to be,

Dorset Street, Manchester Square, etc.,
8 June, 1852 CHARLES BABBAGE

As this question was one of finance and of calculation, the sagacious Premier adroitly turned it over to his Chancellor of the Exchequer – that official being, from his office, *supposed* to be well versed in both subjects.

The opinion pronounced by the novelist and financier was,

'That Mr Babbage's projects appear to be so indefinitely expensive, the ultimate success so problematical, and the expenditure certainly so large and so utterly incapable of being calculated, that the Government would not be justified in taking upon itself any further liability.' (Extract from the Reply of Earl Derby to the application of the Earl of Rosse, K.P., President of the Royal Society.)

The answer of Lord Derby to Lord Rosse was in substance –

That he had consulted the Chancellor of the Exchequer,[a] who pronounced Mr Babbage's project as – /

1. 'Indefinitely expensive.'
2. 'The ultimate success problematical.'
3. 'The expenditure utterly incapable of being calculated.'

---

[a] Benjamin Disraeli.

With regard to the 'indefinite expense', Lord Rosse had proposed to refer this question to the President of the Institution of Civil Engineers, who would have given his opinion after a careful examination of the drawings and notations. These had not been seen by the Chancellor of the Exchequer; and, if seen by him, would not have been comprehended.

The objection that its success was 'problematical' may refer either to its mechanical construction or to its mathematical principles.

Who, possessing one grain of common sense, could look upon the unrivalled workmanship of the then existing portion of the Difference Engine No. 1, and doubt whether a simplified form of the same engine could be executed?

As to any doubt of its mathematical principles, this was excusable in the Chancellor of the Exchequer, who was himself too practically acquainted with the fallibility of his own figures, over which the severe duties of his office had stultified his brilliant imagination. Far other figures are dear to him – those of speech, in which it cannot be denied he is indeed pre-eminent.

Any junior clerk in his office might, however, have told him that the power of computing tables by differences merely required a knowledge of simple addition.

As to the impossibility of ascertaining the expediture, this merges into the first objection; but a poetical brain must be pardoned when it repeats or amplifies. I will recall to the ex-Chancellor of the Exchequer what Lord Rosse really proposed, / namely, that the Government should take the opinion of the President of the Institution of Civil Engineers upon the question, whether a contract could be made for constructing the Difference Engine, and if so, for what sum.

But the very plan proposed by Lord Rosse and refused by Lord Derby, for the construction of the *English* Difference Engine, was adopted some few years after by another administration for the *Swedish* Difference Engine. Messrs Donkin, the eminent engineers, *made an estimate*, and a *contract was* in consequence executed to construct for government a facsimile of the *Swedish* Difference Engine, which is now in use in the department of the Registrar-General, at Somerset House. There were far greater mechanical difficulties in the production of that machine than in the one the drawings of which I had offered to the Government.

From my own experience of the cost of executing such works, I have no doubt, although it was highly creditable to the skill of the able firm who constructed it, but that it must have been commercially unprofitable. Under such circumstances, surely it was harsh on the part of the Government to refuse Messrs Donkin permission to exhibit it as a specimen of English workmanship at the Exhibition of 1862.

But the machine upon which everybody could calculate, had little chance of fair play from the man on whom nobody could calculate.

If the Chancellor of the Exchequer had read my letter to Lord Derby, he would have found the opinion of the Committee of the Royal Society expressed in these words:

They consider the former [the abstract mathematical principle] as not only sufficiently clear in itself, but as already admitted and acted on by the Council in their former proceedings. /

The latter [its public utility] they consider as obvious to every one who considers the immense advantage of accurate numerical tables in all matters of calculation, especially in those which relate to astronomy and navigation. (*Report of the Royal Society*, 12 February, 1829)

Thus it appears:

1. That the Chancellor of the Exchequer presumed to set up his *own idea* of the utility of the Difference Engine in direct opposition to that of the Royal Society.

2. That he *refused* to take the opinion of the highest mechanical authority in the country on its probable cost, and even *to be informed* whether a contract for its construction at a definite sum might not be attainable: he then boldly pronounced the expense to be 'utterly incapable of being calculated'.

This much-abused Difference Engine is, however, like its prouder relative the Analytical, a being of sensibility, of impulse, and of power.

It can not only calculate the millions the ex-Chancellor of the Exchequer squandered, but it can deal with the smallest quantities; nay, it feels even for zeros.* It is as conscious as Lord Derby himself is of the presence of a *negative quantity*, and it is not beyond the ken of either of them to foresee the existence of *impossible ones*.†

---

* It discovers the roots of equations by feeling whether all the figures in a certain column are *zeros*.

† It may be necessary to explain to the unmathematical reader and to the ex-Chancellor of the Exchequer that *impossible quantities* in algebra are something like *mare's-nests* in ordinary life.

Yet should any unexpected course of events ever raise the / ex-Chancellor of the Exchequer to his former dignity, I am sure he will be its *friend* as soon as he is convinced that it can be made *useful* to him.

It may possibly enable him to un-muddle even his own financial accounts, and to –[a]

But as I have no wish to crucify him, I will leave his name in obscurity.

The Herostratus of Science, if he escape oblivion, will be linked with the destroyer of the Ephesian Temple. /

---

[a] *Sic.*

CHAPTER VIII

OF THE ANALYTICAL ENGINE

Man wrongs, and Time avenges.,
Byron, *The Prophecy of Dante*

Built workshops for constructing the Analytical Engine – Difficulties about carrying the tens – Unexpectedly solved – Application of the Jacquard Principle – Treatment of tables – Probable time required for arithmetical operations – Conditions it must fulfil – Unlimited in number of figures, or in extent of analytical operations – The author invited to Turin in 1840 – Meetings for discussion – Plana, Menabrea, MacCullagh, Mosotti – Difficulty proposed by the latter – Observations on the errata of astronomical tables – Suggestions for a reform of analytical signs.

The circular arrangement of the axes of the Difference Engine round the large central wheels led to the most extended prospects. The whole of arithmetic now appeared within the grasp of mechanism. A vague glimpse even of an Analytical Engine at length opened out, and I pursued with enthusiasm the shadowy vision. The drawings and the experiments were of the most costly kind. Draftsmen of the highest order were necessary to economize the labour of my own head; whilst skilled workmen were required to execute the experimental machinery to which I was obliged constantly to have recourse.

In order to carry out my pursuits successfully, I had purchased a house with above a quarter of an acre of ground in a / very quiet locality. My coach-house was now converted into a forge and a foundry, whilst my stables were transformed into a workshop. I built other extensive workshops myself, and had a fireproof building for my drawings and draftsmen. Having myself worked with a variety of tools, and having studied the art of constructing each of them, I at length laid it down as a principle – that, except in rare cases, I would never do anything myself if I could afford to hire another person who could do it for me.

The complicated relations which then arose amongst the various parts of the machinery would have baffled the most tenacious memory. I overcame that difficulty by improving and extending a language of signs, the Mechanical Notation, which in 1826 I had explained in a paper printed in the 'Phil. Trans.'[a] By such means I succeeded in mastering trains of investigation so vast in extent that no length of years ever allotted to one individual could otherwise have enabled me to control. By the aid of the Mechanical Notation, the Analytical Engine became a reality: for it became susceptible of demonstration.

Such works could not be carried on without great expenditure. The fluctuations in the demand and supply of skilled labour were considerable. The railroad mania withdrew from other pursuits the most intellectual and skilful draftsmen. One who had for some years been my chief assistant was tempted by an offer so advantageous that in justice to his own family he could scarcely have declined it. Under these circumstances I took into consideration the plan of advancing his salary to one guinea per day. Whilst this was in abeyance, I consulted my venerable surviving parent. When I had fully explained the circumstances, my excellent mother replied: 'My dear son, you have advanced / far in the accomplishment of a great object, which is worthy of your ambition. You are capable of completing it. My advice is – pursue it, even if it should oblige you to live on bread and cheese.'

This advice entirely accorded with my own feelings. I therefore retained my chief assistant at his advanced salary.

The most important part of the Analytical Engine was undoubtedly the mechanical method of carrying tens. On this I laboured incessantly, each succeeding improvement advancing me a step or two. The difficulty did not consist so much in the more or less complexity of the con-trivance as in the reduction of the *time* required to effect the carriage. Twenty or thirty different plans and modifications had been drawn. At last I came to the conclusion that I had exhausted the principle of successive carriage. I concluded also that nothing but teaching the engine to foresee and then to act upon that foresight could ever lead me to the object I desired, namely, to make the whole of any unlimited number of carriages in one unit of time. One morning, after I had spent many hours in the drawing-office in endeavouring to improve the system of successive carriages, I mentioned these views to my chief assistant, and added that I should retire to my library, and

---

'On a method of expressing by signs the action of machinery' (1826), *Works of Babbage*, Vol. 3.

endeavour to work out the new principle. He gently expressed a doubt whether the plan was *possible*, to which I replied that, not being able to prove its impossibility, I should follow out a slight glimmering of light which I thought I perceived.

After about three hours' examination, I returned to the drawing-office with much more definite ideas upon the subject. I had discovered a principle that proved the possibility, and I had contrived mechanism which, I thought, would accomplish my object. /

I now commenced the explanation of my views, which I soon found were but little understood by my assistant; nor was this surprising, since in the course of my own attempt at explanation, I found several defects in my plan, and was also led by his questions to perceive others. All these I removed one after another, and ultimately terminated at a late hour my morning's work with the conviction that *anticipating* carriage was not only within my power, but that I had devised one mechanism at least by which it might be accomplished.

Many years after, my assistant, on his return from a long residence abroad, called upon me, and we talked over the progress of the Analytical Engine. I referred back to the day on which I had made that most important step, and asked him if he recollected it. His reply was that he perfectly remembered the circumstance; for that on retiring to my library, he seriously thought that my intellect was beginning to become deranged. The reader may perhaps be curious to know how I spent the rest of that remarkable day.

After working, as I constantly did, for ten or eleven hours a day, I had arrived at this satisfactory conclusion, and was revising the rough sketches of the new contrivance, when my servant entered the drawing-office, and announced that it was seven o'clock – that I dined in Park Lane – and that it was time to dress. I usually arrived at the house of my friend about a quarter of an hour before the appointed time, in order that we might have a short conversation on subjects on which we were both much interested. Having mentioned my recent success, in which my host thoroughly sympathized, I remarked that it had produced an exhilaration of the spirits which not even his excellent champagne could rival. Having enjoyed the society of Hallam, of Rogers, and of some few / others of that delightful circle, I retired, and joined one or perhaps two much more extensive reunions. Having thus forgotten science, and enjoyed society for four or five hours, I returned home. About one o'clock I was asleep in my bed, and thus continued for the next five hours.

This new and rapid system of carrying the tens when two numbers are added together, reduced the actual time of the addition of any number of digits, however large, to nine units of time for the addition, and one unit for the carriage. Thus in ten units of time, any two numbers, however large, might be added together. A few more units of time, perhaps five or six, were required for making the requisite previous arrangements.

Having thus advanced as nearly as seemed possible to the minimum of time requisite for arithmetical operations, I felt renewed power and increased energy to pursue the far higher object I had in view.

To describe the successive improvements of the Analytical Engine would require many volumes. I only propose here to indicate a few of its more important functions, and to give to those whose minds are duly prepared for it some information which will remove those vague notions of wonder, and even of its impossibility, with which it is surrounded in the minds of some of the most enlightened.

To those who are acquainted with the principles of the Jacquard loom, and who are also familiar with analytical formulae, a general idea of the means by which the engine executes its operations may be obtained without much difficulty. In the Exhibition of 1862 there were many splendid examples of such looms.

It is known as a fact that the Jacquard loom is capable of / weaving any design which the imagination of man may conceive. It is also the constant practice for skilled artists to be employed by manufacturers in designing patterns. These patterns are then sent to a peculiar artist, who, by means of a certain machine, punches holes in a set of pasteboard cards in such a manner that when those cards are placed in a Jacquard loom, it will then weave upon its produce the exact pattern designed by the artist.

Now the manufacturer may use, for the warp and weft of his work, threads which are all of the same colour; let us suppose them to be unbleached or white threads. In this case the cloth will be woven all of one colour; but there will be a damask pattern upon it such as the artist designed.

But the manufacturer might use the same cards, and put into the warp threads of any other colour. Every thread might even be of a different colour, or of a different shade of colour; but in all these cases the *form* of the pattern will be precisely the same – the colours only will differ.

The analogy of the Analytical Engine with this well-known process is nearly perfect.

The Analytical Engine consists of two parts:

1. The store in which all the variables to be operated upon, as well as all those quantities which have arisen from the result of other operations, are placed.

2. The mill into which the qualities about to be operated upon are always brought.

Every formula which the Analytical Engine can be required to compute consists of certain algebraical operations to be performed upon given letters, and of certain other modifications depending on the numerical value assigned to those letters.

There are therefore two sets of cards, the first to direct the / nature of the operations to be performed – these are called operation cards: the other to direct the particular variables on which those cards are required to operate – these latter are called variable cards. Now the symbol of each variable or constant, is placed at the top of a column capable of containing any required number of digits.

Under this arrangement, when any formula is required to be computed, a set of operation cards must be strung together, which contain the series of operations in the order in which they occur. Another set of cards must then be strung together, to call in the variables into the mill, the order in which they are required to be acted upon. Each operation card will require three other cards, two to represent the variables and constants and their numerical values upon which the previous operation card is to act, and one to indicate the variable on which the arithmetical result of this operation is to be placed.

But each variable has below it, on the same axis, a certain number of figure-wheels marked on their edges with the ten digits: upon these any number the machine is capable of holding can be placed. Whenever variables are ordered into the mill, these figures will be brought in, and the operation indicated by the preceding card will be performed upon them. The result of this operation will then be replaced in the store.

The Analytical Engine is therefore a machine of the most general nature. Whatever formula it is required to develop, the law of its development must be communicated to it by two sets of cards. When these have been placed, the engine is special for that particular formula. The numerical value of its constants must then be put on the columns of wheels below them, and on setting the engine in motion it will calculate and print the numerical results of that formula. /

Every set of cards made for any formula will at any future time recalculate that formula with whatever constants may be required.

Thus the Analytical Engine will possess a library of its own. Every set of cards once made will at any future time reproduce the calculations for which it was first arranged. The numerical value of its constants may then be inserted.

It is perhaps difficult to apprehend these descriptions without a familiarity both with analytical forms and mechanical structures. I will now, therefore, confine myself to the mathematical view of the Analytical Engine, and illustrate by example some of its supposed difficulties.

An excellent friend of mine, the late Professor MacCullagh, of Dublin, was discussing with me, at breakfast, the various powers of the Analytical Engine. After a long conversation on the subject, he enquired what the machine could do if, in the midst of algebraic operations, it was required to perform logarithmic or trigonometric operations.

My answer was, that whenever the Analytical Engine should exist, all the developments of formula would be directed by this condition – that the machine should be able to compute their numerical value in the shortest possible time. I then added that if this answer were not satisfactory, I had provided means by which, with equal accuracy, it might compute by logarithmic or other tables.

I explained that the tables to be used must, of course, be computed and punched on cards by the machine, in which case they would undoubtedly be correct. I then added that when the machine wanted a tabular number, say the logarithm of a given number, that it would ring a bell and then stop itself. On this, the attendant would look at a certain part of the machine, and find that it wanted the logarithm of a given / number, say of 2303. The attendant would then go to the drawing containing the pasteboard cards representing its table of logarithms. From among these he would take the required logarithmic card, and place it in the machine. Upon this the engine would first ascertain whether the assistant had or had not given him the correct logarithm of the number; if so, it would use it and continue its work. But if the engine found the attendant had given him a wrong logarithm, it would then ring a louder bell, and stop itself. On the attendant again examining the engine, he would observe the words, 'Wrong tabular number', and then discover that he really had given the wrong logarithm, and of course he would have to replace it by the right one.

Upon this, Professor MacCullagh naturally asked why, if the machine could tell whether the logarithm was the right one, it should have asked the attendant at all? I told him that the means employed were so ridiculously simple that I would not at that moment explain them; but that if he would come again in the course of a few days, I should be ready to explain it. Three or four days after, Bessel and Jacobi, who had just arrived in England, were sitting with me, enquiring about the Analytical Engine, when fortunately my friend MacCullagh was announced. The meeting was equally agreeable to us all, and we continued our conversation. After some time Bessel put to me the very same question which MacCullagh had previously asked. On this Jacobi remarked that he, too, was about to make the same enquiry when Bessel had asked the question. I then explained to them the following very simple means by which that verification was accomplished.

Besides the sets of cards which direct the nature of the operations to be performed, and the variables or constants / which are to be operated upon, there is another class of cards called number cards. These are much less general in their uses than the others, although they are necessarily of much larger size.

Any number which the Analytical Engine is capable of using or of producing can, if required, be expressed by a card with certain holes in it thus –

Number					*Table*					
2	3	0	3	3	6	2	2	9	3	9
●	●	○	●	●	●	●	●	●	●	○
●	●	○	●	●	●	●	●	●	●	○
○	●	○	●	●	●	○	○	●	●	○
○	○	○	○	○	●	○	○	●	○	○
○	○	○	○	○	●	○	○	●	○	○
○	○	○	○	○	●	○	○	●	○	○
○	○	○	○	○	○	○	○	●	○	○
○	○	○	○	○	○	○	○	●	○	○
○	○	○	○	○	○	○	○	●	○	●

The above card contains eleven vertical rows for holes, each row having nine or any less number of holes. In this example the tabular number is 3 6 2 2 9 3 9, whilst its number in the order of the table is 2 3 0 3. In fact, the former number is the logarithm of the latter.

The Analytical Engine will contain,

1. Apparatus for printing on paper, one, or, if required, two copies of its results.
2. Means for producing a stereotype mould of the tables or results it computes.
3. Mechanism for punching on blank pasteboard cards or metal plates the numerical results of any of its computations.

Of course the engine will compute all the tables which / it may itself be required to use. These cards will therefore be entirely free from error. Now when the engine requires a tabular number, it will stop, ring a bell, and ask for such number. In the case we have assumed, it asks for the logarithm of 2 3 0 3.

When the attendant has placed a tabular card in the engine, the first step taken by it will be to verify the *number* of the card given it by subtracting its number from 2 3 0 3, the number whose logarithm it asked for. If the remainder is zero, then the engine is certain that the logarithm must be the right one, since it was computed and punched by itself.

Thus the Analytical Engine first computes and punches on cards its own tabular numbers. These are brought to it by its attendant when demanded. But the engine itself takes care that the *right* card is brought to it by verifying the *number* of that card by the number of the card which it demanded. The engine will always reject a wrong card by continually ringing a loud bell and stopping itself until supplied with the precise intellectual food it demands.

It will be an interesting question, which time only can solve, to know whether such tables of cards will ever be required for the engine. Tables are used for saving the time of continually computing individual numbers. But the computations to be made by the engine are so rapid that it seems most probable that it will make shorter work by computing directly from proper formulae than by having recourse even to its own tables.

The Analytical Engine I propose will have the power of expressing every number it uses to fifty places of figures. It will multiply any two such numbers together, and then, if required, will divide the product of one hundred figures by number of fifty places of figures. /

92

Supposing the velocity of the moving parts of the engine be not greater than forty feet per minute, I have no doubt that

Sixty additions or subtractions may be completed and printed in one minute.

One multiplication of two numbers, each of fifty figures, in one minute.

One division of a number having 100 places of figures by another of 50 in one minute.

In the various sets of drawings of the modifications of the mechanical structure of the Analytical Engines, already numbering upwards of thirty, two great principles were embodied to an unlimited extent.

1. The entire control over *arithmetical* operations, however large, and whatever might be the number of their digits.

2. The entire control over the *combinations* of algebraic symbols, however lengthened those processes may be required. The possibility of fulfilling these two conditions might reasonably be doubted by the most accomplished mathematician as well as by the most ingenious mechanician.

The difficulties which naturally occur to those capable of examining the question, as far as they relate to arithmetic, are these –

(*a*) The number of digits in *each constant* inserted in the engine must be without limit.

(*b*) The number of constants to be inserted in the engine must also be without limit.

(*c*) The number of operations necessary for arithmetic is only four, but these four may be repeated an *unlimited* number of times.

(*d*) These operations may occur in any order, or follow an *unlimited* number of laws. /

The following conditions relate to the algebraic portion of the Analytical Engine:

(*e*) The number of *literal* constants must be *unlimited*.

(*f*) The number of *variables* must be *without limit*.

(*g*) The combinations of the algebraic signs must *be unlimited*.

(*h*) The number of *functions* to be employed must be *without limit*.

This enumeration includes eight conditions, each of which is absolutely *unlimited* as to the number of its combinations.

Now it is obvious that no *finite* machine can include infinity. It is also certain that no question *necessarily* involving infinity can ever be converted into any other in which the idea of infinity under some shape or other does not enter.

It is impossible to construct machinery occupying unlimited space; but it is possible to construct finite machinery, and to use it through unlimited time. It is this substitution of the *infinity of time* for the *infinity of space* which I have made use of, to limit the size of the engine and yet to retain its unlimited power.

(a) I shall now proceed briefly to point out the means by which I have effected this change.

Since every calculating machine must be constructed for the calculation of a definite number of figures, the first datum must be to fix upon that number. In order to be somewhat in advance of the greatest number that may ever be required, I chose fifty places of figures as the standard for the Analytical Engine. The intention being that in such a machine two numbers, each of fifty places of figures, might be multiplied together and the resultant product of one hundred places might then be divided by another number of fifty / places. It seems to me probable that a long period must elapse before the demands of science will exceed this limit. To this it may be added that the addition and subtraction of numbers in an engine constructed for n places of figures would be equally rapid whether n were equal to five or five thousand digits. With respect to multiplication and division, the time required is greater:

Thus if $a \cdot 10^{50} + b$ and $a' \cdot 10^{50} + b'$ are two numbers each of less than a hundred places of figures, then each can be expressed upon two columns of fifty figures, and a, b, a', b' are each less than fifty places of figures: they can therefore be added and subtracted upon any column holding fifty places of figures.

The product of two such numbers is –

$$aa' \, 10^{100} + (ab' + a'b)10^{50} + bb'.$$

This expression contains four pairs of factors, aa', ab', $a'b$, bb', each factor of which has less than fifty places of figures. Each multiplication can therefore be executed in the engine. The time, however, of multiplying two numbers, each consisting of any number of digits between fifty and one hundred, will be nearly four times as long as that of two such numbers of less than fifty places of figures.

The same reasoning will show that if the numbers of digits of each factor are between one hundred and one hundred and fifty, then the time required for the operation will be nearly nine times that of a pair of factors having only fifty digits.

Thus it appears that whatever may be the number of digits the

Analytical Engine is capable of holding, if it is required to make all the computations with k times that number of digits, then it can be executed by the same engine, but in an amount of time equal to k^2 times the former. Hence the / condition (*a*), or the unlimited number of digits contained in each constant employed, is fulfilled.

It must, however, be admitted that this advantage is gained at the expense of diminishing the number of the constants the engine can hold. An engine of fifty digits, when used as one of a hundred digits, can only contain half the number of variables. An engine containing m columns, each holding n digits, if used for computations requiring kn digits, can only hold m/k constants or variables.

(*b*) The next step is therefore to prove (*b*), viz.: to show that a finite engine can be used as if it contained an unlimited number of constants. The method of punching cards for tabular numbers has already been alluded to. Each Analytical Engine will contain one or more apparatus for printing any numbers put into it, and also an apparatus for punching on pasteboard cards the holes corresponding to those numbers. At another part of the machine a series of number cards, resembling those of Jacquard, but delivered to and computed by the machine itself, can be placed. These can be called for by the engine itself in any order in which they may be placed, or according to *any law* the engine may be directed to use. Hence the condition (*b*) is fulfilled, namely: an *unlimited number of constants* can be inserted in the machine in an *unlimited* time.

I propose in the engine I am constructing to have places for only a thousand constants, because I think it will be more than sufficient. But if it were required to have ten, or even a hundred times that number, it would be quite possible to make it, such is the simplicity of its structure of that portion of the engine.

(*c*) The next stage in the arithmetic is the number of times / the four processes of addition, subtraction, multiplication, and division can be repeated. It is obvious that four different cards thus punched

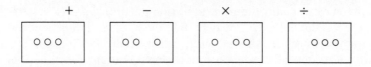

would give the orders for the four rules of arithmetic.

Now there is no limit to the number of such cards which may be strung together according to the nature of the operations required. Consequently the condition (c) is fulfilled.

(d) The fourth arithmetical condition (d), that the order of succession in which these operations can be varied, is itself *unlimited*, follows as a matter of course.

The four remaining conditions which must be fulfilled, in order to render the Analytical Engine as general as the science of which it is the powerful executive, relate to algebraic quantities with which it operates.

The thousand columns, each capable of holding any number of less than fifty-one places of figures, may each represent a constant or a variable quantity. These quantities I have called by the comprehensive title of variables, and have denoted them by V_n, with an index below. In the machine I have designed, n may vary from 0 to 999. But after any one or more columns have been used for variables, if those variables are not required afterwards, they may be printed upon paper, and the columns themselves again used for other variables. In such cases the variables must have a new index; thus, $^mV^n$. I propose to make n vary from 0 to 99. If more variables are required, these may be supplied by variable cards, which may follow each other in unlimited succession. Each card will cause its symbol to be printed with its proper indices. /

For the sake of uniformity, I have used V with as many indices as may be required throughout the engine. This, however, does not prevent the printed result of a development from being represented by any letters which may be thought to be more convenient. In that part in which the results are printed, type of any form may be used, according to the taste of the proposer of the question.

It thus appears that the two conditions, (e) and (f), which require that the number of constants and of variables should be unlimited, are both fulfilled.

The condition (g) requiring that the number of combinations of the four algebraic signs shall be unlimited, is easily fulfilled by placing them on cards in any order of succession the problem may require.

The last condition (h), namely, that the number of functions to be employed must be without limit, might seem at first sight to be difficult to fulfil. But when it is considered that any function of any number of operations performed upon any variables is but a combination of the four simple signs of operation with various quantities, it becomes apparent that any function whatever may be represented by two groups of cards, the first being signs of operation, placed in the order in which they succeed each other, and the second group of cards representing the variables and constants placed in the order of succession in which they are acted upon by the former.

Thus it appears that the whole of the conditions which enable a *finite* machine to make calculations of *unlimited* extent are fulfilled in the Analytical Engine. The means I have adopted are uniform. I have converted the infinity of space, which was required by the conditions of the problem, into the infinity of time. The means I have employed are in / daily use in the art of weaving patterns. It is accomplished by systems of cards punched with various holes strung together to any extent which may be demanded. Two large boxes, the one empty and the other filled with perforated cards, are placed before and behind a polygonal prism, which revolves at intervals upon its axis, and advances through a short space, after which it immediately returns.

A card passes over the prism just before each stroke of the shuttle; the cards that have passed hang down until they reach the empty box placed to receive them, into which they arrange themselves one over the other. When the box is full, another empty box is placed to receive the coming cards, and a new full box on the opposite side replaces the one just emptied. As the suspended cards on the entering side are exactly equal to those on the side at which the others are delivered, they are perfectly balanced, so that whether the formulae to be computed be excessively complicated or very simple, the force to be exerted always remains nearly the same.

In 1840 I received from my friend M. Plana a letter pressing me strongly to visit Turin at the then approaching meeting of Italian philosophers. In that letter M. Plana stated that he had enquired anxiously of many of my countrymen about the power and mechanism of the Analytical Engine. He remarked that from all the information he could collect the case seemed to stand thus:

Hitherto the *legislative* department of our analysis has been all-powerful – the *executive* all feeble.

Your engine seems to give us the same control over the executive which we have hitherto only possessed over the legislative department.

Considering the exceedingly limited information which / could have reached my friend respecting the Analytical Engine, I was equally surprised and delighted at his exact prevision of its powers. Even at the present moment I could not express more clearly, and in

97

fewer terms, its real object. I collected together such of my models, drawings, and notations as I conceived to be best adapted to give an insight into the principles and mode of operating of the Analytical Engine. On mentioning my intention to my excellent friend the late Professor MacCullagh, he resolved to give up a trip to the Tyrol, and join me at Turin.

We met at Turin at the appointed time, and as soon as the first bustle of the meeting had a little abated, I had the great pleasure of receiving at my own apartments, for several mornings, Messrs Plana, Menabrea, Mosotti, MacCullagh, Plantamour, and others of the most eminent geometers and engineers of Italy.

Around the room were hung the formula, the drawings, notations, and other illustrations which I had brought with me. I began on the first day to give a short outline of the idea. My friends asked from time to time further explanations of parts I had not made sufficiently clear. M. Plana had at first proposed to make notes, in order to write an outline of the principle of the engine. But his own laborious pursuits induced him to give up this plan, and to transfer the task to a younger friend of his, M. Menabrea, who had already established his reputation as a profound analyst.

These discussions were of great value to me in several ways. I was thus obliged to put into language the various views I had taken, and I observed the effect of my explanations on different minds. My own ideas became clearer, and I profited by many of the remarks made by my highly gifted friends. /

One day Mosotti, who had been unavoidably absent from the previous meeting, when a question of great importance had been discussed, again joined the party. Well aware of the acuteness and rapidity of my friend's intellect, I asked my other friends to allow me five minutes to convey to Professor Mosotti the substance of the preceding sitting. After putting a few questions to Mosotti himself, he placed before me distinctly his greatest difficulty.

He remarked that he was now quite ready to admit the power of mechanism over numerical, and even over algebraical relations, to any extent. But he added that he had no conception how the machine could perform the act of judgement sometimes required during an analytical enquiry, when two or more different courses presented themselves, especially as the proper course to be adopted could not be known in many cases until all the previous portion had been gone through.

I then enquired whether the solution of a numerical equation of any degree by the usual, but very tedious proceeding of approximation would be a type of the difficulty to be explained. He at once admitted that it would be a very eminent one.

For the sake of perspicuity and brevity I shall confine my present explanation to possible roots.

I then mentioned the successive stages:

Number of operation cards used.

1 *a*. Ascertain the number of possible roots by applying Sturm's theorem to the coefficients.

2 *b*. Find a number greater than the greatest root.

3 *c*. Substitute the powers of ten (commencing with that next greater than the greatest root, and / diminishing the powers by unity at each step) for the value of x in the given equation.

Continue this until the sign of the resulting number changes from positive to negative.

The index of the last power of ten (call it n), which is positive, expresses the number of digits in that part of the root which consists of whole numbers. Call this index $n + 1$.

4 *d*. Substitute successively for x in the original equation 0×10^n, 1×10^n, 2×10^n, 3×10^n, ... 9×10^n, until a change of sign occurs in the result. The digit previously substituted will be the first figure of the root sought.

5 *e*. Transform the original equation into another whose roots are less by the number thus found.

The transformed equation will have a real root, the digit, less than 10^n.

6 *f*. Substitute $1 \times 10^{n-1}$, $2 \times 10^{n-1}$, $3 \times 10^{n-1}$, etc., successively for the root of this equation, until a change of sign occurs in the result, as in process 4.

This will give the second figure of the root.

This process of alternately finding a new figure in the root, and then transforming the equation into another (as in process 4 and 5), must be carried on until as many figures as are required, whether whole numbers or decimals, are arrived at.

7 *g*. The root thus found must now be used to reduce the original equation to one dimension lower. /

8 *h*. This new equation of one dimension lower must now be treated by sections 3, 4, 5, 6, and 7, until the new root is found.

9 *i*. The repetition of sections 7 and 8 must go on until all the roots have been found.

Now it will be observed that Professor Mosotti was quite ready to admit at once that each of these different processes could be performed by the Analytical Machine through the medium of properly arranged sets of Jacquard cards.

His real difficulty consisted in teaching the engine to know when to change from one set of cards to another, and back again repeatedly, at intervals not known to the person who gave the orders.

The dimensions of the algebraic equation being known, the number of arithmetical processes necessary for Sturm's theorem is consequently known. A set of operation cards can therefore be prepared. These must be accompanied by a corresponding set of variable cards, which will represent the columns in the store, on which the several coefficients of the given equation, and the various combinations required amongst them, are to be placed.

The next stage is to find a number greater than the greatest root of the given equation. There are various courses for arriving at such a number. Any one of these being selected, another set of operation and variable cards can be prepared to execute this operation.

Now, as this second process invariably follows the first, the second set of cards may be attached to the first set, and the engine will pass on from the first to the second process, and again from the second to the third process. /

But here a difficulty arises: successive powers of ten are to be substituted for x in the equation, until a certain event happens. A set of cards may be provided to make the substitution of the highest power of ten, and similarly for the others; but on the occurrence of a certain event, namely, the change of a sign from $+$ to $-$, this stage of the calculation is to terminate.

Now at a very early period of the enquiry I had found it necessary to teach the engine to know when any numbers it might be computing passed through zero or infinity.

The passage through zero can be easily ascertained, thus: Let the continually decreasing number which is being computed be placed upon a column of wheels in connection with a carrying apparatus. After each process this number will be diminished, until at last a number is subtracted from it which is greater than the number expressed on those wheels.

Thus let it be	00000,00000,00000,00423
Subtract	00000,00000,00000,00511

99999,99999,99999,99912

100

Now in every case of a carriage becoming due, a certain lever is transferred from one position to another in the cage next above it.

Consequently in the highest cage of all (say the fiftieth in the Analytical Engine), an arm will be moved or not moved accordingly as the carriages do or do not run up beyond the highest wheel.

This arm can, of course, make any change which has previously been decided upon. In the instance we have been considering it would order the cards to be turned on to the next set.

If we wish to find when any number, which is increasing, / exceeds in the number of its digits the number of wheels on the columns of the machine, the same carrying arm can be employed. Hence any directions may be given which the circumstances require.

It will be remarked that this does not actually prove, even in the Analytical Engine of fifty figures, that the number computed has passed through infinity; but only that it has become greater than any number of fifty places of figures.

There are, however, methods by which any machine made for a given number of figures may be made to compute the same formulae with double or any multiple of its original number. But the nature of this work prevents me from explaining that method.

It may here be remarked that in the process, the cards employed to make the substitutions of the powers of ten are *operation* cards. They are, therefore, quite independent of the numerical values substituted. Hence the same set of operation cards which order the substitutions 1×10^n will, if backed, order the substitution of 2×10^n, etc. We may, therefore, avail ourselves of mechanism for backing these cards, and call it into action whenever the circumstances themselves require it.

The explanation of M. Mosotti's difficulty is this: Mechanical means have been provided for backing or advancing the operation cards to any extent. There exist means of expressing the conditions under which these various processes are required to be called into play. It is not even necessary that two courses only should be possible. Any number of courses may be possible at the same time; and the choice of each may depend upon any number of conditions.

It was during these meetings that my highly valued friend, M. Menabrea, collected the materials for that lucid and / admirable description which he subsequently published in the Bibliothèque Universelle de Genève, t. xli, October, 1842.[a]

The elementary principles on which the Analytical Engine rests were thus in the first instance brought before the public by General Menabrea.

Some time after the appearance of his memoir on the subject in the Bibliothèque Universelle de Genève, the late Countess of Lovelace* informed me that she had translated the memoir of Menabrea. I asked why she had not herself written an original paper on a subject with which she was so intimately acquainted? To this Lady Lovelace replied that the thought had not occurred to her. I then suggested that she should add some notes to Menabrea's memoir; an idea which was immediately adopted.[b]

We discussed together the various illustrations that might be introduced: I suggested several, but the selection was entirely her own. So also was the algebraic working out of the different problems, except, indeed, that relating to the numbers of Bernouilli, which I had offered to do to save Lady Lovelace the trouble. This she sent back to me for an amendment, having detected a grave mistake which I had made in the process.

The notes of the Countess of Lovelace extend to about three times the length of the original memoir. Their author has entered fully into almost all the very difficult and abstract questions connected with the subject.

These two memoirs taken together furnish, to those who are capable of understanding the reasoning, a complete demonstration – *That the whole of the developments and operations of analysis are now capable of being executed by machinery.*

There are various methods by which these developments / are arrived at: 1. By the aid of the Differential and Integral Calculus. 2. By the Combinatorial Analysis of Hindenburg. 3. By the Calculus of Derivations of Arbogast.

Each of these systems professes to expand any function according to any laws. Theoretically each method may be admitted to be perfect; but practically the time and attention required are, in the greater number of cases, more than the human mind is able to bestow. Consequently, upon

* Ada Augusta, Countess of Lovelace, only child of the Poet Byron.

[a] L. F. Menabrea, 'Notions sur la machine analytique de M. Charles Babbage' (1842), reprinted in *Works of Babbage*, Vol. 3.
[b] A. A. Lovelace, 'Sketch of the analytical engine' (1843), *Works of Babbage*, Vol. 3.

several highly interesting questions relative to the Lunar theory, some of the ablest and most indefatigable of existing analysts are at variance.

The Analytical Engine is capable of executing the laws prescribed by each of these methods. At one period I examined the combinatorial analysis, and also took some pains to ascertain from several of my German friends, who had had far more experience of it than myself, whether it could be used with greater facility than the differential system. They seemed to think that it was more readily applicable to all the usual wants of analysis.

I have myself worked with the system of Arbogast, and if I were to decide from my own limited use of the three methods, I should, for the purposes of the Analytical Engine, prefer the calcul des derivations.

As soon as an Analytical Engine exists, it will necessarily guide the future course of the science. Whenever any result is sought by its aid, the question will then arise – By what course of calculation can these results be arrived at by the machine in the *shortest time*?

In the drawings I have prepared I proposed to have a thousand variables, upon each of which any number not having more than fifty figures can be placed. This machine would multiply 50 figures by other 50, and print the product / of 100 figures. Or it would divide any number having 100 figures by any other of 50 figures, and print the quotient of 50 figures. Allowing but a moderate velocity for the machine, the time occupied by either of these operations would be about one minute.

The whole of the *numerical* constants throughout the works of Laplace, Plana, Le Verrier, Hansen, and other eminent men whose indefatigable labours have brought astronomy to its present advanced state, might easily be recomputed. They are but the numerical coefficients of the various terms of functions developed according to certain series. In all cases in which these numerical constants can be calculated by more than one method, it might be desirable to compute them by several processes until frequent practice shall have confirmed our belief in the infallibility of mechanism.

The great importance of having accurate tables is admitted by all who understand their uses; but the multitude of errors really occurring is comparatively little known. Dr Lardner, in the 'Edinburgh Review', has made some very instructive remarks on this subject.[a]

---

[a] D. Lardner, 'Babbage's calculating engine' (1834), *Works of Babbage*, Vol. 2.

I shall mention two within my own experience: these are selected because they occurred in works where neither care nor expense were spared on the part of the Government to insure perfect accuracy. It is, however, but just to the eminent men who presided over the preparation of these works for the press to observe, that the real fault lay not in them but in *the nature of things*.

In 1828 I lent the Government an original MS. of the table of Logarithmic Sines, Cosines, etc., computed to every second of the quadrant, in order that they might have it compared with Taylor's Logarithms, Quarto, 1792, of which they possessed a considerable number of copies.[a] Nineteen / errors were thus detected, and a list of these errata was published in the Nautical Almanac for 1832: these may be called

Nineteen errata of the first order   1832

An error being detected in one of these errata, in the following Nautical Almanac we find an

Erratum of the errata in *N. Alm.* 1832   1833

But in this very erratum of the second order a new mistake was introduced larger than any of the original mistakes. In the year next following there ought to have been found

Erratum in the erratum of the errata in *N. Alm.* 1832   1834

In the 'Tables de la Lune', by M. P. A. Hansen, Quarto, 1857,[b] published at the expense of the English Government, under the direction of the Astronomer Royal, is to be found a list of errata amounting to 155. In the 21st of these original errata there have been found *three* mistakes. These are duly noted in a newly-printed list of errata discovered during computations made with them in the Nautical Almanac; so that we now have the errata of an erratum of the original work.

This list of errata from the office of the Nautical Almanac is larger than the original list. The total number of errors at present (1862) discovered in Hansen's 'Tables of the Moon' amounts to above three hundred and fifty. In making these remarks I have no intention of

---

[a] M. Taylor *Tables of logarithms of all numbers from 1 to 101000* . . . (London, 1792).
[b] P. A. Hansen *Tables de la lune* . . . (London, 1857).

imputing the slightest blame to the Astronomer Royal, who, like other men, cannot avoid submitting to inevitable fate. The only circumstance which is really extraordinary is that, when it was demonstrated that all tables are capable of being computed by machinery, and even when a machine existed which / computed certain tables, that the Astronomer Royal did not become the most enthusiastic supporter of an instrument which could render such invaluable service to his own science.

In the Supplementary Notices of the Astronomical Society, No. 9, vol. xxiii, p. 259, 1863, there occurs a paper by M. G. de Ponteculant, in which forty–nine numerical coefficients relative to the Longitude, Latitude, and Radius vector of the Moon are given as computed by Plana, Delaunay, and Ponteculant. The computations of Plana and Ponteculant agree in thirteen cases; those of Delaunay and Ponteculant in two; and in the remaining thirty-four cases they all three differ.

I am unwilling to terminate this chapter without reference to another difficulty now arising, which is calculated to impede the progress of analytical science. The extension of analysis is so rapid, its domain so unlimited, and so many enquirers are entering into its fields, that a variety of new symbols have been introduced, formed on no common principles. Many of these are merely new ways of expressing well-known functions. Unless some philosophical principles are generally admitted as the basis of all notation, there appears a great probability of introducing the confusion of Babel into the most accurate of all languages.

A few months ago I turned back to a paper in the Philosophical Transactions, 1844, to examine some analytical investigations of great interest by an author who has thought deeply on the subject. It related to the separation of symbols of operation from those of quantity, a question peculiarly interesting to me, since the Analytical Engine contains the embodiment of that method. There was no ready, sufficient, and simple mode of distinguishing letters which represented quantity from those which indicated operation. To understand / the results the author had arrived at, it became necessary to read the whole memoir.

Although deeply interested in the subject, I was obliged, with great regret, to give up the attempt; for it not only occupied much time, but placed too great a strain on the memory.

Whenever I am thus perplexed it has often occurred to me that the very simple plan I have adopted in my *Mechanical Notation* for lettering drawings might be adopted in analysis.

On the geometrical drawings of machinery every piece of matter which represents framework is invariably denoted by an *upright* letter; whilst all letters indicating movable parts are marked by *inclined* letters.

The analogous rule would be –

Let all letters indicating operations or modifications be expressed by *upright* letters;

Whilst all letters representing quantity should be represented by *inclined* letters.

The subject of the principles and laws of notation is so important that it is desirable, before it is too late, that the scientific academies of the world should each contribute the results of their own examination and conclusions, and that some congress should assemble to discuss them. Perhaps it might be still better if each academy would draw up its own views, illustrated by examples, and have a sufficient number printed to send to all other academies. /

CHAPTER IX

OF THE MECHANICAL NOTATION

Art of lettering drawings – Of expressing the time and duration of action of every part – A new demonstrative science – Royal medals of 1826.

Soon after I had commenced the Difference Engine, my attention was strongly directed to the imperfection of all known modes of explaining and demonstrating the construction of machinery. It soon became apparent that my progress would be seriously impeded unless I could devise more rapid means of understanding and recalling the interpretation of my own drawings.

By a new system of very simple signs I ultimately succeeded in rendering the most complicated machine capable of explanation almost without the aid of words.

In order thoroughly to understand the action of any machine, we must have full information upon the following subjects, and it is of the greatest importance that this information should be acquired in the shortest possible time.

I. The actual shape and relative position of every piece of matter of which the machine is composed.

This can be accomplished by the ordinary mechanical drawings. Such drawings usually have letters upon them for the sake of reference in the description of the machine. Hitherto such letters were chosen without any principle, / and in fact gave no indication of anything except the mere spot upon the paper on which they were written.

I then laid down rules for the selection of letters. I shall only mention one or two of them:

1. All upright letters, as a, c, d, e, A, B, represent framing.

2. All inclined letters, as *a, c, d, e, A, B*, represent movable parts.

3. All small letters represent working points. One of the most obvious advantages of these rules is that they enable the attention to be more easily confined to the immediate object sought.

By other rules it is rendered possible, when looking at a plan of any complicated machine, to perceive the *relative order* of super-position of any number of wheels, arms, etc., without referring to the elevation or end view.

II. The actual time and duration of every motion throughout the action of any machine can be ascertained almost instantly by a system of signs called the Notations of Periods.

It possesses equal facilities for ascertaining every contemporaneous as well as for every successive system of movements.

III. The actual connection of each movable piece of the machine with every other on which it acts. Thus, taking from any special part of the drawing the indicating letter, and looking for it on a certain diagram, called the trains, the whole course of its movements may be traced, up to the prime mover, or down to the final result.

I have called this system of signs the Mechanical Notation. By its application to geometrical drawing it has given us a new demonstrative science, namely, that of proving that any given machine can or cannot exist; and if it can exist, that it will accomplish its desired object. /

It is singular that this addition to human knowledge should have been made just about the period when it was beginning to be felt by those most eminently skilled in analysis that the time has arrived when many of its conclusions rested only on probable evidence. This state of things arose chiefly from the enormous extent to which the developments were necessarily carried in the lunar and planetary theories.

After employing this language for several years, it was announced, in December 1825, that King William IV had founded two medals of fifty guineas each, to be given annually by the Royal Society according to rules to be laid down by the Council.

On 26 January, 1826, it was resolved,
That it is the opinion of the Council that the medals be awarded for the most important discoveries or series of investigations, completed and made known to the Royal Society in the year preceding the day of the award.

This rule reduced the number of competitors to a very few. Although I had had some experience as to the mode in which medals were awarded, and therefore valued them accordingly, I was simple enough to expect that the Council of the Royal Society would not venture upon a fraud on the very first occasion of exercising the royal liberality. I had also another motive for taking a ticket in this philosophical lottery of medals.

In 1824, the Astronomical Society did me the honour to award to me the first gold medal they ever bestowed. It was rendered still more grateful by the address of that eminent man, the late Henry Thomas Colebrooke, the President, who in a spirit of prophecy anticipated the results of years, at that period, long future.[a] /

It may not, therefore, be deemed too sanguine an anticipation, when I express the hope that an instrument which in its simpler form attains to the extraction of the roots of numbers, and approximates to the roots of equations, may, in a more advanced state of improvement, rise to the approximate solutions of algebraic equations of elevated degrees. I refer to solutions of such equations proposed by Lagrange, and more recently by other analysts, which involve operations too tedious and intricate for use, and which must remain without efficacy, unless some mode be devised of abridging the labour or facilitating the means of performance.[*]

I felt, therefore, that the *first* Royal Medal might fairly become an object of ambition, whatever might be the worth of subsequent ones.

In order to qualify myself for this chance, I carefully drew up a paper, 'On a Method of expressing by Signs the Action of Machinery',[b] which I otherwise should not have published at that time.

This memoir was read at the Royal Society on 16 March, 1826. To the system of signs which it first expounded I afterwards gave the name of 'Mechanical Notation'. It had been used in England and in Ireland, although not taught in its schools. It applies to the description of a combat by sea or by land. It can assist in representing the functions of animal life; and I have had both from the Continent and from the United States, specimens of such applications. Finally, to whatever degree of simplicity I may at last have reduced the Analytical Engine, the course / through which I arrived at it was the most entangled and perplexed which probably ever occupied the human mind. Through the aid of the Mechanical Notation I

---

[*] 'Discourse of the President on delivering the first Gold Medal of the Astronomical Society to Charles Babbage, Esq.', *Memoirs of the Astronomical Society*, vol. i, p. 509.

[a] H. T. Colebrooke, 'On presenting the gold medal of the Astronomical Society to Charles Babbage' (1825), *Works of Babbage*, Vol. 2.

[b] 'On a method of expressing by signs the action of machinery' (1826), *Works of Babbage*, Vol. 3.

examined numberless plans and systems of computing, and I am sure, from the nature of its self-necessary verifications that it is impossible I can have been deceived.

On 16 November, 1826, that very Council of the Royal Society which had made the law took the earliest opportunity to violate it by awarding the two royal medals, the first to Dalton, whose great discovery had been made nearly twenty years before, and the other to Ivory, for a paper published in their 'Transactions' three years before. The history of their proceedings will be found in the 'Decline of Science in England', p. 115, 1830.[a] /

---

[a] *Works of Babbage*, Vol. 7, p. 59.

CHAPTER X

THE EXHIBITION OF 1862

En administration, toutes les sottises sont mères. *Maximes*, par M. G. De Levis.

An abject worship of princes and an unaccountable appetite for knighthood are probably unavoidable results of placing second-rate men in prominent positions. *Saturday Review*, 16 January, 1864.

Whose fault is this? But tallow, toys, and sweetmeats evidently stand high in the estimation of Her Majesty's Commissioners. *The Times*, 13 August, 1862.

Mr Gravatt suggests to King's College the exhibition of the Difference Engine No. 1, and offers to superintend its transmission and return – Place allotted to it most unfit – Not exhibited in 1851 – Its loan refused to New York – Refused to the Dublin Exhibition in 1847 – Not sent to the great French Exhibition in 1855 – Its exhibition in 1862 entirely due to Mr Gravatt – Space for its drawings refused – The payment of six shillings a day for a competent person to explain it refused by the commissioners – Copy of Swedish Difference Engine made by English workmen not exhibited – Loan of various other calculating machines offered – Anecdote of Count Strzelecki's – The Royal Commissioners' elaborate taste for children's toys – A plan for making such exhibitions profitable – Extravagance of the commissioners to their favourite – Contrast between his treatment and that of industrious workmen – The inventor of the Difference Engine publicly insulted by his countrymen in the Exhibition of 1862.

Circumstances connected with the exhibition of the Difference Engine No. 1 in the International Exhibition of 1862

When the construction of the Difference Engine No. 1 was abandoned by the Government in 1842, I was consulted respecting the place in which it should be deposited. Well aware of the unrivalled perfection of its workmanship, and / conscious that it formed the first great step towards reducing the whole science of number to the absolute control of mechanism, I wished it to be placed wherever the greatest number of persons could see it daily.

With this view, I advised that it should be placed in one of the much-frequented rooms of the British Museum. Another locality was, however, assigned to it, and it was confided by the Government

111

to the care of King's College, Somerset House. It remained in safe custody within its glass case in the museum of that body for twenty years. It is remarkable that during that long period no person should have studied its structure, and, by explaining its nature and use, have acquired an amount of celebrity which the singularity of that knowledge would undoubtedly have produced.

The college authorities did justice to their charge. They put it in the place of honour, in the centre of their museum, and would, no doubt have given facilities to any of their members or to other persons who might have wished to study it.

But the system quietly pursued by the Government, of ignoring the existence of the Difference Engine and its inventor doubtlessly exercised its deadening influence* on those who were inclined, by taste or acquirements, to take such a course. /

I shall enumerate a few instances.

1. In 1850, the Government appointed a Commission to organize the Exhibition of 1851.

The name of the author of the *Economy of Manufactures* was not thought worthy by the Government to be placed on that Commission.

2. In 1851, the Commissioners of the International Exhibition did not think proper to exhibit the Difference Engine, although it was the property of the nation. They were as insensible to the greatest mechanical as to, what has been regarded by some, the greatest intellectual triumph of their country.

3. When it was decided by the people of the United States to have an exhibition at New York, they sent a Commissioner to Europe to make arrangements for its success. He was authorized to apply for the loan of the Difference Engine for a few months, and was empowered to give any pecuniary guarantee which might be required for its safe return.

That Commissioner, on his arrival, applied to me on the subject. I

---

* An illustration fell under my notice a few days after this paragraph was printed. A *new* work on geometrical drawing, commissioned by the committee of council on education, was published by Professor Bradley. <Thomas Bradley, *Lecture . . . on practical plane and descriptive geometry, mechanical and machine drawing . . .* (London, 1860).> I have not been able to find in it a single word concerning 'Mechanical Notation', not even the very simplest portion of that science, namely, the art of lettering drawings. It would seem impossible that any *Professor* of so limited a subject could be ignorant of the existence of such an important addition to its powers.

112

explained to him the state of the case, and advised him to apply to the Government, whose property it was. I added that, if his application was successful, I would at my own expense put the machine in good working order, and give him every information requisite for its safe conveyance and use. His application was, however, unsuccessful.

4. In 1847, Mr Dargan nobly undertook at a vast expense to make an exhibition in Dublin to aid in the relief of his starving countrymen. It was thought that the exhibition of the Difference Engine would be a great attraction. I was informed at the time that an application was made to the Government for its loan, and that it was also unsuccessful. /

5. In 1855 the great French Exhibition occurred. Previously to its opening, our government sent commissioners to arrange and superintend the English department.

These Commissioners reported that the English contribution was remarkably deficient in what in France are termed 'instruments de précision', a term which includes a variety of instruments for scientific purposes. They recommended that 'a Committee should be appointed who could represent to the producers of philosophical instruments how necessary it was that they should, upon an occasion of this kind, maintain their credit in the eyes of Europe'. The Government also applied to the Royal Society for advice; but neither did the Royal Society advise, nor the Government propose, to exhibit the Difference Engine.

6. The French Exhibition of 1855 was remarkable beyond all former ones for the number and ingenuity of the machines which performed arithmetical operations.

Pre-eminently above all others stood the Swedish Machine for calculating and printing mathematical tables. It is honourable to France that its highest reward was deservedly given to the inventor of that machine; whilst it is somewhat remarkable that the English Commissioners appointed to report upon the French Exhibition omitted all notice of these calculating machines.

The appearance of the finished portion of the unfinished Difference Engine No. 1 at the Exhibition of 1862 is entirely due to Mr Gravatt. That gentleman had a few years before paid great attention to the Swedish calculating engine of M. Scheutz, and was the main cause of its success in this country.

Being satisfied that it was possible to calculate and print all tables by machinery, Mr Gravatt became convinced that / the time must arrive when no tables would ever be calculated or printed except by machines. He felt that it was of great importance to accelerate the arrival of that period, more especially as numerical tables, which are at present the most expensive kind of printing, would then become the cheapest.

In furtherance of this idea, Mr Gravatt wrote to Dr Jelf, the Principal of King's College, Somerset House, to suggest that the Difference Engine of Mr Babbage, which had for so many years occupied a prominent place in the museum, should be exhibited in the International Exhibition of 1862. He at the same time offered his assistance in the removal and reinstatement of that instrument.

The authorities of the college readily acceded to this plan. On further enquiry, it appeared that the Difference Engine belonged to the Government, and was only deposited with the college. It was then found necessary to make an application to the Treasury for permission to exhibit it, which was accordingly done by the proper authorities.

The Government granted the permission, and referred it to the Board of Works to superintend its placement in the building.

The Board of Works sent to me a copy of the correspondence relative to this matter, asking my opinion whether any danger might be apprehended for the safety of the machine during its transport, and also enquiring whether I had any other suggestion to make upon the subject.

Knowing the great strength of the work, I immediately answered that I did not anticipate the slightest injury from its transport, and that, under the superintendence of Mr Gravatt, I considered it might be removed with perfect safety. The only suggestion I ventured to offer was, that as the Government possessed in the department of the Registrar-General / a copy, made by English workmen, of the Swedish Difference Engine, that it should be exhibited by the side of mine: and that both the engines should be kept constantly working with a very slow motion.

By a subsequent communication I was informed that the Swedish machine could not be exhibited, because it was then in constant use, computing certain tables relating to the values of lives. I regretted this very much. I had intended to alter the handle of my own engine in order to make it movable circularly by the same catgut which I had hoped might have driven both. The tables which the Swedish machine was employed in printing were *not* of any pressing necessity, and their execution could, upon such an occasion, have been postponed for a few months without loss or inconvenience.

Besides, if the Swedish engine had, as I proposed, been placed at work, its superintendent might have continued his table-making with but little delay, and the public would have been highly gratified by the sight.

He could also have given information to the public by occasional explanations of its principles; thus might Her Majesty's Commissioners have gratified thousands of her subjects who came, with intense curiosity, prepared to be pleased and instructed, and whom they sent away amazed and disappointed.

From the experience I had during the first week of the exhibition, I am convinced that if a fit place had been provided for the two calculating machines, so that the public might have seen them both in constant but slow motion, and if the superintendent had occasionally given a short explanation of the principles on which they acted, they would have been one of the greatest attractions within the building. /

On Mr Gravatt applying to the commissioners for space, it was stated that the engine must be placed amongst philosophical instruments, Class XIII.

The only place offered for its reception was a small hole, 4 feet 4 inches in front by 5 feet deep. On one side of this was the *only* passage to the office of the superintendent of the class. The opposite side was occupied by a glass case in which I placed specimens of the separate parts of the unfinished engine. These, although executed by English workmen above thirty years ago, were yet, in the opinion of the most eminent engineers, unsurpassed by any work the building of 1862 contained. The back of this recess was closed in and dark, and only allowed a space on the wall of about five feet by four, on which to place the *whole* of the drawings and illustrations of the Difference Engine. Close above the top of the machine was a flat roof, which deprived the drawings and the work itself of much light.

The public at first flocked to it: but it was so placed that only three persons could conveniently see it at the same time. When Mr Gravatt kindly explained and set it in motion, he was continually interrupted by the necessity of moving away in order to allow access to the numerous persons whose business called them to the superintendent's office. At a very early period various representations were made to the commissioners by the jury, the superintentent, and very strongly by the press, of the necessity of having some qualified person to explain the machine to the public. I was continually informed by the attendants that hundreds of persons had, during my absence asked, when they could get an opportunity of seeing the machine in motion.

Admiring the earnestness of purpose and the sagacity with which Mr Gravatt had steadily followed out the convictions of / his own mind relative to the abolition of all tables except those made and stereotyped by machinery, I offered all the assistance in my power to accelerate the accomplishment of his task.

I lent him for exhibition numerous specimens of the unfinished portions of the Difference Engine No. 1. These I had purchased on the determination of the Government to abandon its construction in 1842.

I proposed also to lend him the mechanical notations of the Difference Engine, which had been made at my own expense, and were finished by myself and my eldest son, Mr B. Herschel Babbage.

I had had several applications from foreigners* for some account of my system of Mechanical Notation, and great desire was frequently expressed to see the illustrations of the method itself, and of its various applications.

These, however, were so extensive that it was impossible, without very great inconvenience, to exhibit them even in my own house.

I therefore wrote to Mr Gravatt to offer him the loan of the following property for the exhibition:

1. A small calculating machine of the simplest order for adding together any number of separate sums of money, provided the total was under £100,000, by Sir Samuel Morland. 1666.

2. A very complete and well-executed machine for answering all questions in plane trigonometry, by Sir Samuel Morland. 1663. /

3. An original set of Napier's bones.

4. A small arithmetical machine, by Viscount Mahon, afterwards Earl Stanhope. Without date.

5. A larger machine, to add, subtract, multiply, and divide, by Viscount Mahon. 1775.

6. Another similar machine, of a somewhat different construction, for the same operations, by Viscount Mahon. 1777.

7. A small Difference Engine, made in London, in consequence of its

---

* One object of the mission of Professor Bolzani was, to take back with him to Russia such an account of the Mechanical Notation as might facilitate its teaching in the Russian Universities. I regret that it was entirely out of my power to assist him.

author having read Dr Lardner's article in the 'Edinburgh Review' of July, 1834, No. CXX.

List of Mechanical Notations proposed to be lent for the exhibition

1. All the drawings explaining the principles of the Mechanical Notation.
2. The complete Mechanical Notations of the Swedish calculating engine of M. Scheutz.

These latter drawings had been made and used by my youngest son, Major Henry P. Babbage, now resident in India, in explaining the principles of the Mechanical Notation at the meeting of the British Association at Glasgow, and afterwards in London, at a meeting of the Institution of Civil Engineers.*

3. The Mechanical Notations of the Difference Engine No. 1. /

These had been made at my own expense, and were finished by myself and my eldest son, Mr B. Herschel Babbage, now resident in South Australia.

4. A complete set of the drawings of the Difference Engine No. 2, for calculating and printing tables, with seven orders of differences, and thirty places of figures. Finished in 1849.
5. A complete set of the notations necessary for the explanation and demonstration of Difference Engine No. 2, finished in 1849.

These drawings and notations would have required for their exhibition about seven or eight hundred square feet of wall. My letter to Mr Gravatt was forwarded to the commissioners with his own application for space to exhibit them. The commissioners declined this offer; yet during the first six weeks of the exhibition there was at a short distance from the Difference Engine an empty space of wall large enough for the greater part of these instructive diagrams. This portion of wall was afterwards filled up by a vast oil-cloth. Other large portions of wall, to the amount of thousands of square feet, were given up to other oil-cloths, and to numberless carpets. It is evident the Royal Commissioners were much better qualified to judge of furniture for the feet than of furniture for the head.

I was myself frequently asked why I did not employ a person to explain the Difference Engine. In reply to some of my friends, I enquired whether, when they purchased a carriage, they expected the builder to pay the wages of their coachman.

But my greatest difficulty was with foreigners; no explanation I could devise, and I tried many, appeared at all / to satisfy their minds. The thing seemed to them entirely incomprehensible.

* See Proceedings of British Association at Glasgow, 1855, p. 203; also Minutes of Proceedings of the Institution of Civil Engineers, vol. xv, 1856.

That the nation possessing the greatest military and commercial marine in the world – the nation which had spent so much in endeavouring to render perfect the means of finding the longitude – which had recently caused to be computed and published at considerable expense an entirely new set of lunar tables should not have availed itself *at any cost* of mechanical means of computing and stereotyping such tables, seemed entirely beyond their comprehension.

At last they asked me whether the commissioners were *bétes*. I assured them that the only *one* with whom I was personally acquainted certainly was not.

When hard pressed by difficult questions, I thought it my duty as an Englishman to save my country's character, even at the expense of my own. So on one occasion I suggested to my unsatisfied friends that commissioners were usually selected from the highest class of society, and that possibly four out of five had never heard of my name.

But here again my generous efforts to save the character of my country and its commissioners entirely failed. Several of my foreign friends had known me in their own homes, and had seen the estimation in which I was held by their own countrymen and by their own sovereign. These were still more astonished.

On another occasion an anecdote was quoted against me to prove that my name was well known even in China. It may, perhaps, amuse the reader. A short time after the arrival of Count Strzelecki in England, I had the pleasure of meeting him at the table of a common friend. Many enquiries were made relative to his residence in China. Much interest was expressed by several of the party to learn on / what subject the Chinese were most anxious to have information. Count Strzelecki told them that the subject of most frequent enquiry was Babbage's calculating machine. On being further asked as to the nature of the enquiries, he said they were most anxious to know whether it would go into the pocket. Our host now introduced me to Count Strzelecki, opposite to whom I was then sitting. After expressing my pleasure at the introduction, I told the Count that he might safely assure his friends in the celestial empire that it was in every sense of the word an *out-of-pocket* machine.

At last the commissioners were moved, not to supply the deficiency themselves, but to address the Government, to whom the Difference Engine belonged, to send somebody to explain it. I received a communication from the Board of Works, enquiring whether I could make any suggestions for getting over this difficulty. I immediately made enquiries, and found a person who formerly had been my amanuensis, and had, under my direction, worked out many most intricate problems. He possessed very considerable knowledge of mathematics, and was willing, for the moderate remuneration of six shillings a day, to be present daily during nine hours to explain the Difference Engine.

I immediately sent this information to the Board of Works, with the name and address of the person I recommended. This, I have little doubt, was directly communicated to the commissioners; but they did not avail themselves of his services.

It is difficult, upon any principle, to explain the conduct of the Royal Commissioners of the Exhibition of 1862. They were appointed by the Government, yet when the Government itself became an exhibitor, and sent for exhibition a Difference / Engine, the property of the nation, these commissioners placed it in a *small hole* in a *dark corner*, where it could, with some difficulty, be seen by six people at the same time.

No remonstrance was of the slightest avail; it was 'Hobson's choice', that or none. It was represented that all other space was occupied.

A trophy of children's toys, whose merits, it is true, the commissioners were somewhat more competent to appreciate, filled one of the most prominent positions in the building. On the other hand, a trophy of the workmanship of English engineers, executed by *machine tools* thirty years before, and admitted by the best judges to be unsurpassed by any rival, was placed in a position not very inappropriate for the authorities themselves who condemned it to that locality.

But no hired aristocratic* agent was employed to excite the slumbering perceptions of the commissioners, who might have secured a favourable position for the Difference Engine, by practising on their good nature, or by imposing upon their imbecility.

It has been urged, in extenuation of the conduct of these commissioners, that their duty as guardians of the funds entrusted to them, and of the interests of the guarantors, compelled them to practice a rigid economy.

Rigid economy is to be respected only when it is under the control of judgement, not of favouritism. If the machinery for making arithmetical calculations which was placed at the disposal of the

---

* See 'The Times', 19 January, 1863, and elsewhere.

119

commissioners had been properly arranged, it might have been made at once a source of high gratification to the public and even of *profit* to the exhibition. /

Such a group of calculating machines might have been placed by themselves in a small court capable of holding a limited number of persons. Round the walls of this court might have been hung the drawings I had offered to lend, containing the whole of those necessary for the Difference Engine No. 2, as well as a large number of illustrations for the explanation of the Mechanical Notation. The Swedish Difference Engine and my own might have been slowly making calculations during the whole day.

This court should have been open to the public generally, except at two or three periods of half an hour each, during which it should have been accessible only to those who had previously secured tickets at a shilling apiece.

During each half hour the person whom I had recommended to the commissioners might have given a short popular explanation of the subject.

This attraction might have been still further increased, and additional profit made, if a single sheet of paper had been printed containing a woodcut of the Swedish machine, an impression from a page of the tables computed and stereotyped by it at Somerset House, and also an impression from a stereotype plate of the Difference Engine exhibited by the Government.

A plate of the Swedish machine is in existence in London. I am confident that, for such a purpose, I could have procured the loan of it for the commissioners, and I would willingly have supplied them with the stereotype plate from which the frontispage of the present volume was printed, together with from ten to twenty lines of necessary explanation.

These illustrations of machinery used for computing and printing tables might have been put up into packets of dozens and half dozens, and also have been sold in single / sheets at the rate of one penny each copy. There can be no doubt the sale of them would have been very considerable. As it was, I found the woodcut representing the Difference Engine No. 1 in great request,[a] and during the exhibition I had numberless applications for it; having given away my whole stock of about 800 copies.

---

[a] See frontispiece to this volume.

The calculating court might have held comfortably from sixty to eighty seats. Each lecture would have produced say £3. This being repeated three times each day, together with the sale of the woodcuts, would have produced about £10 per day, out of which the commissioners would have had six shillings per day to pay the assistant who gave the required explanations.

If the dignity of the commissioners would not permit them to make money by such means, they might have announced that the proceeds of the tickets would be given to the distressed population of the Manchester district, and there would then have been crowds of visitors.

But the rigid economy of the commissioners, who refused to expend six shillings a day for an attendant, although it would most probably have produced a return of several hundred pounds, was entirely laid aside when their patronage was to be extended to a brother official.

Captain Fowke, an officer of engineers, whose high order of architectural talent became afterwards so well known to the public, and whose whole time and services were retained and paid for by the country, was employed to make a design for the exhibition building.

The commissioners approved of this design, which comprised two lofty domes, uniting in themselves the threefold inconvenience of being ugly, useless, and expensive. They then proceeded to pay him five thousand pounds for the job. /

This system of awarding large sums of money to certain favoured public officers who are already paid for their services by liberal salaries seems to be a growing evil. At the period of the Irish famine the Under-Secretary of the Treasury condescended to accept £2500 out of the fund raised to save a famished nation. Some enquiries, even recently, were occasionally made whether any similar deduction will be allowed from the liberal contributions to the sufferers by the cotton famine.

The question was raised and the practice reprobated in the House of Commons by men of opposite party politics. Mr Gladstone remarked:

If there was one rule connected with the public service which more than any other ought to be scrupulously observed, it was this, that the salary of a public officer, more especially if he were of high rank, ought to cover all the services he might be called upon to render. Any departure from this rule must be dangerous. (Hansard, vol. 101, p. 138, 1848. Supply, 14 August, 1848. See also 'The Exposition of 1851', Octavo, p. 271.[a])

[a] *Works of Babbage*, Vol. 10, p. 162.

The following paragraph appeared in 'The Times'* a short time since, under the head Naval Intelligence:

A reply has been received to the memorial transmitted to the Admiralty some few days since from the inspectors employed on the iron frigate 'Achilles', building at Chatham dockyard, requesting that they may be placed on the same footing as regards increased pay as the junior officers and mechanics working on the iron frigate for the additional number of hours they are employed in the dockyard. The Lords of the Admiralty intimate that they cannot accede to the wishes of the memorialists, who are reminded that, as / salaried officers of the establishment, the whole of their time is at the disposal of the Admiralty. This decision has caused considerable dissatisfaction.

It appears that the Admiralty wisely adopted the principle enunciated by Mr Gladstone.

It may, however, not unreasonably have caused dissatisfaction to those who had no interest to back them on finding that such large sums are pocketed by those who are blessed with influential friends in high quarters.

If the commissioners had really wished to have obtained a suitable building at a fair price their course was simple and obvious. They need only have stated the nature and amount of accommodation required, and then have selected half a dozen of the most eminent firms amongst our great contractors, who would each have given them an estimate of the plans they respectively suggested.

The commissioners might have made it one of the conditions that they should not be absolutely bound to give the contract to the author of the plan accepted. But in case of not employing him a sum previously stipulated should have been assigned for the use of the design.

By such means they would have had a choice of various plans, and if those plans had, previously to the decision of the commissioners, been publicly exhibited for a few weeks, they might have been enlightened by public criticism. Such a course would have prevented the gigantic job they afterwards perpetrated. It could therefore find no support from the commissioners.

The present commissioners, however, are fit successors to those who in 1851 ignored the existence of the author of the 'Economy of Manufactures' and his inventions. They seem to have been deluded

* About 20 May, 1863.

into the belief that they possessed / the strength, as well as the desire, quietly to strangle the Difference Engine.

It would be idle to break such butterflies upon its matchless wheels, or to give permanence to such names by reflecting them from its diamond-graven plates.* Though the steam-hammer can crack the coating without injuring the kernel of the filbert it drops upon – the admirable precision of its gigantic power could never be demonstrated by exhausting its energy upon an empty nutshell.

Peace, then, to their memory, aptly enshrined in unknown characters within the penetralia of the temple of oblivion.

These celebrities may there at last console themselves in the enjoyment of one enviable privilege denied to them during their earthly career – exemption from the daily consciousness of being 'found out'.

It is, however, not quite impossible, although deciphering is a brilliant art, that one or other of them may have heard of the dread power of the decipherer. Having myself had some slight acquaintance with that fascinating pursuit, it gives me real pleasure to relieve them from this very natural fear by assuring them that not even the most juvenile decipherer could be so stupid as to apply himself to the interpretation of – characters known to be meaningless.

Yet there is one name amongst, but not of them – a fellow-worshipper with myself at far other fanes, whose hands, like mine, have wielded the hammer, and whose pen, like mine, has endeavoured to communicate faithfully to his fellow-men / the measure of those truths he has himself laboriously extracted from the material world. With such endowments, it is impossible that *he* could have had any cognizance of this part of the proceedings of his colleagues.†

At the commencement of the exhibition, Mr Gravatt was constantly present, and was so kind as to explain to many anxious enquirers the nature and uses of the Difference Engine. This, however, interfered so much with his professional engagements as a civil engineer, that it would have been unreasonable to have expected

---

* For the purpose of testing the steadiness and truth of the tools employed in forming the gun-metal plates, I had some dozen of them turned with a diamond point. The perfect equality of its cut caused the reflected light to be resolved into those beautiful images pointed out by Frauenhofer, and also so much admired in the celebrated gold buttons produced by the late Mr Barton, the Comptroller of the Mint.

† I have since learnt, with real satisfaction, that my friend, Mr Fairbairn, was *not* a member of that incompetent commission.

its continuance. In fact, as not above half a dozen spectators could see the machine at once, it was a great sacrifice of valuable time for a very small result.

During the early part of my own examination of the exhibition I had many opportunities of conversing with experienced workmen, well qualified to appreciate the workmanship of the Difference Engine; these I frequently accompanied to its narrow cell, and pointed out to them its use, as well as the means by which its various parts had received their destined form.

Occasionally also I explained it to some few of my personal friends. When Mr Gravatt or myself were thus engaged, a considerable crowd was often collected, who were anxious to hear about, although they could not see, the engine itself.

Upon one of these occasions I was insulted by impertinent questions conveyed in a loud voice from a person at a distance in the crowd. My taste for music, and especially for organs, was questioned. I was charitable enough to suppose that this was an exceptional case; but in less than a week another instance / occurred. After this experience, of course, I seldom went near the Difference Engine. Mr Gravatt who had generously sacrified a considerable portion of his valuable time for the information and instruction of the public was now imperatively called away by professional engagements, and the public had no information whatever upon a subject on which it was really very anxious to be instructed.

Fortunately, however, the exhibition took place during the long vacation; and a friend of mine, Mr Wilmot Buxton, of the Chancery Bar, very frequently accompanied me in my visits. Possessing a profound knowledge of the mathematical principles embodied in the mechanism, I had frequently pointed out to him its nature and relations. These I soon found he so well apprehended that I felt justified in entrusting him with one of my keys of the machine, in order that he might have access to it without the necessity of my presence.

Whenever he opened it for his own satisfaction or for the instruction of his friends, he was speedily surrounded by a far larger portion of the public than could possibly see it, but who were still attracted by his lucid oral explanation.

It was fortunate for many of the visitors to the exhibition that this occurred, for the demands on his time, when present, were incessant, and hundreds thus acquired from his explanations a popular view of the subject.

After the close of the exhibition, Mr Gravatt and myself attended to prepare the Difference Engine for its return to the museum of King's College. To our great astonishment, we found that it had already been removed to the museum at South Kensington. Not only the Difference Engine itself, but also the illustrations and all the unfinished portions of exquisite workmanship which I had lent to the exhibition for its explanation, were gone. /

On Mr Gravatt applying to the Board of Works, it was stated that the Difference Engine itself had been placed in the Kensington Museum because the authorities of King's College had declined receiving it, and immediate instructions were of course given for the restoration of my own property. /

CHAPTER XI

THE LATE PRINCE CONSORT

'Suum cuique.'

Count Mensdorf mentions to the Duke of Wellington his wish to see the Difference Engine – An appointment made – Prince Albert expresses his intention of accompanying his uncle – Time of appointment altered – Their visit, accompanied by the Duke of Wellington – Portrait of Jacquard – Anecdote of Wilkie – Afghanistan arms – Extract from the author's work on the Exhibition of 1862.[a]

I have had one opportunity of fairly estimating some portion of the character of the late justly lamented Prince Consort; to this I will now venture to allude.

In 1842 Count Mensdorf visited London. A few days after I had a note from the late Duke of Wellington, in which he informed me that on the previous evening he had met at the palace the Queen's uncle, Count Mensdorf, who had expressed to the Duke his wish to see my calculating engine. The Duke then enquired whether I could conveniently make some arrangement for that purpose. I immediately wrote to the Duke, that if he would appoint an hour on any morning of the ensuing week, I should have great pleasure in showing and explaining the Difference Engine to Count Mensdorf. It was afterwards arranged that on the following Tuesday, at two o'clock, Count Mensdorf and the Duke should pay me a visit in Dorset Street. On Monday / morning I received another note from the Duke, informing me that Prince Albert had expressed his intention to accompany Count Mensdorf in the proposed visit, and that it would be more convenient if the hour were changed to one instead of two o'clock.

I must freely admit that I did not greatly rejoice at this addition to the party. I resolved, however, strictly to perform the duties thus

---

[a] *Sic*. The extract is taken from the preface of *The Exposition of 1851*, *Works of Babbage*, Vol. 10.

thrown upon me as a host, as well as all those to which Prince Albert was entitled by his elevated position.

Before I took the Prince into the fireproof building in which the Difference Engine was then deposited, I asked his Royal Highness to allow me to show him a portrait of Jacquard, which was at that time hanging up in my drawing-room, as it would greatly assist in explaining the nature of calculating machines.

When we had arrived in front of the portrait, I pointed it out as the object to which I solicited the Prince's attention. 'Oh! that engraving?' remarked the Duke of Wellington. 'No!' said Prince Albert to the Duke; 'it is not an engraving.' I felt for a moment very great surprise; but this was changed into a much more agreeable feeling, when the Prince instantly added, 'I have seen it before.' I felt at once that the Prince was a 'good man and true', and I resolved that I would not confine myself to the rigid rules of etiquette, but that I would help him with all my heart in whatever line his enquiries might be directed.

The portrait of Jacquard was, in fact, a sheet of woven silk, framed and glazed, but looking so perfectly like an engraving, that it had been mistaken for such by two members of the Royal Academy.

A short time after I became possessed of this beautiful work of art, I met Wilkie, and invited him to come and see / my recent acquisition. He called on me one morning. I placed him at a short distance in front of the portrait, which he admired greatly. I then asked him what he thought it was. He answered, 'An engraving!' On which I asked, 'Of what kind?' To this he replied, 'Line-engraving, to be sure!' I drew him a little nearer. He then mentioned another style of engraving. At last, having placed Wilkie close to the portrait, he said, after a considerable pause, 'Can it be lithography?'

A splendid collection of arms from Afghanistan, recently sent to me from India by Sir Edward Ryan, was lying on the tables in one of the rooms we passed through. These had attracted the notice of the Prince, and on returning, the whole party examined them with the greatest interest.

I now conducted my visitors to the fireproof building in which the Difference Engine was placed. Prince Albert was, I understood, sufficiently acquainted with the higher departments of mathematical science to appreciate the influence of such an instrument on its future progress. But the circumstance that charmed me was – his bearing towards his uncle, Count Mensdorf. It was perfectly natural: it could be felt, admired, and honoured – but not described.

When the sad fact of the nation's loss became known to me, I immediately reverted with some anxiety to a work I had published ten years before on the Exhibition of 1851. I feared lest, in speaking of that event, I might have committed some injustice, whilst I was indignant at that under which I was myself suffering. I willingly reprint it here because it contained no empty words of flattery; but analysed the reasons which commanded our respect.

The merit of the original conception of the present Exposition / [1851] is insignificant in comparison with that of the efforts by which it was carried out, and with the importance of its practical results.

To have seen from afar its effects on the improvement, the wealth, and the happiness of the people – to have seized the fit moment, when, by the right use of the influence of an exalted station, it was *possible* to overcome the deeply rooted prejudices of the upper classes – to remove the still more formidable, because latent, impediments of party – generously to have undertaken great responsibility, and with indefatigable labour to have endeavoured to make the best out of the only materials at hand – these are endowments of no ordinary kind.

To move in any rank of society an exception to its general rules, is a very difficult, and if accompanied by the consciousness of the situation, a very painful position to a reflecting mind.

Whatever may be the cause, whether exalted rank, unbounded wealth, surpassing beauty, or unrivalled wit – the renown of daring deeds, the magic of a world-wide fame; to all within those narrow limits the dangers and the penalties are great. Each exists an isolated spirit; each unconsciously imprisoned within its crystal globe, perceives the colours of all external objects modified by those tints imparted to them by its own surrounding sphere. No change of view can teach it to rectify this partial judgement; throughout its earthward course the same undying rainbow attends to the last its parent drop.

Rarely indeed can some deep-searching mind, after long comparison, perceive the real colours of those translucent shells which encompass kindred spirits; and thus at length enable him to achromatize the medium which surrounds his / own. To one who has thus rectified the 'colour-blindness' of his intellectual vision, how deep the sympathy he feels for those still involved in that hopeless obscurity from which he has himself escaped. None can so justly appreciate that sense of loneliness, that solitude of mind, which surrounds unquestioned eminence on its lofty throne – none, therefore, can make so large an allowance for its errors – none so skilfully assist in guiding its hazardous career. /

128

CHAPTER XII

RECOLLECTIONS OF THE DUKE OF WELLINGTON

Official visit to see the Difference Engine in 1829 – Extract from a letter from the late General Sir William Napier – Loss of the troopship 'Birkenhead' – The author accompanies the Duke to the Exhibition of 1851 – Fixed in the crowd, the Duke plays with a child of two years old – The late Countess of Wilton asks a question about the Difference Engine – The author's explanation – The Duke's remark – Sketch of one portion of the Duke's intellectual character – University addresses – The Duke helps a dumpy fellow to see the Queen – The author saves a Master of Arts from hanging – The Duke and the Ninth Bridgewater Treatise – The Duke an economist of time – Character of the French Marshals.

My acquaintance with the late Duke of Wellington commenced in an official visit from himself and Mr Goulburn, the Chancellor of the Exchequer, to inspect the drawings and works of the Difference Engine No. 1. This was in November, 1829. Afterwards I met the Duke in private society at the houses of one or two of his intimate friends, and subsequently I was honoured not unfrequently by receiving him at my own. During the Exhibition of 1851 I very often accompanied him in his examination of the contents of that building. I made no notes of any of the conversations, some of them highly interesting, which occurred on such occasions, because I felt that the habit of recording privately the conversations with our acquaintances was a breach of faith towards the individual, and tended to destroy all confidence in society. /

I now perceive, when it is too late, that a rigid adherence to that rule has deprived me of the power of relating circumstances of the greatest interest to survivors, and of the highest credit to himself. I should not even have adverted to the subject in the present work, had I not observed in the fourth volume of the life of the late General Sir Charles Napier of Scinde a passage which, if not explained, might lead to the erroneous inference that I had myself proposed to speak to the Duke of Wellington on a certain military subject, whereas I only did so at the repeated desire of Sir Charles himself.

129

The following is a portion of a letter from General Sir Charles Napier to his brother, General Sir William Napier, extracted from 'The Life of Sir Charles Napier', vol. iv, p. 347:[a]

TO GENERAL W. NAPIER

2 May, 1852

I met Babbage at Miss Burdett Coutts. He talked about the 'Birkenhead', and was very eager, saying, 'Cannot you speak to the Duke of Wellington?' 'No; it would seem a criticising of his conduct.' 'Well, I, as a civilian, may.' 'Yes; and you will do good, for the Duke alluded to the subject at the Royal Academy dinner an hour ago.' Babbage did so at once, asking him to move in the matter; and the Duke said he would. I also spoke to Hardinge, who told me he had had a mind to allude to it in his speech at the dinner, but feared it might seem a reflection on the Duke.

. . .

I have been told that the Duke is only awaiting an official despatch from Harry Smith, or Cathcart, about the 'Birkenhead', / to act. This is probable, as being like his cautious way, but, to my thinking, not well in this case.

The matter referred to arose thus. Several years ago a troopship, named the 'Birkenhead', was wrecked on the African coast, near the Cape of Good Hope. A very small portion only of the troops were saved. According to the testimony of the survivors, the discipline and order which prevailed on board up to the final catastrophe was admirable, and almost beyond example. If any human means could have saved those invaluable lives, such discipline would have largely contributed to the result.

Sharing the general regret at this severe loss, and sympathizing deeply with the feelings of the surviving relatives, it occurred to me that very simple and inexpensive means were available, which if employed, would at the least afford a melancholy consolation to the afflicted relatives, might be retained with becoming pride in their families, and would also add to the respectability of the social position of the soldier.

Observing that military offences punished by a court-martial were made public by being read at the head of every regiment, I

---

[a] W. F. P. Napier, *The life and opinions of General Sir C. J. Napier* (London, 1857).

suggested that in certain cases publicity should be given by the same means to noble acts of forbearance or of self-devotion.

In the case of the 'Birkenhead', in which ship small detachments of several regiments were lost, I suggested that an order should be issued, stating –

The circumstances under which the loss occurred, and the nation's approbation of the conduct of the departed.

That their names should be read at the head of their respective regiments.

That an official letter, signed by the colonel or other proper / officer of each regiment, describing the nature of the service under which the loss occurred, and conveying to the nearest surviving relative the expression of the high approbation the Government entertained of such heroic conduct.

Such official testimonials would soothe the feelings of many a relative, would become objects of just pride amongst the relations of the departed, and be handed down as heirlooms in many a village circle.

I mentioned these views to several of my acquaintances, and the idea seemed to meet with general approbation. I found my military friends fully alive to the advantage of such a course for the benefit of the service, and also as a consolation to surviving relatives. Among others, I proposed it to the late General Sir Charles Napier. He highly approved of the plan, about which we had several conversations. In one of these I suggested that he should mention it to the Duke of Wellington; to which Sir Charles replied, 'No, I could not do that: you should tell him yourself.' I smiled at the notion, not thinking that my friend was in earnest.

A short time after I met Sir Charles Napier at a large evening party. We were sitting together on a sofa talking: he resumed the plan I had proposed, spoke of it with much approbation, and concluded by saying, 'You ought to tell the Duke of it.'

I replied that I had thought he was only joking when he had on a former occasion made the same observation.

'No, indeed,' said Sir Charles; 'I am serious. The Duke will attend to what you say more than to any of us.'

'If you really think so,' I replied, 'I will follow your counsel. I hope,' I added, 'the Duke may excuse me as a civilian for speaking about it, but after such an expression of your opinion I feel bound to take that course.' /

The conversation then turned upon other subjects, when shortly after the Duke of Wellington was announced.

'There,' observed Sir Charles, 'is the Duke, now go and talk to him about it.' I promised to do so at a proper opportunity.

After the Duke had made his bow to the lady of the house, and recognized and conversed with many of his friends, I threw myself in his way. On the Duke shaking hands with me, I remarked that I was particularly glad to meet him, because an idea had occurred to me in which I thought he would take an interest. He stepped with me a little out of the crowd, and I then stated shortly my views. The Duke paid great attention to the subject; made several remarks upon it; and when we separated, I felt satisfied that he took a strong interest in it. I thought, however, that he had applied the idea rather more to the officers, whilst my main object was the interests of the privates.

Much later in the evening I was taking some refreshment in another room, when the Duke entering, saw and rejoined me. He reverted to the subject; I observed that though officers and privates should have the same official acknowledgement, yet that the Commander-in-Chief and the Government possessed other more substantial means of benefiting the surviving relatives of the officers than of the privates. We had some further conversation about it, and I then felt quite satisfied that he both understood and approved of it.

I rather think the Duke of Wellington moved in the House of Lords for certain papers, on which he intended to found some measure of the kind; but his death, shortly after, put an end to the question.

During the year 1851 I very frequently accompanied the Duke of Wellington to the Exhibition, or met him there by / appointment at the crystal fountain. Sometimes one or two of his particular friends, usually ladies, were invited to join the party.

On the first occasion I spoke to one of the attending police, simply for the purpose of facilitating our passage if we should get into a great crowd, which, of course, did occasionally happen. In these cases the policeman a little preceded us, and it was very interesting to observe the sudden changes in the countenances of those whom the constable gently touched in order to accelerate our passage. On the first slight pressure of the policeman's hand upon the arm of John Bull, he looked round with indignation: but when the policeman quietly asked him to be so good as to allow the Duke of Wellington to pass, the muscles of John Bull's countenance relaxed into a grateful smile: he immediately made way, and in several cases thanked the officer for

132

giving him an opportunity of seeing the Duke. During the most crowded of those days we at one period became entirely blocked up and stationary for upwards of ten minutes. Our intelligent companion was himself wedged in, at a short distance from us. Just in front of us stood a woman with a child in her arms of about two years old, who was leaning over its mother's shoulder.

The Duke began to play with the infant, pretending to touch its ear with his finger, and then to touch its nose. The mother was gratified – the child was charmed. At last the crowd almost suddenly broke up, and we went on. After we had advanced about a dozen paces I said to the Duke of Wellington, 'I must step back to speak to the mother of your young friend.' I then asked her if she knew the gentleman who had been playing with her child for the last ten minutes: she said 'No, Sir.' I told her it was the Duke of Wellington. Her surprise and delight were equally great. / I desired her to tell her boy when he grew up that, when an infant, the Duke of Wellington had played with him. I then returned and told the Duke the object of my mission. His approbation was indicated by a happy smile.

One morning the Duke of Wellington called in Dorset Street with the late Countess of Wilton, to whom he wished me to show the Difference Engine. Its home was at that period in my drawing-room. We sat round it whilst I explained its mode of action, and made it calculate some small table of numbers.

When I had concluded my explanation, Lady Wilton, addressing me, said, 'Now, Mr Babbage, can you tell me what was your greatest difficulty in contriving this machine?' I had never previously asked myself that question; but I knew the nature of it well.

It arose not from the difficulty of contriving mechanism to execute each individual movement, for I had contrived very many different modes of executing each: but it really arose from the almost innumerable *combinations* amongst all these contrivances – a number so vast, that no human mind could examine them all.

It instantly occurred to me that a similar difficulty must present itself to a general commanding a vast army, when about to engage in a conflict with another army of equal or of greater amount. I therefore thought it must have been felt by the Duke of Wellington, and I determined to make a kind of psychological experiment upon him.

Carefully abstaining from any military term, I commenced my

explanation to Lady Wilton. I soon perceived by his countenance that the Duke was already in imagination again in Spain. I then went on boldly with the explanation of my / own mechanical difficulty; and when I had concluded, the Duke turned to Lady Wilton and said, 'I know that difficulty well.'

The success of this experiment induced me in a subsequent publication* to give an analysis of one portion of the Duke of Wellington's intellectual character, although I made no mention of his name. Many of his admirers, however, perceived at once the truth of those views, and recognized the justice of their application. I therefore place them before my readers in the following extract from the work referred to:

It is now felt and admitted, that it is the civil capacity of the great commander which prepares the way for his military triumphs; that his knowledge of human nature enables him to select the fittest agents, and to place them in the situations best adapted to their powers; that his intimate acquaintance with all the accessories which contribute to the health and comfort of his troops, enables him to sustain their moral and physical energy. It has been seen that he must have studied and properly estimated the character of his foes as well as of his allies, and have made himself acquainted with the personal character of the chiefs of both; and still further, that he must have scrutinized the secret motives which regulated their respective governments.

When directly engaged in the operations of contending armies occupying a wide extent of country, he must be able, with rapid glance, to ascertain the force it is possible to concentrate upon each of many points in any given time, and the greater or less chance of failing in the attempt. He must also be able to foresee, with something more than conjecture, what amount of the enemy's force can be brought to the same spot in the same and in different times. With these elements / he must undertake one of the most difficult of mental tasks, that of classifying and grouping the innumerable combinations to which either party may have recourse for purposes of attack or defence. Out of the multitude of such combinations, which might baffle by their simple enumeration the strongest memory, throwing aside the less important, he must be able to discover, to fix his attention, and to act upon the most favourable. Finally, when the course thus selected having been pursued, and perhaps partially carried out, is found to be entirely deranged by one of those many chances inseparable from such operations, then, in the midst of action, he must be able suddenly to organize a different system of operations, new to all other minds, yet possibly, although unconsciously, anticipated by his own.

* 'The Exposition of 1851', 2nd edition, p. 222. <*Works of Babbage*, Vol. 10, p. 133.>

The genius that can meet and overcome such difficulties *must* be intellectual, and would, under different circumstances, have been distinguished in many a different career.

Nor even would it be very surprising that such a commander, estimating justly the extent of his own powers, and conscious of having planned the best combinations of which his mind is capable, should, having issued his orders, calmly lie down on the eve of the approaching conflict, and find in sleep that bodily restoration so indispensable to the full exercise of his faculties in the mighty struggle about to ensue.

Soon after the Queen came to the throne, the two Universities presented addresses to her Majesty. I accompanied that of Cambridge. The deputation was very numerous, and much unseemly pushing took place. I recollect a very short dumpy fellow pushing much more energetically than any other, for whom I made way, as I retired from the strife in which I was unwillingly involved. He not only pushed, but was continually / jumping up like a parched pea in a heated frying-pan: his object being to get a glimpse of her Majesty, and the effect accomplished being to alight on the toes or graze the heels of his colleagues.

I retired into a window close to the end of the position occupied by the gentlemen-at-arms. The Duke of Wellington, who had a short time before, as Chancellor of the University of Oxford, presented the address of that body, still remained in the state apartments. He joined me in the recess of the window, and we entered into conversation.

After a time the little dumpy fellow, who had been regularly turned out of the crowd for his pushing, came up to us, and, mistaking the Duke of Wellington for a beefeater or some palace attendant, complained, almost in tears, that he wanted to see the Queen, and that they had pushed him out, and that he had not been able to see the Queen.

The Duke very good-naturedly said he would take him to a place where he could see her Majesty without being pushed about. Accordingly, the Duke led him behind the gentlemen-at-arms to a situation in which the little man's wish was gratified, and then returned with him to the window, and resumed the conversation.

On another occasion the University of Cambridge presented an address to the Queen at Buckingham Palace. The crowd was very great. On descending one of the flights of stairs, a short Master of Arts was unluckily caught by the string of his gown hooking itself upon one of the large door-handles. He was carried off his legs by the advancing rush. To bring back the pendant Master of Arts a single inch was impossible from the pressure onwards. So whilst two or three of his colleagues with difficulty supported him, I took out my penknife and cut the imprisoning ribbon. /

When I published the 'Ninth Bridgewater Treatise', I sent my servant to Apsley House with a presentation copy for the Duke of Wellington. The next morning at breakfast my servant informed me that the porter absolutely refused to take it in, although he stated from whom it came.

I remarked to my brother-in-law, who was staying with me, that it was a very odd circumstance, and enquired what was to be done. He replied, 'When a man refuses to receive a parcel, nothing more can be done.' I then observed, that if any other person than the Duke had done so, I should have taken no further step; but, I added, that I knew his character so well, that I was confident there was really a good and sufficient reason, although I could not conjecture its nature.

After breakfast I wrote a short note to the Duke, mentioning the circumstances, taking for granted that it arose entirely from some misconception of his orders. I then requested him not to take the trouble of writing to me to explain it; but added that I would send the volume to Apsley House on the following morning, when, I had no doubt, the mistaken interpretation of his orders would have been rectified.

About three o'clock the same day a servant of the Duke's brought me a note, enquiring if there were any answer to take back. The Duke stated in his note that letters, books, parcels, maps, and even merchandise, were continually sent to him for the purpose of being forwarded to all parts of the world. This, he observed, threw upon his house-steward so great a responsibility, that he had been compelled to give directions that no parcel should be received at Apsley House without a written order with his signature, like that which he now enclosed. As the Duke's servant was waiting, I gave him the book, which he took back, and I retained the slip of paper for any other similar occasion. /

The Duke was habitually an economist of time. One day I was going homeward in a cab to dress for a dinner engagement, when I thought I observed him riding down St James's Street towards the House of Lords. On reaching the house of the friend with whom I was to dine, I found that the Duke of Wellington was expected at dinner.

He arrived punctually. In the course of the evening I took an opportunity of asking him whether I was mistaken in supposing I had seen him a short time before dinner riding down St James's Street. I then expressed my surprise at the rapidity of his movements in getting back to Apsley House in time to dress and be punctual to his engagement. He said, 'No, I did not do that; I had ordered my carriage to meet me at the House of Lords, and I changed my dress whilst it was bringing me here.'

The most interesting conversations generally occurred when only a few of his intimate friends met together.

On one of these occasions, at a very small dinner-party, the characters of the French marshals became the subject of conversation. The Duke, being appealed to, pointed out freely their various qualities, and assigned to each his peculiar excellence.

One question, the most highly interesting of all, naturally presented itself to our minds. I was speculating how I could, without impropriety, suggest it, when, to my great relief, one of the party, addressing the Duke, said –

'Well, sir, how was it that, with such various great qualities, you licked them all, one after another?'

The Duke was evidently taken by surprise. He paused for a moment or two, and then said –

'Well, I don't know exactly how it was; but I think that if any unexpected circumstance occurred in the midst of a / battle, which deranged its whole plan, I could perhaps organize another plan more quickly than most of them.'

This strongly confirms the view of the Duke of Wellington's character given in the preceding pages. After examining all the more important combinations which might be made for the conflict, and having selected those which appeared the best, it is quite natural, if any accident deranged the original plan, that he should perceive, more quickly than another commander, one amongst the many plans previously rejected which was immediately applicable to the new and unexpected circumstances. /

CHAPTER XIII

RECOLLECTIONS OF WOLLASTON, DAVY, AND ROGERS

Secretaryship of Royal Society – Mr Murray of Albemarle Street – Remark
on 'The Decline of Science' – Dr Somerville – Explanation of a job of Sir
Humphry Davy – History of the thaumatrope – Introduction to Mr Rogers –
The poet nearly run over – Anecdote of the 'Economy of Manufactures' –
Teaches the author how to live for ever – Rapidity of composition amongst
poets – Different effects of imagination in the poet and the philosopher –
Consultation about the author's unwritten novel.

In 1826, one of the secretaryships of the Royal Society became
vacant. Dr Wollaston and several others of the leading members of
the Society and of the Council wished that I should be appointed.
This would have been the more agreeable to me, because my early
friend Herschel was at that time the senior Secretary.

This arrangement was agreed to by Sir H. Davy, and I left town
with the full assurance that I was to have the appointment. In the
meantime Sir H. Davy summoned a Council at an unusual hour –
eight o'clock in the evening – for a special purpose, namely, some
arrangement about the Treasurer's accounts.

After the business relating to the Treasurer was got through, Sir H.
Davy observed that there was a secretaryship vacant, and he
proposed to fill it up.

Dr Wollaston then asked Sir Humphry Davy if he claimed the
nomination as a right of the President, to which / Sir H. Davy replied
that he did, and then nominated Mr Children. The President, as
President, has no such right; and even if he had possessed it, he had
promised Mr Herschel that I should be his colleague. There were
upright and eminent men on that council; yet no one of them had the
moral courage to oppose the President's dictation, or afterwards to
set it aside on the ground of its irregularity.

A few years after, whilst I was on a visit at Wimbledon Park, Dr
and Mrs Somerville came down to spend the day. Dr Somerville
mentioned a very pleasant dinner he had had with the late Mr John

138

Murray of Albemarle Street, and also a conversation relating to my book 'On the Decline of Science in England'. Mr Murray felt hurt at a remark I had made on himself (page 107) whilst criticizing a then unexplained job of Sir Humphry Davy's. Dr Somerville assured Mr Murray that he knew me intimately, and that if I were convinced that I had done him an injustice, nobody would be more ready to repair it. A few days after, Mr Murray put into Dr Somerville's hands papers explaining the whole of the transaction. These papers were now transferred to me. On examining them I found ample proof of what I had always suspected. The observation I had made which pained Mr Murray fell to the ground as soon as the real facts were known, and I offered to retract it in any suitable manner. One plan I proposed was to print a supplemental page, and have it bound up with all the remaining copies of the 'Decline of Science'.

Mr Murray was satisfied with my explanation, but did not wish me to take the course I proposed, at least, not at that time. Various objections may have presented themselves to his mind, but the affair was adjourned with the understanding that at some future time I should explain the real state of / the facts which had led to this misinterpretation of Mr Murray's conduct.

The true history of the affair was this: Being on the Council of the Royal Society in 1827, I observed in our accounts a charge of £381.5s. as paid to Mr Murray for 500 copies of Sir Humphry Davy's Discourses.

I asked publicly at the Council for an explanation of this item. The answer given by Dr Young and others was –

'That the Council had agreed to purchase these volumes at that price, in order to *induce* Mr Murray to print the President's speeches.'

To this I replied that such an explanation was entirely inadmissible. I then showed that even allowing a very high price for composing, printing, and paper, if the Council had wished to print 500 copies of those Discourses they could have done it themselves for £150 at the outside. I could not extract a single word to elucidate this mystery, about which, however, I had my own ideas.

It appeared by the papers put into my hands that Sir Humphry Davy had applied to Mr Murray, and had sold him the copyright of the Discourses for 500 guineas, one of the conditions being that the Royal Society should purchase of him 500 copies at the trade price.

Mr Murray paid Sir H. Davy the 500 guineas in three bills at six, twelve, and eighteen months. These bills passed through Drummond's (Sir H. Davy's banker), and I have had them in my own hands for examination.

Thus it appears that Mr Murray treated the whole affair as a matter of business, and acted in this purchase in his usual liberal manner. I have had in my hand a statement of the winding-up of that account copied from Mr Murray's books, and I find that he was a considerable loser by his purchase. / Sir H. Davy, on the other hand, contrived to transfer between three and four hundred pounds from the funds of the Royal Society into his own pocket.*

It was my determination to have called for an explanation of this affair at the election of our President and officers at our anniversary on 30 November if Sir H. Davy had been again proposed as President in 1827.

The Thaumatrope

One day Herschel, sitting with me after dinner, amusing himself by spinning a pear upon the table, suddenly asked whether I could show him the two sides of a shilling at the same moment.

I took out of my pocket a shilling, and holding it up before the looking-glass, pointed out *my* method. 'No,' said my friend, 'that won't do;' then spinning my shilling upon the table, he pointed out *his* method of seeing both sides at once. The next day I mentioned the anecdote to the late Dr Fitton, who a few days after brought me a beautiful illustration of the principle. It consisted of a round disc of card suspended between the two pieces of sewing-silk. These threads being held between the finger and thumb of each hand, were then made to turn quickly, when the disc of card, of course, revolved also.

Upon one side of this disc of card was painted a bird; upon the other side, an empty bird-cage. On turning the thread rapidly, the bird appeared to have got inside the cage. We soon made numerous applications, as a rat on one side and a trap upon the other, etc. It was shown to Captain Kater, Dr Wollaston, and many of our friends, and was, after the lapse of a short time, forgotten. /

Some months after, during dinner at the Royal Society Club, Sir Joseph Banks being in the chair, I heard Mr Barrow, then Secretary to the Admiralty, talking very loudly about a wonderful invention of Dr

* See 'Decline of Science in England', p. 105. Octavo. 1830. <*Works of Babbage*, Vol. 7, p. 53.>

Paris, the object of which I could not quite understand. It was called the thaumatrope, and was said to be sold at the Royal Institution, in Albermarle Street. Suspecting that it had some connection with our unnamed toy, I went the next morning and purchased, for seven shillings and sixpence, a thaumatrope, which I afterwards sent down to Slough to the late Lady Herschel. It was precisely the thing which her son and Dr Fitton had contributed to invent, which amused all their friends for a time and had then been forgotten. There was however *one* additional thaumatrope made afterwards. It consisted of the usual disc of paper. On one side was represented a thaumatrope (the design upon it being a penny-piece) with the motto, 'How to turn a penny'.

On the other side was a gentleman in black, with his hands held out in the act of spinning a thaumatrope, the motto being, 'A new trick from Paris'.

After my contest for Finsbury was decided, Mr Rogers the banker, and the brother of the poet, who had been one of my warmest supporters, proposed accompanying me to the hustings at the declaraton of the poll. He had also invited a party of some of the most influential electors of his district to dine with him in the course of the week, in order that they might meet me, and consider about measures for supporting me at the next opportunity.

On a cold drizzling rainy day in November the final state of the poll was declared. Mr Rogers took me in his carriage to the hustings, and caught a cold, which seemed at first unimportant. On the day of the dinner, when we met at / Mr Rogers's, who resided at Islington, he was unable to leave his bed. Miss Rogers, his sister, who lived with him, and his brother the poet, received us, quite unconscious of the dangerous condition of their relative, who died the next day.

Thus commenced a friendship with both of my much-valued friends which remained unruffled by the slightest wave until their lamented loss. Miss Rogers removed to a house in the Regent's Park, in which the paintings by modern artists collected by her elder brother, and increased by her own judicious taste, were arranged. The society at that house comprised all that was most eminent in literature and in art. The adjournment after her breakfasts to the delightful verandah overlooking the park still clings to my fading memory, and the voices of her poet brother, of Jeffrey, and of Sidney Smith still survive in the vivid impressions of their wisdom and their wit.

I do not think the genuine kindness of the poet's character was sufficiently appreciated. I occasionally walked home with him from

141

parties during the first years of our acquaintance. In later years, when his bodily strength began to fail, I always accompanied him, though sometimes not without a little contest.

I have frequently walked with him from his sister's house, in the Regent's Park, to his own in St James's Place, and he has sometimes insisted upon returning part of the way home with me.

On one of those occasions we were crossing a street near Cavendish Square: a cart coming rapidly round the corner, I almost dragged him over. As soon as we were safe, the poet said, very much as a child would, 'There, now, that was all your fault; you would come with me, and so I was nearly run over.' However, I found less and less resistance to my / accompanying him, and only regretted that I could not be constantly at his side on those occasions.

Soon after the publication of the 'Economy of Manufactures', Mr Rogers told me that he had met one evening, at a very fashionable party, a young dandy, with whom he had had some conversation. The poet had asked him whether he had read that work. To this his reply was, 'Yes: it is a very nice book – just the kind of book that anybody could have written.'

One day, when I was in great favour with the poet, we were talking about the preservation of health. He told me he would teach me how to live forever; for which I thanked him in a compliment after his own style, rather than in mine. I answered, 'Only embalm me in your poetry, and it is done.' Mr Rogers invited me to breakfast with him the next morning, when he would communicate the receipt. We were alone, and I enjoyed a very entertaining breakfast. The receipt consisted mainly of cold ablutions and the frequent use of the flesh brush. Mr Rogers himself used the latter to a moderate extent regularly, three times every day – before he dressed himself, when he dressed for dinner, and before he got into bed. About six or eight strokes of the flesh-brush completed each operation. We then adjourned to a shop, where I purchased a couple of the proper brushes which I used for several years, and still use occasionally, with, I believe, considerable advantage.

Once, at Mr Rogers's table, I was talking with one of his guests about the speed with which some authors composed, and the slowness of others. I then turned to our host, and, much to his surprise, enquired how many lines a day on the average a poet usually wrote. My friend, when his astonishment had a little subsided, very good-naturedly gave us the result of his own

142

experience. He said that he had never written / more than four* lines of verse in any one day of his life. This I can easily understand; for Mr Rogers's taste was the most fastidious, as well as the most just, I ever met with. Another circumstance also, I think, contributed to this slowness of composition.

An author may adopt either of two modes of composing. He may write off the whole of his work roughly, so as to get upon paper the plan and general outline, without attending at all to the language. He may afterwards study minutely every clause of each sentence, and then every word of each clause.

Or the author may finish and polish each sentence as soon as it is written.

This latter process was, I think, employed by Mr Rogers, at least in his poetry.

He then told us that Southey composed with much greater rapidity than himself, as well in poetry as in prose. Of the latter Southey frequently wrote a great many pages before breakfast.

Once, at a large dinner party, Mr Rogers was speaking of an inconvenience arising from the custom, then commencing, of having windows formed of one large sheet of plate-glass. He said that a short time ago he sat at dinner with his back to one of these single panes of plate-glass: it appeared to him that the window was wide open, and such was the force of imagination, that he actually caught cold.

It so happened that I was sitting just opposite to the poet. Hearing this remark, I immediately said, 'Dear me, how odd it is, Mr Rogers, that you and I should make such a very different use of the faculty of imagination. When I go to the house of a friend in the country, and unexpectedly remain / for the night, having no nightcap, I should naturally catch cold. But by tying a bit of pack-thread tightly round my head, I go to sleep imagining that I have a nightcap on; consequently I catch no cold at all.' This sally produced much amusement all around, who supposed I had improvised it; but, odd as it may appear, it is a practice I have often resorted to. Mr Rogers, who knew full well the respect and regard I had for him, saw at once that I was relating a simple fact, and joined cordially in the merriment it excited.

In the latter part of Mr Rogers's life, when, being unable to walk,

---

* I am not quite certain that the number was four; but I am absolutely certain that it was either four or six.

143

he was driven in his carriage round the Regent's Park, he frequently called at my door, and, when I was able, I often accompanied him in his drive. On some one of these occasions, when I was unable to accompany him, I put into his hands a parcel of proof-sheets of a work I was then writing, thinking they might amuse him during his drive, and that I might profit by his criticism. Some years before, I had consulted him about a novel I had proposed to write solely for the purpose of making money to assist me in completing the Analytical Engine. I breakfasted alone with the poet, who entered fully into the subject. I proposed to give up a twelvemonth to writing the novel, but I determined not to commence it unless I saw pretty clearly that I could make about £5000 by the sacrifice of my time. The novel was to have been in three volumes, and there would probably have been reprints of another work in two volumes. Both of these works would have had graphic illustrations. The poet gave me much information on all the subjects connected with the plan, and amongst other things, observed that when he published his beautifully illustrated work on Italy, that he had paid £9000 out of his own pocket before he received any return for that work. /

CHAPTER XIV

RECOLLECTIONS OF LAPLACE, BIOT, AND HUMBOLDT

My first visit to Paris was made in company with my friend John Herschel. On reaching Abbeville, we wanted breakfast, and I undertook to order it. Each of us usually required a couple of eggs. I preferred having mine moderately boiled, but my friend required his to be boiled quite hard. Having explained this matter to the waiter, I concluded by instructing him that each of us required two eggs thus cooked, concluding my order with the words, 'pour chacun deux'.

The garçon ran along the passage halfway towards the kitchen, and then called out in his loudest tone –

'Il faut faire bouillir cinquante-deux oeufs pour Messieurs les Anglais.' I burst into such a fit of uncontrollable laughter at this absurd misunderstanding of *chacun deux*, for *cinquante-deux*, that it was some time before I could explain it to Herschel, and but for his running into the kitchen to countermand / it, the half hundred of eggs would have assuredly been simmering over the fire.

A few days after our arrival in Paris, we dined with Laplace, where we met a large party, most of whom were members of the Institut. The story had already arrived at Paris, having rapidly passed through several editions.

To my great amusement, one of the party told the company that, a few days before, two young Englishmen being at Abbeville, had ordered fifty-two eggs to be boiled for their breakfast, and that they ate up every one of them, as well as a large pie which was put before them.

My next neighbour at dinner asked me if I thought it probable. I replied, that there was no absurdity a young Englishman would not occasionally commit.

One morning Herschel and I called on Laplace, who spoke to us of various English works on mathematical subjects. Amongst others, he mentioned with approbation, 'Un ouvrage de vous deux'. We were both quite at a loss to know to what work he referred. Herschel and I had not written any joint work, although we had together translated the work of Lacroix.[a] The volume of the 'Memoirs of the Analytical Society',[b] though really our joint production, was not known to be such, and it was also clear that Laplace did not refer to that work. Perceiving that we did not recognize the name of the author to whom he referred, Laplace varied the pronunciation by calling him *vous deux*; the first word being pronounced as the French word 'vous', and the second as the English word 'deuce'.

Upon further explanation, it turned out that Laplace meant to speak of a work published by Woodhouse, whose name is in the pronunciation of the French so very like *vous deux*. /

Poisson, Fourier, and Biot were amongst my earliest friends in Paris. Fourier, then Secretary of the Institute, had accompanied the first Napoleon in his expedition to Egypt. His profound acquaintance with analysis remains recorded in his works. His unaffected and genial manner, the vast extent of his acquirements, and his admirable taste conspicuous even in the apartments he inhabited, were most felt by those who were honoured by his friendship.

With M. Biot I became acquainted in early life; he was then surrounded by a happy family. In my occasional visits to Paris I never omitted an opportunity of paying my respects to him: when deprived of those supports and advanced in life, he still earnestly occupied himself in carrying out the investigations of his earlier years.

His son, M. Biot, a profound oriental scholar, who did me the honour of translating 'The Economy of Manufactures', died many years before his father.

In one of my visits to Paris, at a period when beards had become fashionable amongst a certain class of my countrymen, I met Biot.

---

[a] With J. F. W. Herschel and G. Peacock (translators), S. F. Lacroix, *An elementary treatise on the differential and integral calculus* (1816) – extracts in *Works of Babbage*, Vol. 1.

[b] With J. F. W. Herschel, *Memoirs of the Analytical Society* (1813) – extracts in *Works of Babbage*, Vol. 1.

After our first greeting, looking me full in the face, he said, 'My dear friend, you are the best shaved man in Europe'.

At a later period I took with me to Paris the complete drawings of Difference Engine No. 2. As soon as I had hung them up round my own apartments to explain them to my friends I went to the College de France, where M. Biot resided. I mentioned to him the fact, and said that if it was a subject in which he was interested, and had leisure to look at these drawings, I should have great pleasure in bringing them to him, and giving him any explanation that he might desire. I told him, however, that I was fully aware how much the time of every man who really adds to science must be occupied, / and that I made this proposal rather to satisfy my own mind that I had not neglected one of my oldest friends than in the expectation that he had time for the examination of this new subject.

The answer of my friend was remarkable. After thanking me in the warmest terms for this mark of friendship, he explained to me that the effect of age upon his own mind was to render the pursuit of any new enquiry a matter of slow and painful effort; but that in following out the studies of his youth he was not so much impeded. He added that in those subjects he could still study with satisfaction, and even make advances in them, assisted in the working out of his views experimentally by the aid of his younger friends.

I was much gratified by this unreserved expression of the state of the case, and I am sure those younger men who so kindly assisted the aged philosopher will be glad to know that their assistance was duly appreciated.

The last time during M. Biot's life that I visited Paris I went, as usual, to the College de France. I enquired of the servant who opened the door after the state of M. Biot's health, which was admitted to be feeble. I then asked whether he was well enough to see an old friend. Biot himself had heard the latter part of this conversation. Coming into the passage he seized my hand and said 'My dear friend, I would see you even if I were dying'.

Alexander Humboldt

One of the most remarkable characteristics of Humboldt's mind was, that he not merely loved and pursued science for its own sake, but that he derived pleasure from assisting with his information and advice any other enquirer, however humble, who might need it. /

In one of my visits to Paris, Humboldt was sitting with me when a

147

friend of mine, an English clergyman, who had just arrived in Paris, and had only two days to spare for it, called upon me to ask my assistance about getting access to certain MSS. Putting into Humboldt's hand a tract lying on my table, I asked him to excuse me for a few minutes whilst I gave what advice I could to my countryman.

My friend told me that he wanted to examine a MS., which he was informed was in a certain library in a certain street in Paris; that he knew nobody in the city to help him in his mission.

Humboldt having heard this statement, came over to us and said, 'If you will introduce me to your friend, I can put him in the way of seeing the MSS. he is in search of.' He then explained that the MSS. had been removed to another library in Paris, and proposed to give my friend a note of introduction to the librarian, and mentioned other MSS. and other libraries in which he would find information upon the same subject.

Many years after, being at Vienna, I heard that Humboldt was at Töplitz, a circumstance which induced me to visit that town. On my arrival I found he had left it a few days before on his return to Berlin. In the course of a few days, I followed him to that city, and having arrived in the middle of the day, I took apartments in the Linden Walk, and got all my travelling apparatus in order; I then went out to call on Humboldt. Finding that he had gone to dine with his brother William, who resided at a short distance from Berlin, I therefore merely left my card.

The next morning at seven o'clock, before I was out of bed, I received a very kind note from Humboldt, to ask me to breakfast with him at nine. In a postscript he added, 'What / are the moving molecules of Robert Brown?' These atoms of dead matter in rapid motion, when examined under the microscope, were then exciting great attention among philosophers.

I met at breakfast several of Humboldt's friends, with whose names and reputation I was well acquainted.

Humboldt himself expressed great pleasure that I should have visited Berlin to attend the great meeting of German philosophers, who in a few weeks were going to assemble in that capital. I assured him that I was quite unaware of the intended meeting, and had directed my steps to Berlin merely to enjoy the pleasure of his society. I soon perceived that this meeting of philosophers on a very large scale, supported by the King and by all the science of Germany, might itself have a powerful influence upon the future progress of human knowledge. Among my companions at the breakfast-table

148

were Derichlet[a] and Magnus. In the course of the morning Humboldt mentioned to me that his own duties required his attendance on the King every day at three o'clock, and having also in his hands the organization of the great meeting of philosophers, it would not be in his power to accompany me as much as he wished in seeing the various institutions in Berlin. He said that, under these circumstances, he had asked his two young friends, Derichlet and Magnus, to supply his place. During many weeks of my residence in Berlin, I felt the daily advantage of this thoughtful kindness of Humboldt. Accompanied by one or other, and frequently by both, of my young friends, I saw everything to the best advantage, and derived an amount of information and instruction which under less favourable circumstances it would have been impossible to have obtained.

The next morning, I again breakfasted with Humboldt. / On the previous day I had mentioned that I was making a collection of the signs employed in map-making. I now met Von Buch and General Ruhl, both of whom were profoundly acquainted with that subject. I had searched in vain for any specimen of a map shaded upon the principle of lines of equal elevation. Von Buch the next morning gave me an engraving of a small map upon that principle, which was, I believe, at that time the only one existing.

After breakfast we went into Humboldt's study to look at something he wished to show us. In turning over his papers, which, like my own, were lying apparently in great disorder upon the table, he picked up the cover of a letter on which was written a number of names in different parallel columns. 'That,' he observed incidentally, 'is for you.' After he had shown us the object of our visit to his sanctum, he reverted to the envelope which he put into my hands explaining that he had grouped roughly together for my use all the remarkable men then in Berlin, and several of those who were expected.

These he had arranged in classes: Men of science, men of letters, sculptors, painters, and artists generally, instrument-makers, etc. This list I found very convenient for reference.

When the time of the great meeting approached, it became necessary to prepare the arrangements for the convenience of the assembled science of Europe. One of the first things, of course, was the important question, how they were to dine? A committee was therefore appointed to make experiment by dining successively at each of the three or four

---

[a] G. P. L. Dirichlet.

hotels competing for the honour of providing a table d'hôte for the savans.

Humboldt put me on that committee, remarking, that an Englishman always appreciates a good dinner. The committee performed their agreeable duty in a manner quite / satisfactory to themselves, and I hope, also, to the digestions of the Naturforschers.

During the meeting much gaiety was going on at Berlin. One evening previous to our parties, I was walking in the Linden Walk with Humboldt, discussing the singularities of several of our learned acquaintance. My companion made many acute and very amusing remarks; some of these were a little caustic, but not one was ill-natured. I had contributed a very small and much less brilliant share to this conversation, when the clock striking, warned us that the hour for our visits had arrived. I never shall forget the expression of archness which lightened up Humboldt's countenance when shaking my hand he said, in English, 'My dear friend, I think it may be as well that we should not speak of each other until we meet again.' We then each kept our respective engagement, and met again at the most recherché of all, a concert at Mendelssohn's.

Of the Buonaparte family

From my father's house on the coast, near Teignmouth, we could, with a telescope, see every ship which entered Torbay. When the 'Bellerophon' anchored, the news was rapidly spread that Napoleon was on board. On hearing the rumour, I put a small telescope into my pocket, and, mounting my horse, rode over to Torbay. A crowd of boats surrounded the ship, then six miles distant; but, by the aid of my glass, I saw upon the quarter-deck that extraordinary man, with many members of whose family I subsequently became acquainted. Of those who are no more I may without impropriety say a few words.

My first acquaintance with several branches of the family / of Napoleon Buonaparte arose under the following circumstances:

When his elder brother Lucien, to avoid the necessity of accepting a kingdom, fled from his imperial brother, and took refuge in England, his position was either not well understood, or, perhaps, was entirely mistaken. Lucien seems to have been looked upon with suspicion by our government, and was placed in the middle of England under a species of espionage.

Political parties then ran high, and he did not meet with those attentions which his varied and highly cultivated tastes, especially in the fine arts, entitled him to receive, as a stranger in a foreign land.

A family connection of mine, residing in Worcestershire, was in the habit of visiting Lucien Buonaparte. Thus, in my occasional visits to my brother-in-law's place, I became acquainted with the Prince of Canino. In after-years, when he occasionally visited London, I had generally the pleasure of seeing him.

In 1828 I met at Rome the eldest son of Lucien, who introduced me to his sisters, Lady Dudley Stuart and the Princess Gabrielli.

In the same year I became acquainted, at Bologna, with the Princess d'Ercolano, another daughter of Lucien, whom I afterwards met at Florence, at the palace of her uncle Louis, the former king of Holland. During a residence of several months in that city I was a frequent guest at the family table of the Compte St Leu. One of his sons had married the Princess Charlotte, the second daughter of the King of Spain, a most accomplished, excellent, and charming person. They reminded me much of a sensible English couple, in the best class of English society. Both had great taste in the fine / arts. The prince had a workshop at the top of the palace, in which he had a variety of tools and a lithographic printing press. Occasionally, in the course of their morning drives, some picturesque scene, in that beautiful country, would arrest their attention. Stopping the carriage, they would select a favourable spot, and the princess would then make a sketch of it.

At other times they would spend the evening, the prince in extemporizing an imaginary scene, which he described to his wife, who, with admirable skill, embodied upon paper the tasteful conceptions of her husband. These sketches then passed up to the workshop of the Prince, were transferred to stone, and in a few days lithographic impressions descended to the drawing-room. I fortunately possess some of these impressions, which I value highly, not only as the productions of an amiable and most accomplished lady, but of one who did not shrink from the severer duties of life, and died in fulfilling them.

After the melancholy loss of her husband, the Princess Charlotte remained with her father, who resided at one period in the Regent's Park, where I from time to time paid my respects to them. Occasionally I received them at my own house. One summer letters from Florence reached them, announcing the dangerous illness of the Comte de St Leu. The daughter of Joseph immediately set out alone for Florence to minister to the comfort of her uncle and father-in-law. On her return from Italy she was attacked by cholera and died in the south of France. /

151

CHAPTER XV

EXPERIENCE BY WATER

Shooting sea-birds – Walking on the water – A screw being loose – The author nearly drowned – Adventure in the Thames Tunnel – Descent in a diving-bell – Plan for submarine navigation.

The grounds surrounding my father's house, near Teignmouth, extended to the sea. The cliffs, though lofty, admitted at one point of a descent to the beach, of which I very frequently availed myself for the purpose of bathing. One Christmas when I was about sixteen I determined to see if I could manage a gun. I accordingly took my father's fowling-piece, and climbing with it down to the beach, I began to look about for the large sea-birds which I thought I might have a chance of hitting.

I fired several charges in vain. At last, however, I was fortunate enough to hit a sea-bird called a diver; but it fell at some distance into the sea: I had no dog to get it out for me; the sea was rough, and no boat was within reach; also it was snowing.

So I took advantage of a slight recess in the rock to protect my clothes from the snow, undressed, and swam out after my game, which I succeeded in capturing. The next day, having got the cook to roast it, I tried to eat it; but this was by no means an agreeable task, so for the future I left the sea-birds to the quiet possession of their own dominion. /

Shortly after this, whilst residing on the beautiful banks of the Dart, I constantly indulged in swimming in its waters. One day an idea struck me, that it was possible, by the aid of some simple mechanism, to walk upon the water, or at least to keep in a vertical position, and have head, shoulders, and arms above water.

My plan was to attach to each foot two boards closely connected together by hinges themselves fixed to the sole of the shoe. My theory was, that in lifting up my leg, as in the act of walking, the two boards would close up towards each other; whilst on pushing down my foot,

152

the water would rush between the boards, cause them to open out into a flat surface, and thus offer greater resistance to my sinking in the water.

I took a pair of boots for my experiment, and cutting up a couple of old useless volumes with very thick binding, I fixed the boards by hinges in the way I proposed. I placed some obstacle between the two flaps of each book to prevent them from approaching too nearly to each other so as to impede their opening by the pressure of the water.

I now went down to the river, and thus prepared, walked into the water. I then struck out to swim as usual, and found little difficulty. Only it seemed necessary to keep the feet farther apart. I now tried the grand experiment. For a time, by active exertion of my legs, I kept my head and shoulders above water and sometimes also my arms. I was now floating down the river with the receding tide, sustained in a vertical position with a very slight exertion of force.

But unfortunately one pair of my hinges got out of order, and refused to perform its share of the propulsion. The result was that I became lop-sided. I was therefore obliged to swim, which I now did with considerable exertion; but another difficulty soon occurred – the instrument on the / disabled side refused to do its share in propelling me. The tide was rapidly carrying me down the river; my own exertion alone would have made me revolve in a small circle, consequently I was obliged to swim in a spiral. It was very difficult to calculate the curve I was describing upon the surface of the water, and still more so to know at what point, if at any, I might hope to reach its banks again. I became very much fatigued by my efforts, and endeavoured to relieve myself for a time by resuming the vertical position.

After floating, or rather struggling for some time, my feet at last touched the bottom. With some difficulty and much exertion I now gained the bank, on which I lay down in a state of great exhaustion.

This experiment satisfied me of the danger as well as of the practicability of my plan, and ever after, when in the water, I preferred trusting to my own unassisted powers.

At the close of the year 1827, as I anticipated a long absence from England, I paid a visit to the Thames Tunnel, in the construction of which I took a great interest. My eldest son, then about twelve years of age, accompanied me in this visit. I fortunately found the younger Brunel at the works, who kindly took us with him into the workings.

We stood upon a timber platform, distant about fifty feet from the

153

shield, which was full of busy workmen, each actively employed in his own cell. As we were conversing together, I observed some commotion in the upper cell on the right-hand side. From its higher corner there entered a considerable stream of liquid mud. Brunel ran directly to the shield, a line of workmen was instantly formed, and whatever tools or timber was required was immediately conveyed to the spot.

I observed the progress with some anxiety, since but a short time before a similar occurrence had been the prelude / to the inundation of the whole tunnel. I remained watching the fit time, if necessary, to run away; but also noticing what effect the apparent danger had on my son. After a short time it was clear that the ingress of liquid mud had been checked, and in a few minutes more Brunel returned to me, having this time succeeded in stopping up the breach. I then enquired what was really the nature of the danger we had escaped. Brunel told me that unless himself or Gravatt had been present, the whole tunnel would in less than ten minutes have been full of water. The next day I embarked for Holland, and in about a week after I read in Galignani's newspaper, that the Thames had again broken into the tunnel; that five or six of the workmen had been drowned, and that Brunel himself had escaped with great difficulty by swimming.

In 1818, during a visit to Plymouth, I had an opportunity of going down in a diving-bell: I was accompanied by two friends and the usual director of that machine.

The diving-bell in which I descended was a cast-iron vessel about six feet long by four feet and a half wide, and five feet eight inches high. In the top of the bell there were twelve circular apertures, each about six inches in diameter, filled by thick plate-glass fixed by water-tight cement. Exactly in the centre there were a number of small holes through which the air was continually pumped in from above.

At the ends of the bell are two seats, placed at such a height, that the top of the head is but a few inches below the top of the bell; these will conveniently hold two persons each. Exactly in the middle of the bell, and about six inches above its lower edge, is placed a narrow board, on which the feet of the divers rest. On one side, nearly on a level with the shoulders, is a small shelf, with a ledge to / contain a few tools, chalk for writing messages, and a ring to which a small rope is tied. A board is connected with this rope; and after writing any orders on the board with a piece of chalk, on giving it a pull, the superintendent above, round whose arm the other end of the rope is

154

fastened, will draw it up to the surface, and, if necessary, return an answer by the same conveyance.

In order to enter the bell, it is raised about three or four feet above the surface of the water; and the boat in which the persons who propose descending are seated, is brought immediately under it; the bell is then lowered, so as to enable them to step upon the footboard within it; and having taken their seats, the boat is removed, and the bell gradually descends to the water.

On touching the surface , and thus cutting off the communication with the external air, a peculiar sensation is perceived in the ears; it is not, however, painful. The attention is soon directed to another object. The air rushing in through the valve at the top of the bell overflows, and escapes with a considerable bubbling noise under the sides. The motion of the bell proceeds slowly, and almost imperceptibly; and, on looking at the glass lenses close to the head, when the top of the machine just reaches the surface of the water, it may be perceived, by means of the little impurities which float about in it, flowing into the recesses containing glasses. A pain now begins to be felt in the ears, arising from the increased external pressure; this may sometimes be removed by the act of yawning, or by closing the nostrils and mouth, and attempting to force air through the ears. As soon as the equilibrium is established the pain ceases, but recommences almost immediately by the continuance of the descent. On returning, the same sensation of / pain is felt in the ears; but it now arises from the dense air which had filled them endeavouring, as the pressure is removed, to force its way out.

If the water is clear, and not much disturbed, the light in the bell is very considerable; and, even at the depth of twenty feet, was more than is usual in many sitting-rooms. Within the distance of eight or ten feet, the stones at the bottom began to be visible. The pain in the ears still continues to occur at intervals, until the descent of the bell terminates by its resting on the ground. The light is sufficient, after passing through twenty feet of sea water, even for delicate experiments; and a far less quantity is enough for the work which is usually performed in those situations.

The temperatures of the hand and of the mouth, under the tongue, were measured by a thermometer, but they did not seem to differ from those which had been determined by the same instrument previous to the descent; at least, the difference did not amount to one-sixth of a degree of Fahrenheit's scale. The pulse was more frequent.

155

A small magnetic needle did not appear to have entirely lost its directive power, when placed on the footboard in the middle of the bell; but its direction was not the same as that which it indicated on shore. This was determined by directing, by means of signals, the workmen above to move the bell in the direction of one of the co-ordinates; a stick then being pressed against the bottom drew a line parallel to that co-ordinate, its direction by compass was ascertained in the bell, and the direction of the co-ordinate was determined on returning to the surface after leaving the bell.

Signals are communicated by the workmen in the bell to those above, by striking against the side of the bell with a hammer. Those most frequently wanted are indicated by / the fewest number of blows; thus a single stroke is to require more air. The sound is heard very distinctly by those above; but, it must be confessed, that to persons unaccustomed to it, the force with which a weighty hammer is driven against so brittle a material as cast iron is a little alarming.

After ascending a few inches from the bottom, the air in the bell became slightly obscured. At the distance of a few feet this appearance increased. Before it had half reached the surface, it was evident that the whole atmosphere it contained was filled with a mist or cloud, which at last began to condense in large drops on the whole of the internal surface.

The explanation of this phenomenon seems to be, that on the rising of the bell the pressure on the air within being diminished by a weight equal to several feet of water, it began to expand; and some portion of it escaping under the edges of the bell, reduced the temperature of that which remained so much, that it was unable to retain, in the state of invisible vapour, the water which it had previously held in solution. Thus the same principle which constantly produces clouds in the atmosphere filled the diving-bell with mist.

This first led me to consider the much more extensive question of submarine navigation. I was aware that Fulton had already descended in a diving-vessel, and remained under water during several hours. He also carried down a copper sphere containing one cubic foot of space into which he had forced two hundred atmospheres. With these means he remained under water and moved about at pleasure during four hours.

But a closed vessel is obviously of little use for the most important purposes to which submarine navigation would be applied in case of war. In the article Diving-Bell, published in 1826, in the 'Encyclopedia Metropolitana',[a] I gave a description / and drawings of an *open* submarine vessel which would contain sufficient air for the consumption of four persons during more than two days. A few years ago, I understand, experiments were made in the Seine at Paris, on a similar kind of open diving-vessel. Such a vessel could be propelled by a screw, and might enter, without being suspected, any harbour, and place any amount of explosive matter under the bottoms of ships at anchor.

Such means of attack would render even iron and iron-clad ships unsafe when blockading a port. For though chains were kept constantly passing under their keels, it would yet be possible to moor explosive magazines at some distance below, which would effectually destroy them. /

---

[a] 'Diving-bell' (1826), *Works of Babbage*, Vol. 4.

CHAPTER XVI

EXPERIENCE BY FIRE

Baked in an oven – A living volcano – Vesuvius in action – Carried up the cone of ashes in a chair – View of the crater in a dark night – Sunrise – Descent by ropes and rolling into the great crater – Watched the small crater in active eruption at intervals – Measured a base of 330 feet – Depth of great crater 570 feet – Descent into small crater – A lake of red-hot boiling lava – Regained the great crater with the sacrifice of my boots – Lunched on biscuits and Irish whisky – Visit to the hot springs of Ischia – Towns destroyed by earthquake – Coronets of smoke projected by Vesuvius – Artificial mode of producing them – Fire-damp visited in Welsh coal-mine in company with Professor Moll.

Baked in an oven

Calling one morning upon Chantrey, I met Captain Kater and the late Sir Thomas Lawrence, the President of the Royal Academy. Chantrey was engaged at that period in casting a large bronze statue. An oven of considerable size had been built for the purpose of drying the moulds. I made several enquiries about it, and Chantrey kindly offered to let me pay it a visit, and thus ascertain by my own feelings the effects of high temperature on the human body.

I willingly accepted the proposal, and Captain Kater offered to accompany me. Sir Thomas Lawrence, who was suffering from indisposition, did not think it prudent to join our party. In fact, he died on the second or third day after our experiment.

The iron folding-doors of the small room or oven were / opened. Captain Kater and myself entered, and they were then closed upon us. The further *corner* of the room, which was paved with squared stones, was visibly of a dull-red heat. The thermometer marked, if I recollect rightly, 265°. The pulse was quickened, and I ought to have counted but did not count the number of inspirations per minute. Perspiration commenced immediately and was very copious. We remained, I believe, about five or six minutes without very great discomfort, and I experienced no subsequent inconvenience from the result of the experiment.

A living volcano

I have never been so fortunate as to be *conscious* of having experienced the least shock of an earthquake, although, when a town had been destroyed in Ischia I hastened on from Rome in the hope of getting a slight shake. My passion was disappointed, so I consoled myself by a flirtation with a volcano.

The situation of my apartments during my residence at Naples enabled me constantly to see the cone of Vesuvius, and the continual projections of matter from its crater. Amongst these were occasionally certain globes of air, or of some gas, which, being shot upwards to a great height above the cone, spread out into huge coronets of smoke, having a singular motion among their particles.

A similar phenomenon sometimes occurs on a small scale during the firing of heavy ordnance. I have frequently seen such at Plymouth and elsewhere; but I was not satisfied about the cause of this phenomenon. I was told that it occurred more frequently if the muzzle of the gun were rubbed with grease; but this did not always succeed.

Soon after my return to London I made a kind of drum, by / stretching wet parchment over a large tin funnel. On directing the point of the funnel at a candle placed a few feet distant, and giving a smart blow upon the parchment, it is observed that the candle is immediately extinguished.

This arises from what is called an air shot. In fact, the air in the tubular part is projected bodily forward, and so blows out the candle. The statements about persons being killed by cannonballs passing close to but not touching them, if true, are probably the results of air shots.

Wishing to trace the motions of such air shots, I added two small tubes towards the large end of the tin funnel, in order that I might fill it with smoke, and thus trace more distinctly the progress of the ball of air.

To my great delight the first blow produced a beautiful coronet of smoke, exactly resembling, on a small scale, the explosions from cannon or the still more attractive ones from Vesuvius.

If phosphoretted hydrogen or any other gas, which takes fire in air, where thus projected upwards, a very singular kind of firework would be produced.

It is possible in dark nights or in fogs that by such means signals might be made to communicate news or to warn vessels of danger.

159

Vesuvius was then in a state of moderate activity. It had a huge cone of ashes on its summit, surrounding an extensive crater of great depth. In one corner of this was a smaller crater, quite on a diminutive scale, which from time to time ejected red-hot fragments of lava occasionally to the height of from a thousand to fifteen hundred feet above the summit of the mountain.

I had taken apartments in the Chiaja, just opposite the volcano, in order that I might watch it with a telescope. In fact, / as I lay in my bed I had an excellent view of the mountain. My next step was to consult with Salvatori, the most experienced of the guides, from whom I had purchased a good many minerals, as to the possibility of getting a peep down the volcano's throat.

Salvatori undertook to report to me from time to time the state of the mountain, round the base of which I made frequent excursions. After about a fortnight, the explosions were more regular and uniform, and Salvatori assured me that all the usual known indications led him to think that it was a fit time for my expedition. As I wished to see as much as possible, I made arrangements to economize my strength by using horses or mules to carry me wherever they could go. Where they could not carry me, as for instance, up the steep slope of the cone of ashes, I employed men to convey me in a chair.

By these means, I saw in the afternoon and evening of one day a good deal of the upper part of the mountain, then took a few hours' repose in a hut, and reached the summit of the cone long before sunrise.

It was still almost dark: we stood upon the irregular edge of a vast gulf spread out below at the depth of about five hundred feet. The plain at the bottom would have been invisible but for an irregular network of bright-red cracks spread over the whole of its surface. Now and then the silence was broken by a rush upwards of a flight of red-hot scoria from the diminutive crater within the large one. These missiles, however, although projected high above the summit of the cone, never extended themselves much beyond the small cavity from which they issued.

Those who have seen the blood-vessels of their own eye by the aid of artificial light, will have seen on a small scale a / perfect resemblance of the plain which at that time formed the bottom of the great crater of Vesuvius.

As the morning advanced the light increased, and some time

before sunrise we had completed the tour of the top of the great crater. Then followed that glorious sight - the sun when seen rising from the top of some lofty mountain.

I now began to speculate upon the means of getting a nearer view of the little miniature volcano in action at one corner of the gulf beneath us. We had brought ropes with us, and I had observed, in our tour round the crater, every dike of congealed lava by which the massive cone was split. These presented buttresses with frequent ledges or huge steps by which I hoped, with the aid of ropes, to descend into the Tartarus below.

Having consulted with our chief guide Salvatori, I found that he was unwilling to accompany us, and proposed remaining with the other guides on the upper edge of the crater. Upon the whole, I was not discontented with the arrangement, because it left a responsible person to keep the other guides in order, and also sufficient force to lift us up bodily by the ropes if that should become necessary.

The abruptness of the rocky buttresses compelled us to use ropes, but the attempt to traverse the steep inclines of light ashes and of fine sand would have been more dangerous from the risk of being engulfed in them.

Having well examined the several disadvantages of these rough-hewn irregular Titanic stairs, I selected one which seemed the most promising for facilitating our descent into the crater. I was encumbered with one of Troughton's heavy barometers, strapped to my back, looking much like Cupid's quiver, though probably rather heavier. In my pocket I had an excellent box sextant, and in a rough kind of basket / two or three thermometers, a measuring tape, and a glass bottle enclosed in a leather case, commonly called a pocket-pistol, accompanied by a few biscuits.

We began our descent by the aid of two ropes, each supported above by two guides. I proceeded, trusting to my rope to step wherever I could, and then cautiously holding on by the rope to spring down to the next ledge. In this manner we descended until we arrived at the last projecting ledge of the dike. Nothing then remained for us but to slide down a steep and lengthened incline of fine sand. Fortunately, the sand itself was not very deep, and was supported by some solid material beneath it. I soon found that it was impossible to stand, so I sat down upon this moving mass, which evidently intended to accompany us in our journey. At first, to my great dismay, I was relieved from the care of my barometer, of which

161

the runaway sand immediately took charge. I then found myself getting deeper and deeper in the sand, and still accelerating my downward velocity.

Gravity had at last done its work and became powerless. I soon dug myself out of my sandy couch, and rushed to my faithful barometer lying at some distance from me with its head just unburied. Fortunately, it was uninjured. My companion, with more skill or good fortune, or with less incumbrances, had safely alighted on the burning plain we now stood upon.

The area of this plain, for it was perfectly flat, was in shape somewhat elliptical. The surface consisted of a black scoriacious rock, reticulated with ditches from one to three feet wide, intersecting each other in every direction. From some of these, fumes not of the most agreeable odour were issuing. All those above two feet deep showed that at that depth below us everything was of a dull-red heat. It was / these ditches with red-hot bottoms which, in the darkness of the night, had presented the singular spectacle I described as having witnessed on the evening before.

At one extremity of this oval plain there was a small cone, from which the eruptions before described appeared to issue.

My first step, after examining the few instruments I had brought with me, was to select a spot upon which to measure a base for ascertaining the depth of the crater from its upper edge.

Having decided upon my base line, I took with my sextant the angle of elevation of the rim of the crater above a remarkable spot on a level with my eye. Then fixing my walking-stick into a little crack in the scoria, I proceeded to measure with a tape a base line of 340 feet. Arrived at this point, I again took the angle of elevation of the same part of the rim from the same remarkable spot on a level with the eye. Then, by way of verification, I remeasured my base line and found it only differed from the former measure by somewhat less than one foot. But my walking-stick, which had not penetrated the crack more than a few inches, was actually in flames.

Having noted down these facts, including the state of the thermometer and barometer, in my pocket-book, I took first a survey and then a tour about my fiery domain. I afterwards found, from the result of this measurement, that our base line was 570 feet below one of the lowest points of the edge of the crater. Having collected a few mineral specimens, I applied myself to observe and register the eruptions of the little embryo volcano at the further extremity of the elliptical plain.

These periodical eruptions interested me very much. I proceeded to observe and register them, and found they occurred / at tolerably regular intervals. At first, I performed this operation at a respectful distance and out of the reach of the projected red-hot scoria. But as I acquired confidence in their general regularity, I approached from time to time more nearly to the little cone of scoria produced by its own eruptions.

I now perceived an opening in this little cone close to the perpendicular rock of the interior of the great crater. I was very anxious to see real fluid lava; so immediately after an eruption, I rushed to the opening and thus got within the subsidiary crater. But my curiosity was not gratified, for I observed, about forty or fifty feet below me, a huge projecting rock, which being somewhat in advance, effectively prevented me from seeing the lava lake, if any such existed. I then retreated to a respectful distance from this infant volcano to wait for the next explosion.

I continued to note the intervals of time between these jets of red-hot matter, and found that from ten to fifteen minutes was the range of the intervals of repose. Having once more reconnoitred the descent into the little volcano, I seized the opportunity of the termination of one of the most considerable of its eruptions to run towards the gap and cautiously to pick my way down to the rock which hid from me, as I supposed, the liquid lava. I was armed with two phials, one of common smelling salts, and the other containing a solution of ammonia. On reaching the rock, I found it projected over a lake which was really filled by liquid fiery lava. I immediately laid myself down, and looking over its edge, saw, with great delight, lava actually in a state of fusion.

Presently I observed a small bubble swelling up on the surface of the fluid lava: it became gradually larger and larger, but did not burst. I had some vague suspicion that / this indicated a coming eruption; but on looking at my watch, I was assured that only one minute had elapsed since the termination of the last. I therefore watched its progress; after a time the bubble slowly subsided without breaking.

I now found the heat of the rock on which I was reposing, and the radiation from the fluid lava, almost insupportable, whilst the sulphurous effluvium painfully affected my lungs. On looking around, I fortunately observed a spot a few feet above me, from

163

which I could, in a standing position, get a better view of the lake, and perhaps suffer less inconvenience from its vapours. Having reached this spot, I continued to observe the slow formation and absorption of these vesicles of lava. One of them soon appeared. Another soon followed at a different part of the fiery lake, but, like its predecessor, it disappeared as quietly.

Another swelling now arose about halfway distant from the centre of the cauldron, which enlarged much beyond its predecessors in point of size. It attained a diameter of about three feet, and then burst, but not with any explosion. The waves it propagated in the fiery fluid passed on to the sides, and were thence reflected back just as would have happened in a lake of water of the same dimensions.

This phenomenon reappeared several times, some of the bubbles being considerably larger in size, and making proportionally greater disturbance in the liquid of this miniature crater. I would gladly have remained a longer time, but the excessive heat, the noxious vapours, and the warning of my chronometer forbade it. I climbed back through the gap by which I had descended, and rushed as fast as I could to a safe distance from the coming eruption.

I was much exhausted by the heat, although I suffered still greater inconvenience from the vapours. From my / observations of the eruptions before my descent into this little crater, I had estimated that I might safely allow myself six minutes, but not more than eight, if I descended into the crater immediately after an eruption.

If my memory does not fail me, I passed about six minutes in examining it, and the next explosion occurred ten minutes after the former one. On my return to Naples I found that a pair of thick boots I had worn on this expedition were entirely destroyed by the heat, and fell to pieces in my attempt to take them off.

On my return from the pit of burning fire, I sat down with my companion to refresh myself with a few biscuits contained in our basket. Cold water would have been the most refreshing fluid we could have desired, but we had none, and my impatient friend cried out, 'I wish I had a glass of whisky!' It immediately occurred to me to feel in my own basket for a certain glass bottle preserved in a tight leather case, which fortunately being found, I presented to my astonished friend, with the remark that it contained half a pint of the finest Irish whisky. This piece of good luck for my fellow-traveller arose not from my love but from my dislike of whisky. Shortly before my Italian tour I had been travelling in the north of Ireland, and having exhausted my brandy, was unable to replace it by anything but whisky, a drink which I can only tolerate under very exceptional circumstances.

Hot springs

During my residence at Naples in 1828, the Government appointed a commission of members of the Royal Academy of Naples to visit Ischia and make a report upon the hot springs in that island. Being a foreign member of the Academy, they / did me the honour of placing my name upon that commission. The weather was very favourable, the party was most agreeable, and during three or four days I enjoyed the society of my colleagues, the delightful scenery, and the highly interesting natural phenomena of that singular island.

None of the hot springs were deep: in several we made excavations which, in all cases, gave increased heat to the water. In one or two, I believe if we had excavated to a small depth or bored a few feet, we might have met with boiling water.

I took the opportunity of this visit to view the devastations made by the recent earthquake in the small town which had been destroyed.

The greater part of the town consisted of narrow streets formed by small houses built of squared stone. In some of these streets the houses on one side were thrown down, whilst those a few feet distant, on the opposite side, although severely damaged, had their walls left standing.

The landlord of the hotel at which we took up our quarters assured me the effects of the recent earthquake were entirely confined to a small portion of the island which he pointed out from the front of his hotel, and added that it was scarcely felt in other parts.

Earthquakes

At the commencement of this chapter I mentioned that I had never been *consciously* sensible of the occurrence of an earthquake. I think it may perhaps be useful to state that on a recent occasion I really perceived the effects of an earthquake, although at the time I assigned them to a different cause.

On 6 October last, about half-past three, a.m., / most of the inhabitants of London who were awake at that hour perceived several shocks of an earthquake. I also was awake, although not conscious of the shocks of an earthquake.

165

As soon as I read of the event in the morning papers, I was forcibly struck by its coincidence with my own observations, although I had attributed to them an entirely different cause. In order to explain this, it is necessary to premise that I had on a former occasion instituted some experiments for the purpose of ascertaining how far off the passing of a cart or carriage would affect the steadiness of a star observed by reflection. Amongst other methods, I had fixed a looking-glass of about 12 by 16 inches, by a pair of hinges, to the front wall of my bedroom. It was usually so placed that, as I lay in bed, at the distance of about 10 or 12 feet, I could see by reflection a small gaslight burner, which was placed on my left hand.

By this arrangement any tremors propagated through the earth from passing carriages would be communicated to the looking-glass by means of the front wall of the house, which rose about 40 feet from the surface. The image of the small gas-burner reflected in the looking-glass would be proportionally disturbed. In this state of things at about half-past three o'clock of the morning in question, I observed the reflected image of the gaslight move downwards and upwards two or three times. I then listened attentively, expecting to hear the sound of a distant carriage or cart. Hearing nothing of the kind, I concluded that the earth wave had travelled beyond the limit of the sound wave, arising from the carriage which produced it. Presently the image of the gaslight again vibrated up and down, and then suddenly fell about four or five inches lower down in the glass, where it remained fixed for a time. Still thinking the observation of no consequence, / I shut my eyes, and after perhaps another minute, again saw the image in its lower position. It then rose to its former position, vibrated, and shortly again descended: it remained down for some time and then resumed its first position.

Firedamp

An opportunity presented itself several years after my examination of Vesuvius of witnessing another form under which fire occasionally exerts its formidable power.

I was visiting a friend* at Merthyr Tydfil, who possessed very extensive coal-mines. I enquired of my host whether any firedamp existed in them. On receiving an affirmative answer, I expressed a wish to become personally acquainted with the miner's invisible but

---

* The late Sir John J. Guest, Bart.

most dangerous enemy. Arrangements were therefore made for my visit to the subterranean world on the following day. Professor Moll of Utrecht, who was also a guest, expressed a wish to accompany me.

The entrance to the mine is situated in the side of a mountain. Its chief manager conducted our expedition to visit the 'fire-king'.

We found a coal-waggon drawn by a horse, and filled with clean straw, standing on the railway which led into the workings.

The manager, Professor Moll, and myself, together with two or three assistants, with candles, lanterns, and Davy-lamps, got into this vehicle, which immediately entered the adit of the mine. We advanced at a good pace, passing at intervals doors which opened on our approach and then instantly closed. Each door had an attendant boy, whose duty was confined to the regulation of his own door. /

Many were the doors we passed before we arrived at the termination of the tram-road. After travelling about a mile and a half, our carriage stopped and we alighted. We now proceeded on foot, each carrying his own candle, until we reached a kind of chamber where one of our attendants was left with the candles.

We, each holding a Davy-lamp in our hand, advanced towards a small opening in the side of this chamber, which was so low that we were compelled to crawl, one after another, on our hands and knees. A powerful current of air rushed through this small passage. On reaching the end of it, we found ourselves in a much larger chamber from which the coal had been excavated. At a little distance opposite to the path by which we entered was a continuation of the same narrow hole which had led us to the waste in which we now stood. From this opening issued the powerful stream of air which seemed to pass in a direct course from one opening to the other.

On our right hand the large chamber we had entered appeared to spread to a very considerable distance, its termination being lost in darkness. The floor was covered with fragments which had fallen from the roof; so that, besides the risk from explosion, there was also a minor one arising from the possible fall of some huge mass of slate from the roof of the excavation beneath which we stood: an accident which I had already witnessed in the waste of another coal-mine. As we advanced over this flaky flooring it was evident that we were making a considerable ascent. We, in fact, now occupied a vast cavern, which had been originally formed by the extraction of the coal, and then partially filled up by the falling in from time to time of portions of the slaty roof.

167

As we advanced cautiously with our Davy-lamps beyond / the current of air which had hitherto accompanied us, it was evident that a change had taken place in their light: for the flames became much enlarged. Professor Moll and myself mounted a huge heap of these fragments, and thus came into contact with air highly charged with carburetted hydrogen. At this point there was a very sensible difference in the atmosphere, even by a change of three feet in the elevation of the lamp.

Holding up the lamp at the level of my head, I could not see the wick of the lamp, but a general flame seemed to fill the inside of its wire covering. On lowering it to the height of my knee, the wick resumed its large nebulous appearance.

My companion, Professor Moll, was very much delighted with this experiment. He told me he had often at his lectures explained these effects to his pupils, but that this was the first exhibition of them he had ever witnessed in their natural home.

Although well acquainted with the miniature explosions of the experimentalist, I found it very difficult to realize in my own mind the effects which might result from an explosion under the circumstances in which we were then placed. I enquired of the manager, who stood by my side, what would probably be the effect, if an explosion were to take place? Pointing to the vast heap of shale from which I had just descended, he said the whole of that would be blown through the narrow channel by which we entered, and every door we had passed through would be blown down.

We now retraced our steps, and crawling back through the narrow passage, rejoined our carriage, and were rapidly conveyed to the light of day. /

CHAPTER XVII

EXPERIENCE AMONGST WORKMEN

Visit to Bradford – Clubs – Co-operative shops – The author of the 'Economy
of Manufactures' welcomed by the workmen – Visit to the Temple of Aeolus –
The philosopher moralizes – Commiserates the unsuccessful statesmen –
Points to the poet a theme for his verse – Immortalizes both.

During one of my visits to Leeds, combinations and trades unions
were very prevalent. A medical friend of mine, who was going to
Bradford on a professional visit, very kindly offered to take me over
in his carriage and bring me back again in the evening. He had in that
town a friend engaged in the manufactories of the place, to whom he
proposed to introduce me, and who would willingly give me every
assistance. Unfortunately, on our arrival we found that this
gentleman was absent on a tour.

My medical friend was much vexed; but I assured him that I was
never at a loss in a manufacturing town, and we agreed to meet at our
hotel for dinner. I then went into the town to pick up what
information I might be able to meet with.

Passing a small manufactory, I think it was of doormats, I enquired
whether a stranger might be permitted to see it. The answer being in
the affirmative, one of the men accompanied me round the works. Of
course I asked him many questions which he answered as far as he
could; but several of them / puzzled him, and he very good-
humouredly tried to supply the information I wanted by asking
several of his fellow-workmen. One question about which I was
anxious to be informed, puzzled them all. At last one of the men to
whom he applied said, 'Why don't you go and ask Sam Brown?' My
guide immediately went in search of his learned friend, who gave me
full information on the subjects of my enquiry.

Much pleased by the intelligence and acuteness of this man, I
thought it possible he might have read the 'Economy of Manufactures'. On mentioning that work, I found he was well acquainted with
it, and he asked my opinion of its merits. I told him that, having myself

169

written the book, I was not an impartial judge. On hearing that I was its author, his delight was unbounded; he held out his brawny hand, which I cordially grasped. The most gratifying remark to me, however, amongst the many things in it to which he referred with approbation, was the expression he applied to it as a whole. 'Sir,' said my new friend, 'that book made me think.' To make a man think for himself is doing him far higher service than giving him much instruction.

I now told my new friend that I had studied a little the effects of combinations, and also the results of co-operative shops, and that I was very anxious to add to my stock of information upon both subjects, but particularly on the latter. Knowing that there existed a co-operative shop in Bradford, I asked whether it would be possible to see it and make some enquiries as to its state and prospects. He said if he could get permission for half an hour's absence he would accompany me to it, and give me whatever information I wished as to its operation.

Mr Brown accordingly accompanied me to the co-operative / shop, where the information required was most readily given.

As we were returning, my companion exclaimed, 'Oh, how lucky! there is ——, the secretary of all our clubs. He is the man to tell you all about them.' We accordingly crossed over to the other side: the secretary, as soon as he heard my name, held out his hand and greeted me with a hearty grasp.

Having told him the objects of my enquiry, he expressed great anxiety to give me the fullest information. He proposed to take me with him in the course of the evening to all the clubs in Bradford, in each of which he promised me that I should receive a most cordial welcome.

He offered to show me all their rules, with the exception of certain ones which he assured me had no connection whatever with the objects of my enquiries, and which the laws of the respective clubs required to be kept secret. I think it right to mention this fact; but I am bound also to add that I have a strong conviction of the truth and sincerity of my informant. I believe that the one or two rules which I understood could not be communicated to a stranger, were merely secret modes of recognition amongst the members of the different societies by which fellow-members of the same societies might recognize each other in distant places.

However, my limited time was now drawing to a close. It was

impossible to remain at Bradford that night, and my previous arrangements called me in two days to a distant part of the country. I parted with regret from these friendly workmen, and joining my companion at the hotel, after a hasty dinner we were soon on our way back to Leeds.

Our conversation turned upon the large ironworks we should pass on our return, which indeed were clearly indicated / by the columns of fire in front of us – tall chimneys illumining the darkness of the night.

I was told by my friend that in one of the ironworks which we should pass, there was a large tunnel through a rock which had originally been intended for a canal: but that it was now used as an air-chamber, to equalize the supply of the blast furnaces. Also that an engine of a hundred horsepower continually blew air into this stony chamber.

I enquired whether it would be possible to get admission into this Temple of Aeolus. As my friend, fortunately for me, was acquainted with the proprietors, this was not difficult. Our carriage drove up to the manager's house, and my wish was immediately gratified.

A lantern was provided, a small iron door at the end of the cavern was opened, and armed like Diogenes, I entered upon *my* search after truth. I soon ascertained that there was very little current, except close to the tuyeres which supplied the several furnaces, and also at the aperture through which tons of air were driven without cessation by the untiring fiery horse.

I tried to think seriously; and reflecting on Shadrach, Meshach, and Abed-nego, I speculated whether their furnace might have been hotter than the one before me. I was within a foot or two of a white heat, but I had no thermometer with me, and if I had had one, its graduations might not have been upon the same scale as theirs – so I gave up the speculation.

The intensity of the fire was peculiarly impressive. It recalled the past, disturbed the present, and suggested the future. The contemplation of the fiery abyss, which had recalled the history of those ancient Hebrews, naturally turned my attention to the wonderful powers of endurance / manifested by one of their modern representatives. Candour obliges me to admit that my speculations on the future were not entirely devoid of anxiety, though I trust they were orthodox, for whilst I admired the humanity of Origen, I was shocked by the heresy of Maurice.

171

I now began to moralize.

Blown upon by a hundred horsepower, I sympathized with Disraeli refrigerated by his *friends*. Turning from that painful contemplation, I was calmed by the freshness of the breeze. The action of the pumps, the *cool*ness of the place and of the time, for it was *evening*, recalled to my recollection M ... M ...; so I hoped, for the sake of instruction, that he would in his own adamantine verses snatch if possible from oblivion the moral anatomy of that unsuccessful statesman. Yet, lest even the poet himself should be forgotten, I resolved to give each of them his last chance of celebrity preserved in the modest amber of my own simple prose.

Emerging from my reverie, I made the preconcerted signal; the iron door was opened, and we were again on our road to Leeds. /

CHAPTER XVIII

PICKING LOCKS AND DECIPHERING

Interview with Vidocq – Remarkable power of altering his height – A bungler in picking locks – Mr Hobb's lock and the Duke of Wellington – Strong belief that certain ciphers are inscrutable – Davies Gilbert's cipher – The author's cipher both deciphered – Classified dictionaries of the English language – Anagrams – Squaring words – Bishop not easily squared – Lesser dignitaries easier to work upon.

These two subjects are in truth much more nearly allied than might appear upon a superficial view of them. They are in fact closely connected with each other as small branches of the same vast subject of *combinations*.

Several years ago, the celebrated thief-taker, Vidocq, paid a short visit to London. I had an interview of some duration with this celebrity, who obligingly conveyed to me much information, which, though highly interesting, was not of a nature to become personally useful to me.

He possessed a very remarkable power, which he was so good as to exhibit to me. It consisted in altering his height to about an inch and a half less than his ordinary height. He threw over his shoulders a cloak, in which he walked round the room. It did not touch the floor in any part, and was, I should say, about an inch and a half above it. He then altered his height and took the same walk. The cloak then touched the floor and lay upon it in some part or other during the whole / walk. He then stood still and altered his height alternately, several times to about the same amount.

I enquired whether the altered height, if sustained for several hours, produced fatigue. He replied that it did not, and that he had often used it during a whole day without any additional fatigue. He remarked that he had found this gift very useful as a disguise. I asked whether any medical man had examined the question; but it did not appear that any satisfactory explanation had been arrived at.

I now entered upon a favourite subject of my own – the art of

173

picking locks – but, to my great disappointment, I found him not at all strong upon that question. I had myself bestowed some attention upon it, and had written a paper, 'On the Art of Opening all Locks', at the conclusion of which I had proposed a plan of partially defeating my own method. My paper on that subject is not yet published.[a]

Several years after Vidocq's appearance in London, the Exhibition of 1851 occurred. On one of my earliest visits, I observed a very curious lock of large dimensions with its internal mechanism fully exposed to view. I found, on enquiry, that it belonged to the American department. Having discovered the exhibitor, I asked for an explanation of the lock. I listened with great interest to a very profound disquisition upon locks and the means of picking them, conveyed to me with the most unaffected simplicity.

I felt that the maker of that lock surpassed me in knowledge of the subject almost as much as I had thought I excelled Vidocq. Having mentioned it to the late Duke of Wellington, he proposed that we should pay a visit to the lock the next time I accompanied him to the Exhibition. We did so a few days after, when the Duke was equally pleased with the lock and its inventor. Mr Hobbs, the / gentleman of whom I am speaking and whose locks have now become so celebrated, was good enough to explain to me from time to time many difficult questions in the science of constructing and of picking locks. He informed me that he had devised a system for defeating all these methods of picking locks, for which he proposed taking out a patent. I was, however, much gratified when I found that it was precisely the plan I had previously described in my own unpublished pamphlet.

Deciphering

Deciphering is, in my opinion, one of the most fascinating of arts, and I fear I have wasted upon it more time than it deserves. I practised it in its simplest form when I was at school. The bigger boys made ciphers, but if I got hold of a few words, I usually found out the key. The consequence of this ingenuity was occasionally painful: the owners of the detected ciphers sometimes thrashed me, though the fault really lay in their own stupidity.

There is a kind of maxim amongst the craft of decipherers (similar to one amongst the locksmiths), that every cipher can be deciphered.

I am myself inclined to think that deciphering is an affair of time,

---

[a] The paper was never published.

ingenuity, and patience; and that very few ciphers are worth the trouble of unravelling them.

One of the most singular characteristics of the art of deciphering is the strong conviction possessed by every person, even moderately acquainted with it, that he is able to construct a cipher which nobody else can decipher. I have also observed that the cleverer the person, the more intimate is his conviction. In my earliest study of the subject I shared in this belief, and maintained it for many years. /

In a conversation on that subject which I had with the late Mr Davies Gilbert, President of the Royal Society, each maintained that he possessed a cipher which was absolutely inscrutable. On comparison, it appeared that we had both imagined the same law, and we were thus confirmed in our conviction of the security of our cipher.

Many years after, the late Dr Fitton, having asked my opinion of the possibility of making an inscrutable cipher, I mentioned the conversation I had had with Davies Gilbert, and explained the law of the cipher, which we both thought would baffle the greatest adept in that science. Dr Fitton fully agreed in my view of the subject; but even whilst I was explaining the law, an indistinct glimpse of defeating it presented itself vaguely to my imagination. Having mentioned my newly conceived doubt, it was entirely rejected by my friend. I then proposed that Dr Fitton should write a few sentences in a cipher constructed according to this law, and that I should make some attempts to unravel it. I offered to give a few hours to the subject; and if I could see my way to a solution, to continue my researches; but if not on the road to success, to tell him I had given up the task.

Late in the evening of that day I commenced a preparatory enquiry into the means of unravelling this new cipher, and I soon arrived at a tolerable certainty that I should succeed. The next night, on my return from a party, I found Dr Fitton's cipher on my table. I immediately commenced my attempt. After some time I found that it would not yield to my means of treating it; and on further examination I succeeded in proving that it was not written according to the law agreed upon. At first my friend was very positive that I was mistaken; and having taken it to his sister, by whose / aid it was composed, he returned and told me that it *was* constructed upon the very law I had proposed. I then assured him that they *must* have made some mistake, and that my evidence was so irresistible, that if my life depended upon the result I should have no hesitation in making my election.

Dr Fitton again retired to consult his sister; and after the lapse of

175

a considerable interval of time again returned, and informed me that I was right – that his sister had inadvertently mistaken the enunciation of the law. I now remarked that I possessed an absolute demonstration of the fact I had communicated to him; and added that, having conjectured the origin of the mistake, I would decipher the cipher with the erroneous law before he could send me the new cipher to be made according to the law originally proposed. Before the evening of the next day both ciphers had been translated.

This cipher was arranged upon the following principle: Two concentric circles of cardboard were formed, each divided into twenty-six or more divisions.

On the outer were written in regular order the letters of the alphabet. On the inner circle were written the same twenty-six letters, but in any irregular manner.

In order to use this cipher, look for the first letter of the word to be ciphered on the outside circle. Opposite to it, on the inner circle, will be another letter, which is to be written as the cipher for the former.

Now turn round the inner circle until the cipher just written is opposite the letter *a* on the *outer* circle. Proceed in the same manner for the next, and so on for all succeeding letters.

Many varieties of this cipher may be made by inserting / other characters to represent the divisions between words, the various stops, or even blanks. Although Davies Gilbert, I believe, and myself, both arrived at if from our own efforts, I have reason to think that it is of very much older date. I am not sure that it may not be found in the 'Steganographia' of Schott, or even of Trithemius.[a]

One great aid in deciphering is, a complete analysis of the language in which the cipher is written. For this purpose I took a good English dictionary, and had it copied out into a series of twenty-four other dictionaries. They comprised all words of

> One letter,
> Two letters,
> Three letters,
> etc.,
> Twenty-six letters.

Each dictionary was then carefully examined, and all the

---

[a] Gaspar Schott, . . . *Stenographica* . . . (Nuremberg, 1665); Johann Tritheim, *Stenographia* . . . (Frankfurt, 1606).

modifications of each word, as, for instance, the plurals of substantives, the comparatives and superlatives of adjectives, the tenses and participles of verbs, etc., were carefully indicated. A second edition of these twenty-six dictionaries was then made, including these new derivatives.

Each of these dictionaries was then examined, and every word which contained any two or more letters of the same kind was carefully marked. Thus, against the word *tell* the numbers 3 and 4 were placed to indicate that the third and fourth letters are identical. Similarly, the word *better* was followed by the numbers 25, 34. Each of these dictionaries was then rearranged thus: In the first or original one each word was arranged according to the alphabetical order of its *initial* letter.

In the next the words were arranged alphabetically according / to the *second* letter of each word, and so in the other dictionaries on to the last letter.

Again, each dictionary was divided into several others, according to the numerical characteristics placed at the end of each word. Many words appeared repeatedly in several of these subdivisions.

The work is yet unfinished, although the classification already amounts, I believe, to nearly half a million words.

From some of these, dictionaries were made of those words only which by transposition of their letters formed anagrams. A few of these are curious:

Opposite		*Similarity*		*Satirical*	
vote	veto	fuel	flue	odes	dose
acre	care	taps	pats	bard	drab
evil	veil	tubs	buts	poem	mope
ever	veer	vast	vats	poet	tope
lips	slip	note	tone	trio	riot
cask	sack	cold	clod	star	rats
fowl	wolf	evil	vile	wive	view
gods	dogs	arms	mars	nabs	bans
tory	tyro	rove	over	tame	mate
tars	rats	lips	lisp	acts	cats

There are some verbal puzzles costing much time to solve which may be readily detected by these dictionaries. Such, for instance, is the sentence,

I tore ten Persian MSS.,

177

which it is required to form into one word of eighteen letters.

The first process is to put opposite each letter the number of times it occurs, thus: /

i	2	p	1	It contains –	
t	2	s	3	2 triplets	
o	1	a	1	4 pairs	
r	2	m	1	4 single letters	
e	3		—	—	
n	2		6	18	
	—		12		
	12		—		
			18		

Now, on examining the dictionary of all words of eighteen letters, it will be observed that they amount to twenty-seven, and that they may be arranged in six classes:

> 7 having five letters of the same kind
> 5 having four letters of the same kind
> 3 having three triplets
> 7 having two triplets
> 3 having one triplet
> 2 having seven pairs
>
> —
> 27

Hence it appears that the word sought must be one of those seven having two triplets, and also that it must have four pairs; this reduces the question to the two words –

> misinterpretations,
> misrepresentations.

The latter is the one sought, because its triplets are e and s, whilst those of the former are i and t.

The reader who has leisure may try to find out the word of eighteen letters formed by the following sentence:

> Art is not in, but Satan.

Another amusing puzzle may be greatly assisted by these / dictionaries. It is called squaring words, and is thus practised:

Let the given word to be squared be Dean. It is to be written horizontally, and also vertically, thus:

178

```
D  e   a   n.
e   .   .   .
a   .   .   .
n   .   .   .
```

And it is required to fill up the blanks with such letters that each vertical column shall be the same as its corresponding horizontal column, thus:

```
D  e   a   n
e   a   s   e
a   s   k   s
n   e   s   t
```

The various ranks of the church are easily squared; but it is stated, I know not on what authority, that no one has yet succeeded squaring the word bishop.

Having obtained one squared word, as in the case of Dean, it will be observed that any of the letters in the two diagonals, d, a, k, t – n, s, s, n, may be changed into any other letter which will make an English word.

Thus Dean may be changed into such words as

dear	peas	weak	beam
fear	seas	lead	seal
deaf	bear	real	team

In fact there are upwards of sixty substitutes: possibly some of these might render the two diagonals, d, a, k, t, and n, s, s, n, also English words. /

CHAPTER XIX

EXPERIENCE IN ST GILES'S

Deep-snow – Beggar in Belgravia wanted work – He said he was a watchmaker – Gave his address – It was false – Met him months after – The same story – The same untruth – Children hired for the purpose of begging – Cellar in St Giles's – Enquired for a poor woman and child – Landlady told me of a man almost starving in her back kitchen – He turned out to be an accomplished swindler – Pot-boys – Caught him at last – Took him to Bow Street.

Soon after taking up my residence in London, I met with many applications from street-beggars, with various tales of distress. I could not imagine that all these were fictitious, and found great difficulty in selecting the few objects on whom I could bestow my very moderate means of charity. One severe winter I resolved on making my own personal observations on the most promising cases which presented themselves.

The first general principle at which I arrived was, that –

In whatever part of London I might be, if I asked for the residence of a mendicant, it was pretty sure to be in a quarter very remote from the one in which he asked relief.

The next was, that –

Those mendicants who professed to want work and not charity, always belonged to trades in which it was scarcely possible to give them employment without trusting them with valuable property. /

One example will suffice. During a very severe winter, the ground being covered with snow, whilst passing through Belgrave Square, a man accosted me, declaring that he could get no work, and that himself and his family were starving.

I enquired his trade: he was a watchmaker. I asked for his address. I wrote down in my pocket-book his name, the street, and the number, and read it to him: it was in Clerkenwell. The next day I went there, made particular enquiries of the landlord, and was informed that no person of that name lodged in the house, or ever had lodged in it. I spoke to several respectable female lodgers also, who gave me the same information, as far as their knowledge went.

Several months after, I met the same professional mendicant in Portland Road. He did not recollect me, and again told the same story, and again gave me the same address. On this, I recalled to his memory that I had seen him before: that he had given me the same address; and that, having myself been there to enquire, I had found that his story was untrue. This statement had allowed him time to invent a new tale.

With well-feigned surprise he suddenly remembered that his wife, about three months ago, had told him that a strange gentleman had called, and had particularly asked for him; that his wife, knowing that a writ was out against him, and that he was liable to be arrested, had denied that any person of his name resided in the house.

A few days afer I went again to Clerkenwell, and received from the residents the answer they had given me three months before. I then went to one of the large shops for tools used by watchmakers near that locality, and having mentioned the subject to the master, he very readily asked amongst his shopmen whether they knew of such a person. /

He assured me that, even allowing the man had not usually dealt at his shop, it was impossible that he should not have been several times there for some trifling article necessary in the hurry of his business. I then went to two or three other shops of a similar kind, and found that his name was entirely unknown. I therefore concluded that he was an impostor.

I will mention one other case, because it arose entirely out of an accident, and could not have been foreseen.

Living at that time much in society, I usually walked home from the hot rooms of an evening party wrapped in a stout cloak, even though it sometimes rained. On these occasions I was often placed in a most painful situation.

A half-clad miserable female, with an infant in her arms, and sometimes accompanied by another just able to walk, followed me through a drizzling rain to ask charity for her starving children.

I confess it was to me a most painful effort to resist such an application; yet my better reason informed me that in all probability these miserable children were hired for the purpose of exciting the feelings of the charitable. To give money to their heartless conductors could only be considered charitable, inasmuch as it might contribute to shorten the lives of their wretched victims.

I fear I gave wrongfully many a sixpence. I enquired into some cases, but without any result which could enable me to alter the opinion I have expressed. It was in one of these enquiries that the singular case I am now about to relate occurred.

In one of the densest of London fogs on a November night, or rather at between one and two o'clock in the morning, I was enquiring in one of the most disreputable streets in London – George Street, St Giles's, long ago pulled down, / enlarged, and rebuilt – for a female with an infant, who had represented herself to me as a miserable mother, and into the truth of whose story I was anxious to enquire.

I had been into several of the lowest lodging-houses, and into the cellars of that nest of misery and guilt, and was unsuccessful in finding the object I sought.

Only a few of these abodes of wretchedness remained unvisited, when I enquired after the poor woman I was seeking of a somewhat decently clothed woman, who rented one of them.

She was the weekly tenant of one of these houses, and told me that on the preceding night a poor woman, with a child wrapped up in a miserably torn shawl, had applied for a lodging at about eleven o'clock. It was raining hard, and the poor woman possessed only twopence, and the price of a bed in the cellar was at this house threepence. The poor woman went away, remarking that she must then go and pawn the remnant of the shawl that covered her infant. She went, but returned no more.

The ancient weekly tenant then thought it necessary to defend, or rather to explain, her own apparently cruel conduct. I told her that it was unnecessary, and that even in my inmost thoughts I had not cast a reproach upon her. I told her that, from my knowledge of the misery suffered by poor people, I could readily imagine circumstances which might fully explain her conduct.

Her heart, however, was too full, so I sat down and listened to her tale. She was a widow advanced in years, having no relatives, or even friends, to assist her in her old age. She was the weekly tenant of a small house in that villanous street, and was entirely supported by letting out every foot of floor which could be made available for a human being to / sleep upon. But the stern necessity which hung over her with its iron hand was this:

Her weekly rent became due on each Monday, and if not paid on that night, the next morning would see her inexorably turned out of her only home, and deprived of her only means of sustaining life.

182

She was pleased at my attention to her sad tale, and, with a little encouragement, mentioned some of the experience she had had in her painful vocation.

'At this moment,' she said, 'there is lying on a rug in the back kitchen a young man, who has tasted nothing during the last two days but water from the pump on the opposite side of the street. He appears,' she said, 'to have been in better circumstances in other times.'

It was now two o'clock in the morning, in the midst of a dense fog. I enquired whether it would be possible at this hour to get some soup or meat, or anything to sustain life. I went 'down into the close unventilated room, and beheld, stretched on a kind of thing like a couple of sacks, a pale, emaciated man, apparently about two or three and thirty years of age. I desired him to call on me the next morning; and, leaving my address with his landlady, left also a small sum of money to procure for him, if possible, present necessaries.

The next morning this half-starved man called at my house, in garments scarcely covering him. I enquired into his history, and he told me one probably as fabulous as that with which he afterwards deluded me, during my own short acquaintance with him.

I supplied him with a few clothes, shoes, and other things, just to replace the worn-out rags in which I had found him, and desired him in a day or two, when he got them into a / serviceable form, to come to me, that I might see what his capacity was, and by what means he could best earn a subsistence.

It is unnecessary to enter into the long and artful stories he invented. The short result was this: that he had been a steward of a merchant ship – had been in the West Indies, and on other voyages; that having, on his return from some voyage, been reduced by illness to spend all his little earnings, and even to sell his clothes, and having no friends in London, he could not go amongst the merchant captains for want of decent clothes to appear in. This difficulty was partially removed by my giving him a suit. He called one day to tell me that he had succeeded in getting the situation of steward in a small West Indiaman, and that he did not like to sell or exchange a pair of top-boots which I had given him without asking my permission, which, of course, I gave. He told me that if he sold the boots, and purchased light, gaudy-coloured waistcoating, he might do a little profitable business with the niggers. He showed me the card of the shop in Monmouth Street at which he had commenced a negotiation about the sale of the boots, and another, in the same street, at which he proposed to purchase the waistcoats. He gave me the name of his ship, and of its captain, and the day of sailing. I flattered myself that he was now in a fair position to get a fresh start in life.

A few evenings after the ship was supposed to have sailed he called at my house, in the midst of heavy rain, apparently much agitated, and stated that, in raising their anchor, an accident had happened, by which the captain's leg had been broken.

He also said that, being sent up with the ship's boat to fetch the new captain, he could not resist calling at my house / once more to express all his gratitude. I confess I entertained some suspicion about this story; but I said nothing.

The next morning I found that during his visit he had extracted something more from my female servants, upon whose sympathy he had worked, and who had previously contributed very liberally to his wants.

I now went to search for him in his old haunts, and with much difficulty ascertained that he had been living riotously at some public-house in another quarter, and had been continually drunk.

My next step was to go to Bow Street and consult Sir Richard Birnie. Having explained the case, he consulted several of his most skilful officers; but none were acquainted with the man. Sir Richard remarked that he was a very adroit fellow, and that it was doubtful whether he had actually committed an act of swindling. I enquired what I should do in case I found him. The magistrate replied, 'Bring him before me;' but he did not indicate the slightest expectation of my accomplishing that object.

Having thanked Sir Richard, I withdrew, determined, if the fellow were in London, I would catch him.

I now renewed my enquiries, which at first were ineffectual. One day it occurred to me that, as he had shown me two cards of shopkeepers in Monmouth Street, I might possibly, by cautious enquiry, get some clue to his whereabouts.

Although it was Sunday when this idea occurred, I immediately commenced at one end of the street to knock at each door, apologize to the landlord or landlady, and, shortly stating my case, to enquire if they could throw any light upon the subject. I went up one side of the street, and down part of the other, having at two places gained some traces of the fellow. /

I will say, to the credit of the then residents, some of whom I intruded upon at their dinner hour, that I received in no one instance the slightest incivility, nor even coldness.

The most important information I obtained was, that a certain pot-boy (name and name of his public-house both unknown) would probably be able to give me some clue.

I next took my station at the northern end of Monmouth Street, and during three hours accosted every pot-boy who passed. At last I got hold of the right one, and so ultimately obtained the information I wanted.

The fellow was then arrested, and brought before Sir R. Birnie. The magistrate was much surprised that so clever a fellow should not have been known to any of his officers. After a long examination, I stated to the magistrate, that though I was very reluctant to appear before the public in such a case, yet that if he thought it a public duty, I should not shrink from it. Sir Richard remarked, that the inconvenience of my attending two or three days to prosecute would be very great – that the fellow was so accomplished an artist, that it was very doubtful if he could be convicted. He then added, that the best thing to be done for the man himself would be, if I could produce any new evidence, that he should be remanded for a week, to hear it, and then be discharged with a caution from the bench.

As my servants could give additional evidence, the fellow was remanded for a week, then duly lectured and discharged.

In the course of my efforts to inform myself of the real wants of those around me, I profited much by the experience of one or two friends, both most excellent and kind-hearted men, whose official duties rendered them far more conversant than myself with the subject. Mr Walker and Mr Broderip, both of them magistrates, were amongst my intimate friends. / Mr Walker, the author of *The Original*, maintained that no one ever was actually starved in London, except through his own folly or fault.

The result of my own experience leads me to recommend all those who do not possess time and the requisite energies for personal enquiries, to place the means they wish to devote to charity in the hands of some sensible and kind-hearted magistrate.

I have been present, in the course of my life, at many cases brought before our London police magistrates. They possess an immense power of doing good – a power of making the law respected, not by its punishments, but by their own kindliness of

185

manner and thoughtful consideration for the feelings of those brought into close contact with them.

Plain common sense, a kind heart, and, above all, the feelings of a thorough gentleman, are invaluable qualities in a magistrate. They give dignity to the court over which he presides, as well as an example which will be insensibly followed by all its officers. I have seen cases from which my own avocations have imperatively called me away, when I would gladly have remained to admire the kindness and the tact with which entangled questions have been gradually brought to a humane and just conclusion. /

CHAPTER XX

THEATRICAL EXPERIENCE

The philosopher in a tableau at the feet of beauty – Tableau encored – Philosopher at the opera of Don Juan – Visits the waterworks above and the dark expanse below the stage – Seized by two devils on their way up to fetch Juan – Cheated the devils by springing off to a beam at an infinite distance, just as his head appeared to the audience through the trap-door – The philosopher writes a ballet – Its rehearsal – Its high moral tone – Its rejection on the ground of the probable combustion of the opera-house.

I was never particularly devoted to theatrical representations. Tragedy I disliked, and comedy, which I enjoyed, frequently excited my feelings more than the dignity of the philosophic character sanctioned. In fact, I could not stand the reconciliation scenes.

I did, however, occasionally, in one or two rare instances, *assist* in a tableau. I still remember my delight when personating a dead body, with my head towards the audience, I lay motionless at the feet of three angels, entranced by their beauty, and whose charms still fascinate my imagination, and still retain their wonted power over my own sex.

We enacted the scene so admirably that our performance was twice encored. But though thus 'thrice slain', the near proximity of beauty speedily revived the 'caput mortuum' at its feet.

On one occasion having joined a party of friends in their box at the opera of 'Don Juan', I escaped, by half a second, / a marvellous adventure. Somewhat fatigued with the opera, I went behind the scenes to look at the mechanism. One of the scene-shifters of whom I had made an enquiry, found out that I, like himself, was a workman. He immediately offered to take me all over the theatre, and show me every part.

We ascended to the roof to examine the ventilation, by which, if stopped, the spectators, in case of accident or of a row, might be suffocated. Also, the vast water-tanks by which, in case of fire, they might be drowned. After long rambling and descending endless steps, I found myself in a vast dark and apparently boundless area; the flat

187

wooden roof high above my head was supported by upright timbers, some having intermediate stages like large dissecting tables. Here and there three lamps, rivalling rushlights, made the obscurity more visible, and the carpentry more incomprehensible.

Suddenly a little bell rang – the signal for my scene-shifting friend to take his post. He pointed to one of the dismal imitations of a rushlight, and said: 'You see that light; on its left is a door, go through that, and straight on until you arrive at daylight.' Instantly my friend became invisible in the surrounding gloom.

My first step when thus suddenly abandoned, was to mount on a large oblong platform about six feet above the floor. Here I was philosophically contemplating the surrounding obscure vacuity, in order that I might fully 'comprehend the situation'.

Suddenly a flash of lightning occurred. On looking up, high above my head I saw an opening as large as the platform on which I stood. All there was brightness. Whilst I was admiring this new light, and seeking my way to the upper and outer world, two devils with long forked tails jumped upon the platform, one at each end. /

'What do you do here?' said Devil No. 1.

Before I could invent a decent excuse, Devil No. 2 exclaimed:

'You must not come with us.'

This was consolatory and reassuring, so I replied –

'Heaven forbid!'

During this colloquy, the table, the philosopher, and the devils, were all slowly moving upward to the open trap-door of the stage above. Seeing a beam some feet higher at a moderate distance, I enquired whether it was fixed and would bear my weight? 'Yes,' said Devil No. 1.

'But you cannot reach it at a jump,' added Devil No. 2.

'Trust that to me,' said I, 'to get out of your clutches.'

We had now reached the level of the desired beam, though not near enough for a jump. However, still ascending, we passed it: then stooping my head and bending my body to avoid the floor of the stage, which we were fast approaching, I sprang down on the beam of refuge. My two missionary companions continued their course to the world above in order to convey the wicked Juan to the realms below. My transit through the dark, subterranean abyss to my own world above was rapid. I soon rejoined my companions, who congratulated me on what they represented as my 'undeserved escape': kindly hoping that I might be equally fortunate upon some future occasion.

188

Presence of mind frequently arises from having previously considered a variety of possible events. I had never contemplated such a situation, and have often asked myself and others what should have been my conduct, in case I had not escaped from my satanic companions; but no satisfactory conclusion has yet presented itself.

During one season, I had a stall at the German Opera. / One evening, in the cloister scene by moonlight, in the convent, I observed that the white bonnet of my companion had a pink tint: so also had the paper of our books and every white object around us.

This contrast of colour suggested to me the direct use of coloured lights. The progress of science in producing intense lights by the oxy-hydrogen blowpipe, and by electricity under its various forms, enabled me to carry out the idea of producing coloured lights for theatrical representations. I made many experiments by filling cells formed by pieces of parallel plate glass with solutions of various salts of chrome, of copper, and of other substances.

The effects were superb. I then devised a dance, in which they might be splendidly exhibited. This was called the rainbow dance. I proposed to abolish the footlights, and instead of them to substitute four urns with flowers. These urns would each conceal from the audience an intense light of one of the following colours: blue, yellow, red, or any others which might be preferable.

The rays of light would be projected from the vases towards the stage, and would form four cones of red, blue, yellow, and purple light passing to its further end.

Four groups, each of fifteen danseuses in pure white, would now enter on the stage. Each group would assume the colour of the light in which it was placed. Thus four dances each of a different colour would commence. Occasionally, a damsel from a group of one colour would spring into another group, thus resembling a shooting star.

After a time, the coloured lights would expand laterally and overlap each other, thus producing all the colours of the rainbow. In the meantime the sixty damsels in pure white forming one vast ellipse, would dance round, each in turn / assuming, as it passed through them, all the prismatic colours.

I had mentioned these experiments and ideas to a few of my friends, one of whom spoke of it to Mr Lumley, the lessee of the Italian Opera House. He thought it promised well, and ultimately I made a series of experiments in the great concert-room.

Ropes were stretched across the room, on which were hung in

189

innumerable forms large sheets of patent net. The various folds and bendings displayed the lights under endless modifications. Some brilliant greens, some fiery reds, blues of the brightest hue. Another of these was an almost perfect resemblance of the dead purple powdery coating of the finest grapes.

Things being thus prepared, I had a consultation with the eminent *chef-de-ballet* as to the kind of dance and the nature of the steps to be adapted to these gorgeous colours. Thus having invented the 'Rainbow Dance' I became still more ambitious, and even thought of writing a story to introduce it, and to give it a moral character. Hence arose the beautiful ballet of 'Alethes and Iris'.

Alethes, a priest of the sun, surrounded by every luxury that earth can lay at the feet of its god, feels, like all before him, that the most glorious life is sad without a companion to sympathize with his feelings and share in his enjoyments. He makes, therefore, a magnificent sacrifice to the god of this visible creation, and prays for the gratification of his solitary desire.

Apart from all the inferior orders of his class, in the midst of clouds of incense, the high priest himself becomes entranced.

He beholds in a vision a distant and lonely spot of bright / light. Advancing towards him, it assumes a circular form, having a small yellow centre surrounded by a deep blue confined within a brilliant red circle.

Retaining its shape, but slowly enlarging in size, it becomes a circular rainbow, out of which emerges a form of beauty more resplendent than mortal eyes might bear. Approaching the Book of Fate, which lies closed upon a golden pedestal in this the deepest and most sacred portion of the Temple of the Sun, she opens it and inscribes in purple symbols these mystic signs.

. . . .
. . . .
. . . .
. . . .

Then waving her graceful arm over the entranced high priest, she re-enters the aerial circle: it closes and retires.

Alethes, recovering from the magic spell his powerful art had wrought, rushes to the Book of Fate, opens, and reads the revelation it unfolds.

Through ocean's depths to southern ice-fields roam,
Through solid strata seek earth's central fire,
Cull from each wondrous field, each distant home,
An offering meet for her thy soul's desire.

This gives rise to a series of moving and most instructive dioramas, in which the travels of Alethes are depicted.

1. A representation of all the inhabitants of the ocean, comprising big fishes, lobsters, and various crustacea, mollusca, coralines, etc.

2. A view of the Antarctic regions – a continent of ice with an active volcano and a river of boiling water, supplied by geysers cutting their way through cliffs of blue ice.

3. A diorama representing the animals whose various / remains are contained in each successive layer of the earth's crust. In the lower portions symptoms of increasing heat show themselves until the centre is reached, which contains a liquid transparent sea, consisting of some fluid at a white heat, which, however, is filled up with little infinitesimal eels, all of one sort, wriggling eternally.

This would have produced a magnificent spectacle considered merely as a show, but the moralist might, if he pleased, have discovered in it a profound philosophy.

The ennui and lassitude felt by the priest of the sun arose from the want of occupation for his powerful mind. The remedy proposed in the ballet was – look into all the works of creation.

The central ocean of frying eels was added to assist the teaching of those ministers who prefer the doctrine of the eternity of bodily torments.*

The night proposed for the experiment of the dance at length arrived. Two fire-engines duly prepared were placed on the stage under the care of a portion of the fire brigade.

About a dozen danseuses in their white dresses danced and

---

* An ancester of mine, Dr Burthogge, a great friend of John Locke, wrote, I regret to say it, a book to prove the eternity of torments; so I felt it a kind of hereditary duty to give him a lift. The arguments, such as they are, of my wealthy and therefore revered ancestor are contained in a work whose title is 'Causa Dei; or, an Apology for God', wherein the perpetuity of infernal torments is evinced, and Divine justice (that notwithstanding) defended. By Richard Burthogge, M.D. London: Imprinted at the Three Daggers, Fleet Street, 1675.

The learned Tobias Swinden, M.A., late rector of Cuxton, in his 'Enquiry into the Nature and Place of Hell', 2nd edition, 1727, has discovered that its locality is in the sun. The accurate map he gives of that luminary renders it highly probable that the red flames so well observed and photographed by Mr De La Rue during a recent total eclipse have a *real* existence.

191

attitudinized in the rays of powerful oxy-hydrogen blowpipes. / The various brilliant hues of coloured light had an admirable effect on the lovely fireflies, especially as they flitted across from one region of coloured light to another.

A few days after I called on Mr Lumley, to enquire what conclusion he had arrived at. He expressed great admiration at the brilliancy of the colours and the effect of the Rainbow Dance, but much feared the danger of fire. I tried to reassure him; and to show that I apprehended no danger from fire, added, that I should myself be present every night. Mr Lumley remarked that if the house were burnt his customers would also be burnt with it. This certainly was a valid objection, for though he could have insured the building, he could not have insured his audience. /

CHAPTER XXI

ELECTIONEERING EXPERIENCE

The late Lord Lyndhurst candidate for the University of Cambridge – The philosopher refuses to vote for him – The reason why – Example of unrivalled virtue – In 1829 Mr Cavendish was a candidate for that university – The author was chairman of his London committee – Motives for putting men on committees – Of the pairing sub-committee – Motives for voting – Means of influencing voters – Voters brought from Berlin and from India – Elections after the Reform Bill, 1832 – The author again requested to be chairman of Mr Cavendish's committee – Reserves three days in case of a contest for Bridgenorth – It occurs, but is arranged – Bridgenorth being secure, the author gets up a contest for Shropshire – Patriot Fund sends £500 to assist the contest – It lasts three days – Reflections on squibs – Borough of Finsbury – Adventure in an omnibus – A judicious loan – Subsequent invitation to stand for Stroud – Declined – Reflections on improper influence on voters.

When the late Lord Lyndhurst[a] was a candidate for the representation of the University of Cambridge, I met Mr ——, a Whig in politics, and a great friend of Dr Wollaston. After the usual salutation, he said, 'I hope you will go down to Cambridge and vote for our friend Copley.' I made no answer, but, looking full in his face, waited for some explanation. 'Oh,' said Mr ——, 'I see what you mean. You think him a Tory; Copley still is what he always has been – a republican.' I replied that I was equally unable to vote for him upon that ground, and wished my friend good morning. /

A few evenings after I met the beautiful Lady Copley, who also canvassed me for my vote for her husband. I had the energy to resist even this temptation, which I should not have ventured to mention did not the poll-book enable me to refer to it as a witness of my unrivalled virtue.

Some years after, in 1829, a vacancy again arose in the representation of the University of Cambridge. Mr Cavendish[b] having recently waived the privilege of his rank, which entitled him, after a residence

---

[a] John Singleton Copley (Lord Lyndhurst), 1772–1863.
[b] William Cavendish (7th Duke of Devonshire), 1808–91.

of two years, to take the degree of Master of Arts, had entered into competition with the whole of the young men of his own standing, and had obtained the distinguished position of second wrangler and senior Smith's prize man. Under such circumstances, it was quite natural that all those who felt it important that the accidental aristocracy of birth should be able to maintain its position by the higher claim of superior knowledge; as well as all those who took a just pride in their Alma Mater, should wish to send such a man as their representative to the House of Commons.

A very large meeting of the electors was held in London, over which the Earl of Euston presided. It was unanimously resolved to nominate Mr Cavendish as a proper person to represent the University of Cambridge in the House of Commons. A committee was appointed to carry on the election, of which I was nominated chairman. Similar proceedings took place at Cambridge. The family of the young but distinguished candidate were not at first very willing to enter upon the contest. As it advanced, the committee-room became daily more and more frequented. Ultimately, in the midst of the London season, and during the sitting of the House of Commons, this single election excited an intense interest amongst men of all parties, whilst those who supported / Mr Cavendish upon higher grounds were not less active than the most energetic of his political supporters.

At all elections some few men, perhaps from four or five up to ten or twelve, do all the difficult and real work of the committee. The committee itself is, for several reasons, generally very numerous.

All who are supposed to have weight are, of course, put upon it.

Many who wish to appear to have weight get their names upon it.

Some get put upon it thinking to establish a political claim upon the *party*.

Others because they like to see their names in the newspapers.

Others again, who, if not on *his* committee, would vote against the candidate.

There are also idlers and busybodies, who go there to talk or to carry away something to talk about, which may give them importance in their own circle.

Young lawyers, of both departments of the profession, are very numerous, possessing acute perceptions of professional advantage.

A jester and a good story-teller are very useful; but a jolly and enterprising professor of rhodomontade is on some occasions invaluable – more especially if he is not an Irishman.

194

Occasionally a few simply honest men are found upon committees. These are useful as adjuncts to give a kind of high moral character to the cause; but the rest of the committee generally think them bores, and when they differ upon any point from the worldly members, it is invariably whispered that they are crotchety fellows. /

When any peculiarly delicate question arises, it is sometimes important to eliminate one or more of them temporarily from the *real* committee of management. This is accomplished (as in graver matters) by sending him on an embassy, usually to one of the adepts, with a confidential mission on a subject represented to him as of great importance. The adept respectfully asks for his view of the subject, rather opposes it, but not too strongly; is at last convinced, and ultimately entirely adopts it. The adept then enters upon the honest simpleton's crotchet, trots it out in the most indulgent manner, and at length sends him back, having done the double service of withdrawing him from a consultation at which he might have impeded the good cause, and also of enabling him at any future time to declare truly, if necessary, that he never was present at any meeting at which even a questionable course had been proposed.

One of the most difficult as well as of the most important departments of some elections is the pairing sub-committee. When I had myself to arrange it, I generally picked out two of the cleverest and most quick-witted of the committee. I told them I had perfect confidence in their judgement and discretion, and therefore constituted them a sub-committee, with absolute power on all questions of pairing. I also entirely forbade any appeal to myself. I then advised them to have attached to them a couple of good and entertaining talkers, to hold in play the applicants while they retired to ascertain the policy of the proposed pair.

Upon one occasion, when both my persuasive gentlemen were absent, I was obliged to officiate myself. I soon discovered that the adverse vote was very lukewarm in his own cause, and was also very averse to the prospect of missing a great cricket match if he went to the poll. Whilst my / pairing committee were making the necessary enquiries, I was so fortunate as to secure the promise of his vote for my own candidate at the succeeding election. In the meantime the pairing committee had kindly taken measures to save him from missing his cricket match without, however, wasting a pair.

Yet notwithstanding all my efforts to introduce primitive virtue into electioneering, I did not always succeed. About a dozen years had elapsed after one of the elections I had managed, when the subject was mentioned at a large dinner-table. A supporter of the adverse political party, referring to the contest, stated as a *merit* in his friends that they had succeeded in outwitting their opponents, for on one occasion they had got a man on their side who had unluckily just broken his arm, whom they succeeded in pairing off against a sound man of their adversaries. Remembering my able coadjutors in that contest, I had little doubt that a good explanation existed; so the next time I met one of them I mentioned the circumstance. He at once admitted the fact, and said, 'We knew perfectly well that the man's arm was broken; but our man, whom we paired off against him, had *no vote*.' He then added, 'We were afraid to tell you of our success.' To which I replied, 'You acted with great discretion.'

University elections are of quite a different class from all others. The nature of the influences to be brought to bear upon the voters is of a peculiar kind: the clerical element is large, and they are for the greater part expectant of something better hereafter.

The first thing to be done in any election contest is to get as exact a list as possible of the names and addresses of the voters. In a university contest the chairman should adopt / certain letters or other signs to be used in his own private copy attached to the names of the clerical voters. These should indicate –

> The books such voter may have written
> The nature of his preferment
> The source whence derived
> The nature of his expectations
> The source whence expected
> The age of the impediment
> The state of its health
> The chance of its promotion

Possessed of a full knowledge of all these circumstances, a paragraph in a newspaper regretting the alarming state of health of some eminent divine will frequently decide the oscillation even of a cautious voter.

This dodge is the more easily practised because some eminent divines, on the approach of an university election, occasionally become ill, and even take to their bed, in order to avoid the bore of being canvassed, or of committing themselves until they see 'how the land lies'.

The motives which induce men to act upon election committees are various. The hope of advancement is a powerful motive. It was stated to me by some of my committee, that every really working member of the committee which a few years before had managed the election of Copley for the University of Cambridge had already been rewarded by place or advancement.

My two most active lieutenants in the two contests for Cambridge, to which I have referred, were not neglected. One of them shortly after became a Master in Chancery, and the other had a place in India, producing £10,000 a year. /

The highest compliment, however, that party can pay to those who thus assist them is entirely to ignore their service, and pass them over on every occasion. This may be done with impunity to the very few who have such strong convictions that no amount of neglect or ill-usage can cause them to desert those principles of the soundness of which their reason is convinced. This course has also the great advantage of economizing patronage.

Always ascertain who are the personal enemies of the opposing candidate. If skilfully managed, you may safely depend upon their becoming the warmest friends of your own. Their enthusiasm can be easily stimulated: their zeal in the cause may shame some of your own lukewarm friends into greater earnestness. Men will always give themselves tenfold more trouble to crush a man obnoxious to their hatred than they will take to serve their most favoured ally.

When I have been chairman of an election committee I have found it advantageous to commence my duties early in the morning, and to remain until late at night. There is always something to be done for the advancement of the cause. In the first Cambridge election in which I took part I invariably remained at my post until midnight; and in the second, I was seldom absent at that hour.

One evening, being alone, I employed myself in looking through our lists to find the names of all voters at that period unaccounted for. The first name which attracted my attention was that of a liberal with whom I was personally unacquainted. The next day I set at work one of my investigating committee. In the course of the following day, he had traced out the voter, who at that time was at Berlin. As there was ample time for his return, a friend was employed to write to him, and he returned and voted for our candidate. /

On another evening, the name of Minchin turned up on the list. I remembered the man, whom I had met very frequently at the rooms

197

of one of my most intimate friends; but I had not seen him for nearly twenty years.

The next day, after many enquiries, I found that he had been lost sight of for a long time, and it was believed that he had gone out to India. I immediately sent a note to a friend of mine, Captain Robert Locke, who commanded an Indiaman, to beg him to look in upon me at the committee-room. In two hours he called and informed me that Minchin was a barrister at Calcutta, and was about to return to England. On my expressing a wish for further particulars, he kindly went into the City to procure information, and on his return told me that Minchin was on his voyage home in the 'Herefordshire', an excellent ship. It was due on a certain day, about a fortnight thence, and would in all probability not be three days behind its time.

In the evening, being again alone in the committee-room, I resumed the Minchin question, and found that he might possibly arrive on the second of the three days' polling. I therefore wrote the following letter:

Dear Minchin,
If twenty years have not altered your political principles, we have now an opportunity of getting in a Liberal to represent our University.
The three days of polling are ——   ——   ——
If you arrive in time, pray come immediately to my committee-room in Cockspur Street.

Yours truly,

C. BABBAGE

I addressed this letter to Minchin at Portsmouth, and / making two copies of it, directed them to two other seaports. When I put these letters into the basket, I smiled at my own simplicity in speculating on the triple improbability –

1. That Minchin should ever get my letter.

2. That his ship, which was expected, should really arrive on the second or third day of the three days of polling.

3. That a young lawyer should not have changed his political principles in twenty years.

However, I considered that the chance of this election lottery ticket winning for us a vote, although very small, was at least worth the three sheets of letter-paper which it cost our candidate.

Amidst the bustle of the election this subject was entirely forgotten. The first day of polling arrived, and was concluded, and as usual I was sitting, at midnight, alone in the large committee-room, when the door opened, and there entered a man enveloped in a huge box-coat, who advanced towards me. He held out his hand, and grasping mine, said, 'I have not altered my political principles.' This was Minchin, to whom the pilot, cruising about on the look-out for the 'Herefordshire', had delivered a packet of letters.

The first letter Minchin opened was mine. He immediately went below, told his wife that he must get into the boat which had just put the pilot on board, and hasten to Cambridge, whilst she remained with the children to pursue their voyage to London. Minchin returned in the pilot-boat to Portsmouth found a coach just ready to start, got up on the roof, borrowed a box-coat, and on arriving in London, drove directly to the committee-room. Finding that it / would be most convenient to Minchin to start immediately for Cambridge, I sent off a note to the Temple for the most entertaining man* upon the committee; I introduced him to Minchin, and they posted down to Cambridge, and voted on the second day.

Greatly to the credit and to the advantage of the University, Mr Cavendish was elected on this occasion.

In May, 1832, after the passing of the Reform Bill, there was a dissolution of Parliament. At the general election which ensued, Lord Palmerston and Mr Cavendish, the two former members, again became candidates. Two of the most active members of Mr Cavendish's former committee called upon me, one of whom began speaking in somewhat complimentary phrases of our young candidate. I was listening attentively to all that could be said in favour of the Cavendish family, when his companion, suddenly interrupting him, said, 'No, —— that won't do for Babbage.' He then continued, in terms which I have no wish to repeat, to speak of our candidate, and concluded by saying, that they expressed the opinion of all the working members of the former committee, and came by their desire to request me again to take the chair during the approaching contest; stating, also, that there was no other man under whom they would all willingly act. He then entreated me to be their chairman, not for the sake of the Cavendishes, but for the sake of the cause.

This appeal was irresistible. I immediately acceded to their request,

* My friend, John Elliott Drinkwater, afterwards Bethune.

but with one reservation, in case my brother-in-law's[a] seat was contested, that I should have three days to help him at Bridgenorth.

Under such circumstances the contest commenced. I can / truly add, that amongst the many elections in which I have taken an active working share, none was ever carried on with greater zeal, nor were greater efforts ever made to attain success.

I had good reason at its commencement to doubt the success of our candidate: not from any defect on his part, but entirely on political grounds. The same reasons induced me to suppose that Lord Palmerston's seat was equally in danger. Of course, a tone of perfect confidence was sustained, and, but for a very inopportune petition signed by a considerable number of members of the University, I believe that we might have managed, by a compromise with the other party, to have secured one seat for our own. As it was, however, both the Liberal candidates were defeated.

The contingency I had anticipated did occur. I was sent for, and went down by the mail to assist Mr Wolryche Whitmore. On my arrival, I found that circumstances had entirely changed, and not only my brother-in-law, but also Mr Foster, a large iron-master, was to be returned for Bridgenorth without a contest.

As soon as I was informed of this arrangement, I took immediate measures for rejoining my committee in Cockspur Street. On reaching Bridgenorth, it appeared that four hours would elapse before the mail to London could arrive. I fortunately found a great number of Mr Foster's most influential supporters assembled at the hotel, comprising amongst them many of the largest iron-masters and manufacturers in the county. They were naturally elated at the success of their friend, which secured to their class a certain amount of influence in the House of Commons. In the course of conversation, mention was made of the utter neglect of the manufacturing interests of the district by their county members. / I remarked, that it depended upon themselves to remedy this evil, and enquired whether they were seriously disposed to work. One of the party, who had greatly assisted me when I was managing another contest, and who had ridden over four counties in search of votes for us, appealed to my own experience of their energy. After some discussion, I suggested that they should start a rival candidate of their own for the county.

I then proposed to retire into another room and draw up an address

---

[a] Wolryche Whitmore.

200

to the freeholders, and also placards, to be stuck up in every town and village in the county. I desired them, in the meantime, to divide the county into districts, of such size that one of our party could in the course of a day go to every town and large village in his district, and arrange with one or more tradesmen in our interest to exhibit the address in their shop windows. I also desired them to make an estimate of the number of large and small placards necessary for each town and village, in order that we might ascertain how many of each need be printed.

I returned with the addresses to the freeholders. In these the characters of their late members were lightly sketched, and the public were informed that a committee in the liberal interest was sitting in every town in the county, and that at the proper time the name of a fit candidate would be announced.

My friends cordially concurring in these sentiments, unanimously adopted the addresses, undertook to publish them in the newspapers, to arrange their distribution, and organize committees throughout the county. They were, of course, very anxious to know who was to be their candidate. I told them at once that it was not to be expected that they could succeed in their first attempt, but that such a course would / assuredly secure for them in future much more attention to their interests from their county members. With respect to a candidate, if they could not themselves find one, these placards and advertisements would without doubt produce one.

I may here mention that a member of the Cambridge committee in Cockspur Street had taken rooms at the Crown and Anchor, and, in conjunction with many other Liberals, instituted the Patriotic Fund, for the purpose of collecting subscriptions for the support of liberal candidates at the first elections under the Reform Bill. A very large sum was soon subscribed.

In the broadsides and placards issued in Shropshire, I had taken care to allude to this fund in large capitals.

I now got into the mail for London, amidst the hearty congratulations of my Shropshire friends. During the few minutes' rest at Northampton, I had an opportunity of seeing a member of the Liberal committee and of informing him of our proceedings in Shropshire, and afterwards of conveying his report of the prospects of the contest in that town to our friends in London.

Two or three days after every town, and almost every village in Shropshire, was enlightened by my placards; and in the course of a few days more, three candidates were in the field.

On my return to London I communicated with the Patriotic Fund, who sent down £500 to support the party in Shropshire. After a short contest the Liberal party was of course beaten; but the diversion produced the intended effect.

One portion of electioneering tactics is thought to consist in the manufacture of squibs. These should never give pain nor allude to any personal defect or inevitable evil. They / ought either to produce a broad laugh or that involuntary smile which true wit usually provokes. They are productive of little effect except the amusement of the supporters engaged in carrying on the contest.

My own share in elections has generally been in more serious departments. I remember, however, a very harmless squib which I believed equally amused both parties, and which, I was subsequently informed, was concocted in Mr Cavendish's committee-room.

High mathematical knowledge is by no means a very great qualification in a candidate for the House of Commons, nor is the absence of it any disparagement. In the contest to which I refer, the late Mr Goulburn was opposed to Mr Cavendish. The following paragraph appeared in the 'Morning Post':

The Whigs lay great stress on the academical distinction attained by Mr Cavendish. Mr Goulburn, it is true, was not a candidate for university honours; but his scientific attainments are by no means insignificant. He has succeeded in the exact rectification of a circular arc; and he has likewise discovered the equation of the lunar caustic, a problem likely to prove of great value in nautical astronomy.

It appears that late one evening a cab drove up in hot haste to the office of the 'Morning Post', delivered the copy as coming from Mr Goulburn's committee, and at the same time ordered fifty *extra* copies of the 'Post' to be sent next morning to their committee-room.

During my own contest for the borough of Finsbury few incidents worth note occurred. One day, as I was returning in an omnibus from the City, an opportunity presented itself by which I acquired a few votes. A gentleman at the extreme end of the omnibus being about to leave it, asked the conductor / to give him change for a sovereign. Those around expressed their opinion that he would acquire bad silver by the exchange. On hearing this remonstrance, I thought it a good opportunity to make a little political capital, which might

202

perhaps be improved by a slight delay. So I did not volunteer my services until a neighbour of the capitalist who possessed the sovereign had offered him the loan of a sixpence. It was quite clear that the borrower would ask for the address of the lender, and tolerably certain that it would be in some distant locality. So, in fact, it turned out: Richmond being the abode of the benevolent one. Other liberal individuals offered their services, but they only possessed half-sovereigns and half-crowns.

In the meantime I had taken from my well-loaded breast-pocket one of my own charming addresses[a] to my highly-cultivated and independent constituents, and having also a bright sixpence in my hand, I immediately offered the latter as a loan, and the former as my address for repayment. I remarked at the same time that my committee-room on Holborn Hill, at which I was about to alight, would be open continually for the next five weeks. This offer was immediately accepted, and further extensive demands were instantly made upon my pocket for other copies of my address.

My immediate neighbour, having read its fascinating contents, applied to me for more copies, saying that he highly agreed with my sound and patriotic views, would at once promise me six votes, and added that he would also immediately commence a canvass in his own district. On arriving at my committee-room I had already acquired other supporters. Indeed, I am pretty sure I carried the whole of my fellow-passengers with me: for I left the omnibus amidst the hearty cheers of my newly acquired friends. /

About a year or two after this long-forgotten loan, I received a letter from a gentleman whose name I did not recognize as being one of my too numerous correspondents. It commenced thus: 'Sir, I am the gentleman to whom you lent sixpence in the omnibus.' He then went on to state, in terms too flattering for me to repeat, that he had watched the Finsbury election with the greatest interest, and much deplored the taste of the electors in rejecting so, etc., a candidate. My friend then informed me of an approaching vacancy in the borough of Stroud, in which town he resided. He proceeded to give me an outline of the state of opinion, and of the wants of the electors, and concluded by saying he was certain that my opinions would be very favourably received. He also assured me, if I decided on offering

---

[a] 'Mr Babbage's address to the electors of the Borough of Finsbury', (1832), *Works of Babbage*, Vol. 4.

my services to the constituency, that he should have great pleasure in giving me every support in his power. In reply, I cordially thanked him for his generous offer, but declined the proposed honour. In fact, I was not peculiarly desirous of wasting my time for the benefit of my country. The constituency of Finsbury had already expressed their opinion that Mr Wakley and Mr Thomas Duncombe were fitter than myself to represent them in Parliament, and in that decision I most cordially concurred.

During some of the early contests for the borough of Marylebone, it too frequently occurred that ladies drove round to their various tradesmen to canvass for their votes, threatening, in case of refusal, to withdraw their custom. This unfeminine conduct occasionally drew upon them unpleasant though well-deserved rebukes.

In one of those contests I took a considerable interest in favour of a candidate who I shall call Mr A. Meeting / a very respectable tradesman – a plumber and painter, whom I had employed in decorating my own house – I asked him how he intended to vote. He replied that he wished to vote for Mr A., but that one of his customers had been to his shop and asked him to vote for Mr Z., threatening, in case he declined, never to employ him again.

I enquired whether his customer's house was larger than mine, to which he replied that mine was twice the size of the other. I then asked whether his customer was a younger man than myself, to this he replied, 'He is a much older man.'

I then asked him what he would do if I adopted the same line of conduct, and insisted on his voting for my friend Mr A. This query was unanswerable. Of course I did not attempt to make him violate his extorted promise.

Such conduct is disgraceful, and if of frequent occurrence would have a tendency to introduce the vote by ballot; a mode of voting for representatives which, in my opinion, nothing short of the strongest necessity could justify.

The election for Finsbury gave occasion to the following *jeu d'esprit*, which, as a specimen of the electioneering *squibs* of the day, I give *in extenso*: /

204

CHAPTER XXII

SCENE FROM A NEW AFTER-PIECE

CALLED

Politics and Poetry or *The Decline of Science*

DRAMATIS PERSONAE

PEOPLE OF FASHION:
TURNSTILE, *a retired Philosopher, M.P. for Shoreditch.*
LORD FLUMM, *a Tory nobleman of ancient family.*
COUNTESS OF FLUMM, *his wife.*
LADY SELINA, *their daughter.*
HON. MRS FUBSEY, *sister of the Countess.*

WHIGS:
LORD A., *Prime Minister.*
CLOSEWIND, *First Lord of the Admiralty.*
SHIFT, *Secretary at War.*
SMOOTH, *Secretary for the Colonies; also M.P. for Shoreditch.*

TORIES:
LORD GEORGE,
LORD CHARLES,
MARQUIS OF FLAMBOROUGH, } *Members of the Conservative Club*
DICK TRIM, *a former Whipper-in,*

SHOREDITCH ELECTORS:
HIGHWAY, *a Radical.*
GRISKIN, *Colonel of the Lumber Troop.*
TRIPES, *his Lieutenant.*

PHILOSOPHERS:
  SIR ORLANDO WINDFALL, Knt. R. Han. Guelph. Order, *an Astronomical Observer.*
  SIR SIMON SMUGG, Knt. R. Han. Guelph. Order, *Professor of Botanism.*
  ATALL, *an Episcopizing Mathematician, Dean of Canterbury.*
  BYEWAYS, *a Calculating Officer.*

  Other Lords – Conservative and Whig.

  —

The Scene is laid in London; principally at the West end of the town.

The time is near the end of May, 1835. /

206

SCENES, ETC., EXTRACTED

ACT I

SCENE I. *Committee-room of the Conservatives, Charles Street;* LORD FLUMM; MARQUIS OF FLAMBOROUGH; LORD GEORGE; LORD CHARLES; *other Tory Lords, and* TRIM. *A table covered with papers;* LORD CHARLES *smoking a cigar;* LORD GEORGE *half asleep in an armchair;* TRIM *busy in looking over a list of the House of Commons.*

Trim. It will be a devilish close run I see! – yet I think we might manage some of them (*pause*). Does anybody know *Turnstile*?

Marquis. Never heard of him!

Lord George. (*Mumbling*) The reform Member for Puddledock, isn't he? – the author of a book on Pinmaking, and things of that kind. An ironmonger in Newgate Street!

Trim. No, no! Member for Shoreditch – with Smooth, the Colonial Secretary.

Lord Charles. (*Taking the cigar from his mouth*) I think I've heard something of him at Cambridge: he was Newtonian Professor of Chemistry when I was at College.

Trim. Can't we talk him over?

Lord Charles. No, no! he is too sharp for that.

Trim. Will anybody speak to him? And if he won't vote with us, keep him out of the way.

Marquis. Perhaps a hint at an appointment!

Lord Charles. Nor that either; he is a fellow of some spirit; and devilish proud. /

Lord Flumm. ·But what are his tastes? How does he employ himself? Who are his friends?

Trim. Why he's – a sort of a – philosopher – that wants to be a man of the world!

Lord Flumm. Oh! – now I begin to recollect – I must have seen him

207

at Sir Phillip's. Leave him to me – I think Lady Flumm and my daughter can manage to keep him quiet on Thursday night.

Trim. But for Tuesday – my Lord?

Lord Flumm. Two nights! Then I must try what I can do for you, myself. [*Exit*

SCENE IV. *Grosvenor Square*

Enter TURNSTILE, *musing*

Turnstile. This will never do! They make use of me, and laugh at me in their sleeves – push me round and go by. That breakdown *was* a devil of a business! They didn't laugh out to be sure; but they coughed and looked unutterably!! And where is this to end? What shall I have to show for it? Confounded loss of time – to hear those fellows prosing, instead of seeing the occultation last night. And that book of L's.; so much that *I* had begun upon – and might have finished! It never will do! (*Rousing himself after a pause*) But knowledge, after all, *is* power! That at least is certain – power – to do what? to refuse Lord Doodle's invitation; and to ask Lord Humbug for a favour, which it is ten to one he will refuse! But the Royal Society is defunct! That I *have* accomplished. Gilbert, and the Duke! and the Secretaries! – I have driven them all before me! and, now, though *I* must not be a knight of the Guelphic order, (yet a riband is a pretty looking thing! and / a star too!) I will show that I can teach *them* how to make knights; and describe the decorations that other men are to wear. But here comes Lord Flumm, and I am saved the bore of calling upon him.

SCENE V

Enter LORD FLUMM

Lord Flumm. Mr Turnstile, if I do not mistake! My dear Turnstile: how glad I am to see you again! It *was* kind of Sir Phillip to introduce me. You know that you are near our house; and Lady Flumm will be so happy –

Turnstile. In truth, my Lord, I was about to call upon you. After what you were so good as to say last night, I took the first opportunity.

Lord Flumm. Well, that *is* kind. But you did not speak last night.

How came that? I don't find you in the paper, yet the subject was quite your own. Tallow and bar-iron, raw materials and machinery. Ah, my dear sir! when science condescends to come amongst us mortals, the effects to be expected *are* wonderful indeed!

Turnstile. My Lord, you flatter. But we have reached your door. (*Aside*) [Confound him! – But I am glad he was not in the house. It's clear he hasn't heard of the breakdown.]

Lord Flumm. While I have you to myself, Turnstile, remember that you dine with me on Tuesday. I am to have two friends, Lord S——and Sir George Y——, who wish very much to be acquainted with you. Half-past seven.

Turnstile. You are very good, my lord. I dare not refuse so kind an invitation.   [*Exeunt /*

SCENE VI. LADY FLUMM'S *drawing room.* LADY FLUMM *at the writing-table.* MRS FUBSEY *at work on a sofa.*

Enter LORD FLUMM *and* TURNSTILE

Lord Flumm. Lady Flumm, this is Mr Turnstile, whom you have so long wished to know. Mr Turnstile – Lady Flumm.

Lady Flumm. The Mr Turnstile. My dear sir, I am too happy to see you. We had just been speaking of your delightful book. Selina! (*Calling*) [*Enter* LADY SELINA] This is Mr Turnstile.

Lady Selina. Indeed!

Lady Flumm. Yes, indeed! You see he is a mortal man after all. Bring me, my love, the book you will find open on the table in the boudoir. I wish to show Mr Turnstile the passages I have marked this morning.

Lady Selina. (*Returning with the book, and running over the leaves*) 'Lace made by caterpillars.' – 'Steam-engines with fairy fingers.' – 'Robe of nature.' – 'Sun of science.' – 'Faltering worshipper.' – 'Altar of truth.' It *is, indeed,* delightful! The taste, the poetical imagination, are surprising. I hope, Mr Turnstile – indeed I am sure, that you love music?

Turnstile. Not *very* particularly, I must acknowledge (*smiling*); a barrel-organ is the instrument most in my way.

Lady Flumm. (*Smiling*) Music and machinery, Mr Turnstile.

Polite literature and mathematics. You *do* know how to combine. Others must judge of the profounder parts of your works; but the style, and the fancy, are what I should most admire. You dine with Lord Flumm, he tells me, on Tuesday. Now you *must* come to *me* on Thursday night.

Turnstile. I am sorry to say, that, on recollection, I *ought* to / have apologized to Lord Flumm. The Pottery Question stands for Tuesday; and I should be there, as one of the Committee; and Thursday, your Ladyship knows, is the second reading of the Place and Pension Bill.

Lady Flumm. Oh, we are Staffordshire people! *that* will excuse you to the pottery folks; and, for Thursday, I *will* absolutely take no excuse. We have Pasta and Donzelli! perhaps a quadrille afterwards – (you dance, Mr Turnstile?) – and Lady Sophia C—— and her cousin, Lord F——, you have said *so much* about those beautiful passages at the end of your book, that they will be quite disappointed if I do not keep my promise to introduce them (*touching his arm with her finger*).

Turnstile. Your Ladyship knows how to conquer: I feel that I *cannot* refuse.   [*Exit*

SCENE VII. *Grosvenor Square; before* LORD FLUMM'S *house.*

Enter TURNSTILE, *from the house*

Turnstile. This is all very delightful; but what will they say at Shoreditch? – twice in one week absent from the House, and at two Tory parties.

Enter GRISKIN, *hastily, heated; his hat in his left hand; a pocket-handkerchief in his right.*

Griskin. Mr Turnstile, I'm glad to find you; just called on you, as I came to this quarter to look after a customer – long way from the City – sorry not to hear from you.

Turnstile. Why, really, Mr Griskin, I am very sorry; but I am not acquainted with the Commander-in-chief. And I must say that I should not know how to press for the contract, / knowing that your nephew's prices are 30 per cent., at least, above the market.

Griskin. That's being rather nice, I should say, Mr Turnstile. My nephew is as good a lad as ever stood in shoe-leather; and has six

210

good wotes in Shoreditch – and, as to myself, Mr Turnstile, I must say that, after all I did at your election – and in such wery hot weather – I did not expect you'd be so wery particular about a small matter. Sir, I wish you a good morning.

Turnstile. (*Bowing and looking after him*) So this fellow, like the rest of them, thinks that I am to do his jobs, and to neglect my own. And this is your *reformed* Parliament.

SCENE IX. *The street, near* TURNSTILE'S *house*

Enter TRIPES *and* SMOOTH, *meeting*

Smooth. (*Taking both* TRIPES' *hands*) My dear Tripes, how d'ye do? Pray, how is your good lady? What a jolly party at your house last night! and Mrs Tripes, I hope, is none the worse for it?

Tripes. Oh dear sir, no! Mrs Tripes and my daughters were *so* pleased with your Scotch singing.

Smooth. And your boys, how are they? – fine, promising, active fellows. You've heard from MacLeech?

Tripes. Just received the note as I left home.

Smooth. All is quite right, you see, your cousin has the appointment at the Cape. I knew MacLeech was just the man for the details. A ship, I find, is to sail in about three weeks; and (*significantly*) I don't think your cousin need be *very* scrupulous about freight and passage.

Tripes. You are too good, Mr Smooth. I'm sure if anything that I can do – my sense of all your kindness — /

Smooth. I was thinking, when I saw those fine lads of yours, that another assistant to my under secretary's deputy – but (between you and me) Hume thinks that one is more than enough. We must wait a little.

Takes TRIPES' *arm*   [*Exeunt*

SCENE X. TURNSTILE'S *parlour,* 11½ A.M. *Breakfast on the table; pamphlets and newspapers. In the corners of the room, books and philosophical instruments, dusty and thrown together; heaps of Parliamentary Reports lying above them.* TURNSTILE *alone, musing, and looking over some journals.*

Turnstile. This headache! Impossible to sleep when one goes to bed by daylight. Experiments by Arago! Ah! a paper by Cauchy, on my own subject. But here is this cursed committee in Smithfield to be attended; and it is already past eleven (*rising*).

[*Knock at the hall door*]

Enter Servant

Servant. Mr Tripes, sir.
Turnstile. Show him in. He comes, no doubt, to say that my election is arranged. A good, fat-headed, honest fellow.

Enter TRIPES

Well Mr Tripes, I'm glad to see you. Pray take a chair.
Tripes. We hoped to have seen you at the meeting yesterday, sir. Capital speech from Mr Smooth. You know, of course, that Mr Highway is a candidate; and Mr MacLeech is talked of; very sorry, indeed, you weren't there.
Turnstile. A transit of Venus, Mr Tripes, is a thing that does not happen every day. Besides, my friend, Stellini / from Palermo, is here; and I had promised to go with him to Greenwich.
Tripes. Almost a pity, sir, to call off your attention from such objects. But in the City we are men of business, you know – plain, everyday people.
Turnstile. It was unlucky; but I could not help it. The committee, I hope, is by this time at work?
Tripes. It was just that, I called about. I wished to tell you myself how very sorry I am that I cannot be your chairman. But – my large family – press of business – in short – you must excuse me; and, if I should be upon Mr Smooth's committee, I don't well see how I can attend to both.
Turnstile. Smooth! – but he and I go together, you know – at least, I understood it so.
Tripes. I'm glad to hear it; I feared there might be some mistake. And, if Mr MacLeech comes forward – being a fellow-townsman of Mr Smooth, and a good deal in the Glasgow interest; a commercial man too, Mr Turnstile; a *practical* man – Mr Turnstile; I am not quite sure that you can count upon Mr Smooth's assistance; and Government, you know, is strong.
Turnstile. Assistance, Mr Tripes – from Smooth! – why I came in

212

on my own ground; on the *Independent* interest. Assistance from Smooth! Besides – Smooth knows very well that *our* second votes secured him.

Tripes. Very true, sir; but these Independent people are hard to deal with; and Mr Highway, I assure you, hit very hard in his speech at the meeting yesterday. He talked of amateur politicians – attention to the business of the people – dinners with the opposite party. In short, I fear, they will say – like the others – that what they want is something / of 'a *practical man*', Mr Turnstile. I'm sorry that I must be going. Sir, your servant.

Turnstile. (*Rising and ringing*) [*Enter servant*] Open the door for Mr Tripes. [*Exit* TRIPES] D——d, double-faced, selfish blockhead!

SCENE XI. *The street, as before*

Enter TRIPES, *from* TURNSTILE'S *house*

Tripes. (*Putting on his hat*) He might have been more civil, too; though he did count upon me for his chairman. But I'll show him that I'm not to be insulted; and if, MacLeech manages the matter well for Charles, this *Mr Philosopher Turnstile*, though he thinks himself so clever, may go to the devil.   [*Exit*

213

ACT II

SCENE I. *Downing Street, after a Cabinet Meeting.* LORD A.; CLOSE-
WIND; SHIFT; SMOOTH; *and other Members of the Cabinet.*

Lord A. That point being settled, gentlemen, the sooner you are at
your posts the better. The King comes down to dissolve on Friday.*
But, before we part, we had better / decide about this Presidency of the
Board of Manufactures. The appointment requires an able man; of
rather peculiar attainments. Mr Turnstile has been mentioned to me;
and his claims I am told, are strong: long devotion to science – great
expense and loss of time for public objects – high reputation, and
weight of opinion, as a man of science.

Smooth. I believe that he has left *science*; at least, he wishes it to be
so considered. He is my colleague at Shoreditch; and, of course, I wish
to support him; but – when business is to be done; and men – and
things, to be brought together – I own – I *doubt* – whether a more
practical man – might not—

Shift. And *that* poor Turnstile certainly is not. He must always have *a*
reason; nothing but the *quod erat demonstrandum*; a romancer; if you
have anything to do, his first object is *to do it well*. I am quite sure he
will not answer our purpose.

Closewind. He talks too much about consistency; and on party
questions, you are never sure of him: last week he did not divide with
us, on either night.

---

* Parliament is ordinarily dissolved by Proclamation, after having been previously
prorogued. However, there is at least one modern instance to justify the historical
consistency of the text, namely, that which occurred on 10 June, 1818, when the Prince
Regent, afterwards George IV, dissolved the Parliament in person. The Dramatist
cannot therefore be properly accused of drawing heedlessly upon his imagination,
though even had he thus far transgressed the boundaries of historical truth, Horace's
maxim might have been pleaded in excuse:

'Pictoribus atque Poetis
Quidlibet audendi semper fuit æqua potestas.'

<*Translation:* To Painters and Poets / Anything of daring has always been an equal
power.>

Lord A. Well; *I* am quite different. I did hear of his being at Lord Flumm's; and after what had just passed in the Lords, a personal friend of mine would, perhaps, have kept away from that quarter. Is there no other person?

Smooth. (*Hesitatingly*) Davies Gilbert.

Shift. (*Laughing*) Pooh! Pooh! Poor Gilbert! No, that will never do.

Smooth. Or – Warburton?

Shift. (*Sneering*) Worse and worse! – if *ever* there was an impracticable—

Closewind. But we don't know that Turnstile is sure of his seat. Smooth, hasn't MacLeech been talked of for Shoreditch? /

Smooth. He's *certain* of succeeding! The independent gentlemen don't quite like Turnstile – they wish for Highway – and the split will foil them both. MacLeech – now that he has been mentioned – I must acknowledge, does seem to me to be the *very* man for the manufactures – a practical, persevering man of business – never absent from the House – excellent Scottish connections – a cousin of the Duke of Y.'s—

Lord A. That is a good point, certainly. An appointment given there would be candid and liberal; it might be conciliate—

Closewind. A very civil, excellent fellow, too. MacLeech, *I* should say, is the man.

Shift. I quite agree with you.

Smooth. I confess, I think he will fill the office well. And if it is thought quite necessary that Hume's motion to reduce the salary – though it is not large—

Closewind. Oh, no! The salary had better remain; £2000 is not too much. Besides, the *principle* of giving way is bad.

Lord A. Well, gentlemen, let it be so. Smooth, you will let MacLeech know that he has the office.

Smooth. And at the present salary?

Lord A. Agreed.   [*Exeunt*

SCENE IV. *The Athenaeum Club.* SMOOTH *and* ATALL *at a table.*

Smooth. I saw it this morning on the breakfast table at Lord A's; it is an admirable article, and I was told is yours.

Atall. (*Decliningly*) These things, you know, are always supposed to be anonymous. But I am not sorry that you liked the paper. Did his lordship speak of it? /

215

Smooth. The book was open at the article upon the table. It does you honour. Hits *just* the happy point – hints probable *intentions*, without giving any pledge – enough to please the Liberals – and full room for *explanation*, if any change becomes expedient. The true plan, believe me, for a ministry, in times like these, is to proceed *en tâtonnant*. Pray, Mr Dean, how is the Bishop of Hereford?

Atall. I didn't know that he was particularly ill. He has long been feeble.

Smooth. These complainers do sometimes hold out. But they cannot last forever. We meet I hope tomorrow at the levee. You *ought* to be there.

Atall. I have come to town for the purpose; having secured, I think Closewind's election at Cambridge.

Smooth. Well done, my very good friend! Men of talent should always pull together. Sorry that I must go; but we meet tomorrow (*shaking hands very cordially*). [*Exit*

SCENE VI. BYEWAYS' *lodgings*. BYEWAYS *alone, writing*.

Enter TURNSTILE

Turnstile. My dear Byeways; I want your assistance. Deserted by those shabby dogs the Radicals, and tricked, I fear, by the Whigs, I find I have no chance of a decent show of numbers at the next election, if my scientific friends do not support me with spirit. Even so, it *can* be only an honourable retreat. I count upon *you* – you understand the world; and as soon as we can muster a committee, you must be my chairman.

Byeways. My good friend, don't be in a hurry; sit down and tell me all about it. I know you don't care much about your seat – and after all – it is – to you, a waste of time; / but, with the Independents at your back, you are secure. As to me, my dear fellow, you know that I am—

Turnstile. But man! the Independents, as you call them, have taken up Highway; he blusters, and goes any length.

Byeways. But Smooth, you know, is strong in Shoreditch – Government interest – you brought him in last time; and you and he, together—

Turnstile. I know it; but he says he is not *strong enough* to run any risk. If you will be my chairman, with a good committee, we may at least die game.

216

Byeways. My dear Turnstile, you know how glad I always am to serve you – and you know what *I think*; but in my situation, my dear fellow, it is quite impossible that I can *oppose* the ministers. MacLeech too, they say, is a candidate; and his brother-in-law's uncle was very civil, last year, in Scotland, to my wife's cousin. But I *have* a plan for you. There is Atall, just come to town; make *him* your chief, and bring the Cambridge men together. The clergy were always strong in Shoreditch. Atall can speak to them. I am obliged to go to the War Office. And you had better lose no time in seeing Atall. Sorry to bid you goodbye.   [*Exit*

Turnstile. Well, this *is* strange! yet I thought I might have counted upon Byeways.   [*Exit*

SCENE VIII. LADY FLUMM'S *drawing room*. LADY FLUMM; LADY SELINA; HON. MRS FUSBEY

Mrs Fusbey. But, my dear sister; how *can* you so beflatter that poor man? You don't know all the mischief you may do to him.

Lady Flumm. 'Poor man!' I cannot pity him. His maxim is, that knowledge is power; and he thinks *his* knowledge / is all that can be known. He has to learn that *our* knowledge, also, is power; and that we know how to use it too.

Enter LORD FLUMM

Lord Flumm. There, Lady Selina, so much for your philosophic friend. Poor Turnstile! What a business he *has* made of it. Here is 'The Times', with the report of the Shoreditch election meeting. Turnstile has no chance. The Scotchmen coalesce; Highway none of us can think of; and Smooth and MacLeech walk over the ground in triumph; and then, the Presidency of Manufactures, the *very* appointment for which poor Turnstile was fitted (and, to do the poor devil justice, he could have filled it well), is given to MacLeech, a Scotch hanger on, or distant cousin of Smooth's, and with the old salary, in spite of all that Hume could say against it. Bravo! Reform, and the Whigs for ever! We Tories could not have done the business in a better style.

Enter a footman

Footman. Mr Turnstile, my Lady, sends up his card.

217

Lady Flumm. Oh, not at home! And Sleek, put a memorandum in the visiting-book, that we arc 'out of town', whenever Mr Turnstile calls.

SCENE XII. TURNSTILE'S *parlour. Night.* TURNSTILE *alone.*

Turnstile. Then all is up. What a fool have I been to embark upon this sea of trouble! Two years of trifling and lost time; whilst others have been making discoveries and adding to their reputation. Those *rascal* Whigs, my blood boils to think of them. I can forgive the Shoreditch people / – the greasy, vulgar, money-getting beasts; but my *friends*, the men of principle— (*getting up and walking about*).

Is it still too late to return? (*Looking round upon his books and instruments*) There you are, my old friends, whom I *have* treated rather ungratefully. What a scene at that cursed meeting! Highway's bullying; and the baseness of Smooth; the sleek, sly, steering of that knave MacLeech; and yet they *must* succeed. There's no help for it. I *am* fairly beaten – thrown overboard, with not a leg to stand upon; and all I have to do is to go to bed now, to sleep off this fever; and tomorrow, take leave of politics, and try to be myself once more.

END OF THE EXTRACTS

Note. The reader will doubtlessly have already discovered that *Byeways*, with the other *dramatis personae* of this squib, are living characters not unknown in the fashionable and political circles. In a future edition, if it can be done without offence, I may perhaps be induced to present them to the public without their masks and buskins. /

218

CHAPTER XXIII

EXPERIENCE AT COURTS

Pension to Dr Dalton – Inhabitants of Manchester subscribe for a Statue by Chantrey – The author proposed that he should appear at a levee – Various difficulties suggested and removed – The Chancellor approves and offers to present him – Mentions it to King William IV – Difficulties occur – Dalton as a Quaker could not wear a sword – Answer, he may go in his robes as a Doctor of Laws of Oxford – As a Quaker he could not wear Scarlet Robes – Answer, Dalton is afflicted with colour-blindness – Crimson to him is dirt-colour – Dr Dalton breakfasts with the author – First rehearsal – Second rehearsal at Mr Wood's – At the levee – The Church in danger – Courtiers jealous of the Quaker – Conversation at Court sometimes interesting, occasionally profitable.

The following letter was addressed by me to Dr Henry, the biographer of Dalton, in reply to enquiries respecting the part I had taken in procuring a pension for that distinguished philosopher. It was printed in the 'Life of Dalton', and is now reprinted from its illustration of the subject of this chapter:[a]

My dear sir,
I have now examined my papers, as far as I can, to find any traces of Dalton amongst them. I find only two letters, of which I send you copies.

I well remember taking a great interest in Dalton's pension, as you will see by several passages in 'The Decline of Science', pp. 20 and 22, and note; but I have no recollection of any of the circumstances, or through what channel it was applied for. /

I find several letters of that date from Mr Wood,* and it appears from them that I went with him to Poulett Thomson;† but I only gather this fact from those letters. I send them in the enclosure, as they may be of use. You can return them at your own convenience.

When the inhabitants of Manchester had subscribed £2000 for a statue of

---

* Member for South Lancashire.
† Afterwards Lord Sydenham.

---

[a] W. C. Henry, *Memoirs of the life and scientific researches of John Dalton* (London, 1854), pp. 185–9; the footnotes do not appear in the original text.

219

Dalton, he came up to London, and was the guest of Mr Wood. He sat to Chantrey for the statue. I consequently saw much of my friend. It occurred to me that, as his townsmen were having a statue of him – as the University of Oxford had given him the honorary degree of Doctor of Laws – and as the Government had given him a pension – if it were not incompatible with his feelings, it would be a fit thing that he should be presented at a levee. It appeared to me that if William the Fourth were informed of it, it would afford him an opportunity of saying a few words to the venerable philosopher, which would be gratifying to the inhabitants of Manchester, the University of Oxford, and the world of science.

Accordingly I wrote a note to Mr Wood, suggesting the idea, and proposing that he should ascertain from Doctor Dalton whether it would be unpleasant to him to go through the usual forms.

Dalton not objecting, my note was sent on by Mr Wood to Lord Brougham, who at that time was Lord Chancellor. He approved highly of the plan, and offered to present Doctor Dalton. He also mentioned the circumstance to the King.

I had had some conversation with Mr Wood upon the subject, when several difficulties presented themselves to him. Doctor Dalton, as a Quaker, could not appear in a court-dress / because he must wear a sword. To this I replied, that being aware of the difficulty, I had proposed to let him wear the robes of a Doctor of Laws of Oxford.

Mr Wood remarked, that those robes being *scarlet*, they were not of a colour admissible by Quakers.

To this I replied, that Doctor Dalton had a kind of *colour-blindness*, and that all red colours appeared to him to be the colour of dirt. Besides, I had found that our friend entertained very reasonable views of such mere matters of form. The velvet cap of the Doctor again was not an obstacle, as he was informed that it was usually held in the hand, and was rather a mark of office than a covering for the head.

These difficulties being surmounted, Doctor Dalton came one morning to breakfast with me. We were alone; and after breakfast he went up with me into the drawing-room, in order to see the Difference Engine. After we had made several series of calculations, he recollected that he had in his pocket a note to me from Mr Wood. On hastily looking it over, I found that it was to announce to me that our friend acquiesced in the plan.

I now mentioned the forms usual at a levee, and placing several chairs in order to represent the various officers in the Presence-chamber, I put Doctor Dalton in the middle of the circle to represent the King. I then told my friend that I should represent a greater man than the King; that I intended to personate Doctor Dalton, and would re-enter at the further door, go round the circle, make my obeisance to the King, and thus show him the kind of ceremony at which he was to assist.

220

On passing the third chair from the King's, I put my card on the chair, at the same time informing Doctor Dalton / that this was the post of a Lord in Waiting, who takes the cards, and gives them to the next officer, who announces them to the King.

On passing the philosopher I kissed his hand, and then passing round the rest of the circle of chairs, I thus gave him his first lesson as a courtier.

It was arranged that I should take Doctor Dalton with me to the levee, and put on his card, 'Doctor Dalton, presented by the Lord Chancellor.'

When the morning arrived I went to Mr Wood's residence, and found Doctor Dalton quite ready for the expedition. In order to render the chief actor perfect in his part, we again had a rehearsal; Mrs Wood personating the King, and the rest of the family, with the assistance of sundry chairs and stools, representing the great Officers of State. I then entered the room, preceding my excellent friend, who followed his instructions as perfectly as if he had been repeating an experiment.

Being now quite satisfied with the performance, we drove off to St. James's. The robes of a Doctor of Laws are rarely made use of, except at a University Address: consequently Dr Dalton's costume attracted much attention, and compelled me to gratify the curiosity of many of my friends, by explaining who he was. The prevailing opinion had been that he was the Mayor of some corporate town come up to get knighted. I informed my enquirers, that he was a much more eminent person than any Mayor of any city, and having won for himself a name which would survive when orders of knighthood should be forgotten, he had no ambition to be knighted.

At a short distance from the Presence-chamber, I observed close before me several dignitaries of the Church, in / the full radiance of their vast lawn sleeves. The Bishop of Gloucester,* who was nearest, accidentally turning his head, I recognized a face long familiar to me from its cordiality and kindness. A few words were interchanged between us, and also by myself with the rest of the party, the remotest of whom, if I remember rightly, was the Archbishop of Dublin. The dress of my friend seemed to strike the Bishop's attention; but the quiet costume of the Quaker beneath his scarlet robe was entirely unnoticed. I therefore confided to the Bishop of Gloucester the fact that I had a Quaker by my side, at the same time assuring him that my peaceful and philosophic friend was very far from meditating any injury to the Church. The effect was electric upon the whole party; episcopal eyes had never yet beheld such a spectacle in such society, and I fear, notwithstanding my assurance, some portion of the establishment thought the Church really in danger.

We now entered the Presence-chamber, and having passed the King, I retired very slowly, in order that I might observe events. Doctor Dalton having kissed hands, the King asked him several questions, all which the

* Dr Monk.

philosopher duly answered, and then moved on in proper order to join me. This reception, however, had not passed with sufficient rapidity to escape jealousy, for I heard one officer say to another, 'Who the d —l is that fellow whom the King keeps talking to so long?'

Conversations at Courts are not always thought to be the most interesting things in the world; although, doubtless, they must be so to the parties engaged in them. In the midst of crowded levees and drawing-rooms, one is often compelled to become the confidant of strangers around us. / The amusement derived from this source predominates over the instruction. I have heard much anxious enquiry as to certain pieces of clerical preferment – who is to have certain military or colonial commands, and what promotions will take place from the consequent vacancies? – many political queries have been proposed, and how 'the party' would act in certain contingent cases? I once heard a gentleman receive at a levee the first announcement of a legacy; on another occasion, on my return from the Continent, I was myself informed at a levee of a similarly gratifying, and to me entirely unexpected, event.

Doctor Dalton having now passed through the formal part of a levee, had a better opportunity of viewing the details. He enquired the names of several of the portraits, and I took the opportunity of pointing out to him many of the living celebrities.

We then returned to Mr Wood's residence, and the whole party were highly gratified at the success of the undertaking.

I am, my dear Sir, very truly yours,

Dorset Street, Manchester Square,　　　　　　　　　　　　C. BABBAGE
7 February, 1854 /

CHAPTER XIV

EXPERIENCE AT COURTS

The author invited to a meeting at Turin of the philosophers of Italy, 1840 – The King, Charles Albert – Reflections on shyness – Question of dress – Electric telegraph – Theory of storms – Remark of an Italian friend in the evening at the opera – Various instruments taken to the palace, and shown to the young princes – The Queen being absent – The reason why – The young princes did great credit to their governor – The General highly gratified – The philosopher proposes another difficult question – It is referred to the King himself – An audience is granted to ask the King's permission to present the woven silk engraving of Jacquard to her Majesty – Singular but comic scene – The final capture of the butterflies – Visit to Raconigi – The vintage.

About a quarter of a century ago the Court of Turin had the reputation of being the most formal and punctilious of any in Europe. It was dull to the diplomatic officials, who were doomed like planets to circulate around it, though not without interest to the enquiring traveller, whose orbit, like that of a comet, passed through its atmosphere only at distant intervals.

In 1840 I received a gratifying invitation to meet the *élite* of the science of Italy at Turin. On my arrival I immediately took measures to pay my respects in the usual manner to the sovereign of the country. Having enquired of a nobleman* high in the confidence of the King, when there / would occur a levee, in order that I might have the honour of being presented, I was informed that his Majesty was aware of my arrival, and would receive me at a private audience. Two days after I had a formal visit from Count Alessandro Saluzzo to inform me that the King would receive me the next day at two o'clock.

I then made enquiries as to the usual dress, and found that a Court dress was not considered essential on such occasions, especially for a

---

* Conte D. Alessandro Saluzzo di Monesiglio, Grande di Corona, Presid. della sexiare dell' interno nel consiglio di stato, etc.

foreigner, and that I might with perfect propriety go in plain clothes. I was glad to avail myself of this permission; but in order to prevent any misapprehension, I drove up to the palace about a quarter of an hour before the appointed time, and called upon General Cesare de Salluce'* the governor of the two young princes, the present King of Italy and the late Duke of Genoa, then respectively about eighteen and seventeen years of age.

The General kindly offered to accompany me to the ante-chamber. In the course of our conversation I took an opportunity of mentioning that, having been informed I might appear in plain clothes, I had thought it most respectful to his sovereign to wear the same dress I had worn a few days before I left England, when I had the honour of being invited to the first party† given by a subject to my own sovereign.

I had already been informed that the King, Charles Albert, took a great interest in the success of the meeting; that he was a very good man, but remarkably shy; and that he probably would not detain me more than perhaps five minutes.

I had myself experienced the misery of that affliction, and / felt how much more painful it must inevitably become when it fell to the lot of a person placed in the most exalted rank.

On entering the ante-room I found a number of the most distinguished people of the country waiting for audience, the King at that time being occupied, as I was informed, with one of his ministers. On his exit the master of the ceremonies announced that his Majesty would receive me.

I then entered the royal reception-room, and was presented to the King. He was a remarkably tall person, dressed in military costume, having a very peculiar expression of countenance, which I was at a loss how immediately to interpret. The King invited me to sit down, and I followed his Majesty to a large bay-window, where we immediately sat down on two stools opposite to each other.

The King expressed his satisfaction that I had come from so considerable a distance to assist at the councils of the men of science then assembling in his own capital. Of course I replied by remarking that the advancement of the sciences contributed to the material as well as to the intellectual progress of every nation, and that when a

---

* Saluzzo di Monesiglio, Car. Cesare, Luogoten, Gen., Gran Mastro d'Artiglieria et Governatore de Reali Principi, etc.; the younger brother of the Count Alexander.
† The déjeûné at Wimbledon Park, the residence of the late Duke of Somerset.

sovereign, intimately convinced of this truth, took measures for the extension and diffusion of knowledge, it was the duty of all those engaged in its cultivation respectfully to assist as far as their individual circumstances permitted.

After a short pause, the King put some question which I do not remember, except that it was one of the conventional topics of society: perhaps it might have related to my journey. I now felt that unless I could raise some question of curiosity in his Majesty's mind, to overcome his natural reserve, the interview would soon terminate precisely in the manner predicted. I therefore, in replying to this question, / contrived to introduce a remarkable fact relative to the electric telegraph. I soon perceived that it had taken hold of the King's imagination, and the next question confirmed my view. 'For what purposes,' said the King, 'will the electric telegraph become useful?'

I must here request the reader to go back in his memory to the state of our knowledge in 1840, when electricity and other subjects, now of everyday application, were just commencing their then eccentric but now regulated course.

The King put the very question I had wished. Carefully observing his countenance, I felt that I was advancing in a tract in which he was interested. At each pause the proper question was suggested, and at last I pointed out the probability that, by means of the electric telegraphs, his Majesty's fleet might receive warning of coming storms. This led to the new theory of storms, about which the King was very curious. By degrees I endeavoured to make it clear. I cited, as an illustration, a storm which had occurred but a short time before I left England. The damage done by it at Liverpool was very great, and at Glasgow immense. On one large property in the west coast of Scotland thirty thousand timber-trees had been thrown down.

I then explained that by subsequent enquiries it had been found that this storm arose from the overlapping of two circular whirlwinds, one of them coming up from the Atlantic bodily at the rate of twenty miles an hour, the other passing at the rate of twelve miles an hour, in a north-westerly direction, to Glasgow, where they coalesced, and destroyed property to the value of above half a million sterling. I added that if there had been electric communication between Genoa and a few other places the people of Glasgow might have had information of one of those storms twenty-four hours previously to its / arrival, and could then have taken effective measures for the security of much of their shipping.

225

During this conversation I had felt rather uneasy at occupying the King's time so long when several of his own ministers were waiting in his ante-room for an audience, perhaps upon important business. Urged by this truly conscientious motive, I committed a *gaucherie* of the deepest water – I half rose from my stool to take leave of his Majesty. The King, as well he might, lifted up both his hands and then expressed the greatest interest in the continuance of the subject.

After a conversation of about five-and-twenty minutes the King rose, and, walking with me to the door, I made my bow. The King then held out his hand.

Here might have arisen a puzzling question, what I ought to have done; but previously to the interview I had taken the precaution of enquiring of one of my Sardinian friends what were the usual forms, and whether it was customary to kiss hands on being presented to the sovereign. The answer was in the negative. The ceremony of kissing hands, he informed me, never took place except when a native subject was appointed to some very high office.

I therefore immediately perceived that the King had done me the honour of adopting the salutation of my own country. Under these circumstances I shook hands as an Englishman does, and then, bowing profoundly, retired.

In the course of the evening of that day, being at the opera, I visited the box of one of my Italian acquaintances. A great friend of mine, also an Italian, who had been dining at the palace, came in soon after. He said to me, 'What an extraordinary person you are! You have perfectly fascinated our King, who has done nothing but talk of you and the things you have told him during the whole of dinner time.' /

I admit I felt great satisfaction at this announcement of the complete success of my daring experiment. It assured me that my unusual deviation from the routine of a Court was fully justified by the interest the matter communicated had awakened in the King's mind.

I had brought with me to Turin several models and various instruments connected with science and mechanical art, which of course had been examined by many of my scientific and personal friends. Unfortunately, on two occasions, when General de Salluce, who was much my senior in years, called upon me, I happened to be absent from the house. Knowing how fully his time was occupied by his illustrious pupils, I much regretted that I had not been at home when he called, and during one of my visits at the palace I offered to bring with me, on another occasion, some of the things I thought might be most interesting.

The General could not think of giving me that trouble, and at first very courteously declined the proposal. But after a moment or two he said, 'On second thoughts, I will accept your kind offer, because I think it may be useful to my young pupils.'

On the morning proposed I drove up to the palace with some boxes containing the various apparatus, and was immediately shown into a large room nearly at the top of the palace. After opening the boxes and giving the General a glance at the various articles, I remarked that several of them were interesting to ladies, and that possibly the Queen, if made acquainted with it, might like to accompany her sons; in which cause it would, perhaps, be more convenient for her Majesty if they were placed in a lower room of the palace.

The idea appeared a happy one; the General was much / pleased at it, and said he would go immediately and take her Majesty's pleasure on the subject. After considerable delay General de Salluce returned, evidently much disappointed, and said he was commanded by the Queen to thank me for the attention, and to express her Majesty's regret that she was prevented by an engagement from accompanying the young princes.

When everything was arranged, and the hour appointed had arrived, the young Princes, accompanied by, I presume, various members of the royal household, and their Governor, arrived. Altogether there might have been about a dozen or fourteen persons of both sexes present.

I pointed out the use and structure of most of the instruments. Some objects belonged to mechanical art, such as patent locks and tools; a few were related to the Fine Arts.

The whole party seemed much pleased; the young Princes particularly took a great interest in them, whereat the General was highly gratified. Before his young pupils retired, I took the General aside and enquired whether it was consistent with their customs that I should present to each of his two pupils one of the various (but in a pecuniary sense trifling) articles which they had examined. I was glad to find that I might be permitted to leave behind me two little souvenirs of a most agreeable day.

The whole party, with the exception of General de Salluce, had now retired. We walked up and down the room together for some time, conversing upon the success of the meeting. My excellent friend was justly delighted with the intelligent enquiries made by his pupils.

I thought I now perceived a favourable opportunity of ascertaining the cause of the Queen's absence.

After some kind expression towards me, I suddenly stopped, / and, looking enquiringly into his countenance, said, 'Now, General, just before this very agreeable party met you went to invite the Queen, and you returned, and then told me the *official*. Now pray do tell me the *real*.'

The surprise of the General was certainly great, but, with a most agreeable smile, he immediately consented.

It appears that its history was thus. The General went to the Queen's apartments and asked, through her lord-in-waiting, to be permitted to see her Majesty. This request was immediately granted. The General then informed the Queen that amongst the things her sons were going to see were several which might, perhaps, interest her Majesty. The Queen said she would accompany her sons, and then directed her own lord-in-waiting to go and ask the King's permission.

Accordingly the Queen's lord-in-waiting went to the King's apartments, and found that he was sitting in Council. He proceeded to the ante-room of the Council-chamber, and there found the King's lord-in-waiting, to whom he communicated his mission.

The King's lord-in-waiting then informed the Queen's lord-in-waiting that important news* had just arrived, and that a special council had been called; that of course he was ready to convey the Queen's message immediately, but he suggested whether, under these circumstances, the Queen would wish it.

The Queen's lord-in-waiting now returned to her Majesty for further instructions.

Of course the Queen, like a good wife, at once gave up the intention of accompanying her sons in their interview with the philosopher. I felt much regret at this disappointment. The Queen of Sardinia was the sister of the Grand Duke of Tuscany (Leopold II), from whom I had, many years before, / when under severe affliction from the loss of a large portion of my family, received the most kind and gratifying attention.

On my road to Turin I had passed a few days at Lyons, in order to examine the silk manufacture. I was specially anxious to see the loom

---

* The Syrian question.

in which that admirable specimen of fine art, the portrait of Jacquard, was woven. I passed many hours in watching its progress.

I possessed one copy, which had been kindly given to me by a friend; but as I had proposed to visit Florence after the meeting at Turin, I wished to procure another copy to present to the Grand Duke of Tuscany.

These beautiful productions were not made for sale; but, as a favour, I was allowed to purchase one of them.

Whilst the General was giving me this illustration of Court etiquette, it occurred to me that the silken engraving would be an appropriate offering to a lady.

I therefore again asked my friend whether, consistently with the usages of the country, I might be permitted to offer the engraving to the Queen.

The sudden change of his countenance from gay to grave was very remarkable. I feared I had proposed something of the most unusual kind. The General then slowly replied, 'I will take the King's pleasure on the subject.'

Two days after the General informed me that the King would give me an audience the next day, in order that I might ask permission to present the woven engraving to the Queen.

Accordingly, at the appointed hour, I went to the palace with the large cartoon-case containing the portrait of Jacquard.* On being admitted into the presence of the King, I placed the case upon a sofa, and, opening it carefully, unfolded / the woven portrait from a crowd of sheets of silver paper of the most ethereal lightness. I then placed it in his Majesty's hands. The King examined it minutely on both sides, enquired about its structure, and appeared much pleased at the sight.

I now went over to replace the engraving in its travelling-carriage. The instant it approached its paper case a multitude of sheets of silver paper were disturbed in their snug repose, and forthwith flew up into the air. I made many ineffectual efforts to catch these runaways. The King most condescendingly came to my assistance, took the portrait out of my hands, and endeavoured himself to replace it in its nest, whilst I was attempting to catch the flying covey.

But these volatile papers had no proper respect even for royalty. The quires of silver paper which had remained in the case now came out in all directions, whether to do honour to the King by rising to

* The dimensions were 2 ft. 8 in. by 2 ft. 2 in.

receive him, or to recall their flighty sisters to their deserted couch I know not; but somehow or other both the King and myself were on the floor upon our knees, having secured some few of the fallen angels, whilst a cloud of others, still on the wing, continually eluded our grasp.

At last I gave up the idea of grabbing at the flying sheets, and confined my attention to seizing on the fallen ones. Whilst still on my knees, I suddenly felt an obstacle presented to my right foot. On looking round I perceived that the heel of royalty had come into contact with the toe of philosophy.

A comic yet kindly smile beamed upon the countenance of the King, whilst an irrepressible but not irreverent one, lightened up my own.

The whole army of butterflies being at last captured, and / the engraving replaced, the King entered into a conversation with me upon various subjects.

The processes of wine-making then became the subject of conversation. I believe I may have observed incidentally in reply to some question, that my information was only derived from books, as I had not had an opportunity of seeing any of its processes. About a week after this, one of the officers of the household called upon me, and told me that the vintage of Raconigi, one of the King's beautiful domains, at about a dozen miles from Turin, would commence in the following week; that he was commanded by his Majesty, in case I should wish to examine the processes, to inform me of the circumstance, and to accompany me for the purpose of explaining them – a mission, he was so kind as to add, which would personally be highly gratifying to himself.

I willingly accepted this most agreeable proposition, and the day was fixed upon. At an early hour my friend was at my door in one of the royal carriages. The weather was magnificent, and we drove through a beautiful country.

On arriving at the vineyard we found several of the processes in full operation. Each in succession was explained; and after spending a most instructive morning, we found an excellent dinner prepared for us at the palace, where I had the pleasure of meeting General ——, who presided, and who had spent several years in England.

On our return in the evening I observed a dragoon apparently accompanying the carriage. At first I took it for granted that his road happened to be the same as ours; but after a mile or two had been passed over, seeing him still close to us, I enquired of my companion if he knew whither the soldier was going. It then appeared that he had been sent by the General as a complimentary escort. /

However gratified I felt by this attention, I still was quite uncomfortable at the idea of having a man galloping after our carriage for ten miles. I therefore appealed to my friend to suspend this unnecessary loss of *vis viva*. With some reluctance the dragoon was exempted from further attendance upon the philosopher.

Shortly before I left Turin, one of my Italian friends remarked, with evident feelings of pride and satisfaction, upon the attentions I had received from his sovereign. 'The King, he observed, has done three things for you, which are very unusual –

'He has shaken hands with you.

'He has asked you to sit down at an audience.

'He has permitted you to make a present to the Queen. This last,' he added, 'is the rarest of all.'

Two days before my departure from Turin, I had an audience, to take leave of his Majesty. The King enquired in what direction I intended to travel homeward. I mentioned my intention of taking the mail to Geneva, because it traversed a most remarkable suspension-bridge over a deep ravine. The span of this bridge, which is named, after the king, Pont Charles Albert, is six hundred French feet, and the depth of the chasm over which it is suspended is also six hundred French feet. The King immediately opened a drawer, and, taking out a small bronze medal, struck to celebrate the opening of the bridge, presented it to me.

I now took the opportunity of expressing to the King my gratitude for the many and kind attentions I had received from his subjects, and more especially for the honour he had himself recently done me by sending one of his ministers officially to convey to me his Majesty's high approbation of my conduct. /

The King then entered upon another course of enquiry, more immediately connected with his Government. I had on several occasions, when a favourable opportunity presented itself, drawn the King's attention to the doctrine of free trade – a subject on which he evidently felt a great desire to be informed. The questions put to me, though necessary for assisting the King to arrive at right conclusions, were of such a nature that I considered them confidential, and therefore forbear to relate them.

231

Two days after I started by the mail for Geneva. I shared the Coupé of the Malle Poste with the courier, a very intelligent officer. On mentioning my wish to see the celebrated bridge, he informed me that he was already aware of my wishes, and that he had received orders to detain the mail a quarter of an hour, that I might have a good opportunity of seeing it.

The scene which presented itself on my approach to the Pont Charles Albert was singularly grand. We had been driving for some time along a road skirting the edge of an immense chasm, six hundred and forty English feet in depth. The opposite side was hid from our view by a mist which hung over it. At the next bend in the road a portion of the bridge suddenly became visible to us. It appeared to spring from a massive pier on which the chains on our side of the ravine rested. The bridge itself was nearly level, and was visible for about three-quarters only of its length as it traversed the valley far beneath it. The termination of the ascending portion of the chains on the further pier, and that part of the bridge itself, were completely concealed by the mist. It really seemed like a bridge springing from a lofty cliff spanning the sea beneath and suspended on the distant clouds. When we had descended from the mail at the commencement, / we had directed the postilions to drive slowly across the bridge, then about a third of a mile distant from us.

We were singularly favoured by circumstances. We saw the carriage which had just left us apparently crossing the bridge, then penetrating into the clouds, and finally becoming entirely lost to our view. At the same time the dissolving mist in our own immediate neighbourhood began to allow us to perceive the depth of the valley beneath, and at last even the little wandering brook, which looked like a thread of silver at its bottom.

The sun now burst out from behind a range of clouds, which had obscured it. Its warm rays speedily dissipated the mist, illuminated the dark gulf at our own side, and discovered to us the mail on terra firma on the opposite side of the chasm waiting to convey us to our destination.

On our arrival at Annecy, my thoughtful companion informed me that the mail would wait five-and-forty minutes. He suggested, as I was not in good health, that I should immediately on my arrival get into bed, whilst he would order tea, or supper, or any refreshment I might prefer, and that he would be answerable for calling me at the proper time to enable me to get comfortably whatever I might require, and be ready to start again with the mail.

I have frequently attempted to assign in my own mind the reasons of the singularly favourable reception I met with from the King of Sardinia. The reputation arising from the Analytical Engine could scarcely have produced that effect. The position of a sovereign is a very exceptional one. He is surrounded by persons each of whom has always one or more objects to gain. It is scarcely within the limits of possibility / that he can have a real friend, or if he have that rarest commodity, that he can know the fact.

A certain amount of distrust must therefore almost always exist in his mind. But this habitual distrust applies less to foreigners than to his own subjects. The comet which passes through the thick atmosphere of a Court may be temporarily disturbed in its path though it may never revisit it again.

Perhaps the first element of my success was, that having been the victim of shyness in early life, I could sympathize with those who still suffered under that painful complaint.

Another reason may have been, that I never stated more than I really knew. This is, I believe, a very unusual practice in Courts of *every* kind; and when it happens to be obviously sincere, it commands great influence.

There might be yet another reason: it was well known that I had nothing to ask for – to expect – or to desire. /

CHAPTER XXV

RAILWAYS

Opening of Manchester and Liverpool Railway – Death of Mr Huskisson –
Plate-glass manufactory – Mode of separating engine from train – Broad-
gauge question – Experimental carriage – Measure the force of traction, the
vertical, lateral, and end shake of carriage, also its velocity by chronometer
– Fortunate escape from meeting on the same line Brunel on another engine
– Sailed across the Hanwell Viaduct in a waggon without steam – Meeting of
British Association at Newcastle – George Stephenson – Dr Lardner –
Suggestions for greater safety on railroads – George Stephenson's opinion of
the gauges – Railways at national exhibitions.

At the commencement of the railway system I naturally took a great
interest in the subject, from its bearings upon mechanisms as well as
upon political economy.

I accompanied Mr Woolryche Whitmore, the member for Bridgenorth, to Liverpool, at the opening of the Manchester and Liverpool
Railway. The morning previous to the opening, we met Mr Huskisson
at the Exchange, and my friend introduced me to him. The next day
the numerous trains started with their heavy loads of travellers. All
went on pleasantly until we reached Parkside, near Newton. During
the time the engines which drew us were taking in their water and their
fuel, many of the passengers got out and recognized their friends in
other trains.

At a certain signal all resumed their seats; but we had / not
proceeded a mile before the whole of our trains came to a standstill
without any ostensible cause. After some time spent in various
conjectures, a single engine almost flew past us on the other line of
rail, drawing with it the ornamental car which the Duke of
Wellington and other officials had so recently occupied. Instead of its
former numerous company it appeared to convey only two, or at
most three, persons; but the rapidity of its flight prevented any close
observation of the passengers.

A certain amount of alarm now began to pervade the trains, and
various conjectures were afloat of some serious accident. After a

while Mr Whitmore and myself got out of our carriage and hastened back towards the halting place. At a little distance before us, in the middle of the railway, stood the Duke of Wellington, Sir Robert Peel, and the Boroughreeve of Manchester, discussing the course to be pursued in consequence of the dreadful accident which had befallen Mr Huskisson,[a] whom I had seen but a few minutes before standing at the door of the carriage conversing with the Duke of Wellington. The Duke was anxious that the whole party should return to Liverpool; but the chief officer of Manchester pressed upon them the necessity of continuing the journey, stating that if it were given up he could not be answerable for the safety of the town.

It was at last mournfully resolved to continue our course to Manchester, where a luncheon had been prepared for us; but to give up all the ceremonial, and to return as soon as we could to Liverpool.

For several miles before we reached our destination the sides of the railroad were crowded by a highly excited populace shouting and yelling. I feared each moment that some still greater sacrifice of life might occur from the people / madly attempting to stop by their feeble arms the momentum of our enormous trains.

Having rapidly taken what refreshment was necessary, we waited with anxiety for our trains; but hour after hour passed away before they were able to start. The cause of this delay arose thus. The Duke of Wellington was the guest of the Earl of Wilton, the nearest station to whose residence was almost halfway between Manchester and Liverpool. A train therefore was ordered to convey the party to Heaton House. Unfortunately, our engines had necessarily gone a considerable distance upon that line to get their supply of water, and were thus cut off by the train conveying the Duke, from returning direct to Manchester.

There was not yet at this early period of railway history any sidings to allow of a passage, or any crossing to enable the engines to get upon the other line of rails. Under these circumstances the drivers took the shortest course open to them. Having taken in their water, they pushed on as fast as they could to a crossing at a short distance from Liverpool. They backed into the other line of rails, and thus returned to Manchester to pick up their trains.

In the meantime the vague rumour of some great disaster had reached

---

[a] William Huskisson M.P. was run over and killed by Stephenson's Rocket at the opening of the Manchester and Liverpool Railway, 15 September, 1830.

Liverpool. Thousands of persons, many of whom had friends and relatives in the excursion trains, were congregated on the bridges and at the railway station, anxious to learn news of their friends and relatives.

About five o'clock in the evening they perceived at a distance half-a-dozen engines without any carriages, rushing furiously towards them – suddenly checking their speed – then backing into the other line of rail – again flying away towards Manchester, without giving any signs or explanation of the mystery in which many of them were so deeply interested. /

It is difficult to estimate the amount of anxiety and misery which was thus unwillingly but inevitably caused amongst all those who had friends, connections, or relatives in the missing trains.

When these engines returned to Manchester, our trains were unfortunately connected together, and three engines were attached to the front of each group of three trains.

This arrangement considerably diminished their joint power of traction. But another source of delay arose: the couplings which were strong enough when connecting an engine and its train were not sufficiently strong when three engines were coupled together. The consequence was that there were frequent fractures of our couplings and thus great delays arose.

About half-past eight in the evening I reached the great building in which we were to have dined. Its tables were half filled with separate groups of three or four people each, who being strangers in Liverpool, had no other resource than to use it as a kind of coffee-room in which to get a hasty meal, and retire.

The next morning I went over to see the plate-glass manufactory at about ten miles from Liverpool.

On my arrival I found, to my great disappointment, that there were orders that nobody should be admitted on that day, as the Duke of Wellington and a large party were coming over from Lord Wilton's. This was the only day at my disposal, and it wanted nearly an hour to the time appointed: so I asked to be permitted to see the works, promising to retire as soon as the Earl of Wilton's party arrived. I added incidentally that I was not entirely unknown to the Duke of Wellington.

On the arrival of the party I quietly made my retreat unobserved, / and had just entered the carriage which had conveyed me from Liverpool, when a messenger arrived with the Duke's compliments, hoping that I would join his party. I willingly accepted the invitation; the Duke presented me to each of his friends, and I had the advantage of having another survey of the works. This was my first acquaintance with the late Lady Wilton, who afterwards called on me with the Duke of Wellington, and put that sagacious question relative to the Difference Engine which I have mentioned in another part of this volume. Amongst the party were Mr and Mrs Arbuthnot, with the former of whom I afterwards had several interesting discussions relative to subjects connected with the ninth 'Bridgewater Treatise'.

A few days after, I met at dinner a large party at the house of one of the great Liverpool merchants. Amongst them were several officers of the new railway, and almost all the party were more or less interested in its success.

In these circumstances the conversation very naturally turned upon the new mode of locomotion. Its various difficulties and dangers were suggested and discussed. Amongst others, it was observed that obstacles might be placed upon the rail, either accidentally or by design, which might produce expensive and fatal effects.

To prevent the occurrence of these evils, I suggested two remedies.

1. That every engine should have just in advance of each of its front wheels a powerful framing, supporting a strong piece of plate-iron, descending within an inch or two of the upper face of the rail. These iron plates should be fixed at an angle of 45° with the line of rail, and also at the same angle with respect to the horizon. Their shape would be something like that of ploughshares, and their effect would / be to pitch any obstacle obliquely off the rail unless its heavier portion were between the rails.

Some time after, a strong vertical bar of iron was placed in front of the wheels of every engine. The objection to this is, that it has a tendency to throw the obstacle straight forward upon another part of the rail.

2. The second suggestion I made, was to place in front of each engine a strong leather apron attached to a powerful iron bar, projecting five or six feet in front of the engine and about a foot above the ballast. The effect of this would be, that any animal straying over the railway would be pitched into this apron, probably having its legs broken, but forming no impediment to the progress of the train.

I have been informed that this contrivance has been adopted in America, where the railroads, being unenclosed, are subject to frequent obstruction from cattle. If used on enclosed roads, it still might occasionally save the lives of incautious persons, although possibly at the expense of broken limbs.

237

Another question discussed at this party was, whether, if an engine went off the rail, it would be possible to separate it from the train before it had dragged the latter after it. I took out my pencil and sketched upon a card a simple method of accomplishing that object. It passed round the table, and one of the party suggested that I should communicate the plan to the directors of the railway.

My answer was, that having a great wish to diminish the dangers of this new mode of travelling, I declined making any such communication to them; for, I added, unless these directors are quite unlike all of whom I have had any experience, I can foresee the inevitable result of such a communication. /

It might take me some time and trouble to consider the best way of carrying out the principle and to make the necessary drawings. Some time after I have placed these in the hands of the company, I shall receive a very pretty letter from the secretary, thanking me in the most flattering terms for the highly ingenious plan I have placed in their hands, but regretting that their engineer finds certain practical difficulties in the way.

Now, if the same company had taken the advice of some eminent engineer, to whom they would have to pay a large fee, no practical difficulties would ever be found to prevent its trial.

It was evident from the remarks of several of the party that I had pointed out the most probable result of any such communication.

It is possible that some report of this plan subsequently reached the directors; for about six months after, I received from an officer of the railway company a letter, asking my assistance upon this identical point. I sent them my sketch and all the information I had subsequently acquired on the subject. I received the stereotype reply I had anticipated, couched in the most courteous language; in short, quite a model letter for a young secretary to study.

Several better contrivances than mine were subsequently proposed; but experience seems to show that the whole train ought to be connected together as firmly as possible.

Not long after my return from Liverpool I found myself seated at dinner next to an elderly gentleman, an eminent London banker. The new system of railroads, of course, was the ordinary topic of conversation. Much had been said in its favour, but my neighbour did not appear to concur with the majority. At last I had an opportunity of asking his / opinion. 'Ah,' said the banker, 'I don't approve of this new mode of travelling. It will enable our clerks to plunder us, and then be

238

off to Liverpool on their way to America at the rate of *twenty* miles an hour.' I suggested that science might perhaps remedy this evil, and that possibly we might send lightning to outstrip the culprit's arrival at Liverpool, and thus render the railroad a sure means of arresting the thief. I had at the time I uttered those words no idea how soon they would be realized.

In 1838 and 1839 a discussion of considerable public importance had arisen respecting the Great Western Railway. Having an interest in that undertaking, it was the wish of Mr Brunel and the directors that I should state my own opinion upon the question. I felt that I could not speak with confidence without making certain experiments. The directors therefore lent me steam-power, and a second-class carriage to fit up with machinery of my own contrivance, and appointed one of their officers to accompany me, through whom I might give such directions as I deemed necessary during my experiments.

I removed the whole of the internal parts of the carriage. Through its bottom firm supports, fixed upon the framework below, passed up into the body of the carriage, and supported a long table entirely independent of its motions.

On this table slowly rolled sheets of paper, each a thousand feet long. Several inking pens traced curves on this paper, which expressed the following measures:

1. Force of traction.
2. Vertical shake of carriage at its middle.
3. Lateral   „
4. End   „
5, 6, and 7. The same shakes at the end of the carriage. /
8. The curve described upon the earth by the centre of the frame of the carriage.
9. A chronometer marked half seconds on the paper.

Above two miles of paper were thus covered. These experiments cost me about £300, and took up my own time, and that of all the people I was then employing, during five months.

I had previously travelled over most of the railways then existing in this country, in order to make notes of such facts as I could observe during my journeys.

The result of my experiments convinced me that the broad gauge was most convenient and safest for the public. It also enabled me fearlessly to assert that an immense array of experiments which were exhibited round the walls of the meeting-room by those who opposed the directors were made with an instrument which could not possibly measure the quantities proposed, and that the whole of them were worthless for the present argument. The production of the work of such an instrument could not fail to damage even a good cause.

On the discussion at the general meeting at the London Tavern, I made a statement of my own views, which was admitted at the time to have had considerable influence on the decision of the proprietors. Many years after I met a gentleman who told me he and a few other proprietors holding several thousand proxies came up from Liverpool intending to vote according to the weight of the arguments adduced. He informed me that he and all his friends decided their votes on hearing my statement. He then added, 'But for that speech, the broad gauge would not now exist in England.'

These experiments were not unaccompanied with danger. / I sometimes attached my carriage to a public train to convey me to the point where my experiments commenced, and I had frequently to interrupt their course, in order to run on to a siding to avoid a coming train.

I then asked to be allowed to make such experiments during the night when there were no trains; but Brunel told me it was too dangerous to be permitted, and that ballast-waggons, and others, carrying machinery and materials for the construction and completion of the railroad itself, were continually traversing various parts of the line at uncertain hours.

The soundness of this advice became evident a very short time after it was given. On arriving one morning at the terminus, the engine which had been promised for my experimental train was not ready, but another was provided instead. On further enquiry, I found that the 'North Star', the finest engine the company then possessed, had been placed at the end of the great polygonal building devoted to engines, in order that it might be ready for my service in the morning; but that, during the night, a train of twenty-five empty ballast-waggons, each containing two men, driven by an engine, both the driver and stoker of which were asleep, had passed right through the engine-house and damaged the 'North Star'.

Most fortunately, no accident happened to the men beyond a severe shaking. It ought, however, in extenuation of such neglect, to be observed that engine-drivers were at that period so few, and so thoroughly overworked, that such an occurrence was not surprising.

It then occurred to me, that being engaged on a work which was anything but profitable to myself, but which contributed to the safety of all travellers, I might, without impropriety, / avail myself of the repose of Sunday for advancing my measures. I therefore desired Brunel to ask for the director's permission. The next time I saw Brunel, he told me the directors did not like to give an official permission, but it was remarked that having put one of their own officers under my orders, I had already the power of travelling on whatever day I preferred.

I accordingly availed myself of the day on which, at that time, scarcely a single train or engine would be in motion upon it.

Upon one of these Sundays, which were, in fact, the only really safe days, I had proposed to investigate the effect of considerable additional weight. With this object, I had ordered three waggons laden with thirty tons of iron to be attached to my experimental carriage.

On my arrival at the terminus a few minutes before the time appointed, my aide-de-camp informed me that we were to travel on the north line. As this was an invasion of the usual regulations, I enquired very minutely into the authority on which it rested. Being satisfied on this point, I desired him to order my train out immediately. He returned shortly with the news that the fireman had neglected his duty, but that the engine would be ready in less than a quarter of an hour.

A messenger arrived soon after to inform me that the obstructions had been removed, and that I could now pass upon the south, which was the proper line.

I was looking at the departure of the only Sunday train, and conversing with the officer, who took much pains to assure me that there was no danger on whichever line we might travel; because, he observed, when that train had departed, there can be no engine except our own on either line until five o'clock in the evening. /

Whilst we were conversing together, my ears, which had become peculiarly sensitive to the distant sound of an engine, told me that one was approaching. I mentioned it to my railway official: he did not hear it, and said, 'Sir, it is impossible.' 'Whether it is possible or impossible,' I said, 'an engine *is* coming, and in a few minutes we shall see its steam.' The sound soon became evident to both, and our eyes were anxiously directed to the expected quarter. The white cloud of steam now faintly appeared in the distance; I soon perceived the line it occupied, and then turned to watch my companion's countenance. In a few moments more I saw it slightly change, and he said, 'It *is*, indeed, on the north line.'

Knowing that it would stop at the engine-house, I ran as fast as I could to that spot. I found a single engine, from which Brunel, covered with smoke, and blacks, had just descended. We shook hands, and I enquired what brought my friend here in such a plight. Brunel told me that he had posted from Bristol, to meet the only train at the furthest point of the rail then open, but had missed it.' Fortunately, he said, 'I found this engine with its fire up, so I ordered it out, and have driven it the whole way up at the rate of fifty miles an hour.'

I then told him that but for the merest accident I should have met him on the *same* line at the rate of forty miles, and that I had attached to my engine my experimental carriage, the three waggons with thirty tons of iron. I then enquired what course he would have pursued if he had perceived another engine meeting him upon his own line.

Brunel said, in such a case he should have put on all the steam he could command, with a view of driving off the opposite engine by the superior velocity of his own. /

If the concussion had occurred, the probability is, that Brunel's engine would have been knocked off the rail by the superior momentum of my train, and that my experimental carriage would have been buried under the iron contained in the waggons behind.

These rates of travelling were then unusual, but have now become common. The greatest speed which I have personally witnessed, occurred on the return of a train from Bristol, on the occasion of the floating of the 'Great Britain'. I was in a compartment, in conversation with three eminent engineers, when one of them remarked the unusual speed of the train: my neighbour on my left took out his watch, and noted the time of passage of the distance posts, whence it appeared that we were then travelling at the rate of seventy-eight miles an hour. The train was evidently on an incline, and we did not long sustain that dangerous velocity.

One very cold day I found Dr Lardner making experiments on the Great Western Railway. He was drawing a series of trucks with an engine travelling at known velocities. At certain intervals, a truck was detached from his train. The time occupied by this truck before it came to rest was the object to be noted. As Dr Lardner was short of assistants, I and my son offered to get into one of his trucks and note for him the time of coming to rest.

242

Our truck having been detached, it came to rest, and I had noted the time. After waiting a few minutes, I thought I perceived a slight motion, which continued, though slowly. It then occurred to me that this must arise from the effect of the wind, which was blowing strongly. On my way to the station, feeling very cold, I had purchased three yards of coarse blue woollen cloth, which I wound round my person. This I now unwound; we held it up as a sail, and gradually acquiring / greater velocity, finally reached and sailed across the whole of the Hanwell viaduct at a very fair pace.

The question of the best gauge for a system of railways is yet undecided. The present gauge of 4 ft. 8½ in. was the result of the accident that certain tram-roads adjacent to mines were of that width. When the wide gauge of the Great Western was suggested and carried out, there arose violent party movements for and against it. At the meeting of the British Association at Newcastle, in 1838, there were two sources of anxiety to the Council – the discussion of the question of steam navigation to America, and what was called 'the battle of the gauges'. Both these questions bore very strongly upon pecuniary interests, and were expected to be fiercely contested.

On the Council of the British Association, of course, the duty of nominating the presidents and vice-presidents of its various sections devolves. During the period in which I took an active part in that body, it was always a principle, of which I was ever the warm advocate, that we should select those officers from amongst the persons most distiguished for their eminence in their respective subjects, who were born in or connected with the district we visited.

In pursuance of this principle, I was deputed by the council to invite Mr George Stephenson to become the President of the Mechanical Section. In case he should decline it, I was then empowered to offer it to Mr Buddle, the eminent coal-viewer; and in case of these both declining, I was to propose it to the late Mr Bryan Donkin, of London, a native of that district, and connected with it by family ties.

On my arrival at Newcastle, I immediately called on George Stephenson, and represented to him the unanimous wish of the Council of the British Association. To my great / surprise, and to my still greater regret, I found that he at once declined the offer. All my powers of persuasion were exercised in vain. Knowing that the two great controverted questions to be discussed most probably formed the real obstacle, I mentioned them, and added that, as I should be one of his vice-presidents, I would, if he wished it, take the chair upon either or upon both the discussions of the gauges and of the Atlantic steam voyage, or upon any other occasion that might be agreeable or convenient to himself: I found him immovable in his decision. I made another attempt the next day, and renewed the expression of my own strong feeling, that we should pay respect and honour to the most distinguished men of the district we visited. I then told him the course I was instructed by the Council to pursue.

My next step was to apply to Mr Buddle. I need not repeat the arguments I employed: I was equally unsuccessful with each of the eminent men the Council had wished to honour. I therefore now went back to George Stephenson, told him of the failure of my efforts, and asked him, if he still persisted in declining the chair, would he do me the favour to be one of the vice-presidents as the Council had now no resource but to place me in the chair, which I had hoped would have been occupied by a more competent person.

To this latter application he kindly acceded; and I felt that, with the assistance of George Stephenson's and Mr Donkin's professional knowledge, and their presence by my side, I should be able to keep order in these dreaded discussions.

The day before the great discussion upon Atlantic Steam Navigation, I had a short conversation with Dr Lardner: I told him that in my opinion some of his views were hasty; / but that much stronger opinions had been assigned to him than those he had really expressed, and I recommended him to admit as much as he fairly could.

At the appointed hour the room was filled with an expectant and rather angry audience. Dr Lardner's beautiful apparatus for illustrating his views was before them, and the doctor commenced his statement. He was listened to with the greatest attention, and was really most judicious as well as very instructive. At the very moment which seemed to me the most favourable for it, he turned to the explanation of the instruments he proposed to employ, and having concluded his statement, it became my duty to invite discussion upon the question.

I did so in very few words, merely observing that several opinions had been attributed to Dr Lardner which he had never maintained, and that additional information had induced him candidly to admit that some of those doctrines which he had supported were erroneous. I added, that nothing was more injurious to the progress of truth than

244

to reproach any man who honestly admitted that he had been in error.

The discussion then commenced: it was continued with considerable energy, but with great temper; and after a long and instructive debate the assembled multitude separated. Some few who attended in expectation of a scene were sorely disappointed. As I was passing out, one of my acquaintance remarked, 'You have saved that —— —— Lardner': to which I replied, 'I have saved the British Association from a scandal.'

Before I terminate this chapter on railways, it will perhaps be expected by some of my readers that I should point out such measures as occur to me for rendering this universal system more safe. Since the long series of experiments I / made in 1839, I have had no experience either official or professional upon the subject. My opinions, therefore, must be taken only at what they are worth, and will probably be regarded as the dreams of an amateur. I have indeed formed very decided opinions upon certain measures relative to railroads; but my hesitation to make them public arises from the circumstance, that by publishing them I may possibly delay their adoption. It may happen, as is now happening to my system of distinguishing lighthouses from each other, and of night telegraphic communication between ships at sea – that although officially communicated to all the great maritime governments, and even publicly exhibited for months during the Exhibition of 1851, it will be allowed to go to sleep for years, until some official person, casually hearing of it, or perhaps re-inventing it, shall have *interest* with the higher powers to get it quietly adopted as his own invention. I have given, in a former page, a list of the self-registering apparatus I employed in my own experiments.

In studying the evidence given upon the enquiries into the various lamentable accidents which have occurred upon railways, I have been much struck by the discordance of that evidence as to the speed with which the engines were travelling when they took place.

Even the best and most unbiassed judgement ought not to be trusted when mechanical evidence can be produced. The first rule I propose is, that:

Every engine should have mechanical self-registering means of recording its own velocity at every instant during the whole course of its journey.

In my own experiments this was the first point I attended to. I took

245

a powerful spring clock, with a chronometer movement, which every half second lifted a peculiar pen, and left / a small dot of ink upon the paper, which was moving over a table with the velocity given to it by the wheels of the carriage.

Thus the comparative frequency of these dots indicated the rate of travelling at the time. But the instrument was susceptible of giving different scales of measurement. Thus it might be that only three inches of paper passed under the pen in every mile, or any greater length of paper, up to sixty feet per mile, might be ordered to pass under the paper during an equal space. Again, the number of dots per second could, if required, be altered.

The clock was broken four or five times during the earliest experiments. This arose from its being fixed upon the platform carrying the axles of the wheels. I then contrived a kind of parallel motion, by which I was enabled to support the clock upon the carriage-springs, and yet allow it to impress its dots upon the paper, which did not require that advantage. After this, the clock was never injured.

The power of regulating the length of paper for each mile was of great importance; it enabled me to examine, almost microscopically, the junctions of the rails. When a large scale of paper was allowed, every joining was marked upon the paper.

I find, on referring to my paper records, that on 3 March, 1839, the 'Atlas' engine drew my experimental carriage, with two other carriages attached behind it, from Maidenhead to Drayton, with its paper travelling only eleven feet for each mile of journey; whilst from Drayton to Slough, forty-four feet of paper passed under the pen during each mile of progress.

The inking pens at first gave me some trouble, but after successively discovering their various defects, and remedying / them at an expense of nearly £20, they performed their work satisfactorily. The information they gave might be fully relied upon.

We had an excellent illustration of this on one occasion when we were returning, late in the evening, from Maidenhead, after a hard day's work. The pitchy darkness of the night, which prevented us from seeing any objects external to our carriage, was strongly contrasted with the bright light of four argand lamps within it. I was accompanied by my eldest son, Mr Herschel Babbage, and three assistants. A roll of paper a thousand feet in length was slowly unwinding itself upon the long table extended before us, and winding

246

itself up on a corresponding roller at its other extremity. About a dozen pens connected with a bridge crossing the middle of the table were each marking its own independent curve gradually or by jumps, as the circumstances attending our railway course was dictating. The self-feeding pens, which the self-acting roller of blotting-paper continually followed, but never overtook, were quietly marking their inevitable courses. All had gone on well for a considerable time amidst perfect silence, if the steady pace of thirty miles an hour, the dogged automatic action of the material, and the muteness of the living machinery, admitted of such a term. Being myself entirely ignorant of our position upon the rail, I disturbed this busy repose by enquiring whether anyone knew where we were? To this question there was no reply. Each continued to watch in silence for the duties which his own department might at any moment require, but no such demands were made.

After some minutes, as I was watching the lengthening curves, I perceived a slight indication of our position on the railroad. I instantly looked at my son, and saw, by a faint / smile on his countenance, that he also perceived our situation on the line. I had scarcely glanced back at the growing curves upon the paper, to confirm my interpretation, when each of my three assistants at the same instant called out 'Thames Junction'.

At the period I speak of the double line of a small railway, called the Thames Junction, crossed the Great Western line on a level at between two and three miles from its terminus. The interruption caused certain jerks in several of our curves, which, having once noticed, it was impossible to mistake.

I would suggest that every engine should carry a spring clock, marking small equal intervals of time by means of a needle-point impinging upon paper, the speed of whose transit should be regulated by the speed of the engine. It might, perhaps, be desirable to have a differently formed mark to indicate each five minutes. Also, two or more studs on the driving-wheel should mark upon the same paper the number of its revolutions. Besides this, it might be imperative on the engine-driver to mark upon the paper a dot upon passing each of certain prescribed points upon the railway. This latter is not absolutely necessary, but may occasionally supply very valuable information.

The second point which I consider of importance is, that:

Between every engine and its train there should be interposed a dynamometer, that is, a powerful spring to measure the force exerted by the engine.

It may, perhaps, be objected that this would require a certain amount of movement between the engine and its train. A very small quantity would be sufficient, say half an inch, or less. The forces in action are so very large, that even a still smaller amount of motion than this might be sufficiently magnified. Its indications should be marked by / self-acting machinery governing points impinging upon the paper on which the velocity is marked.

Whenever any unusual resistance has opposed the progress of the train, it will thus be marked upon the paper. It will indicate in some measure the state of the road, and it will assuredly furnish valuable information in case an accident happens, and the train or the engine gets off the rails.

The third recommendation I have to make is:

That the curve described by the centre of the engine itself upon the plane of the railway should be laid down upon the paper.

Finding this a very important element, I caused a plate of hardened steel to be pressed by a strong spring against the inner edge of the rail. It was supported by a hinge upon a strong piece of timber descending from the platform supporting the carriage itself. The motion of this piece of steel, arising from the varying position of the wheels themselves upon the rail, was conveyed to a pen which tranferred to the paper the curve traversed by the centre of the carriage referred to the plane of the rail itself.

The contrivance and management of this portion of my apparatus was certainly the most difficult part of my task, and probably the most dangerous. I had several friendly cautions, but I knew the danger, and having examined its various causes, adopted means of counteracting its effect.

After a few trials we found out how to manage it, and although it often broke four or five times in the course of the day's work, the fracture inevitably occurred at the place intended for it, and my first notice of the fact often arose from the blow the fragment made when suddenly drawn by a strong rope up to the underside of the floor of our experimental carriage.

I have a very strong opinion that the adoption of such / mechanical registrations would add greatly to the security of railway travelling, because they would become the unerring record of facts, the incorruptible witnesses of the immediate antecedents of any catastrophe.

248

I have, however, little expectation of their adoption, unless directors can be convinced that the knowledge derived from them would, by pointing out incipient defects, and by acting as a check upon the vigilance of all their officers, considerably diminish the repairs and working expenses both of the engine and of the rail. Nor should I be much surprised even if they were pronounced impracticable, although they existed very nearly a quarter of a century ago.

The question of the gauges has long been settled. A small portion of broad gauge exists, but it is probable that it will ultimately be changed. The vast expense of converting the engines and the rolling stock for use on the narrower gauge presents the greatest obstacle.

It may, however, be interesting to learn the opinion of the father of railways at an early period of their progress. I have already mentioned the circumstances under which my acquaintance with George Stephenson began. They were favourable to that mutual confidence which immediately arose. I was naturally anxious to ascertain the effect of the existing experience upon his own mind, but I waited patiently until a favourable opportunity presented itself.

At a large public dinner, during the meeting of the British Association at Newcastle, I sat next to George Stephenson. It occurred to me that the desired opportunity had now arrived. I said little about railways until after the first glass of champagne. I mentioned several that I had travelled upon, and the conclusions I had drawn relative to the mechanical department. I then referred to the economy of / management, and pointed out one railway in which the accounts were so well managed, that I had been able to arrive at a testing point of an opinion I had formed from my own observations.

One great evil of the narrow gauge was, that when some trifling derangement in the engine occurred, which might be repaired at the expense of two or three shillings, it frequently became necessary to remove uninjured portions of the machine, in order to get at the fault; that the remaking the joints and replacing these parts thus temporarily removed, frequently led to an expense of several pounds.

The second glass of champagne now interrupted a conversation which was, I hope, equally agreeable to both, and was certainly very instructive for me. I felt that the fairest opportunity I could desire of ascertaining my friend's real opinion of the gauge had now arrived. Availing myself of the momentary pause after George Stephenson's glass was empty, I said:

249

'Now, Mr Stephenson, will you allow me to ask you to suppose for an instant that no railways whatever existed, and yet that you were in full possession of all that large amount of knowledge which you have derived from your own experience. Under such circumstances, if you were consulted respecting the gauge of a system of railways about to be inaugurated, would you advise the gauge of 4 feet 8½ inches?'

'Not exactly that gauge,' replied the creator of railroads; 'I would take a few inches more, but a very few.'

I was quite satisfied with this admission, though I confess it reminded me of the frail fair one who, when reproached by her immaculate friend with having had a child – an ecclesiastical licence not being first obtained – urged, as an extenuating circumstance, that it was a very small one. /

In this age of invention, it is difficult to predict the railroads of the future. Already it has been suggested to give up wheels and put carriages upon sledges. This would lower the centre of gravity considerably, and save the expense of wheels.[a] On the other hand, every carriage must have an apparatus to clean and grease the rails, and the wear and tear of these latter might overbalance the economy arising from abolishing wheels.

Again, short and much-frequented railways might be formed of a broad, continuous strap, always rolling on. At each station means must exist for taking up and putting down the passengers without stopping the rolling strap.

The exhaustion of air in a continuous tunnel was proposed many years ago for the purpose of sucking the trains along. This has recently been applied with success to the transmission of parcels and letters.

Possibly in the next International Exhibition a light railway might be employed within the building.*

1. A quick train to enable visitors to get rapidly from end to end, avoiding the crowd and saving time, say at the expense of a penny.

2. A very slow train passing along the most attractive line, and

---

* A gallery, elevated about seven feet, in the centre of each division of the new National Gallery, might be used either for a light railway, or for additional means of seeing the pictures on the walls.

[a] The proofs of *Passages from the life of a philosopher* (Buxton MSS 10–12, Museum of the History of Science, Oxford) include the following autograph addition: 'Drags might then grasp the rails on both sides and thus the velocity might be effectually checked with the greatest rapidity.'

occasionally stopping, to enable persons not capable of bearing the fatigue of pushing on foot through crowds.

If such railways were considered in the original design of the building, they might be made to interfere but little with the general public, and would bring in a considerable revenue to the concern.[a] /

---

[a] See 'Additions to the chapter on railroads', pp. 368–9.

A CHAPTER

ON

STREET NUISANCES.

[*Extracted from* "Passages in the Life of a Philosopher."]

BY

CHARLES BABBAGE, Esq.

THIRD EDITION.

LONDON:

LONGMAN, GREEN, LONGMAN, ROBERTS, & GREEN.

1864.

CHAPTER XXVI

STREET NUISANCES[a]

Various classes injured – Instruments of torture – Encouragers; servants, beer-shops, children, ladies of elastic virtue – Effects on the musical profession – Retaliation – Police themselves disturbed – Invalids distracted – Horses run away – Children run over – A cab-stand placed in the author's street attracts organs – Mobs shouting out his name – Threats to burn his house – Disturbed in the middle of the night when very ill – An average number of persons are always ill – Hence always disturbed – Abusive placards – Great difficulty of getting convictions – Got a case for the Queen's Bench – Found it useless – A dead sell – Another illustration – Musicians give false name and address – Get warrant for apprehension – They keep out of the way – Offenders not yet found and arrested by the police – Legitimate use of highways – An old lawyer's letter to 'The Times' – Proposed remedies; forbid entirely – Authorize police to seize the instrument and take it to the station – An association for prevention of street music proposed.

During the last ten years, the amount of street music has so greatly increased that it has now become a positive nuisance to a very considerable portion of the inhabitants of London. It robs the industrious man of his time; it annoys the musical man by its intolerable badness; it irritates the invalid; deprives the patient, who at great inconvenience has visited London for the best medical advice, of that repose which, under such circumstances, is essential for his recovery, and it destroys the time and the energies of all the intellectual classes of society by its continual interruptions of their pursuits. /

Instruments of torture permitted by the Government to be in daily and nightly use in the streets of London

Organs		Bagpipes
Brass bands		Accordions
Fiddles		Halfpenny whistles
Harps		Tom-toms
Harpsichords		Trumpets
Hurdy-gurdies	*The human*	Shouting out objects for sale
Flageolets	*voice in*	Religious canting
Drums	*various forms*	Psalm-singing

---

[a] *Editor's note:* This chapter of *Passages from the life of a philosopher* was published in advance of the book as a pamphlet *A chapter on street nuisances*.

253

I have very frequently been disturbed by such music after eleven and even after twelve o'clock at night. Upon one occasion a brass band played, with but few and short intermissions, for five hours.

Encouragers of street music

Tavern-keepers	Ladies of doubtful virtue
Public-houses	
Gin-shops	Occasionally titled ladies;
Beer-houses	but these are almost
Coffee-shops	invariably of recent
Servants	elevation, and deficient in
Children	that taste which their sex
Visitors from the country	usually possess.

The habit of frequenting public-houses, and the amount of intoxication, is much augmented by these means. It therefore finds support from the whole body of licensed victuallers, and from all those who are interested, as the proprietors of public-houses.

The great encouragers of street music belong chiefly to the lower classes of society. Of these, the frequenters of public-houses and beer-shops patronize the worst and the most / noisy kinds of music. The proprietors of such establishments find it a very successful means of attracting customers. Music is kept up for a longer time, and at later hours, before the public-house, than under any other circumstances. It not unfrequently gives rise to a dance by little ragged urchins, and sometimes by half-intoxicated men, who occasionally accompany the noise with their own discordant voices.

Servants and children are great admirers of street music; also people from the country, who, coming up to town for a short time, often encourage it.

Another class who are great supporters of street music, consists of ladies of elastic virtue and cosmopolitan tendencies, to whom it affords a decent excuse for displaying their fascinations at their own open windows. Most ladies resident in London are aware of this peculiarity, but occasionally some few to whom it is not known have found very unpleasant inferences drawn, in consequence of thus gratifying their musical taste.

Musicians	*Instruments*
Italians	Organs
Germans	Brass bands
Natives of India	Tom-toms
English	Brass bands, fiddles, etc.
The lowest class of clubs	Bands with double drum

The most numerous of these classes, the organ-grinders, are natives of Italy, chiefly from the mountainous district, whose language is a rude *patois*, and who are entirely unacquainted with any other. It is said that there are above a thousand of these foreigners usually in London employed in tormenting the natives. They mostly reside in / the neighbourhood of Saffron Hill, and are, of course, from their ignorance of any other language than their own, entirely in the hands of their padrones. One of these, a most persevering intruder with his organ, gave me a false address. Having ascertained the real address, he was sought for by the police for above a fortnight, but not discovered. His *padrone* becoming aware of his being '*wanted*', sent him on a country circuit. I once met, within a few miles of the Land's End, one of these fellows whom I had frequently sent away from my own street.

The amount of interruption from street music, and from other occasional noises, varies with the nature and the habits of its victims. Those whose minds are entirely unoccupied receive it with satisfaction, as filling up the vacuum of time. Those whose thoughts are chiefly occupied with frivolous pursuits or with any other pursuits requiring but little attention from the reasoning or the reflective powers, readily attend to occasional street music. Those who possess an impaired bodily frame, and whose misery might be alleviated by *good* music at proper intervals, are absolutely driven to distraction by the vile and discordant music of the streets waking them, at all hours, in the midst of that temporary repose so necessary for confirmed invalids.

By professional musicians its effects are most severely felt. It interrupts them in their own studies, and entirely destroys the value of the instructions they are giving their domestic pupils. When they leave their own house to give lessons to their employers, the '*infernal*' organ still pursues them. Their Belgravian employer is obliged, at every lesson, to bribe the itinerant miscreant to desist – his charge for this act of mercy being from a shilling to half-a-crown for each lesson. /

It is, however, right to hint to the members of the musical profession, that their immediate neighbours do not quite so much enjoy even the most exquisite professional music when filtered through brick walls, or transmitted circuitously and partially through open windows into the houses of their neighbours. I know of no remedy to propose for the benefit of the latter class, but I think that a proper self-respect should induce the professional musician himself to close his windows, and even to suffer the inconvenience of heat, rather than permanently annoy his neighbours.

The law of retaliation, which is only justified when other arguments fail, was curiously put in force in a case which was brought under my notice a few years ago. An artist of considerable eminence, who resided in the west end of London, had for many a year pursued his own undisturbed and undisturbing studies, when one fine morning his professional studies were interrupted by the continuous sound of music transmitted through the wall from his neighbour's house.

Finding the noise continuous and his interruption complete, he rang for his servant, and putting his maul into the man's hand desired him to continue knocking against the wall from whence the disturbance proceeded until he returned from a walk in the park. He added that he should probably be absent for an hour, and that if any person called and wished to see him, he should be at home at the end of that time.

On his return he was informed that the new tenant of the adjacent house had called during his absence, and that on being informed of the hour of his master's return, he had expressed his intention of calling again. A short time after this the new tenant of the adjacent house was introduced. He apologized for this visit to a stranger, but said that during the last hour he had been annoyed by a most extraordinary knocking / against the wall, which entirely interrupted his professional pursuits.

To this the artist replied in almost precisely the same words, that during the previous hour he had been annoyed by a most extraordinary and unusual sound which entirely interrupted *his* professional pursuits. After some discussion it was settled that the piano should be removed to the opposite wall, and that it should be covered with a stratum of blankets.

This arrangement went on for a few months; but the pupils and their relatives disapproving of a dumb piano gradually left the professor, who found it desirable to give up the house and retire to a more music-tolerating neighbourhood. In this case the evil was equal on both sides, and it was reasonable that the newcomer should retire.

In my own case it has often been suggested to me to retaliate; and as many of my interruptions have been *intentional*, that course might be justifiable. But as they have been confined to one or two of the lowest persons in the neighbourhood, I thought it not right to disturb my more respectable neighbours. The means at my command for producing the most hideously discordant noises are ample, having a considerable collection of shrill organ pipes, with appropriate bellows, and an indefatigable steam-engine ever ready to work them whilst I might be 'taking a walk in the park'. I hope by the timely amendment of the law no person may be driven to practise what it refuses to prevent, and thus test the laws of the country by the *reductio ad absurdum*.

It is difficult to estimate the misery inflicted upon thousands of persons, and the absolute pecuniary penalty imposed upon multitudes of intellectual workers by the loss of their time, destroyed by organ-grinders and other similar nuisances.

I have witnessed much and suffered more; many communications / on the subject have reached me, and I fear that I may appear to have neglected several of them. I hope, however, that the great sacrifice of my own time, which has been forced upon me in order to secure the remainder, may be accepted as my excuse. I will now mention some few of the results.

Even policemen have frequently told me that organs are a great nuisance to them personally. A large number of the police are constantly on night duty, and of course these can only get their sleep during the day. On such occasions their rest is constantly broken by the nuisance of street music.

A lady, the wife of an officer on half-pay, writes to me, stating her own sad case. Her husband, suffering under a painfully nervous affection, is brought up to London for the benefit of medical advice. Under these circumstances a sensible improvement takes place, but it requires time and constant attention to advance the cure. In order to profit by the eminent skill which London supplies, the lady and her husband, at considerable sacrifice, take a very small house in a very quiet little square. Unfortunately, the organ-grinders had possession of it, and no entreaties would banish them. The irritation produced on the invalid was frightful, and I feel it some relief not to have known its almost inevitable termination.

Various accidents occur as the consequence of street music. It occasionally happens that horses are frightened, and perhaps their riders thrown; that carriages are run away with, and their occupiers dreadfully alarmed and possibly even bruised.

The following casualties were reported, about three years ago, in most of the daily newspapers:

SHOCKING OCCURENCE – SIX CHILDREN RUN OVER AND MUTILATED – Yesterday afternoon, shortly after four o'clock, a German band, whilst / performing in the Old St Pancras Road, was the cause of a most dreadful accident. At the time mentioned, the band referred to was playing at the corner of Aldenham Terrace, when a man named Charles Field was driving one of Atcherley's (the horse-slaughterer's) carts down Aldenham Street. At the end of Aldenham Street there is a great declivity into the St Pancras Road, and just as the cart was turning it, laden with a dead horse, the big drum was beaten with extraordinary violence. A cart was standing on the opposite side of the road, to avoid which a short turn on the part of the driver of Atcherley's cart was necessary. The sudden beating of the drum caused the horse to take fright, and the driver being pitched head foremost from his seat, caused him to lose control over the animal he was driving, which dashed in amongst the children and others who were standing in the road listening to the music, knocking them down right and left. When the consternation created by the occurrence had subsided, no less than six poor children were found lying on the ground in a helpless condition, the vehicle having passed over some part of their persons. They were conveyed as fast as possible into the adjacent surgery of Dr Sutherin, of 28, Aldenham Terrace, who, with his assistant, promptly attended upon them.

William Hill, aged nine, of 34, Stanmore Terrace, who had sustained fractured ribs and other injuries; and

Charles Harwood, aged eleven years, of 4, Clarendon Square, with fracture of the left arm and groin, as well as right leg, caused by the vehicle passing over them, were removed, by direction of Dr Sutherin, to University College Hospital.

The other sufferers are Robert Thwaites, of 2, St Pancras Square, aged seven years, injury to leg and one of his feet;

James Gunn, 34, Stanmore Street, crushed toes;

William Young, 8, Percy Terrace, aged six years, contusion to head and face; and

A child, name unknown, considerably injured.

The persons who witnessed the occurrence do not attribute any blame to the driver; but as soon as it took place the German band were off with as little delay as possible. (*Daily Telegraph*, 3 October, 1861)

If this sad accident had fortunately happened in Belgravia, there can be little doubt that the law would have been altered, in order to prevent the recurrence of such frightful misery.

No attempt, however, has yet been made to remove the cause; and I have myself more recently seen a German brass band playing in a very narrow, crowded street, close to the / Bank of England, at three o'clock in the afternoon, making it difficult to pass, as well as dangerous to one's pocket.

On another occasion, at two o'clock, a German band was playing in Piccadilly, at that crowded part, the Circus. In both instances the police were looking on, and seemed to enjoy the music they were not directed to stop.

I have obtained, in my *own* country, an unenviable celebrity, not by anything I have done, but simply by a determined resistance to the tyranny of the lowest mob, whose love, not of music, but of the most discordant noises, is so great that it insists upon enjoying it at all hours and in every street. It may therefore be expected that I should in this volume state at least the outline of my own case.

I claim no merit for this resistance; although I am quite aware that I am fighting the battle of every one of my countrymen who gains his subsistence by his intellectual labour. The simple reason for the course I have taken is, that however disagreeable it has been, it would have been still more painful to have given up a great and cherished object, already fully within my reach. I have been compelled individually to resist this tyranny of the lowest mob, because the Government itself is notoriously afraid to face it.

On a careful retrospect of the last dozen years of my life, I have arrived at the conclusion that I speak within limit when I state that one-fourth part of my working power has been destroyed by the nuisance against which I have protested. Twenty-five per cent is rather too large an additional income tax upon the brain of the intellectual workers of this country, to be levied by permission of the Government, and squandered upon its most worthless classes.

The effect of a *uniform* and *continuous* sound, in distracting the attention or in disturbing intellectual pursuits, is almost / insensible. Those who reside near a waterfall – even Niagara – have their organs soon seasoned and adapted to its monotony. It is the *change* from quietness to noise, or from one kind of noise to another, which instantly distracts the attention. It would be equally distracted by the reverse – by the sudden change from the hum of the busy world to the stillness of the desert.

259

The injurious effect of noisy interruptions upon our attention also varies with the nature of the investigations upon which we are engaged. If they are of a kind requiring but a very small amount of intellectual effort, as, for instance, the routine of a public office, they will be little felt. If, on the other hand, those subjects are of such a character as to require the highest efforts of the thinker, then their examination is interrupted by the slightest change in the surrounding circumstances.

When the work to be done is proportioned to the powers of the mind engaged upon it, the painful effect of interruption is felt as deeply by the least intellectual as by the most highly gifted. The condition which determines the maximum of interruption is – that the mind disturbed, however moderate its powers, shall be working up to its full stretch.

Finding, many years ago, the increasing interruption of my pursuits from street music, as it is now tolerated, I determined to endeavour to get rid of it by putting in force our imperfect law, as far it goes. I soon found how very imperfect it is.

The first step is to require the performer to desist, and to assign illness or other sufficient reason for the request. If a female servant is sent on this mission it is quite useless. The organ-player is scarcely ever acquainted with more than four or five words of our language: but these always the most / vulgar, the most offensive, and the most insulting. If a manservant is sent, the Italians are often very insolent, and constantly refuse to depart. But there are multitudes of sufferers who are ill and are in lodgings, and have no servant to send. Besides, the servants must occasionally be absent, being sent by their employers on their various duties.

The principle on which I proposed to act is, whenever it can be fully carried out, usually very effective. It was simply this – to make it more unprofitable to the offender to do the wrong than the right.

Whenever, therefore, an itinerant musician disturbed me, I immediately sent out, or went out myself, to warn him away. At first this was not successful; but after summoning and convicting a few, they found out that their precious time was wasted, and most of them deserted the immediate neighbourhood. This would have succeeded had the offenders been few in number; but their name is legion: upwards of a thousand being constantly in London, besides those on their circuit in the provinces.

It was not, however, the interest of those who deserted my station to inform their countrymen of its barrenness; consequently, the freshly imported had each to gain his own experience at the expense of his own and of my time. Perhaps I might have succeeded at last in banishing the Italian nuisance from the neighbourhood of my residence; but various other native professors of the art of tormenting with discords increased as the licence of these Italian itinerants was encouraged. Another event, however, occurred, which added much more seriously to my difficulty.

Many years before I had purchased a house in a very quiet locality, with an extensive plot of land, on part of which I had erected workshops and offices, in which I might carry / on the experiments and make the drawings necessary for the construction of the Analytical Engine. Several years ago the quiet street in which I resided was invaded by a hackney-coach stand. I, in common with most of the inhabitants, remonstrated and protested against this invasion of our comfort and this destruction of the value of our property. Our remonstrance was ineffectual: the hackney-coach stand was established.

The immediate consequence was obvious. The most respectable tradesmen, with some of whom I had dealt for five-and-twenty years, saw the ruin which was approaching, and, wisely making a first sacrifice, at once left their deteriorated property as soon as they could find for it a purchaser. The neighbourhood became changed: coffee-shops, beer-shops, and lodging-houses filled the adjacent small streets. The character of the new population may be inferred from the taste they exhibit for the noisiest and most discordant music.

I have looked in vain for any public advantage to justify this heavy injury to private property. It will scarcely be believed that another hackney-coach stand actually exists within two hundred yards,* namely, that in Paddington Street, which has a very large space unoccupied by any houses on either side of the street, and which had frequently cabs on it plying for hire during the whole night.

In endeavouring to put in force the existing law, imperfect as it is, I have met with sundry small inconveniences which a cabinet minister might perhaps think trivial, but which, in a slight degree, try the temper even of a philosopher. /

* The distance of the most eastern cab on the stand in Dorset Street from the spot in Paddington Street, on which cabs might stand without being opposite any houses, is in reality less than 140 yards. I am not aware of any two cab-stands placed so near each other as those in question.

Some of my neighbours have derived great pleasure from inviting musicians, of various tastes and countries, to play before my windows, probably with the pacific view of ascertaining whether there are not some kinds of instruments which we might both approve. This has repeatedly failed, even with the accompaniment of the human voice divine, from the lips of little shoeless children, urged on by their ragged parents to join in a chorus rather disrespectful to their philosophic neighbour.

The enthusiasm of the performer, excited by such applause, has occasionally permitted him to dwell too long upon the already forbidden notes, and I have been obliged to find a policeman, to ascertain the residence of the offender. In the meantime the crowd of young children, urged on by their parents, and backed at a judicious distance by a set of vagabonds, forms quite a noisy mob, following me as I pass along, and shouting out rather uncomplimentary epithets. When I turn round and survey my illustrious tail, it stops; if I move towards it, it recedes: the elder branches are then quiet – sometimes they even retire, wishing perhaps to avoid my future recognition. The instant I turn, the shouting and the abuse are resumed, and the mob again follow at a respectful distance. The usual result is that the deluded musicians find themselves left in the lurch at the police court by their enthusiastic encouragers, and have to pay a heavier fine for having contributed to collect this unruly and ungenerous mob.

Such occurrences have unfortunately been by no means rare. In one case there were certainly above a hundred persons, consisting of men, women, and boys, with multitudes of young children, who followed me through the streets before I could find a policeman. To such an extent has this annoyance / of shouting out my name, without or with insulting epithets, been carried, that I can truly affirm, unless I am detained at home by illness, no week ever passes without many instances of it.

The police tell me that the children, 'who are put up to the trick by their parents', belong chiefly to several ragged-schools in my neighbourhood. I have myself repeatedly traced numbers of them into the Portman Chapel School, in East Street. In one instance I went into that school and made a formal complaint to the teacher, who expressed great regret for it, and requested me, if I could see any of the offenders, to point them out; but amongst the number of children then present I was unable to identify the offenders.

The insults arising from boys, set on by their parents, and from other older, and therefore less pardonable offenders, shouting out my name under my windows, or as I pass along the streets, and even in the middle of the night, are of almost constant occurrence. Of course, I always appear to take no notice of such circumstances. Only a few days ago, whilst I was engaged upon the present chapter, I had occasion to pass down Manchester Street: when I was about halfway down, I heard from that end of the street I had left, loud and repeated cries of 'Stop thief'. I naturally turned round, when I saw two young fellows at the corner, who repeated the cry twice, as loudly as they could, and then ran, as hard as they were able, round the corner out of my sight. There could be no mistake that this was intended to annoy me, because it happened at a time when there was no person except myself in the upper part of the street.

Another source of annoyance, fortunately only of a very limited amount, arises from a perverse disposition of some of my neighbours, who, in two or three instances, have gone to / the expense of purchasing worn-out or damaged wind instruments, which they are incapable of playing, but on which they produced a discordant noise for the purpose of annoying me. One of these appearing at the police court as a witness for an organ-grinder, was questioned by the magistrate, and informed that he would render himself liable to an indictment by the continuance of such conduct. Another foolish young fellow purchased a wind instrument with a hole in it, with which he made discordant noises purposely to annoy me. Travelling in a third-class carriage to Deptford, he described, with great zest to the person sitting opposite to him, the instrument, its price, and the use he made of it. The listener to this confidence was one of the best of my own draftsmen, who was quite as much disturbed by the street music as myself. The police were made acquainted with the fact, and I believe still have, from time to time, their eyes upon the young vagabond.

Another wilful disturber of my quiet, was a workman inhabiting an attic in a street which overlooked my garden. When he returned daily to his dinner, this fellow, possessing a penny tin whistle, opened his window, and leaning out of it, blew his shrill instrument in the direction of my garden for about half-an-hour. I simply noted the fact in a memorandum book, and then employed the time he thought he was destroying, in taking my daily exercise, or in any other outdoor mission my pursuits required. After a perseverance in this course during many months, he discontinued the annoyance, but for what reason I never knew.

263

At an early period when I was putting the law in force, as far as I could, for the prevention of this destruction of my time, I received constantly anonymous letters, advising, and even threatening me with all sorts of evils, such as / destruction of my property, burning my house, injury to myself. I was very often addressed in the streets with similar threats. On one occasion, when I was returning home from an affair with a mob whom the police had just dispersed, I met, close to my own door, a man, who, addressing me, said, 'You deserve to have your house burnt, and yourself in it, and I will do it for you, you old villain.' I aked him if he had any objection to give me his address. Of course he refused. I then followed him at a short distance, looking out for a policeman. Whenever he saw one at a distance he turned rapidly up the next street; this chase continued above half-an-hour; he was then joined by a companion, an ill-looking fellow. They still continued to turn off into another street whenever a constable became visible in the distance. At last we saw a great crowd, into which they both rushed, and further pursuit became impossible.

I will not describe the smaller evils of dead cats, and other offensive materials, thrown down my area; of windows from time to time purposely broken, or from occasional blows from stones projected by unseen hands.

The last annoyance I shall mention, occurred in the month of December of the past year. I had been suffering considerably from ill-health, and it became necessary that I should undergo a painful surgical operation. Late in the night of that day, I got into a refreshing sleep, when at one o'clock in the morning I was suddenly awakened by the crash of a brass band, which continued playing whilst I was unable to move, and was compelled passively to submit to the tormentors.

By a most singular accident, many weeks after, I became possessed of evidence, that the musicians held a consultation in Manchester Square about going to the top of the street to wake me up. I am glad, however, to add, for the credit of / human nature, that *one* of the party advised them not to do it, and that he himself immediately left them.

It has been found, upon undoubted authority, by returns from benefit societies, that in London, about 4·72 persons per cent are constantly ill. This approximation may be fairly assumed as the nearest yet attained for the population of London. It follows, therefore, that about forty-seven out of every thousand inhabitants are always ill. The number of persons per house varies in different parts. In my own district it averages ten to each house; in a neighbouring district the average is thirteen per house.

In Manchester Street, which faces my own residence, there are fifty-six houses. This, allowing the above average of ill-health, will show that about twenty-six persons are usually ill in that street. Now the annoyance from street music is by no means confined to the performers in the street in which a house is situated. In my own case, there are portions of five other streets in which street music constantly interrupts me in my pursuits. If the portions of these five streets are considered to be only equal in population to that of Manchester Street, it will appear that upwards of fifty people who are ill, are constantly disturbed by the same noises which so frequently interrupt my own pursuits.

The misery inflicted upon those who are really ill is far greater than that which arises from the mere destruction of time, however valuable. A friend of mine, himself an excellent magistrate, suffering under a severe and fatal complaint, was almost driven to distraction during the last six months of his painful existence, by the constant occurrence of the organ nuisance, which he was entirely unable to stop.

I have at times made attempts to register the number of such interruptions in my pursuits; but these have been very / partial and imperfect. I find by some notes, that during about eighty days, I registered one hundred and sixty-five instances, the greater part of which I went out myself to put a stop to the nuisance. In several of these cases my whole day's work was destroyed, for they frequently occurred at times when I was giving instruction to my workmen relative to some of the most difficult parts of the Analytical Engine.

At one period after I had succeeded in getting two or three convictions, some of my neighbours put themselves to the expense of having large placards printed, in which they abused me for having put the law in force against the destroyers of my time. These placards they stuck up in the windows of their little shops, at intervals from Edgware Road to Tottenham Court Road. Some of them attempted verse and thought it poetry; though the only part really imaginative was their prose statements.

Unfortunately for my comfort, a few years ago, Mr X——, one of the magistrates of Marylebone Office, was succeeded by Mr Y——.

Now the taste of the new magistrate, like that of his predecessor, was favourable to the Italian organ: his predecessor might, however, have been excused, as he was deaf. Possibly Mr Y—— thinks that all Italian music is high art, and therefore ought to be encouraged.

I soon discovered that it was useless to bring any musical offender before him, and I had for some time to endure the most intolerable interruption of my pursuits.

Upon one occasion, when I had summoned an organ-grinder before him, his decision was, in my opinion, so unsatisfactory, that I determined to address to the Home Secretary a remonstrance against it.

The case was heard by Mr Y—— about the middle of July. My letter to Sir George Grey, accompanied by a series / of the placards, was sent to the Home Office about the middle of August. I waited patiently for a reply, but, receiving none, I took it for granted that my letter could not have reached the Home Secretary. At last, on 17 December, I wrote to his private secretary, in order to ascertain the fact: the reply to my note was – the simple admission that *the letter had been received*. I confess that this event baffled all my calculations. I had observed that high officials, distinguished by their intellectual powers, were occasionally oblivious upon minor points; but that high officials distinguished only by the office they held were usually most rigidly courteous and exact.

After this I abstained for a long time from bringing any case before Mr Y——. At last a case occurred, which it appeared to me could not be resisted. I brought it before that magistrate; it was heard, and the charge was dismissed. Believing the decision to be erroneous in law, I consulted a solicitor who had much experience in the Metropolitan Police Courts, with the view of getting the opinion of the Court of Queen's Bench upon the subject.

My legal adviser had no doubt that the decision would be favourable, but urged upon me the great expense, and advised me not to proceed. On enquiry as to the probable amount, he suggested that it might reach fifty pounds. I immediately replied that it would be good economy to purchase my own time at that expense, and I desired him to take the necessary steps.

The first was to get some housekeeper to enter with me into a bond for twenty pounds to pay the magistrate's costs, in case I failed. Having wasted some time upon this, the magistrate granted a case for the Queen's Bench, a copy of which my solicitor immediately sent me. /

The grounds of My Y——'s decision, were:

1. That the man was not *legally* in custody.
2. That he was not within reasonable distance of my house.
3. That he did not understand the English language.

On receiving this, I felt quite relieved, and thought that a clear decision upon these three points would be very cheaply purchased by an expenditure of fifty pounds.

However, on mentioning the subject to several of my personal friends, who were themselves high in the profession of the law, I was destined to be grievously disappointed. I was informed that the Court of Queen's Bench would not decide upon any one of the questions, but would decide generally that the magistrate's decision was right or was wrong, without giving me the least intimation on which of the grounds it rested.

I now perceived the *dodge* that had been practised upon me, and I felt compelled to admit that Mr Y—— was a *clever fellow*. A regard for truth, however, forbids me to extend the application of this observation to anybody else concerned in this matter.

I have spared neither expense nor personal trouble in endeavouring to put a stop to this nuisance. During one twelve-month those expenses amounted, within a few shillings, to one hundred and four pounds. I was not, however, the only sufferer; that amount would otherwise have been expended in giving a year's employment to a skilled workman, whose wages are about two pounds a week.

I shall now give one illustration from my own experience of the utterly imperfect state of the law for suppressing the nuisance of street music:

On Monday, 29 February, in the present year, at 3 p.m., in the midst of a thick fog, a brass band struck up / close under my windows. I was in ill-health, and engaged in a subject requiring much attention. I knocked at the window; but the band continued their performance. Then I opened the window and desired them to desist; they still continued, and I then sent my servant to desire them to go away. Having finished their tune, they removed about five doors from my residence, and commenced another performance. My patience being exhausted, I then went out myself to desire my tormentors to depart. My servant went on to the station before he could get a constable. In the meantime the band had removed about six doors further, and began another tune. At last my servant arrived with a policeman, who took down the names and addresses of the nine musicians constituting the band.

The next day I paid twenty-seven shillings for summonses. The day after, the police informed me that all the addresses given, which were either in Richmond or Brentford, were false. I applied to the police, who watched at certain haunts; but they only succeeded in identifying two of them. I then obtained warrants to apprehend those two, and came up from the country expressly to attend at the police court; but the men were not to be found. I am still waiting in the hope that our police is not quite so inefficient as to allow them to escape. I have already been put to the charge of employing a solicitor and to other expenses. But the band itself is, I believe, still going about in London and playing every day.

Now, if it had been legal for the police to have taken possession of the instruments of those disturbers of the public peace, a false address would have been useless, for it would have been cheaper to have paid the penalties than to have lost their instruments.

It is, I presume, admitted that streets and high roads are not / the property of those who use them. They are the Queen's highways, and were devoted to the public for certain uses only.

The public have an undoubted right to traverse them, and convey over them persons, goods, materials, etc. The adjacent householders must bear any amount of noise which is fairly required for the legitimate use of roads; but no individual has any right to use them for other purposes, as for instance:

Theatrical representations – as Punch, gymnastics

Playground and games

Religious services

Music – as organs and brass bands

These not merely interfere with their proper use, but disturb the householders and are in most cases a positive nuisance.

The following letter, from an 'Old Lawyer', recently appeared in *The Times*. It states the law briefly, and with authority:

STREET MUSIC

To the Editor of The Times

Sir, Whether street music in London ought to be put down or not, I, living in the country, am not concerned to answer. I suppose it is a question, like smoking, on which the public will always be divided; but as the law on the subject is so clear and simple, I am surprised how legislators and justices can be puzzled about it.

Every public road or street belongs to the Sovereign, as embodying the nation, and is accordingly called the King's or Queen's highway. The interest of each individual is limited to a right of passing and repassing over such highway, and he is no more entitled to use it for business or amusement than he is to build upon it or dig for ore beneath its surface. / Hence the keeping of stalls for sale is illegal, and, though often winked at, is sometimes denounced and punished. Hence, the police are justified in desiring you to 'move on', if you loiter, in looking at a shop window or conversing with a friend, so as to bar the progress of passengers. *A fortiori*, a band of musicians has no *locus standi* on the ground.

There is, in my neighbourhood, a right of way over a gentleman's park. But I have only the privilege of passage, and none of remaining on the path for the purpose of reading, sketching, or playing the violin.

I am, Sir, your obedient Servant,

'AN OLD LAWYER'

At most, the tolerance of noisy occupants of the streets, such as organ-grinders, German bands, *et hoc genus omne*, is on sufferance only, and neither the municipal law nor common sense justifies the invasion or curtailment of a man's liberty to use his brain, and exert his mental energies as the occasion may require; and that, too, even within the very recesses of the 'Englishman's castle'.

With respect to the remedies against street music, I am not at all sanguine. The only one which is certain is, positively to forbid it in all cases, and with it also that varied multitude of vocal noises made by persons parading the streets singing, relating tales, praying, offering trifling articles for sale, etc., all of them with the transparent object of begging.

In all these cases which admit of it, the police ought to be directed to take possession of the offensive instrument and convey it to the police court, there to await the decision of the magistrate.

Certain street nuisances reappear periodically every few years: thus the game called 'tip-cat' again prevails. /

After a certain number of eyes have been knocked out, the police will probably have orders to stop the nuisance. It will then be put down in a few weeks, and, perhaps, after a year or two it may break out afresh, and be again as easily put down.

A similar cycle occurs with children's hoops: they are trundled about until they get under horses' legs. Now if, as it frequently happens, they are made of iron, not only is the rider thrown as well as the horse, but the poor animal is almost sure to have his leg broken.

269

In these and other similar cases, the offending instrument should invariably be detained by the police and taken to the station to be destroyed, or only to be returned on payment of a small fine by the offending party within three days after the seizure.

If this were the case, a multitude of daily street nuisances would very soon disappear. Boys with accordions and other noisy instruments, small children with shrill tin whistles would then be obliged to ask their parents to go to the police-office and pay a fine for the recovery of toys, and the parents themselves would prevent their children from destroying the time of other persons as soon as they were made to feel that it incurred an equal penalty on their own.

Every kind of noisy instrument, whether organ or harp, or trumpet or penny whistle, if sounded, should be seized by the police and taken to the station, also all hoops and instruments for playing games. The effect of this would ultimately be to diminish the labours of the police. At first they would have some additional trouble; but a few months would make the disturbers feel that it was a very unprofitable practice; and after that, if the police did their duty, they would only occasionally have to seize a stray instrument or two. / Proper warning of this intention to enforce the law ought to be given. The multitude of music-halls now established in all parts of London is such that those who enjoy street music may have a much larger quantity of it, and of a better kind, at a cheaper rate than that which in their own street disturbs all their neighbours.

If street music is to be at all tolerated by law, against which I protest in the strongest manner, then every performer ought to carry on his back or upon his instrument his name and address, or an authorized number, by which the public might be saved from wasting their time by false addresses, now so frequently given.

I have received several suggestions about organizing a society, to endeavour to put a stop to these street nuisances. My reply has been that such a combination well managed would probably have a very considerable effect, but that it would be impossible for me to give up to it any of my own time. I would willingly subscribe to it, and offer it any suggestions that might assist its operations. Its most important duty would be to ascertain whether the present law is sufficient to put down the nuisance. In case it is not, then it would become necessary to get it amended, and for that purpose to consult with influential members about the introduction of a Bill for that purpose.

Among the legal difficulties are the following: The magistrates in different districts interpret the law differently. Might it not be expedient that police magistrates should meet from time to time and discuss such differences of opinion, and agree to act upon that of the majority? Or ought they not to apply to the Home Secretary for his authority how to interpret it?

If I am right in the opinion which is confirmed in the / letter of the 'Old Lawyer', that the Queen's highways can only be legally used by her subjects for the passage of themselves and the transport of their property, then it is desirable to ascertain how that principle of the common law can be enforced. Hitherto all proceedings have been under certain clauses of the Metropolitan Police Act.

In case any association should be formed to endeavour to procure an Act of Parliament to put an end to the music nuisance, it would be desirable to apply distinctly to each of the members for the Metropolitan Boroughs, in order that it might be known on which side of the question they intended to vote.

As upon all other subjects, men differ upon street nuisances. An ancient philosopher divided all mankind into *two* sections, namely, fools and philosophers; and, unhappily for the race, the one cannot enjoy his whistle except at the expense of the other. I was once asked by an astute and sarcastic magistrate whether I seriously believed that a man's brain would be injured by listening to an organ; my reply was, *'Certainly not'*; for the obvious reason that no man having brain ever listened to street musicians.

> The opera, like the pillory, may be said
> To nail the ears down, but expose the head.

I believe that the greater part of the householders of London would gladly assist in putting a stop to street music. The proportion of cases prosecuted compared with the number of interruptions, is, in my own case, less than one in a thousand. If the annoyance is not absolutely prohibited by law, the number of the police must be at least double, to give quiet working people any repose. /

271

CHAPTER XXVII

WIT

Poor dogs – Puns double and triple – History of the silver lady –
Disappointed by the milliner – The philosopher performs her functions –
Lady Morgan's criticism – Allsop's beer – Sydney Smith – Toss up a bishop –
Lady M . . . and the gipsy in Spain – Epigram on the planet Neptune –
Epigram on Henry Drummond's attack upon Catholics in the House of
Commons – On Catholic miracles.

It has often struck me that an analysis of the causes of wit would be a
very interesting subject of enquiry. With that view I collected many
jest-books, but fortunately in this one instance I had resolution to
abstain from distracting my attention from more important enquiries.

I may, however, note some illustrations of it which occur to my
memory. The late Sir Harris Nicolas used to practice rather strongly
upon some of his friends. I was not an unwilling victim. The pleasure
derived from the wit far exceeded any pain it inflicted. Indeed, Sir
Harris himself one day expressed his disappointment at my
insensibility, by saying that he had never in his whole life been able
really to hit me.

The late Lord S—— was sitting with him one morning listening to a
very astute but rather dry explanation of some matter about which
his Lordship had enquired. At last he threw himself back in his armchair and said, 'My dear Nicolas, I am very stupid this morning: my
brains are all / gone to the dogs.' On which Sir Harris pathetically
exclaimed, 'Poor dogs!'

It is evident in this case, that the wit of the reply arose from
sympathy expressed on the wrong side. The peer expected sympathy
from the knight: but the knight gave it to the dogs.

Another remarkable feature of jokes formed upon this principle is,
that they generally depend upon the intimate meaning of the words
employed, and not either upon their sound or their arrangement;
consequently, they possess the rare quality of being translatable into
all languages.

One of the principles of discovery in many subjects is, to generalize

272

from the individual case up to the species, and thence to descend to other individual instances.

Puns are detestable. The greater number of them depend on the double meaning of the same word, or on the similar pronunciation of words differently spelt. The following may serve as an example of a triple pun:

A gentleman calling one morning at the house of a lady whose sister was remarkably beautiful, found her at the writing-table. Putting his hand upon the little bell used for calling the attendant, he enquired of the lady of the house what relationship existed between his walking-stick, her sister, and the instrument under his finger.

$$\text{His walking-stick was} \begin{cases} \text{cane} \\ \text{Cain} \end{cases}\text{, the brother of} \begin{cases} \text{a bell} \\ \text{a belle} \\ \text{Abel.} \end{cases}$$

I mentioned, in an early chapter, my boyish admiration of an automaton in the shape of a silver lady, who attitudinized in the most graceful manner. Her fate was singular: at the death of her maker she was sold with the rest of his collection / of mechanical toys, and was purchased by Weekes, who had a mechanical exhibition in Cockspur Street. No attempt appears to have been made to finish the automaton; and it seems to have been placed out of the way in an attic uncovered and utterly neglected.

On the sale by auction of Weeke's Museum, I met again the object of my early admiration. Having purchased the silver figure, I proceeded to take to pieces the whole of the mechanism, and found a multitude of small holes which had been stopped up as not having fulfilled their intended object. In fact, it appeared tolerably certain that scarcely any drawings could have been prepared for the automaton, but that the beautiful result arose from a system of continual trials.

I myself repaired and restored all the mechanism of the Silver Lady, by which title she was afterwards known to my friends. I placed her under a glass case on a pedestal in my drawing-room, where she received, in her own silent but graceful manner, these valued friends who so frequently honoured me with their society on certain Saturday evenings.

This piece of mechanism formed a striking contrast with the unfinished portion of the Difference Engine, No. 1, which was placed in the adjacent room: the whole of the latter mechanism existed in drawings upon paper before any portion of it was put together.

The external surface of the figure, which was beautiful in form, was made of silver. It was, therefore, necessary to supply her with robes suitable to her station. This would have been rather difficult for a philosopher, but it was made easy by the aid of one or two of my fair friends who kindly intervened. These generously assisted with their own peculiar skill and taste at the *toilette* of their rival Syren. /

Sketches were made and modists of the purest water were employed. The result was, upon the whole, highly satisfactory. One evening, however, the arrival of the new dress was postponed to so late a period, that I feared it had entirely escaped the recollection of the executive department. The hour at which my friends usually arrived was rapidly approaching.

In this difficulty it occurred to me that there were a few remnants of beautiful Chinese crêpe in the silver lady's wardrobe. Having selected two strips, one of pink and the other of light green, I hastily wound a plaited band of bright auburn hair round the block on which her head-dresses were usually constructed, and then pinned on the folds of coloured crêpe. This formed a very tolerable turban, and was not much unlike a kind of head-dress called a toke, which prevailed at that period. Another larger piece of the same pink Chinese crêpe I wound round her person, which I thought showed it off to considerable advantage. Fortunately, I found in her wardrobe a pair of small pink satin slippers, on each of which I fixed a single silver spangle: then placing a small silver crescent in the front of her turban, I felt I had accomplished all that time and circumstances permitted.

The criticisms on the costume of the Silver Lady were various. In the course of the evening, Lady Morgan communicated to me confidentially her own opinion of the dress.

Holding up her fan, she whispered, 'My dear Mr Babbage, I think your Silver Lady is rather slightly clad tonight; shall I lend her a petticoat?' to which I replied, 'My dear Lady Morgan, I am much indebted for your very considerate offer, but I fear you have not got *one* to spare.'

This retort was not a pun, but merely a 'double-entendre'. It might mean either that her Ladyship had on invisibles, but / not enough to be able to spare one: or it might imply that, having no garment of that kind, she was unable to lend one to a friend.

About the time of the attempt to assassinate the Emperor of the

French by Orsini, an Englishman named Alsop was arrested in London, and afterwards tried and acquitted of a connection with the assassins.

At a distinguished dinner-party, amongst whom was the Attorney-General of that day, there arose a question as to who Mr Alsop was. One of the company asked, 'Whether it was Allsop's beer?' meaning, whether the prisoner was the concoctor of that delightful beverage. The gentleman to whom the question was addressed, immediately replied, 'It is not at present Allsop's *beer*, but,' said he, turning to the Attorney-General, 'if your prosecution succeeds, it is very likely to become Alsop's *bier*.'

Sydney Smith occasionally called upon me in the morning, and was ever a most welcome visitor. The conversation usually commenced upon grave subjects, and I was always desirous of profiting by the light his powerful mind threw upon the most difficult questions.

When railways first came into existence much reasonable alarm arose from the rapidity of the trains and the immense masses of matter in motion. One morning my friend called and asked my opinion on the subject. I pointed out what then appeared to me the chief sources of danger, and entered upon some of the precautions to be attended to, and of remedies to be applied.

Sydney Smith then asked me why I did not go and inform the Government of the danger and of the means of remedying it. My answer was, that such a mission would be a pure waste of time, that nothing whatever would be done until / some great man, a Prime Minister for instance, were smashed. I then continued, 'Perhaps a bishop or two would do; for you know,' said I, looking slyly at my friend, 'they are so much better prepared for the change than we are'.

I have heard this view of the subject assigned to Sydney Smith. It is very seldom that it should have occurred to him, although I scarcely imagine he would have given the reason I did for the preference. His celebrated suggestion to the person who asked him how a man could find which way the wind blew when there was no weathercock in sight,* adds to the probability of Sydney Smith's originality. On the other hand, I may support my own pretensions to independent invention by referring to a parallel remark I made many years before:

At a large dinner party the subject of duelling was discussed. Various opinions were propounded as to its absolute necessity. I had

* Toss up a bishop.

275

made no remark upon the question, but during a slight pause somebody on the opposite side of the table asked my opinion on the subject. My reply was, I always wished that the injured man should fall. On being asked my reason for that wish, I answered, 'Because he is so much better prepared for the change than the wrongdoer.' I afterwards learned, with great satisfaction, that when the ladies retired to the drawing-room, the discussion was much criticized and my reply highly applauded.

The late Lady M——, having a great desire to see Mr Borrow, asked me to invite him to one of my Saturday evening parties. I expressed my regret that, not having the pleasure of his acquaintance, I was unable to ask him to my house, as I never made 'lions' of my guests.

A short time after, a friend who was coming to me on the / following Saturday, called to ask me to allow him to bring Mr Borrow who dined with him on that day, to my party in the evening. Of course, I willingly gave the invitation, and then wrote a note to inform Lady M—— of the occurrence of the opportunity she wished for.

On the following Saturday evening Lady M—— was announced, and immediately asked me whether Mr Borrow had arrived. I said that he had, and that he was in the further room. I then added, that in the course of a few moments I should have great pleasure in presenting to her Mr Borrow.

Lady M——, who had several other engagements that evening, said, 'Only tell me what sort of a person he is, and I will go and find him out myself.'

I observed that he was a remarkably tall, straggling person, with a very intelligent countenance. With these instructions her ladyship left me, and finding, as she imagined, exactly the man I had described, immediately accosted him. The conversation was highly interesting, and included a great variety of widely different subjects. It concluded by Lady M—— expressing her delight with her new acquaintance, from whom she parted with this remark, 'What a delightful gipsying life you must have led!'

A slight mistake had, however, occurred, which was not discovered until long after: the person thus addressed was not Mr Borrow, but Dr Whately, the Archbishop of Dublin.

In this chapter may be placed one or two epigrams which, though upon subjects of transitory interest, may amuse those who are acquainted with the attending circumstances.

It will be remembered that great discussion arose about the conflicting claims of Adams and Le Verrier to the discovery / of the planet Neptune. A great controversy resulted, which was at last summed up in the following couplet:

> When Airy was told, he wouldn't believe it;
> When Challis saw, he couldn't believe it.

The clever and eccentric member for East Surrey, the late Henry Drummond, who founded a professorship of Political Economy at Oxford, made in the House of Commons a most amusing, though rather strong speech against the modern miracles of the Roman Catholic Church, in which he spoke of 'their bleeding pictures, their winking statues, and the Virgin's milk'. On this some profane wag wrote the following couplet:

> Sagacious Drummond, explain, with your divinity:
> Why reject the milk, yet swallow the virginity?

Probably some clever fellow of that faith was at the bottom of this mischief; for I have observed that the cleverest fellows seem to think that the merit of adhering to a cause entitles them to the right of quizzing it.

I was particularly struck with this idea when I saw, for the first time, at Cologne, the celebrated picture of St Ursula and her eleven thousand virgins. The artist has quietly made every one of them more or less matronly. /

CHAPTER XXVIII

HINTS FOR TRAVELLERS

New inventions – Stomach-pump – Built a carriage – Description of Thames tunnel – Barton's iridescent buttons – Chinese orders of nobility – Manufactory of gold chains at Venice – Pulsations and respirations of animals – Punching a hole in glass without cracking it – Specimen of an enormous smash – Proteus Anguineus – Travellers' hotel at Sheffield – Wentworth House.

In this chapter I propose to throw together a few suggestions, which may assist in rendering a tour successful for its objects and agreeable in its reminiscences.

Money is the fuel of travelling. I can give the traveller a few hints how to get money, although I never had any skill in making it myself.

In one tour, extending over more than a twelvemonth, I took with me two letters of credit, each for half the sum I should probably require. My reasons for this were, that in case one was lost the other might still be available. One of these was generally kept about my person, the other concealed in my writing-case. Another reason was, that if I were unluckily carried off and detained for a ransom, it might thus be mitigated.

It is of great advantage to a traveller to have some acquaintance with the use of tools. It is often valuable for his own comfort, and sometimes renders him able to assist a friend. I met at Frankfort the eldest son of the coachmaker / of the Emperor of Russia. He had been travelling over the western part of Europe, and showed me drawings he had made of all the most remarkable carriages he had met with. Some of these were selected for their elegance, others for the reverse; take, as an example, the Lord Mayor's.

We travelled together to Munich, and I took that opportunity of discussing, seriatim, with my very intelligent young friend, every part of the structure of a carriage.

I made notes of certain portions in case I should find occasion to have a carriage built for my own use.

The young Russian was on his way to Moscow, and was very anxious to prevail on me to accompany him thither, for which purpose he offered to wait my own time at Munich. As, however, I wished to reach Italy as soon as possible, I declined his proposition with much regret.

However, in the following year, I profited by the information I then gained. I had built for me at Vienna, from my own design, a strong light four-wheeled calèche in which I could sleep at full length. Amongst its conveniences were a lamp by which I occasionally boiled an egg or cooked my breakfast. A large shallow drawer in which might be placed, without folding, plans, drawings, and dress-coats. Small pockets for the various kinds of money, a larger one for travelling books and telescopes, and many other conveniences. It cost somewhat about sixty pounds. After carrying me during six months, at the expense of only five francs for repair, I sold it at the Hague for thirty pounds.

It is always advantageous for a traveller to carry with him anything of use in science or in art if it is of a portable nature, and still more so if it has also the advantage of novelty. At the time I started on a lengthened tour the stomach-pump had just been invented. It appeared to give / promise of great utility. I therefore arranged in a small box the parts of an instrument which could be employed either as a syringe, a stomach-pump, or for cupping. As a stomach-pump, it was in great request from its novelty and utility. I had many applications for permission to make drawings of it, to which I always most willingly acceded. At Munich, Dr Weisbrod, the King's physician, was greatly interested with it, and at his wish I lent it to the chief surgical instrument-maker who produced for him an exact copy of the whole apparatus.

Having visited the Thames Tunnel a day or two before I started for the Continent, I purchased a dozen copies of the very lucid account of that most interesting work. Six of the copies were in French and the other six in the German language. I frequently lent a copy, and upon some occasions I gave one away; but if I had had twice that number I should have found that I might have distributed them with advantage as acknowledgements of the many attentions I received.

Another most valuable piece of travelling merchandise consisted of a dozen large and a dozen small gold buttons stamped by Barton's steel dies. These buttons displayed the most beautiful iridescence, especially in the light of the sun. They were formed by ruling the steel die in parallel lines in various forms. The lines were from the four to the ten thousandth of an inch apart.

I possessed a die which Mr Barton had kindly given me. This I kept in my writing-case; but I had had a small piece of steel ruled in the same way, though not with quite the same perfection, which I always kept in my waistcoat pocket; it was also accompanied by a small gold button in a sandalwood case. These were frequently of great service. The / mere sight of them procured me many little attentions in diligences and steamboats.

Of course I never appeared to be the possessor of more than one of these treasured buttons; so that if any one had saved my life, its gift would have been thought a handsome acknowledgement. If I had travelled in the East, as I had originally intended until the battle of Navarino prevented me, my buttons might have given me unlimited success in the celestial empire.

The Chinese, like ourselves, have five orders of nobility. They are indicated by spherical buttons. The Chinese nobles, however, wear them on the top of their caps, whilst our nobility wear their pearls and strawberry-leaves in their armorial bearings.

It is a curious circumstance that the most anciently civilized nation should have invented an order of knighthood almost exactly similar to our own – the order of the Peacock's Feather – which, like our own Garter, is confined to certain classes of nobility of the highest rank. Of the two the decoration of the Chinese noble is certainly the more graceful.

One out of many illustrations may show the use I made of a button. During my first visit to Venice I wished to see a manufactory of gold chains for which that city is justly celebrated. I readily got permission, and the proprietor was so good as to accompany me round his factory. I had enquired the price of various chains, and had expressed my wish to purchase a few inches of each kind; but I was informed that they never sold less than a braccia of any one chain. This amount would have made my purchase more costly than I proposed, so I gave it up.

In the meantime we proceeded through several rooms in which various processes were going on. Observing some / tools in one of the shops, I took up a file and asked whence it was procured. This led to a conversation on the subject, in which the proprietor gave me some account of files from various countries, but concluded by observing that the Lancashire files, when they could be got, were by far the

280

best. I took this opportunity of asking him whether he had seen any of our latest productions in steel: then pulling out of my waistcoat-pocket the piece of hardened steel, ruled by a diamond, I put it into his hands. The sun was shining brightly, and he was very much interested with it. I remarked that in a darkened room, and with a single lamp, it would be seen with still greater advantage. A room was soon darkened, and a single lamp produced, and the effect was still more perfect. My conductor then observed that his managing man was a very skilful workman, and if I could afford the time, he should much wish to show him this beautiful sight. I said it always gave me pleasure to see and converse with a skilful workman, and that I considered it as time well spent. The master sent for his superintendent, who, being of a judicious turn of mind, was lavish in admiring what his master approved. The master himself, gratified by this happy confirmation, turning to me, said that he would let me have pieces of any or all of his gold chains of any length, however short I might wish them to be.

I thanked him for thus enabling me to make my countrymen appreciate the excellence of Venetian workmanship, and purchased small samples of every kind of chain then manufactured. These, on my return to London, I weighed and measured, and referred to them in the economy of manufactures as illustrations of the different proportions in which skilled labour and price of raw material occur in the same class of manufactured articles. /

A friend of mine, then at Venice, again visited that city about five years afterwards. He subsequently informed me that he had purchased, at the manufactory I visited, samples of gold chains about an inch or two long, fixed on black velvet, and that it formed a regular article of trade in some demand.

A man may, without being a proficient in any science, and indeed with only the most limited knowledge of a small portion of it, yet make himself useful to those who are most instructed. However limited the path he may himself pursue, he will insensibly acquire other information in return for that which he can communicate. I will illustrate this by one of my own pursuits. I possess the slightest possible acquaintance with the vast fields of animal life, but at an early period I was struck by the numerical regularity of the pulsation and of the breathings. It appeared to me that there must exist some relation between these two functions. Accordingly, I took

281

every opportunity of counting the numbers of the pulsations and of the breathings of various animals. The pig fair at Pavia and the book fair at Leipsic equally placed before me menageries in which I could collect such facts. Every zoological collection of living animals which I visited thus gained an additional interest, and occasionally excited the attention of those in charge of it to making a collection of facts relating to that subject. This led me at another period to generalize the subject of enquiry, and to print a skeleton form for the constants of the class mammalia. It was reprinted by the British Association at Cambridge in 1833, and also at Brussels in the 'Travaux du Congress Général de Statistique', Brussels, 1853.[a]

I have so frequently been mortified by having the utterly undeserved / reputation of knowing everything that I was led to enquire into the probable grounds of the egregious fallacy. The most frequent symptom was an address of this kind: 'Now, Mr Babbage, will you, who know everything, kindly explain to me . . .' Perhaps the thing whose explanation was required might be the metre of some ancient Chinese poem: or whether there were any large rivers in the planet Mercury.

One of the most useful accomplishments for a philosophical traveller with which I am acquainted, I learned from a workman, who taught me how to punch a hole in a sheet of glass without making a crack in it.

The process is very simple. Two centre-punches, a hammer, an ordinary bench-vice, and an old file, are all the tools required. These may be found in any blacksmith's shop. Having decided upon the part of the glass in which you wish to make the hole, scratch a cross (X) upon the desired spot with the point of the old file; then turn the bit of glass over, and scratch on the other side a similar mark exactly opposite to the former.

Fix one of the small centre-punches with its point upwards in the vice. Let an assistant gently hold the bit of glass with its scratched point exactly resting upon the point of the centre-punch.

Take the other centre-punch in your own left hand and place its point in the centre of the upper scratch, which is of course nearly, if not exactly, above the fixed centre-punch. Now hit the upper centre-punch a *very* slight blow with the hammer: a mere touch is almost sufficient.

---

[a] The most complete version of this paper, 'On tables of the constants of nature and art' (1857), appears in *Works of Babbage*, Vol. 5. The paper does not appear in the 1833 report of the BAAS.

This must be carefully repeated two or three times. The result of these blows will be to cause the centre of the cross to be, as it were, gently pounded. /

Turn the glass over and let the slight cavity thus formed rest upon the fixed centre-punch. Repeat the light blows upon this side of the glass, and after turning it two or three times, a very small hole will be made through the glass. It not unfrequently happens that a small crack occurs in the glass; but with a little skill this can be cut out with the pane of the hammer.

The next process is to enlarge the hole and cut it into the required shape with the pane of the hammer. This is accomplished by supporting the glass upon the point of the fixed centre-punch, very close to the edge required to be cut. A light blow must then be struck with the pane of the hammer upon the edge to be broken. This must be repeated until the required shape is obtained.

The principles on which it depends are, that glass is a material breaking in every direction with a conchoidal fracture, and that the vibrations which would have caused cracking or fracture are checked by the support of the fixed centre-punch in close contiguity with the part to be broken off.

When by hastily performing this operation I have caused the glass to crack, I have frequently, by using more care, cut an opening all round the cracked part, and so let it drop out without spreading.

This process is rendered still more valuable by the use of the diamond. I usually carried in my travels a diamond mounted on a small circle of wood, so that I could easily cut out circles of glass with small holes in the centre. The description of this process is sufficient to explain it to an experienced workman; but if the reader should wish to employ it, his readiest plan would be to ask such a person to show him how to do it.

The above technical description will doubtless be rather / dry and obscure to the general reader; so I hope to make him amends by one or two of the consequences which have resulted to me from having instructed others in the art.

In the year 1825, during a visit to Devonport, I had apartments in the house of a glazier, of whom one day I enquired whether he was acquainted with the art of punching a hole in glass, to which he answered in the negative, and expressed great curiosity to see it done. Finding that at a short distance there was a blacksmith whom he sometimes employed, we went together to pay him a visit, and having selected from his rough tools the centre-punches and the hammer, I proceeded to explain and execute the whole process, with which my landlord was highly delighted.

On the eve of my departure I asked for the landlord's account, which was duly sent up and quite correct, except the omission of the charge for the apartments which I had agreed for at two guineas a week. I added the four weeks for my lodgings, and the next morning, having placed the total amount upon the bill, I sent for my host in order to pay him, remarking that he had omitted the principal article of his account, which I had inserted.

He replied that he had intentionally omitted the lodgings, as he could not think of taking payment for them from a gentleman who had done him so great a service. Quite unconscious of having rendered him any service, I asked him to explain how I had done him any good. He replied that he had the contract for the supply and repair of the whole of the lamps of Devonport, and that the art in which I had instructed him would save him more than twenty pounds a year. I found some difficulty in prevailing on my grateful landlord to accept what was justly his due.

The second instance I shall mention of the use to which I / turned this art of punching a hole in glass occurred in Italy, at Bologna.

I spent some weeks very agreeably in that celebrated university, which is still proud of having had the discoverer of the circulation of the blood amongst its students. One morning an Italian friend accompanied me round the town, to point out the more remarkable shops and manufactories. Passing through a small street, he remarked that there was a very well-informed man who kept a little shop for the sale of needles and tape and a few other such articles, but who also made barometers and thermometers, and had a very respectable knowledge of such subjects. I proposed that we should look in upon him as we were passing through the street. On entering his small shop, I was introduced to its tenant, who conversed very modestly and very sensibly upon various mathematical instruments.

I had invited several of my friends and professors to spend the evening with me at my hotel, for the purpose of examining various instruments I had brought with me. I knew that the sight of them would be quite a treat to the occupier of this little shop, so I mentioned the idea to my friend, and enquired whether my expected guests in the evening would think I had taken a liberty with them in inviting the humble constructor of instruments at the same time.

My friend and conductor immediately replied that he was well known to most of the professors, and much respected by them, and that they would think it very kind of me to give him that opportunity of seeing the instruments I possessed. I therefore took the opportunity of asking him to join the very agreeable party which assembled in my apartments in the evening.

We now made a tour of the city, and reached the factory / of the chief philosophical instrument-maker of Bologna. He took great pleasure in showing me the various instruments he manufactured; but still there was a certain air of presumption about him, which seemed to indicate a less amount of knowledge than I should otherwise have assigned to him. I had on the preceding day mentioned to my Italian friend, who now accompanied me, that there existed a very simple method of punching a hole in a piece of glass, which, as he was much interested about it, I promised to show him on the earliest opportunity.

Finding myself in the workshop of the first instrument-maker in Bologna, and observing the few tools I wanted, I thought it a good opportunity to explain the process to my friend; but I could only do this by applying to the master for the loan of some tools. I also thought it possible that the method was known to him, and that, having more practice, he would do the work better than myself.

I therefore mentioned the circumstance of my promise, and asked the master whether he was acquainted with the process. His reply was, 'Yes; we do it every day.' I then handed over to him the punch and the piece of glass, declaring that a mere amateur, who only occasionally practised it could not venture to operate before the first instrument-maker in Bologna, and in his own workshop.

I had observed a certain shade of surprise glance across the face of one of the workmen who heard the assertion of this daily practice of his master's, and, as I had my doubts of it, I contrived to put him in such a position that he must either retract his statement or else attempt to do the trick.

He then called for a flat piece of iron with a small hole in it. Placing the piece of glass upon the top of this bit of iron, and holding the punch upon it directly above the aperture, / he gave a strong blow of the hammer, and smashed the glass into a hundred pieces.

I immediately began to console him, remarking that I did not myself always succeed, and that unaccountable circumstances sometimes defeated the skill even of the most accomplished workman. I then advised him to try a larger* piece of glass. Just after

* The larger the piece of glass to be punched the more certainly the process succeeds.

the crash I had put my hand upon a heavier hammer, which I immediately withdrew on his perceiving it. Thus encouraged, he called for a larger piece of glass, and a bit of iron with a smaller hole in it. In the meantime all the men in the shop rested from their work to witness this feat of everyday occurrence. Their master now seized the heavier hammer, which I had previously just touched. Finding him preparing for a strong and decided blow, I turned aside my head, in order to avoid seeing him blush – and also to save my own face from the coming cloud of splinters.

I just saw the last triumphant flourish of the heavy hammer waving over his head, and then heard, on its thundering fall, the crash made by the thousand fragments of glass which it scattered over the workshop.

I still, however, felt it my duty to administer what consolation I could to a fellow-creature in distress; so I repeated to him (which was the truth) that I, too, occasionally failed. Then looking at my watch, and observing to my companion that these tools were not adapted to my mode of work, I reminded him that we had a pressing engagement. I then took leave of this celebrated instrument-maker, with many thanks for all he had shown me.

After such a misadventure, I thought it would be cruel to / invite him to meet the learned professors who would be assembled at my evening party, especially as I knew that I should be asked to show my friends a process with which he had assured me he was so familiar. The unpretending maker of thermometers and barometers did however join the party; and the kind and considerate manner in which my guests of the university and of the city treated him raised both parties in my estimation.

I will here mention another mode of treating glass, which may occasionally be found worth communicating.

Ground glass is frequently employed for transmitting light into an apartment, whilst it effectually prevents persons on the outside from seeing into the room. Rough plate-glass is now in very common use for the same purpose. In both these circumstances there is a reciprocity, for those who are within such rooms cannot see external forms.

It may in some cases be desirable partially to remedy this difficulty. In my own case, I cut with my diamond a small disc of window-glass, about two inches in diameter, and cemented it with Canada balsam to the rough side of my rough plate-glass. I then suspended a circular piece of card by a thread, so as to cover the circular disc. When the Canada balsam is dry, it fills up all the little inequalities of the rough glass with a transparent substance, of nearly the same refracting power; consequently, on drawing aside the suspended card, the forms of external objects become tolerably well defined.

The smooth surface of the rough plate-glass, not being perfectly flat, produces a slight distortion, which might, if it were worth while, be cured by cementing another disc of glass upon that side. In case the ground glass itself happens to be plate-glass, the image of external objects is perfect. /

Occasionally I met, in the course of my travels, with various things which, though not connected with my own pursuits, might yet be highly interesting to others. If the cost suited my purse, and the subject was easily carried, or the specimen of importance, I have in many instances purchased them. Such was the case with respect to that curious creature the *proteus anguineus*, a creature living only in the waters of dark caverns, which has eyes, but the eyelids cannot open.

When I visited the caves of Adelsburg, in Styria, I enquired whether any of these singular creatures could be procured. I purchased all I could get, being six in number. I conveyed them in large bottles full of river water, which I changed every night. During the greater part of their journey the bottles were placed in large leathern bags lashed to the barouche seat of my calash.

The first of these pets died at Vienna, and another at Prague. After three months, two only survived, and reached Berlin, where they also died – I fear from my servant having supplied them with water from a well instead of from a river.

At night they were usually placed in a large wash-hand basin of water, covered over with a napkin.

They were very excitable under the action of light. On several occasions when I have visited them at night with a candle, one or more have jumped out of their watery home.

These rare animals were matters of great interest to many naturalists whom I visited in my rambles, and procured for me several very agreeable acquaintances. When their gloomy lives terminated I preserved them in spirits, and sent the specimens to the collections of our own universities, to India, and some of our colonies.

When I was preparing materials for the 'Economy of Manufactures', / I

287

had occasion to travel frequently through our manufacturing and mining districts. On these occasions I found the travellers' inn or the travellers' room was usually the best adapted to my purpose, both in regard to economy and to information. As my enquiries had a wide range, I found ample assistance in carrying them on. Nobody doubted that I was one of the craft; but opinions were widely different as to the department in which I practised my vocation.

In one of my tours I passed a very agreeable week at the Commercial Hotel at Sheffield. The society of the travellers' room is very fluctuating. Many of its frequenters arrive at night, have supper, breakfast early the next morning, and are off soon after: others make rather a longer stay. One evening we sat up after supper much later than is usual, discussing a variety of commercial subjects.

When I came down rather late to breakfast, I found only one of my acquaintance of the previous evening remaining. He remarked that we had had a very agreeable party last night, in which I cordially concurred. He referred to the intelligent remarks of some of the party in our discussion, and then added, that when I left them they began to talk about me. I merely observed that I felt myself quite safe in their hands, but should be glad to profit by their remarks. It appeared, when I retired for the night, they debated about what trade I travelled for. 'The tall gentleman in the corner,' said my informant, 'maintained that you were in the hardware line; whilst the fat gentleman who sat next to you at supper was quite sure that you were in the spirit trade.' Another of the party declared that they were both mistaken: he said he had met you before, and that you were travelling for a great iron-master. 'Well,' said I, 'you, I presume, knew my vocation better than our friends.' – 'Yes,' / said my informant, 'I knew perfectly well that you were in the Nottingham lace trade.' The waiter now appeared with his bill, and announced that my friend's trap was at the door.

I had passed nearly a week at the Commercial Inn without having broken the eleventh commandment; but the next day I was doomed to be found out. A groom, in the gay livery of the Fitzwilliams, having fruitlessly searched for me at all the great hotels, at last in despair thought of enquiring for me at the Commercial Hotel. The landlady was sure I was not staying in her house; but, in deference to the groom's urgent request, went to make enquiries amongst her guests. I was the first person she questioned, and was, of course, obliged to admit the impeachment. The groom brought a very kind note from the late Lord Fitzwilliam, who had heard of my being in Sheffield, to invite me to spend a week at Wentworth.

I gladly availed myself of this invitation, and passed it very agreeably. During the few first days the party in the house consisted of the family only. Then followed three days of open house, when their friends came from great distances, even as far as sixty or eighty miles, and that at a period when railroads were unknown.

On the great day upwards of a hundred persons sat down to dinner, a large number of whom slept in the house. This was the first time the ancient custom of open house had been kept up at Wentworth since the death of the former Earl, the celebrated Whig Lord Lieutenant of Yorkshire. /

CHAPTER XXIX

MIRACLES

Difference Engine set so as to follow a given law for a vast period – Thus to change to another law of equally vast or of greater duration, and so on – Parallel between the successive creations of animal life – The author visited Dublin at the first meeting of the British Association – Is the guest of Trinity College – Innocently wears a waistcoat of the wrong colour – Is informed of the sad fact – Rushes to a tailor to rectify it – Finds nothing but party-colours – Nearly loses his breakfast, and is thought to be an amazing dandy – The Dean thinks better of the philosopher, and accompanied him to Killarney – The philosopher preaches a sermon to the divine by the side of the lake.

After that portion of the Difference Engine which was completed had been for some months promoted from the workshop to my drawing-room, I met two of my friends from Ireland – Dr Lloyd, the present Provost of Trinity College, and Dr Robinson, of Armagh. I invited them to breakfast, that they might have a full opportunity of examining its structure. I invited also another friend to meet them – the late Professor Malthus.

After breakfast we adjourned to the drawing-room. I then proceeded to explain the mechanism of the engine, and to cause it to calculate tables. One of the party remarked two axes in front of the machine which had not hitherto been performing any work, and enquired for what purpose they were so placed. I informed him that these axes had been so placed in order to illustrate a series of calculations of the / most complicated kind, to which they contributed. I observed that the tables thus formed were of so artificial and abstract a nature, that I could not foresee the time when they would be of any use.

This remark additionally excited their curiosity, and they requested me to set the machine at work to compute such a table.

Having taken a simple case of this kind, I set the engine to do its work, and then told them:

That it was now prepared to count the natural numbers; but that it would obey this law only as far as the millionth term.

That after that term it would commence a series, following a different, but known law, for a very long period.

That after this new law had been fulfilled for another long period, it would then suddenly abandon it, and calculate the terms of a series following another new law, and so on throughout all time.

Of course it was impossible to verify these assertions by making the machine actually go through the calculations; but, after having made the engine count the natural numbers for some time, I proceeded to point out the fact, that it was impossible, by its very structure, that the machine could record any but the natural numbers before it reached the number 999,990. This I made evident to my friends, by showing them the actual structure of the engine. Having demonstrated this to their entire satisfaction, I put the machine on to the number 999,990, and continued to work the engine, when the result I had predicted soon arrived. After the millionth term a new law *was* taken up, and my friends were convinced that it must, from the very structure of the machine, continue for a very long time, and then / inevitably give place to another new law, and so on throughout all time.

When they were quite satisfied about this fact, I observed that, in a new engine which I was then contemplating, it would be possible to set it so that:

1. It should calculate a table for any given length of time, according to any given law.

2. That at the termination of that time it should cease to compute a table according to that law; but that it should commence a new table according to any other given law that might be desired, and should then continue this computation for any other given period.

3. That this succession of a new law, coming in and continuing during any desired time, and then giving place to other new laws, in endless but known succession, might be continued indefinitely.

I remarked that I did not conceive the time ever could arrive when the results of such calculations would be of any utility. I added, however, that they offered a striking parallel with, although at an immeasurable distance from, the successive creations of animal life, as developed by the vast epochs of geological time. The flash of intellectual light which illuminated the countenances of my three friends at this unexpected juxtaposition was most gratifying.

Encouraged by the quick apprehension with which these views had been accepted, I continued the subject, and pointed out the application of the same reasoning to the nature of miracles.

291

The same machine could be set in such a manner that these laws might exist for any assigned number of times, whether large or small; also, that it was not necessary that these laws should be different, but the same law might, when / the machine was set, be ordered to reappear, after any desired interval.

Thus we might suppose an observer watching the machine, to see a known law continually fulfilled, until after a lengthened period, when a new law has been appointed to come in. This new law might after a single instance cease, and the first law might again be restored, and continue for another interval, when the second new law might again govern the machine as before for a single instance, and then give place to the original law.

This property of a mere piece of mechanism may have a parallel in the laws of human life. That all men die is the result of a vast induction of instances. That one or more men at given times shall be restored to life, may be as much a consequence of the law of existence appointed for man at his creation, as the appearance and reappearance of the isolated cases of apparent exception in the arithmetical machine.

But the workings of machinery run parallel to those of intellect. The Analytical Engine might be so set, that at definite periods, known only to its maker, a certain lever might become moveable during the calculations then making. The consequence of moving it might be to cause the then existing law to be violated for one or more times, after which the original law would resume its reign. Of course the maker of the calculating engine might confide this fact to the person using it, who would thus be gifted with the power of prophecy if he foretold the event, or of working a miracle at the proper time, if he withheld his knowledge from those around until the moment of its taking place.

Such is the analogy between the construction of machinery to calculate and the occurrence of miracles. A further illustration may be taken from geometry. Curves are represented / by equations. In certain curves these are portions, such as ovals, disconnected from the rest of the curve. By properly assigning the values of the constants, these ovals may be reduced to single points. These singular points may exist upon a branch of a curve, or may be entirely isolated from it; yet these points fulfil by their positions the law of the curve as perfectly as any of those which, by their juxtaposition and continuity, form any of its branches.

Miracles, therefore, are not the breach of established laws, but they are the very circumstances that indicate the existence of far higher laws, which at the appointed time produce their pre-intended results.

In 1835, the British Association visited Dublin. I had been anxious to promote this visit, from political as well as scientific motives. I had several invitations to the residences of my friends in that hospitable country; but I thought I could be of more use by occupying apartments in Trinity College, which had kindly been placed at my disposal by the provost and fellows.

After I had enjoyed the college hospitality during three or four days, I was walking with an intimate friend, who suggested to me that I was giving great cause of offence to my learned hosts. Not having the slightest idea how this could have arisen, I anxiously enquired by what inadvertence I had done so. He observed that it arose from my dress. I looked at the various articles of my costume with a critical eye, and could discover nothing exaggerated in any portion of it. I then begged my friend to explain how I had unconsciously offended in that respect. He replied, 'Your waistcoat is of a bright green.' I became still more puzzled, until he remarked that I was wearing O'Connell's colours in the midst of the Protestant University, whose guest I was. /

I thanked my friend sincerely, and requested him to accompany me to my rooms, that I might change the offending waistcoat. My travelling wardrobe was not large, and, unfortunately, we found in it no entirely unobjectionable waistcoat. I therefore put on an under-waistcoat with a light-blue border, and requested him to accompany me to a tailor's, that I might choose an inoffensive colour. As I was not to remain long in Dublin, I wished to select a waistcoat which might do double service, as not too gay for the morning, and not too dull for the evening.

On arriving at the tailor's, he placed before me a profusion of beautiful silks, which I was assured contained all the newest and most approved patterns. Out of these I selected ten or a dozen, as best suiting my own taste. I then requested him to remove from amongst them any which might be considered as a party emblem. He took each of them rapidly up, and tossing it to another part of the counter, pronounced the whole batch to appertain to one party or the other.

Thus limited in my choice, I was compelled to adopt a waistcoat of all work, of rather gayer colours than good taste would willingly have

293

selected for morning use. I explained to the knight of the thimble my dilemma. He swore upon the honour of his order that the finished waistcoat should be at my rooms in the college punctually as the clock struck eight the next morning.

During the rest of the day I buttoned up my coat, and the broad light-blue border of my thin under-waistcoat was alone visible. My modesty, however, was a little uneasy, lest it should be thought that I was wearing the decoration of a Guelphic knight.

I rose early the next morning: eight o'clock arrived, but no waistcoat. The college breakfast in the hall was punctual / at a quarter past eight; 8·20 had arrived, but still no waistcoat. At last, at half-past eight, the squire of the faithless knight of the thimble arrived with the vest.

Thus equipped, I rushed to the hall, and found that my college friends had waited for my arrival. I explained to the Dean* that I had been detained by an unpunctual tailor, who had not brought home my waistcoat until half an hour after the appointed time. We then commenced the serious business which assembled us together. The breakfast was superb, and the society delightful. I enjoyed them both, being fortunately quite unconscious that every eye was examining the artistic and aesthetic garment with which I had been so recently invested. I thus acquired for a time the character of a dandy of the first water. It has not unfrequently been my fate in life to have gained a character for worth or worthlessness upon grounds quite as absurd, which I have afterwards seldom taken the trouble to explain.

The Dean, however, quickly saw through the outer covering, and before the meeting was over I felt that a friendship had commenced which time could only strengthen. One day, whilst we were walking together, MacLean told me that he had heard with great interest from one of his colleagues of some views of mine relative to miracles, which he wished much to hear from my own lips.

I remarked that the explanation of them would require much more time than we could afford during the bustle of the Association; but that I should afterwards, at any quiet time, be delighted to discuss them with him.

After the meeting of the British Association terminated, I made a short tour to visit some of my friends in the north of Ireland. On my

---

* The Rev. S. J. MacLean, Fellow Trinity College, Dublin.

return to Dublin I again found MacLean, / and had the good fortune to enjoy his society in a tour which we took to Killarney.

One fine morning, as we were walking together, it being Sunday, MacLean, looking somewhat doubtfully at me, asked whether I had any objection to go to church. I replied, 'None whatever,' and turned towards the church. Before we reached it an idea occurred to my mind, and I said, 'MacLean, you asked me, in the midst of the bustle at Dublin, about my views respecting miracles. Have you any objection to take a walk with me by the side of the lake, and I will give you a sermon upon that subject.' – 'Not the least,' replied my friend; and we turned immediately towards the banks of that beautiful lake.

I then proceeded to explain that those views of the apparently successive creations opened out to us by geology are in reality the fulfilment of one far more comprehensive law. I pointed out that a miracle, instead of being a violation of a law, is in fact the most eminent fulfilment of a vast law – that it bears the same relation to an apparent law that singular points of a curve bear to the visible form of that curve. My friend enquired whether I had published anything upon these subjects. On my answering in the negative, he strongly urged me to do so. I remarked upon the extreme difficulty of making them intelligible to the public. Reverting again to the singular points of curves, I observed that the illustration, which in a few words I had placed before him, would be quite unintelligible even to men of cultivated minds not familiar with the doctrine of curves.

We had now arrived at a bench, on which we sat. MacLean wrapt up in the new views thus opened out to his mind, remained silent for a long interval. At last, turning towards me, he made these remarks: 'How wonderful it is! Here / am I, bound by the duties of my profession to enquire into the attributes of the Creator; bound still more strongly by an intense desire to do so; possessing, like yourself, the same powerful science to aid my enquiries; and yet, within this last short half hour, you have opened to me views of the Creator surpassing all of which I have hitherto had any conception!'

These views had evidently made a very deep impression on his mind. Amidst the beautiful scenery in the south of Ireland he frequently reverted to the subject; and, having accompanied me to Waterford, offered to cross the channel with me if I could spend one single day at Milford Haven.

Unfortunately, long previous arrangements prevented this delay. I parted from my friend, who, though thus recently acquired, seemed, from the coincidence of our thoughts and feelings, to have been the friend of my youth. I little thought, on parting, that one whom I so much admired, so highly esteemed, would in a few short months be separated for ever from the friends who loved him, and from the society he adorned. /

CHAPTER XXX

RELIGION

Before thy holy altar, sacred Truth,
I bow in manhood, as I knelt in youth;
There let me bend till this frail form decay,
And my last accents hail thine opening day.

The *à priori* proof of the existence of a deity – Proof from revelation – Dr Johnson's definition of inspiration – Various meanings assigned to the word 'revelation' – Illustration of transmitted testimony – The third source of proof of the existence of a Deity – By an examination of His works – Effect of hearing the Athanasian Creed read for the first time.

There are three sources from which it is stated that man can arrive at the knowledge of the existence of a deity.

1. The *à priori* or metaphysical proof. Such is that of Dr Samuel Clarke.

2. From revelation.

3. From the examination of the works of the Creator.

1. The first of these, the *à priori* proof, is of such a nature that it can only be apprehended in a high state of civilization, and then only by the most intellectual. Even amongst that very limited class it does not, as an argument, command universal assent.

2. The argument deduced from revelation is advanced in many countries and for several different forms of faith. / When it is sincerely adopted it deserves the most respectful examination. It must, however, on the other hand, be submitted to the most scrutinizing enquiry. As long as the believer in any form of revelation maintains it by evidence or by argument, it is only by such means that it ought to be questioned.

When, however, professed believers dare to throw doubt upon the motives of those whose arguments they are unable to refute, and still more, when, availing themselves of the imperfections of language, they apply to their opponents epithets which they can defend in one

297

sense but know will be interpreted in another – when they speak of an adversary as a disbeliever, because, though he believes in the same general revelation, he doubts the accuracy of certain texts, or believes in a different interpretation of others – when they apply the term infidel, meaning thereby a disbelief in their *own* view of revelation, but knowing that it will be understood as disbelief in a deity – then it is at least allowable to remind them that they are richly paid for the support of their own doctrines, whilst those they revile have no such motives to influence or to mislead their judgement.

Before, however, we enter upon that great question it is necessary to observe that belief is not a voluntary operation. Belief is the result of the influence of a greater or less preponderance of evidence acting upon the human mind.

It ought also to be remarked that the word revelation assumes, as a fact, that a being exists from whom it proceeds; whilst, on the other hand, the existence of a deity is possible without any revelation.

The first question that arises is the meaning of the word revelation. In its ordinary acceptation it is said to be a direct communication from the Deity to an individual human / being. Dr Johnson remarks, 'Inspiration is when an overpowering impression of any propositions is made upon the mind by God Himself, that gives a convincing and indubitable evidence of the truth and divinity of it.' Be it so; but then, as such, it is not revelation to any *other* human being. All others receive it from the statement of the person to whom the revelation was vouchsafed. To all others its truth depends entirely on human testimony. Now in a certain sense all our faculties being directly given to us by the Supreme Being might be said to be revelations. But this is clearly not the religious meaning of the word. In the latter sense it is a direct special communication of knowledge to one or more persons which is not given to the rest of the race.

Before any person can admit the truth of a revelation asserted by another, he must have clearly established in his own mind what evidence he would require to believe in a special revelation to himself.

But when he communicates this revelation to his fellow-creatures that which may truly be a revelation to him is not revelation to them. It is to them merely human testimony, which they are bound to examine more strictly from its abnormal nature.

Let us now suppose that this believer in his own special revelation offers to work a miracle in proof of the truth of his doctrine, and even, further, that he does perform a miracle. Those who witness it have now before them far higher evidence of inspiration than that of the prophet's testimony. They have the evidence of their own senses that an act contrary to the ordinary laws of nature has been performed.

But even here the amount of conviction will be influenced by the state of knowledge the spectator of the miracle himself / possesses of the laws of nature which he *believes* he has thus seen violated.*

Granting him, however, the most profound knowledge, the evidence influencing his own mind will be inferior to that which acts upon the mind of the inspired worker of the miracle. If there are more witnesses than one thus qualified, this will to a certain extent augment the evidence, although a large number might not give it a proportional addition of weight.

It would be profane to compare evidence derived directly from the Almighty, which must necessarily be irresistible, with the testimony of man, which must always be carefully weighed by taking into account the state of his knowledge, his prejudices, his interests, and his truthfulness. On the other hand, it would lead to endless confusion, and be destructive to all reasoning on the subject, to apply the same word 'revelation' to things so different in their nature as:

The immediate act of the Deity.

The impression produced by that act on the mind of the person inspired.

The description of it given by him in the language of the people he addressed.

The record made of his description by those who heard it.

The transmission of this through various languages and people to the present day.

We have now arrived at the highest external evidence man can have – the declaration of inspiration by the prophet, supported / by an admitted miracle performed before competent witnesses, to prove the truth of his inspiration.

But to all who were not present, the evidence of this is entirely

* I have adopted in the text that view of the nature of miracles which prevailed many years ago. In 1838, I published, in the 'Ninth Bridgewater Treatise', my own views on those important subjects – the nature of miracles and of prophecy. Those opinions have been received and adopted by many of the most profound thinkers of very different religious opinions.

dependent on the truth and even upon the accuracy of *human testimony*.

At every step of its transmission it undergoes some variation in the words in which it is related; and without the least want of good faith at any stage, the mere imperfection of language will necessarily vary the terms by which it is described. Even when written language has conveyed it to paper as a MSS., there may be several different manuscripts by different persons. Even in the extraordinary case of two MSS. agreeing perfectly there remains a perpetual source of doubt as to the exact interpretation arising from the continually fluctuating meaning of the words themselves.

Few persons who have not reflected deeply, or had a very wide experience, are at all aware of the errors arising from this source.

There is a game occasionally played in society which eminently illustrates the value of testimony transmitted with the most perfect good faith through a succession of truthful persons. It is called Russian Scandal, and is thus played:

One of the party writes a short simple tale, perhaps a single anecdote. The original composer of the tale, whom we will call A, retires into another room with B, to whom he communicates it. A then returns to the party, and sends in C, who is told by B the tale he had just learnt. B then returns to the party and sends in D, who is informed of the anecdote by C, and so on until the story has been transmitted through twelve educated and truthful witnesses.

The twelfth then relates to the whole party the story he has just heard: after that the original written document is read. / The wit or fun of the transmitted story is invariably gone, and nothing but an unmeaning platitude generally remains.

One very interesting case occurred a few years ago in which the wit of the original story had evidently been lost, but had afterwards been revived in a different form in the latter part of its transmission. The story at starting consisted of the following anecdote:

The Duke of Rutland and Theodore Hook having dined with the Lord Mayor, were looking for their hats previously to their departure. The Duke, unable to find his own, said to his friend: 'Hook, I have lost my castor.' The Lord Chief Baron, Sir Frederick Pollock, was at that moment passing down the stairs. Hook perceiving him, replied instantly, 'Never mind, take Pollock's' (Pollux).

The story told at the conclusion, after a dozen transmissions, was thus:

Theodore Hook and the Duke of Rutland were dining with the Bishop of Oxford. Both being equally incapable of finding their respective hats, the Duke said to the wit, 'Hook, you have stolen my castor.' 'No,' replied the prince of jokers, 'I haven't stolen your castor, but I should have no objection to take your beaver'; alluding to Belvoir Castle, the splendid seat of the Duke of Rutland, which in the language of the day is pronounced precisely in the same way as the name of that animal whom man robs of his greatcoat in order to make a covering for his own skull.

It requires considerable training to become an accurate witness of facts. No two persons, however well trained, ever express, in the same form of words, the series of facts they have both observed.

3. There remains a third source from which we arrive at / the knowledge of the existence of a Supreme Creator, namely, from *an examination of His works*. Unlike transmitted testimony, which is weakened at every stage, this evidence derives confirmation from the progress of the individual as well as from the advancement of the knowledge of the race.

Almost all thinking men who have studied the laws which govern the animate and the inanimate world around us, agree that the belief in the existence of one Supreme Creator, possessed of infinite wisdom and power, is open to far less difficulties than the supposition of the absence of *any* cause, or of the existence of a *plurality* of causes.

In the *works* of the Creator ever open to our examination, we possess a firm basis on which to raise the superstructure of an enlightened creed. The more man enquires into the laws which regulate the material universe, the more he is convinced that all its varied forms arise from the action of a few simple principles. These principles themselves converge, with accelerating force, towards some still more comprehensive law to which all matter seems to be submitted. Simple as that law may possibly be, it must be remembered that it is only one amongst an infinite number of simple laws: that each of these laws has consequences at least as extensive as the existing one, and therefore that the Creator who selected the present law must have foreseen the consequences of all other laws.

The *works* of the Creator, ever present to our senses, give a living and perpetual testimony of his power and goodness far surpassing any evidence transmitted through human testimony. The testimony of man becomes fainter at every stage of transmission, whilst each new enquiry into the works of the Almighty gives to us more exalted views of His wisdom, His goodness, and His power. /

When I was between sixteen and seventeen years of age, I heard, or rather I attended, for the first time, to the words of the Athanasian Creed. I felt the utmost disgust at the direct contradiction in terms which its words implied; and during several weeks I recurred, at intervals, to the prayer-book to assure myself that I rightly remembered its singular and self-contradictory assertions. On enquiry amongst my seniors, I was assured that it was all true, and that it was part of the Christian religion, and that it was most wicked to doubt a single sentence of it. Whereupon I was much alarmed, seeing that I found it absolutely impossible to believe it, and consequently, if it were an essential dogma, I clearly did not belong to that faith.

In the course of my enquiries, I met with the work upon the Trinity,[a] by Dr Samuel Clarke. This I carefully examined, and although very far from being satisfied, I ceased from further enquiry. This change arose probably from my having acquired the much more valuable work of the same author, on the being and attributes of God.[b] This I studied, and felt that its doctrine was much more intelligible and satisfactory than that of the former work. I may now state, as the result of a long life spent in studying the *works* of the Creator, that I am satisfied they afford far more satisfactory and more convincing proofs of the existence of a Supreme Being than any evidence transmitted through human testimony can possibly supply.

If I were to express my opinion of the Athanasian Creed merely from my experience of the motives and actions of mankind, I should say that it was written by a clever, but most unscrupulous person, who did not believe one syllable of the doctrine – that he purposely asserted and reiterated propositions which contradict each other in terms, in order that / in after and more enlightened times, he should not be supposed to have believed in the religion which he had, from worldly motives, adopted.

The Athanasian Creed is a direct contradiction in terms: if three things can be one thing, then the whole science of arithmetic is at once annihilated, and those wonderful laws, which, as astronomers have shown, govern the solar system, are mere dreams. If, on the other ic

---

[a] Samuel Clarke *et al., An account of. . . the controversy concerning the Trinity* (1720).
[b] Samuel Clarke, *A demonstration of the being and attributes of God* (London, 1705, etc.).

hand, it is attempted to be shown that there may be some mystic sense in which three and one are the same thing, then all language through which alone man can exert his reasoning faculty becomes useless, because it contradicts itself and is untrue.*

The great basis of virtue in man is *truth* – that is, the constant application of the same word to the same thing.

The first element of accurate knowledge is *number* – the foundation and the measure of all he knows of the material world.

I believe these views of the Athanasian Creed are by no means singular – that they are indeed very generally held, although very rarely asserted. If such is the case, it were wise to take the opportunity which the new commission for the revision of the liturgy presents, to remove from the rubric doctrines so thoroughly destructive of all true religion, and about which the author, doubtless in mockery, so complacently tells us, that whosoever does not believe them 'without doubt, he shall perish everlastingly'.

The true value of the Christian religion rests, not upon speculative views of the Creator, which must *necessarily* be different in each individual, according to the extent of the knowledge of the finite being, who employs his own feeble powers in contemplating the infinite: but it rests upon those / doctrines of kindness and benevolence which that religion claims and enforces, not merely in favour of man himself, but of every creature susceptible of pain or of happiness.

A curious reflection presents itself when we meditate upon a state of rewards and punishments in a future life. We must possess the memory of what we did during our existence upon this earth in order to give them those characteristics.

In fact, memory seems to be the only faculty which must of necessity be preserved in order to render a future state possible.

If memory be absolutely destroyed, our personal identity is lost.

Further reflection suggests that in a future state we may, as it were, awake to the recollection that, previously to this our present life, we existed in some former state, possibly in many former ones, and that the then state of existence may have been the consequences of our conduct in those former stages.

It would be a very interesting research if naturalists could devise any means of showing that the dragonfly, in its three stages of a grub beneath the soil – an animal living in the water – and that of a flying

* See Appendix, Note B.

insect – had in the last stage any memory of its existence in its first.

Another question connected with this subject offers still greater difficulty. Man possesses five sources of knowledge through his senses. He proudly thinks himself the highest work of the Almighty Architect; but it is quite *possible* that he may be the very lowest. If other animals possess senses of a different nature from ours, it can scarcely be possible that we could ever be aware of the fact. Yet those animals, having other sources of information and of pleasure, might, though despised by us, yet enjoy a corporeal as well as an intellectual existence far higher than our own. /

CHAPTER XXXI

A VISION

How, when, and where this vision occurred it is unnecessary for me at present to state. It did not arise under the action of the laughing gas or of chloroform, but by some much more real and immediate spiritual action. I had no perception of body or of matter, yet I felt that I was in the presence of a reasoning being of a different order from man. Language was not the means of our communication; yet it became necessary, in order to be intelligible, when I wrote down the facts immediately after that singular event – but language itself is quite insufficient to give an adequate idea of its immense apparent duration.

The first difficulty I felt in this communion with an unearthly spirit was the notion of space. Our views of it differed widely. On many points, as, for instance, measure, we apprehended each other perfectly, for each referred to the height of an individual of his own race – of course about six feet. At last I discovered that my idea of space, which was founded upon vacuity, was exactly the reverse of that of the spirit, which was based upon solidity. I will now, as far as I can, place before my reader the information I received.

The first desire I expressed to the spirit was to learn, if possible, his view of the origin of all things. He stated that / the records of his race, which he declared was the highest in creation, went back, with great certainty, for myriads of years before all other created beings: that previously to this, their history was somewhat obscure, but had recently been placed upon a much surer footing by some of their most prominent spirits.

(a) In the beginning all space was fluid – apparently one universal whitish liquid extended in all directions through what we should call space; so I thought at first that this might have some relation to the 'milky way'. Its temperature was considerable; and in about every thousand years a torrent of this fluid, of a still higher temperature,

305

passed through space with a kind of gushing noise. It was peopled by myriads of happy spirits floating about in it.

After long ages of happiness a dispute arose between two spirits as to the possibility of the existence of matter under any other form than that of a fluid. The power which controlled their destiny, justly angry at their presumption, threw into the fluid a very small piece of what, as far as I could understand, was like organic matter.

(b) The effect was astounding: all the fluid in contact with this intrusive piece of matter gradually lost its fluidity, and a new state of matter or of space arose which had been unknown in all past time. The change advanced slowly but certainly, on every side of the intruded matter. In its new form, as far as I could make out, space became elastic gelatinous matter. The two quarrelsome spirits were the first to be surrounded in it. None in the immediate presence of this new kind of space could move away, and absorption went on rapidly imprisoning millions of beings.

A great controversy arose as to the state of those embedded in the jelly. Some supposed that they were miserably squeezed, / and maintained that they deserved to be thoroughly wretched. Whilst others asserted, that being entirely relieved from movement, theirs must be a state of perfect blessedness, their whole faculties being absorbed in contemplation. In the midst of these discussions the process of jellification was advancing more and more rapidly, and in ten thousand years the whole of infinite fluidity throughout all space, with all its myriads of beings embedded in it, was transformed into this new form of space. From the description conveyed to me by the spirit, I should infer that the whole of what we call infinite space had now become more nearly like *blancmange* than any other subaerial substance.

(c) After a state of repose of many hundred thousand years a new catastrophe occurred. Space became too large even for itself. It then suffered, for many hundred thousand years, enormous compression. During this long period all its embedded spirits perished, and space itself, during six hundred thousand years, became one vast and solid desert, containing no living beings.

But the vast periods of the past were as nothing compared with the long series of cycles which now succeeded – each in itself comprising millions of years.

About this time recorded history began, and is believed, by the spirit with whom I was in conference, to be as authentic as the nature of the circumstances admit.

306

One solitary survivor seems to have escaped the crash of systems and the condensation of space. He proceeded to cut himself into two parts, and to advise each part to follow out the same course, directing them to transmit the command of their first parent throughout all time. Alone, in the midst of infinite solidity, the newly severed beings, setting themselves back to back, exerted force. Thus urged, matter itself gave / way, and they occupied an elongated hollow space. Then again bisecting themselves, they further lengthened the path. After ten thousand years they began to exert their energies in the transverse directions of that path, and thus widened it. The race then began to form chambers, each for himself, into which he might retire for abstruse calculations, the nature of which seemed almost beyond the remotest reach of utility, although not beyond the power of the Analytical Engine. Thus vast cities, as it were, became formed, penetrating in every direction through solid space.

(d) After millions of years of industry, quietness and calculations, a most extraordinary catastrophe occurred. It was with the greatest difficulty that I could discover its nature, or how to explain it in ordinary language. The nearest approach I can make towards its explanation is this: It seemed, from what my spiritual informant communicated, that the whole universe was lifted up bodily, and then borne rapidly back with a great shock, thus disarranging everything, and destroying millions of their race.

But the most incomprehensible part of this historic narration was, that on the survivors recovering their senses, they found that everything which had formerly been on their right hand was now on their left. They also observed, to their still greater dismay, that every abode in the universe was turned topsy-turvy, so that the surviving philosophers, who had retired to their attics to study, suddenly found themselves in their cellars.

I have conveyed, as carefully as the nature of the subject admits, the impressions this relation made upon me, sometimes assisted in my slow apprehensions by another unembodied spirit, whom, to distinguish from the relator, I shall call Mathesis. /

Whenever a man can get hold of numbers, they are invaluable: if correct, they assist in informing his own mind, but they are still more useful in deluding the minds of others. Numbers are the masters of the weak, but the slaves of the strong. I therefore earnestly pressed for more exact information as to the possible number of years; but it appeared beyond the spirit's power to estimate it, even within a few millions. He mentioned incidentally that the last vast period he had just described was merely one of many others of similar extent: also, that though these periods were not actually equal, the difference, which even in extreme cases only reached a hundred thousand years, was not worth considering.

To gratify my longing desire for information on this most important subject, the spirit proceeded to inform me that their histories recorded a large number of these successive catastrophes, and that they were succeeded by a new and more terrible one, which he was proceeding to explain, when I interrupted him by asking for an approximate estimate of their number. Aware of my anxious desire for numerical accuracy, he said he could, in this one instance, gratify it fully. 'If there is,' said my informant, 'any one point better established than all others, it is that there had occurred exactly one hundred and twenty-one of these avatars of destruction.'

I now felt as if I had discovered one solitary fixed point in the vast chaos of time. My guide described to me that, after the termination of this system of one hundred and twenty-one cycles, a new and more terrific system of events followed each other.

First, however, he said he must mention an interregnum, irregular in its progress, but still of vast duration; / in fact, some of his race had been able to prove that it occupied at least three times as long as any one of those just described.

(e) It commenced by a motion very like that to which space itself had been submitted at the end of each avatar, finishing with a smash, and followed by a period of repose of about ten thousand years. It however differed from those avatars inasmuch as there was no inversion of the position of cellar and attic.

(f) A new form of shaking of universal solid space now arose, much more frequent but less destructive than the former. It occurred about once in two years, and was repeated many hundred thousand times.

(g) Again a period exactly similar to that recorded in *(e)* occurred.

(h) This was followed by a long series of movements of all solidity, approaching, as far as I could understand it, to an oscillating or wave motion. This continued without intermission during exactly three of those cycles whose precise number had been preserved.

(i) During the whole of this period there was a great destruction of the race. A universal sickness arose and continued more or less, so that multitudes actually perished, and those who escaped could scarcely carry on the ordinary calculations necessary for their existence.

(j) Another period followed, ending with a smash excessively like *(e)*.

(k) Then followed a period of shaking like that in *(f)*.

(l) Then another smash like *(e)*.

(m) Period of long repose.

After this came a long state of absolute rest.

Such was the dawn of the most terrible, as well as the / most recent, of these vast changes in the universe which had been so well related by my ethereal guide.

(n) The temperature of the universe had been uniform throughout many millions of years: it now began to change in different isolated places. Increased cold in some parts drove the inhabitants from their dwellings. This was followed by torrents of invisible air, bringing infection and death to millions of their race. Public opinion was roused, and their academics of science and of arts were urged to devise a remedy. An expedition was sent by their school of science and of geology to endeavour to trace the origin of this plague.

The commission, after long investigation, reported that they had penetrated solid space in their usual way, putting each other back to back, and pressing the foremost forward. It also stated that one of them had invented a method of arrangement of the members in a kind of wedge form, which they found much more effective for their object. The result of this, however, was that the leader of the column got so many squeezes, that all their best spirits declined a position for which coarser animals were better fitted. Consequently, most of their presidents of scientific bodies were selected from what we should call the '*demi-monde*' of science.

The first report of this commission stated that, after penetrating space (by pushing) through many thousand miles, they had reached the cause of all the evil. They had ascertained that it arose from the fact they had discovered – that space itself was discontinuous: that they had reached a spot where there was a kind of chasm in it, into which some of them tumbled, and were with difficulty extricated: in fact, they reported that it was only necessary to send proper persons to fill up this chasm in order to restore the universe to health. /

Great rejoicings were made on the return of this commission. Public meeting were held, speeches were made, papers were read, and medals were lavished. Those who had interest used their services on this committee to justify their promotion, each in his own different line. Those who had no interest as well as those who had, were

309

anointed daily during twelve months with what I can but very imperfectly describe by calling it *lip-salve*. All this while they were fed at the public expense with *royal food*, which was highly coveted; but as far as I could make out, its taste must have been somewhat intermediate between rancid butter and flummery. Whatever this may have been, they relished it highly, and in truth it seems to have been well suited to their organs of digestion.

Time, however, went on; the pestilence increased. Strange reports arose: first, that space itself was decaying; then, that there existed somewhere in decayed space an immense dragon whose breath produced the pestilence, and who swallowed up thousands of spirits at each mouthful.

Another commission was sent, with instructions to fill up the hole in space. This was supposed to be a great step in advance. Having penetrated a very short distance beyond the celebrated chasm, they found another just like it, and on the same level. They found the first chasm slightly curved, which had indeed been remarked by an unpretending member of the former commission: but so simple a remark was not thought worth reporting. The second chasm also was found slightly curved, but its curvature was in an opposite direction, presenting rudely the appearance of two parentheses, thus ( ). Upon this discovery the commission were inclined to return and report that a series of chasms occurred in advance of the first, and that it would be useless – indeed, / that it would be highly dangerous – to open more chasms. One of the most modest of the commissioners, who had been snubbed on the former occasion, suggested, however, that these slightly curved chasms might possibly be portions of some vast circular crack: an idea which was ridiculed as a wild hypothesis by the chairman, quizzed by the secretary, and laughed at by all the rest. Fortunately they were persuaded to excavate a few yards more on the second vertical chasm or crack, when it became probable that the single dissentient was right. It soon became certain, and before half the circle had been uncovered, each member of the commission thought he had himself been the first to discover its circular shape.

But the chairman was a person of large experience. He quietly left the commissioners to fight amongst themselves about the discovery of the circle, and if they chose, even about its quadrature. On his return, however, he reported that from some very extensive calculations of his own he had anticipated an elliptic cavity; that he had directed the attention of the commissioners to the subject; and that they had

310

succeeded in verifying his prediction. He also stated that the same theory led him to the knowledge of the fact, that in certain cases the ellipse might approach very nearly to a circle, although it could never actually reach it, whilst on the other hand it might become so flat as to approach a straight line – an approximation to which nobody ever suggested that the chairman himself could have attained. The chairman then, with singular modesty, alluding in his report to one of his colleagues possessing high rank, great influence and a very moderate knowledge of science, remarked that it was fortunate for him (the chairman) that that distinguished member had been so fully occupied with much more valuable / investigations, otherwise he would certainly have anticipated the important discovery it had fallen to his own lot to make.

In the meantime the commissioners, who had each wished to appropriate to himself the discovery of the circle, *now* thought that this usurpation of it by their chairman was most unjust towards the unpretending member who had really made it. They therefore advised him to claim his own discovery, and promised to back him in asserting it.

But their chairman really was a *clever fellow*,* and deep as silurian rocks. Aware of the importance of the discovery thus appropriated, he had already visited the modest commissioner – had overwhelmed him with compliments, and had also prevailed upon that other influential commissioner whom he had so well buttered in his report, to give him a small piece of preferment, which had been accepted by his victim: thus putting a padlock upon his lips, which his brother commissioners were unable either to unlock or to pick.

After the report was presented, more speeches were made – more medals given, but the plague continued, and their universe was depopulated.

A third commission was afterwards sent, who reported that they found at the spot previously reached, on either side, two vast circles, the diameter of each of which was one hundred times the height of an ordinary individual; that the material occupying space within the circle differed slightly from that without it; and that it appeared as if a vast cylinder of space had been pushed through without disturbing the matter external to it. They also reported that the former

---

* A *clever fellow* may occasionally snatch our applause; but a *clever man* can alone command our respect.

311

commissioners had never approached the origin of the mischief, but had simply worked their way, at right angles, to a / line which might terminate in it at the distance of a thousand miles, more or less, either on the right or on the left hand of the point they had reached.

At this moment a sound like the roll of distant thunder recalled me to this lower world, and interrupted my interesting communion with the world of spirits. That noise arose from the chimes of the cathedral clock. Spending a few days at Salisbury, I had wandered into the cathedral, and being much fatigued, had selected the luxurious pew of the dean as a place of temporary rest. Reposing on elastic cushions, with my head resting on an eider-down pillow, the vision I have related had taken place.

On removing the pillow I observed a small piece of matter beneath it. This, upon examination, turned out to be a morsel of decayed Gloucester cheese. The whole vision was now very clearly explained. The verger had evidently retired to the most commodious pew to eat his dinner, and had inadvertently left the small bit of cheese upon the very spot I had selected for my temporary repose. It was clear that my spirit had been put, *en rapport*, with the soul of a mite, one of the most cultivated of his race.

If the reader will glance over the following brief explanation, he will be fully convinced that my solution of this vision is the true one.

Parallel passages in the creation of the universe and in the birth and education of a Gloucester cheese
- (a) Milk gushing into the milk pail at the rate of twenty gushes per minute. Alternations of greater and less heat.
- (b) Rennet being thrown in, the milk curdles.
- (c) Curds compressed into cheese. /
- (d) Cheese turned over daily during 121 days.
    A few minutes' difference in the time of the dairyman's attendance to perform this operation made the days slightly unequal.
- (e) Cheese lifted up and pitched into a cart.
- (f) Cheese *jolted* in cart during half a day on its way to be shipped at Gloucester.
- (g) Cheese pitched from cart into ship.
- (h) Ship sails with the cheese for Southampton.
- (i) The motion of the waves makes the mites seasick for three days. Multitudes die.

(j) Cheese taken from ship and pitched into a cart; as in the period *(e)*.

(k) Cheese conveyed in cart to cheesemonger at Salisbury – the mites dreadfully *jolted*.

(l) Cheese pitched into cheesemonger's shop, as in *(e)*.

(m) Long period of repose of the cheese on the cheesemonger's shelf.

(n) A cylindrical cavity made and piece taken out for a customer to taste. Portion of cylinder replaced. Air being let in, a part of the cheese becomes rotten, in which large worms are produced, giving rise to the story of the dragon.

In order to discover the month in which the cheese was made, I remarked that, since it was turned over on its shelf in the cheese-room exactly 121 times, it must have been first placed there in some month which, together with the three succeeding months, had a number of days exactly equal to 121. /

I then computed the following table:

Table of the number of days contained in each four months, commencing on the first day of each month and ending on the last day of the fourth following month

		Number of days
1 January	to 30 April	120
1 February	„ 31 May	120
1 March	„ 30 June	122
1 April	„ 31 July	122
1 May	„ 31 August	123
1 June	„ 30 September	122
1 July	„ 31 October	123
1 August	„ 30 November	122
1 September	„ 31 December	122
1 October	„ 31 January	123
1 November	„ 28 February	120
1 December	„ 31 March	121

Now, from the preceding table it appears that there is only one month in the year fulfilling this condition, namely, the month of March. It follows, therefore, that the cheese must have been made four months before, that is, in the month of December.

Shortly after this vision I received a visit from that great geologist, the erudite Professor Ponderdunder,* a member of all existing academies, and Secretary of the most celebrated How-and-wi Academy for the *Reconstruction of Primeval Time*. I was anxious to have the opinion of this learned person upon my recent experience: but he was evidently envious of my vision, which he treated disrespectfully. Possessed / of an intellect which was anything but precocious, I had with much labour at last made him apprehend the arithmetic by which I had discovered the exact month of December in the date of the great series of 121 cataclysms, and I felt much mortified that he did not appreciate my ingenuity. All of a sudden he seemed intuitively to perceive the use that might be made of this vision. He then asked me with great earnestness whether I had communicated this new method of reasoning to any other person. On my answering in the negative, he entreated me not to say a word about it. He was especially anxious that Gardner Wilkinson, Layard, and Rawlinson should not get hold of it, lest they might anticipate the discovery which it would enable him to complete. He assured me that he could, by visiting Nineveh, and taking the pyramids and Jericho on his road, with the aid of my formula, restore the true chronology from the Creation.

Having given him this promise, he left me, and immediately telegraphed to a very influential friend, the Vice-President who *managed* the How-and-wi Academy, suggesting that not a moment should be lost in authorizing him to set out on this expedition, which although painfully laborious to himself personally and not without peril, he was willing to undertake for the glory of the Academy, and from the religious conviction that it would enable him to refute the frightful heresy of Bishop Colenso. Within twenty-four hours the faithful telegraph brought him back the order to start and the credit necessary for his equipment. He soon completed the latter, and was *en route* within the time I have mentioned.

It is with deep regret I have now to state, that just ten days after the active Secretary had started on his pious mission, I discovered that my reasoning about the month of December with all its consequences was completely vitiated / by not having taken into consideration the existence of leap years, in which case the magic number 121 occurs in no less than four cases; so that nothing at all is decided by it.

* Author of the celebrated treatise 'On the Entity of Space', the basis of all *sound* metaphysical reasoning.

I can only add my hope that, if any of my readers should become acquainted with the whereabouts of the learned Ponderdunder, he would kindly communicate by electric telegraph this painful intelligence to that energetic traveller.

I have subsequently been informed that Professor Ponderdunder's honorarium is only £800 a year, and the payment of all travelling expenses. The former is doubled upon dangerous travel. I was told that he also enjoys a snug sinecure of considerable value recently instituted in his own country; being at the head of the department for the promotion of 'Small Science and Low Art'. The family of the Ponderdunders possess the peculiar gift of 'manipulating learned bodies. The Flowery–Rhetorical, and the Zoo-Ethnological Societies barely escaped perdition under their costly autocracy. I regret also to add (but truth forbids me to conceal the interesting fact) that Ponderdunder is *not* a member of *all* existing academies as his visiting card indicated.

On searching the list of the members of the Roman Academy 'Dei Lynxcii', I find that he is not a Lynx. This, the oldest of European academies, originally existed in the time of Galileo. About a quarter of a century ago I had the honour of receiving its diploma. /

315

CHAPTER XXXII

VARIOUS REMINISCENCES

On preventing the forgery of bank-notes

In 1836 imitations of bank-notes were so easily made, and the forgeries so numerous, that the directors of the Bank of England resolved on appointing a small committee to examine the subject, and advise them upon a remedy.

The Governor of the Bank wrote to ask me whether I would consent to act upon that committee. Not being myself a professional engineer, I entertained some doubts whether my presence would be agreeable to the profession. Having consulted Sir Isambard Brunel and the late Mr Bryan Donkin, who had been also applied to, they both pressed me to join them in the enquiry.

We examined the existing means of preventing forgery, which were certainly very defective. The system of the Bank of Ireland which had recently been greatly improved, was then discussed. Not many months before, I had carefully examined the whole plan at Dublin. After a full deliberation on the subject, I drew up our report, which unanimously recommended its adoption. The identity of the steel plates from which the bank-notes were to be printed was secured by Perkins's plan of multiplying the number of such plates by impressing them all from one roll of hardened steel.

This plan answered its purpose fully at that time. It has, / however, been superseded within the last few years. I had, through the kindness of the late Governor of the Bank of England, an opportunity of examining their most recent improvement. The discovery of the process of making facsimiles of a wood engraving, by means of the electrochemical deposit of copper, has now enabled the Bank to return to the more rapid process of surface printing.

It is probable, from the great progress of the mechanical arts, that these periods for revising methods of preventing forgery will occur at more frequent intervals.

I derived great pleasure from being permitted, as an amateur, to join in this interesting enquiry with my professional friends, whose knowledge and character I highly valued.

Subsequently I received the unexpected gratification of a vote of thanks from the Governor and Company of the Bank of England – an honour usually reserved for warriors and statesmen.

An émeute[a]

On one of my visits to Paris I had the pleasure of dining at the Bank of France. During dinner, in the midst of an interesting conversation, the chairman received a note: having glanced over it he put it down by his side on the table.

On the occurrence of a pause in the conversation, thinking the note might possibly require an immediate reply, I enquired whether such was the case. 'No,' said my host, 'it is of no consequence. It is only an émeute'; which he then informed me was occurring in a distant part of Paris.

Letters of credit

Letters of credit are specially addressed to certain bankers at various places with whom your own banker is in correspondence. /

It has on several occasions happened to me to want cash either for myself or to accommodate some friend at places where my own letters were not addressed to any firm. At Frankfort I made a purchase of books. I had a certain amount of the usual circular letters, but as these were payable in a great many cities, and as I proposed visiting Egypt, I did not wish to part with them. I therefore went to the house of Rothschild, hoping to get an advance on my letter of credit, although it was not addressed to that firm. But it being Saturday, no business was done. I therefore enquired for another banker of reputation, and was directed to M. Koch.

I accordingly called at his counting-house, stated my reason for wanting the money, showed him my circular notes and letters of credit, and asked whether, under these circumstances, he would cash my cheque for twenty pounds. He immediately remarked that he had frequently visited England, and that most probably we had several

---

[a] *Translation:* a riot.

common friends, as it soon appeared, for the first person was Professor Sedgwick.

M. Koch not only advanced me the money, but he was so kind as to invite me to dinner on the following day, and to give me a seat in his box at the opera on the first appearance of Madamoiselle Sontag on the Frankfort stage.

I remember at least three other occasions in which I got money for some of my English friends at towns where my letter of credit was not addressed to any banker. In those cases I only asked them to take my cheque, send it to London, and when they had received the amount, to pay it over to me. I also mentioned that I was known to several persons resident in Geneva and in Berlin where these occurrences happened. In each case the banker immediately let me have the money my friends wanted. /

The only instance in which I was refused amused me very much. I spent a few weeks at Modena, where I had purchased a microscope and several other philosophical instruments. One morning I went to the wealthy firm of Sanguinetti, and mentioning my object to one of the partners, at the same time showing him my letter of credit, asked if, under these circumstances, he would give me cash for a draft of twenty pounds on my banker in London. He replied very courteously that it was the rule of their house to give credit only upon letters addressed to them by their *own* correspondent in London. I remarked that it was quite necessary in matters of business to adhere to fixed rules, and that when made aware of their practice I should be the last person to ask them to deviate from it.

Early the next morning a carriage drove up to the door of my lodgings and an elderly gentleman was announced. This was M. Sanguinetti, the senior partner of the firm. He told me he came to apologize for the refusal of his junior partner on the preceding day, and to offer to give me cash for my cheque to whatever amount I might require.

I replied that, a near relative of my own having formerly been a banker in London, I was aware of the necessity of a rigid observance of rules of business, and that his young partner had not only done his duty, but, I added, that he had done it in the most courteous manner. M. Sanguinetti was so obliging and so pressing, that I found it difficult to accept the advance of so small a sum: however, it was all arranged, and he left me.

I then sent for my landlord and enquired whether he had had any

318

communication with M. Sanguinetti. He replied that the old gentleman, the head of the firm, had called the preceding evening, and asked him who I was. 'And what,' / said I to my landlord, 'was your answer?' – 'I told him you were a Milord Anglais,' replied my host. – 'I am not a Milord Anglais,' I observed; 'but why did you tell him so?' – 'Because,' said my landlord, 'when the minister paid you a visit, you sat down in his presence.'

The explanation of the affair was this. Soon after my arrival at Modena, I called on the Marquis Rangoni, a distinguished mathematician, who had written a profound comment on Laplace's 'Théorie des Fonctions Génératrices'.[a] I had not brought any letter of introduction, but had merely sent up my card. The Marquis Rangoni received me very cordially, and we were soon in deep discussion respecting some of the most abstract questions of analysis. He returned my visit on the following day, when he resumed the discussion, and I showed him some papers connected with the subject. I was aware of the title of the Marquis Rangoni to respect, as arising from his own profound acquaintance with analysis, but I was now, for the first time, informed that he was a man of great importance in the little Dukedom of Modena, for he was the Prime Minister of the Grand Duke – in fact, the Palmerston of Modena. This at once explained the attention I received from the wealthy banker.

The speaker

One Saturday morning an American gentleman who had just arrived from Liverpool, where he had landed from the United States on the previous day, called in Dorset Street. He was very anxious to see the Difference Engine, and quite fitted by his previous studies for understanding it well. I took him into the drawing-room in which the machine then resided and gave him a short explanation of its structure. As I expected a large party of my friends in the evening, / amongst whom were a few men of science, I asked him to join the party.

It so happened on that day that the speaker had a small dinner-party. The Silver Lady was accidentally mentioned, and greatly excited the curiosity of the lady of the house. As the whole of this

---

[a] L. Rangoni, *Sulle funzioni generatrici* (Modena, 1824).

small party, comprising three or four of my most intimate friends, were coming to my house in the evening, they proposed that the speaker and his wife should accompany them to my party, assuring them truly that I should be much gratified by the visit.

The Silver Lady happened to be in brilliant attire, and after mentioning the romance of my boyish passion, the unexpected success of her acquisition, and the devoted cultivation I bestowed upon her education, I proceeded to set in action her fascinating and most graceful movements.

A gay but by no means unintellectual crowd surrounded the automaton. In the adjacent room the Difference Engine stood nearly deserted: two foreigners alone worshipped at that altar. One of them, but just landed from the United States, was engaged in explaining to a learned professor from Holland what he had himself in the morning gathered from its constructor.

Leaning against the doorway, I was myself contemplating the strongly contrasted scene, pleased that my friends were relaxing from their graver pursuits, and admiring the really graceful movements produced by mechanism; but still more highly gratified at observing the deep and almost painful attention of my Dutch guest, who was questioning his American instructor about the mechanical means I had devised for accomplishing some arithmetical object. The deep thought with which this explanation was attended to, suddenly / flashed into intense delight when the simple means of its accomplishment were made apparent.

My acute and valued friend, the late Lord Langdale, who had been observing the varying changes of my own countenance, as it glanced from one room to the other, now asked me, 'What new mischief are you meditating?' – 'Look,' said I, 'in that further room – England. Look again at this – two foreigners.'

Ancient music

Many years ago some friends of mine invited me to accompany them to the concert of ancient music, and join their supper-party after it was over.

My love of music is not great, but for the pleasure of the society I accepted the invitation. On our meeting at the supper-table, I was overwhelmed with congratulations upon my exquisite appreciation of the treat we had just had. I was assured that though my expression of feeling was of the quietest order, yet that I was the earliest to approve all the most beautiful passages.

I accepted modestly my easily won laurels, and perhaps my taste for music might have survived in the memory of my friends, when my taste for mechanism had been forgotten. I will, however, confide to the public the secret of my success. Soon after I had taken my seat at the concert, I perceived Lady Essex at a short distance from me. Knowing well her exquisitely sensitive taste, I readily perceived by the expression of her countenance, as well as by the slight and almost involuntary movement of the hand, or even of a finger, those passages which gave her most delight. These quiet indications, unobserved by my friends, formed the electric wire by which I directed the expressions of my own countenance / and the very modest applause I thought it prudent to develop.

After receiving the congratulations of my friends upon my great musical taste, I informed them how easily that reputation had been acquired. Such are the feeble bases on which many a public character rests.

<Philosophy of invention>
During my residence with my Oxford tutor, whilst I was working by myself on mathematics, I occasionally arrived at conclusions which appeared to me to be new, but which from time to time I afterwards found were already well known. At first I was much discouraged by these disappointments, and drew from such occurrences the inference that it was hopeless for me to attempt to invent anything new. After a time I saw the fallacy of my reasoning, and then inferred that when my knowledge became much more extended I might reasonably hope to make some small additions to my favourite science.

This idea considerably influenced my course during my residence at Cambridge by directing my reading to the original papers of the great discoverers in mathematical science. I then endeavoured to trace the course of their minds in passing from the known to the unknown, and to observe whether various artifices could not be connected together by some general law. The writings of Euler were eminently instructive for this purpose. At the period of my leaving Cambridge I began to see more distinctly the object of my future pursuit.

It appeared to me that the highest exercise of human faculties consisted in the endeavour to discover those laws of thought by which man passes from the known to that which / was unknown. It might

321

with propriety be called the philosophy of invention. During the early part of my residence in London, I commenced several essays on induction, generalization, analogy, with various illustrations from different sources. The philosophy of signs always occupied my attention, and to whatever subject I applied myself I was ever on the watch to perceive and record the links by which the new was connected with the known.

Most of the early essays I refer to were not sufficiently matured for publication, and several have appeared without any direct reference to the great object of my life. I may, however, point out one of my earlier papers in the *Philosophical Transactions* for 1817, which, whilst it made considerable additions to a new branch of science, is itself a very striking instance of the use of analogy for the purpose of invention. I refer to the 'Essay on the Analogy between the Calculus of Functions and other Branches of Analysis' (*Philosophical Transactions*, 1817).[a] /

---

[a] 'Observations on the analogy which subsists between the calculus of functions and other branches of analysis' (1817), *Works of Babbage*, Vol. 1.

CHAPTER XXXIII

THE AUTHOR'S CONTRIBUTIONS TO
HUMAN KNOWLEDGE

Scientific societies – Analytical Society – Astronomical Society – Grand Duke
of Tuscany, Leopold II – Scientific meeting at Florence – Also at Berlin – At
Edinburgh – At Cambridge – Origin of the Statistical Society – Statistical
congress at Brussels – Calculus of functions – Division of labour – Verification
part of cost – Principles of taxation – Extension to elections – The two pumps –
Monopoly – Miracles

Of the part taken by the author in the formation
of various scientific societies[a]

The origin of the Analytical Society has been already explained in the
fourth chapter. In the year 1820 the author of this volume, joining with
several eminent men attached to astronomical pursuits, instituted the
Royal Astronomical Society. At the present time only three of the
original founders survive. The meetings, and still more the publications of that society, have contributed largely to extend the taste for
astronomy.

In 1827 I visited Italy, and during my residence at Florence had
many opportunities of observing the strong feeling of the reigning
Grand Duke Leopold II, not only for the fine arts, but for the progress
of science, and for its application to the advancement of the arts of life.

After a long tour in Italy, I found myself in the following year again
in Florence, and again I was received with a kindness and consideration which I can never forget. The Grand / Duke was anxious to know
my opinion respecting the state of science in Italy. At one of the many
interviews with which I was honoured, he asked me whether I could
point out any way in which he could assist its progress.

The question was unexpected; but it immediately recalled to me a
recent circumstance, which I then mentioned, namely, that in three of

---

[a] Most of the text of this passage was previously published as 'Letter to Dr Farr, on the
origin of the International Statistical Conference' (1860), *Works of Babbage*, Vol. 5.

the great cities of Italy I had been consulted confidentially by three distinguished men of science upon the same subject, on which each was separately engaged without being aware of the fact that the other two were employed on the same enquiry. The result, I remarked, would probably be that Italy would thus make *one* step in science, and that the discovery might probably be accompanied by painful discussions respecting priority; whilst with better means of inter-communication amongst its men of science Italy might have made *three* steps in advance. The idea of a periodical meeting of men engaged in scientific pursuits naturally arose out of these remarks. At parting, the Grand Duke requested me to draw up a minute of the conversation. I therefore drew up a note on the subject, in which I shadowed out an annual meeting of learned men in the various cities of Italy.

On finally taking leave, previous to my visit to Germany, the Grand Duke assured me that he had read the minute of our conversation with much attention, that he saw the evils pointed out, and agreed with me as to the remedy. He then observed that 'the time for such a meeting had not yet arrived; but', added the Grand Duke, 'when it does arrive, you may depend upon me'.

Eleven years after, in 1839, I was honoured by an invitation from the Grand Duke of Tuscany to meet the men of science of Italy, then about to assemble at Florence. In this communication it was observed, that 'the time had *now* arrived'. /

In the autumn of 1828 I reached Berlin, and unexpectedly found, from M. Humboldt, that in the course of a few weeks the philosophers of Germany were to hold a meeting in that capital.

I then learnt for the first time that, some years before, Dr Oken had proposed and organized an annual congress of German naturalists, meeting in each succeeding year in some great town.

I remained to witness the enlarged meeting at Berlin, which was very successful, and wrote an account of it to Sir D. Brewster, who published the description of it in 'The Edinburgh Journal of Science'.* This was, I believe, the first communication to the English public of the existence of the German society.

A few years after, Sir David Brewster, Sir John Robison, Secretary of the Royal Society of Edinburgh, and the Rev. William Vernon Harcourt, undertook the foundation of a similar periodical and itinerant society in our own country.

* Vol. x, p. 225, 1829. <'Account of the great congress of philosophers at Berlin on 18th September 1828', reprinted in *Decline of science* (1830), *Works of Babbage*, Vol. 7, Appendix 1.>

It appeared to me that the original organization of the British Association, as developed at York and at Oxford, was defective – that its basis was not sufficiently extended. In fact, that other sciences besides the physical were wanting for the harmony and success of the whole. There was no section to interest the landed proprietors or those members of their families who sat in either house of parliament. Nor was there much to attract the manufacturer or the retail dealer. A purely accidental circumstance enabled me to remedy one of these defects.* /

At the third meeting of the British Association at Cambridge in 1833, I happened, one afternoon, to call on my old and valued friend the Rev. Richard Jones, Professor of Political Economy at Haileybury, who was then residing in apartments at Trinity College. He informed me that he had just had a long conversation with our mutual friend M. Quételet, who had been sent officially by the Belgian Government to attend the meeting of the British Association. That M. Quételet had brought with him a budget of statistical facts, and that as there was no place for it in any section, he (Professor Jones) had asked M. Quételet to come to him that evening, and had invited Sir Charles Lemon, Professor Malthus, Mr Drinkwater (afterwards Mr Bethune),† and one or two others interested in the subject, to meet him, at the same time requesting me to join the party. I gladly accepted this invitation and departed. I had not, however, reached the gate of Trinity College before it occurred to me that there was now an opportunity of doing good service to the British Association. I returned to the apartments of my friend, explained to him my views, in which he fully coincided, and I suggested the formation of a statistical section. We both agreed that unless some *unusual* course were taken, it would be impossible to get such a section organized until the meeting in the following year. I therefore proposed that when we met in the evening we should consider the question of constituting ourselves provisionally a statistical section, and afterwards, at the general meeting in the Senate House, that I should explain the circumstance which had

---

* I afterwards succeeded in getting the British Association to adopt the plan of having an exhibition of specimens of the various manufactures and commercial products of the districts it successively visited. This commenced at Newcastle in 1838, and was carried to a much greater extent in the following year at Birmingham. I am not aware that this fact was ever referred to by those who got up the Exhibition of 1851.

† I have reason to believe, from the notebook of Mr Drinkwater (Bethune), that this meeting was held on Wednesday, 26 June, 1833.

arisen, and the / great advantage to the British Association of rendering such a section a permanent branch of its institution. After further explanations its utility was fully admitted; certain rather stringent rules were laid down in order to confine its enquiries to collections of facts. The sanction of the general meeting was then given to the establishment of the statistical section, and before the termination of the congress, a larger audience was collected in its meeting-room than in those of any of its sister sciences.

The interest of our discussions, and the mass of materials which now began to open upon our view, naturally indicated the necessity of forming a more permanent society for their collection. The British Association approved of the appointment of a permanent committee of this section. I was requested to act as chairman, and Mr Drinkwater as secretary. On 15 March, 1834, at a public meeting held in London, the Marquis of Lansdowne in the chair, it was resolved to establish the Statistical Society of London.

The Committee of the British Association, in reporting this fact to the Council, observe that: 'though the want of such a society has been long felt and acknowledged, the successful establishment of it, after every previous attempt had failed, has been due altogether to the impulse given by the last meeting of the Association. The distinguished foreigner (M. Quételet) who contributed so materially to the formation of the Statistical Section, was attracted to England principally with a view of attending that meeting; and the Committee hail this as a signal instance of the beneficial results to be expected from that personal intercourse amongst the enlightened men of all countries, which it is a principal object of the British Association to encourage and facilitate.'

M. Quételet, on his return to his own country, continued to / direct by his counsel, and to advance, by his own indefatigable industry, those statistical enquiries of which the Belgian Government so well appreciated the advantage.

At length the conviction of the importance of the value of statistical science becoming widely extended in other countries, M. Quételet saw that a fit time had arrived for summoning a European Congress. The results of such meetings are invaluable to all sciences, but more peculiarly to statistics, in which names have to be defined, signs to be invented, methods of observation to be compared and rendered uniform; thus enhancing the value of all future observations by making them more comparable as well as more expeditiously collected.

The proposal was adopted by the Belgian Government, and the first International Statistical Congress was held at Brussels in September, 1853.

The result was most successful; all the cultivators of statistical science are deeply indebted to M. Quételet for the unwearied pains he took to insure its success. He was assisted in this arduous task by the Ministers of the Crown, and supported by the high approbation of an enlightened sovereign.

Calculus of functions

This was my earliest step, and is still one to which I would willingly recur if other demands on my time permitted. Many years ago I recorded, in a small MS. volume, the facts, and also extracts of letters from Herschel, Bromhead, and Maule, in which I believe I have done justice to my friends if not to myself. It is very remarkable that the Analytical Engine adapts itself with singular facility to the development and numerical working out of this vast department of analysis.

In the list of my printed papers, at the end of this volume, will be found my various contributions to that subject. /

POLITICAL ECONOMY

My contributions to *political economy* are chiefly to be found in 'The Economy of Machinery and Manufactures', which consists of illustrations and developments of the principles regulating a very large section of that important subject.

Division of labour

It is singular that in the analysis of the *division of labour*, given by Adam Smith in 'The Wealth of Nations', the most efficient cause of its advantage is entirely omitted. The three causes assigned in that work are:

1. The increase of dexterity in every particular workman.

2. The saving of time lost in passing from one species of work to another.

3. The invention of a great number of machines which facilitate

327

and abridge labour, and enable one man to do the work of many.

These are undoubtedly true cases, but the most important cause is entirely omitted.

The most effective cause of the cheapness produced by the division of labour is this:

By dividing the work to be executed into different processes, each requiring different degrees of skill, or of force, the master manufacturer can purchase exactly that precise quantity of both which is necessary for each process. Whereas if the whole work were executed by one workman, that person must possess sufficient skill to perform the most difficult, and sufficient strength to execute the most laborious, of those operations into which the art is divided.

Needle-making is perhaps the best illustration of the overpowering effect of this cause. The operatives in this manufacture / consist of children, women, and men, earning wages varying from three or four shillings up to five pounds per week. Those who point the needles gain about two pounds. The man who hardens and tempers the needles earns from five to six pounds per week. It ought also to be observed that one man is sufficient to temper the needles for a large factory; consequently the time spent on each needle by the most expensive operative is excessively small.

But if a manufacturer insist on employing one man to make the whole needle, he must pay at the rate of five pounds a week for every portion of the labour bestowed upon it.*

Cost of any article

Besides the usual elements which contribute to constitute the price of anything, there exists another which varies greatly in different articles. It is this:

The cost and difficulty of verifying the fact that the article is exactly what it professes to be.

This is in some cases very small; but in many instances it is scarcely possible for the purchaser to verify the genuineness of certain articles. In these cases the public pay a larger price than they otherwise would do to those tradesmen whose character and integrity are well established.

* See 'Economy of Manufactures'.

Principles of taxation

In a pamphlet printed in 1848, I published my views of taxation, especially with reference to an income tax.[a]

The principle there supported was entertained and examined by the French Minister of Finance, M. Passy. The pamphlet itself was subsequently translated into Italian and published at Turin, under the auspices of the Sardinian Finance Minister. /

The principle there maintained admits, I think, of an extension to the election of representatives.

In that case, each person would have one vote on the ground of his personality, and other votes in proportion to his income. Whenever any further extension of our representative system becomes necessary, the dangers arising from the extension of the personal suffrage may fairly be counterbalanced by giving a plurality of votes to property. Such a course would have a powerful tendency to good, by supporting the national credit and by preventing the destructive waste of capital by war, and it might even make us a highly conservative people.

As the subject of political economy will be considered rather dry by most readers, I will endeavour to enliven it by an extract from that pamphlet, which singularly illustrates the question of direct and indirect taxation. I had mentioned the productive pump of my Italian friend to the late Lord Lansdowne, who supplied me with the counterpart in the unproductive pump erected by the late William Edgeworth, at Edgeworth Town, in Ireland.

That proprietor, whose country residence was much frequented by beggars, resolved to establish a test for discriminating between the idle and the industrious, and also to obtain some small return for the alms he was in the habit of bestowing. He accordingly added to the pump by which the upper part of his house was supplied with water, a piece of mechanism so contrived that, at the end of a certain number of strokes of the pump-handle, a penny fell out from an aperture to repay the labourer for his work. This was so arranged, that labourers who continued at the work, obtained very nearly the usual daily wages of labour in that part of the country. The idlest of the vagabonds of course refused this new labour test: but the greater part

---

[a] 'Thoughts on the principles of taxation, with reference to a property tax, and its exceptions' (1848); third edition, 1852, in *Works of Babbage*, Vol. 5.

of the beggars, whose / constant tale was that '*they could not earn a fair day's wages for a fair day's work*', after earning a few pence, usually went away *cursing* the hardness of their taskmaster.

An Italian gentleman, with greater sagacity, devised a more productive pump, and kept it in action at far less expense. The garden wall of his villa adjoined the great high road leading from one of the capitals of northern Italy,* from which it was distant but a few miles. Possessing within his garden a fine spring of water, he erected on the outside of the wall a pump for public use, and chaining to it a small iron ladle, he placed near it some rude seats for the weary traveller, and by a slight roof of climbing plants protected the whole from the midday sun. In this delightful shade the tired and thirsty travellers on that well-beaten road ever and anon reposed and refreshed themselves, and did not fail to put in requisition the service of the pump so opportunely presented to them. From morning till night many a dusty and wayworn pilgrim plied the handle, and went on his way, *blessing* the liberal proprietor for his kind consideration of the passing stranger.

But the owner of the villa was deeply acquainted with human nature. He knew in that sultry climate that the liquid would be more valued from its scarcity, and from the difficulty of acquiring it. He therefore, to enhance the value of the gift, wisely arranged the pump, so that its spout was of rather contracted dimensions, and the handle required a moderate application of force to work it. Under these circumstances the pump raised far more water than could pass through its spout; and, to prevent its being wasted, the surplus was conveyed by an invisible channel to a large reservoir judiciously placed for watering the proprietor's own house, stables, and garden – into which about five pints were poured for every spoonful passing out of the spout for the / benefit of the weary traveller. Even this latter portion was not entirely neglected, for the waste-pipe conveyed the part which ran over from the ladle to some delicious strawberry beds at a lower level. Perhaps, by a small addition to this ingenious arrangement, some kind-hearted travellers might be enabled to indulge their mules and asses with a taste of the same cool and refreshing fluid; thus paying an additional tribute to the skill and sagacity of the benevolent proprietor. My accomplished friend would doubtless make a most popular chancellor of the exchequer, should his Sardinian Majesty require his services in that department of administration.

* Turin.

Monopoly

In the course of my examination of this question I arrived at what I conceive to be a demonstration of the following principle:

That even under circumstances of the most absolute monopoly, the monopolist will, if he KNOWS *his own interest and* PURSUES *it, sell the article he produced at exactly the same price as the freest competition would produce.*

I devoted a chapter to this subject in an edition which I prepared several years ago for a new Italian translation of the 'Economy of Manufactures'; but I am not aware whether it has yet been published.[a]

Miracles

The explanation which I gave of the nature of miracles in *The Ninth Bridgewater Treatise*, published in May, 1837, has now stood the test of more than a quarter of a century, during which it has been examined by some of the deepest thinkers in many countries. Its adoption by those writers who have referred to it has, as far as my information goes, been unanimous. /

---

[a] The only Italian edition of the *Economy of machinery and manufactures* was a translation of the third edition (Florence, 1834).

CHAPTER XXXIV

THE AUTHOR'S FURTHER CONTRIBUTIONS
TO HUMAN KNOWLEDGE

Glaciers – Uniform postage – Weight of the Bristol bags – Parcel post – Plan for transmitting letters along aerial wires – Cost of verification is part of price – Sir Rowland Hill – Submarine navigation – Difference Engine – Analytical Engine – Cause of magnetic and electric rotations – Mechanical notation – Occulting lights – Semi-occultation may determine distances – Distinction of lighthouses numerically – Application from the United States – Proposed voyage – Loss of the ship and Mr Reid – Congress of naval officers at Brussels in 1853 – My portable occulting light exhibited – Night signals – Sun signals – Solar occulting lights – Afterwards used at Sebastopol – Numerical signals applicable to all dictionaries – Zenith light signals – Telegraph for ships on shore – Greenwich time signals – Theory of isothermal surfaces to account for the geological facts of the successive uprising and depression of various parts of the earth's surface – Games of skill – Tit-tat-to – Exhibitions – Problem of the Three Magnetic Bodies.

Of glaciers

Much has been written upon the subject of glaciers. The view which I took of the question on my first acquaintance with them still seems to me to afford a sufficient explanation of the phenomena. It is probable that I may have been anticipated in it by Saussure and others; but, having no time to enquire into its history, I shall give a very brief statement of those views.

The greater part of the material which ultimately constitutes a glacier arises from the rain falling and the snow deposited in the higher portions of mountain ranges, which / naturally first fill up the ravines and valleys, and rests on the tops of the mountains, covering them to various depths.

The chief facts to be explained are – first, the causes of the descent of these glaciers into the plains; second, the causes of the transformation of the opaque consolidated snow at the sources of the glacier into pure transparent ice at its termination.

The glaciers usually lying in valleys having a steep descent, gravity must obviously have a powerful influence; but its action is considerably increased by another cause.

The heat of the earth and that derived from the friction of the glacier and its broken fragments against the rock on which it rests, as well as from the friction of its own fragments, slowly melts the ice, and thus diminishing the amount of its support, the ice above cracks and falls down upon the earth, again to be melted and again to be broken.

But as the ice is upon an inclined plane, the pressure from above, on the upper side of the fragment, will be greater than that on the lower; consequently, at every fall the fallen mass will descend by a very small quantity further into the valley. Another consequence of the melting of the lower part of the centre of the glacier will be that the centre will advance faster than the sides, and its termination will form a curve convex towards the valley.

The above was, I believe, the common explanation of the formation of glaciers. The following part explains my own views:

Of the causes of the transformation of condensed snow into transparent ice

It is a well-known fact that water rapidly frozen retains all the air it held in solution, and is opaque. /

It is also known that water freezing very slowly is transparent.

Whenever, by the melting of the lower portion of any part of a glacier, a piece of it cracks and falls to a lower level, the friction of the broken sides will produce heat, and melt a small portion of water. This water, trickling down very slowly, will form a thin layer on the broken surface, and a portion will be retained in the narrowest part of the crack. But, since the temperature of a glacier is very near the freezing point, that water will freeze very slowly. It will, therefore, become transparent ice, and will, as it were, solder together the two adjacent surfaces by a thin layer of transparent ice.

But the transparent ice is much stronger and more difficult to break than opaque ice; consequently, the next time the soldered fragments are again broken, they will not break in the strongest part, which is the transparent ice: but the next fracture will occur in the opaque ice, as it was at first.

Thus, by the continued breaking and falling downward of the fragments of the glacier, as it proceeds down the valley, a series of vertical, rudely parallel veins of transparent ice will be formed. As

333

these masses descend the valley, fresh vertical layers of transparent ice will be interposed between those already existing until the whole takes that beautiful transparent cerulean tint which we so frequently see at the lower termination of a glacier. Another effect of this vertical fracture at the surfaces of least resistance will be alternate vertical layers of opaque and transparent ice shading into each other. This would, in some of its stages, give a kind of ribboned appearance to the ice. Probably traces of it would still be exhibited even in the most transparent ice. Speaking roughly, this ribboned structure ought to be closer together the nearer the piece examined is to the end of the glacier. It / ought also to be more apparent towards the centre of the glacier than towards the sides. The effect of this progress downward is to produce a very powerful friction between the masses of ice and the earth over which they are pushed, and consequently, a continual accession to that stream of water which is found issuing from all glaciers.

The result of this continual breaking up is to cause all the water melted by the friction of the blocks of ice which is not retained in the interstices to fall towards the lowest part of the descending valley, and thus increase the stream, and so take away more and more of the support of the central part of the glacier. Hence the advance of the surface of the glacier will be much quicker towards its middle than near the sides.

The consequences of these actions is, that cracks in the ice will occur generally in planes perpendicular to its surface. The rain which falls upon the glacier, the water produced from its surface by the sun's rays and by the effect of the temperature of the atmosphere, as well as the water produced by the friction of its descending fragments, will penetrate through these cracks, and be retained by capillary action on the surfaces, and still more where the distance of the adjacent surfaces is very small. The rest of this unfrozen water will reach the rocky bottom of the glacier, and give up some of its heat to the bed over which it passes, to be again employed in melting away the lowest support of the glacier ice. Although the temperature of the glacier should differ but by a very small quantity from that of the freezing point of water, yet these films will only freeze the more slowly, and therefore become more solid and transparent ice. Their very thinness will enable all the air to be more readily extricated by freezing.

The question of the *regelation* of pounded ice, if by that / term is meant anything more than welding ice by heat, or of joining its parts by a process analogous to that which is called *burning together* two separate portions of a bronze statue, has always appeared to me unsatisfactory.

The process of 'burning together' is as follows: Two portions of a large statue, which have been cast separately, are placed in a trough of sand, with their corresponding ends near to each other. A channel is made in the sand, leading through the junction of the parts to be united.

A stream of melted bronze is now allowed to run out from the furnace through the channel between the contiguous ends which it is proposed to unite. The first effect of this is to heat the ends of the two fragments. After the stream of melted metal has continued some time, the ends of those fragments themselves begin to melt. When a small quantity of each end is completely melted, the further flow of the melted metal is stopped, and as soon as the pool of melted metal connects, the two ends of the pieces to be united begins to consolidate: the whole is covered up with sand and allowed to cool gradually. When cold, the unnecessary metal is cut away, and the fragments are as perfectly united as if they had been originally cast in one piece.

The sudden consolidation, by physical force, of pounded ice or snow appears to me to arise from the first effect of the pressure producing heat, which melts a small portion into water, and brings the particles of ice or snow nearer to each other. The portion of water thus produced then, having its heat abstracted by the ice, connects the particles of the latter more firmly together by freezing.

If two flat surfaces of clear ice had a heated plate of metal put between them, two very thin layers of water would be formed between the ice and the heated plate. If the hot / plate were suddenly withdrawn, and the two plates of ice pressed together, they would then be frozen together. This would be equivalent to welding. In all these cases the temperature of the ice must be a very little lower than the freezing-point. The more nearly it approached that point the slower the process of freezing would be, and therefore the more transparent the ice thus formed.

In the Exhibition of 1862 there were two different processes by which ice was produced in abundance, even in the heat of the machinery annex, in which they were placed.

In both the water was quickly converted into ice, and in both cases the ice was opaque.

In one of them the ice was produced in the shape of long hollow cylinders These were quite opaque, and were piled up in stacks. The temperature of the place caused the ice to melt slowly; consequently, the interstices where the cylinders rested upon each other, received and retained a small portion of the water, which, trickling down, was detained by capillary attraction. Here it was very slowly frozen, and formed at the junction of the cylinders a thin film of transparent ice. This gradually increased as the upper cylinders of the ice melted away, and, after several hours' exposure, I have seen clear transparent ice a quarter of an inch thick, where, at the commencement, there had not been even a trace of translucency.

On enquiring of the operator why the original cylinders were opaque, he told me, because they were frozen quickly. I then pointed out to him the small portions of transparent ice, which I have described, and asked him the cause. He immediately said, because they had been frozen slowly.

It appeared to be an axiom, derived from his own experience, that water quickly frozen is always opaque, and water / slowly frozen always transparent. I pointed out this practical illustration to many of the friends I accompanied in their examination of the machinery of the annex.

It would follow from this explanation, that glaciers on lofty mountains and in high latitudes may, by their own action, keep the surface of the earth on which they rest at a higher temperature than it would otherwise attain.

Book and parcel post

When my friend, the late General Colby, was preparing the materials and instruments for the intended Irish survey, he generally visited me about once a week to discuss and talk over with me his various plans. We had both of us turned our attention to the Post Office, and had both considered and advocated the question of a uniform rate of postage. The ground of that opinion was, that the actual *transport* of a letter formed but a small item in the expense of transmitting it to its destination; whilst the heaviest part of the cost arose from the *collection* and *distribution*, and was, therefore, almost independent of the length of its journey. I got some returns of the weight of the Bristol mail-bag for each night during one week, with a view to ascertain the possibility of a more rapid transmission. General Colby arrived at the conclusion that, supposing every letter paid sixpence, and that the same number of letters were posted, then the revenue would remain the same. I believe, when an official comparison was subsequently made, it was found that the equivalent sum was fivepence halfpenny. I then devised means for transmitting letters enclosed in small cylinders, along wires suspended from posts, and from towers, or from church steeples. I made a little model of such an apparatus, and thus transmitted notes from my front drawing-room, through the house, / into my workshop, which was in a room above my stables. The date of these experiments I do not exactly recollect, but it was certainly earlier than 1827.

I had also, at a still earlier period, arrived at the remarkable economical principle, *that one element in the price of every article is the cost of its verification*. It arose thus:

In 1815 I became possessed of a house in London, and commenced my residence in Devonshire Street, Portland Place, in which I resided until 1827. A kind relative of mine sent up a constant supply of game. But although the game cost nothing, the expense charged for its carriage was so great that it really was more expensive than butchers' meat. I endeavoured to get redress for the constant overcharges, but as the game was transferred from one coach to another I found it practically impossible to discover where the overcharge arose, and thus to remedy the evil. These efforts, however, led me to the fact that *verification*, which in this instance constituted a considerable part of the *price of the article, must form a portion of its price in every case.*

Acting upon this, I suggested that if the Government were to become, through the means of the Post Office, parcel carriers, they would derive a greater profit from it than any private trader, because the whole price of verification would be saved by the public. I therefore recommended the enlargement of the duties of the Post Office by employing it for the conveyance of books and parcels.

I mention these facts with no wish to disparage the *subsequent* exertions of Sir Rowland Hill. His devotion to the subject, his unwearied industry, and his long and at last successful efforts to overcome the notorious official friction of that department, required all the enduring energy he so constantly bestowed upon the subject. The benefit conferred / upon the country by the improvements he introduced is as yet scarcely sufficiently estimated.

These principles were published afterwards in the 'Economy of Manufactures'. See First Edition, 8 June, 1832; Second Edition, 22

337

November, 1832. See chapter on the 'Influence of Verification on Price', p. 134, and 'Conveyance of Letters', p. 273.[a]

Submarine navigation

Of this it is not necessary to do more than mention the title and refer for the detail to the chapter on Experience by Water: and also to the article Diving Bell in the 'Encyclopaedia Metropolitana'.[b]

I have only to add my opinion that in open inverted vessels it may probably be found, under certain circumstances, of important use.

Difference Engine

Enough has already been said about that unfortunate discovery in the previous part of this volume. The first and great cause of its discontinuance was the inordinately extravagant demands of the person whom I had employed to construct it for the Government. Even this might, perhaps, by great exertions and sacrifices, have been surmounted. There is, however, a limit beyond which human endurance cannot go. If I survive some few years longer, the Analytical Engine will exist, and its works will afterwards be spread over the world. If it is the will of that Being, who gave me the endowments which led to that discovery, that I should not survive to complete my work, I bow to that decision with intense gratitude for those gifts: conscious that through life I have never hesitated to make the / severest sacrifices of fortune, and even of feelings, in order to accomplish my imagined mission.

The great principles on which the Analytical Engine rests have been examined, admitted, recorded, and demonstrated. The mechanism itself has now been reduced to unexpected simplicity. Half a century may probably elapse before anyone without those aids which I leave behind me, will attempt so unpromising a task. If, unwarned by my example, any man shall undertake and shall succeed in really constructing an engine embodying in itself the whole of the executive department of mathematical analysis upon different principles or by simpler mechanical means, I have no fear of leaving my reputation in his charge, for he alone will be fully able to appreciate the nature of my efforts and the value of their results.

---

[a] Chapter XV and article 334 in the 4th edition of the *Economy of machinery and manufactures* (1835), *Works of Babbage*, Vol. 8.

[b] 'Diving-bell' (1826), *Works of Babbage*, Vol. 4.

Explanation of the cause of magnetic and electric rotations

In 1824 Arago published his experiments on the magnetism manifested by various substances during rotation. I was much struck with the announcement, and immediately set up some apparatus in my own workshop in order to witness the facts thus announced.

My friend Herschel, who assisted at some of the earliest experiments, joined with me in repeating and varying those of Arago. The results were given in a joint paper on that subject, published in the 'Transactions of the Royal Society' in 1825.[a]

I had previously made some magnetic experiments on a large magnet which would, under peculiar management, sustain about 32½ lbs. It was necessary to commence with a weight of about 28 lbs., and then to add at successive intervals additional weights, but each less and less than the former. / This led me to an explanation of the cause of those rotations, which I still venture to think is the true cause, although it is not so recognized by English philosophers.

The history is a curious one, and whether the cause which I assigned is right or wrong, the train of thought by which I was led to it is valuable as an illustration of the mode in which the human mind works in its progress towards new discoveries.

The first experiment, showing that the weight suspended might be increased at successive intervals of time, was stated in most treatises on magnetism. But the visible fact impressed strongly on my mind the conclusion that the production and discharge of magnetism is not instantaneous, but requires time for its complete action. It appeared, therefore, to me that this principle was sufficient for the explanation of the rotations observed by Arago.

In the following year it occurred to me that electricity possessed the same property, namely, that of requiring time for its communication. I then instituted a new series of experiments, and succeeded, as I had anticipated, in producing electric rotations. But a new fact now presented itself: in certain cases the electric needle moved back in the contrary direction to that indicated by the influences to which it was subjected. Whenever this occurred the retrograde motion was always very slow. After eliminating successively by experiment every cause which I could imagine, the fact which remained was, that in certain cases there occurred a motion in the direction opposite to that which

---

[a] 'Account of the repetition of M. Arago's experiment on the magnetism manifested by various substances during the act of rotation' (1825), *Works of Babbage*, Vol. 4.

was expected. But whenever such a motion occurred it was always very slow. Upon further reflection, I conjectured that it might arise from the screen, interposed between the electric and the needle itself, becoming electrified possibly in the opposite direction. New experiments confirmed this view and proved / that the original cause was sufficient for the production of all the observed effects.

These experiments and their explanation were printed in the 'Philosophical Transactions' 1826.[a] But they met with so little acceptance in England that I had ceased to contend for them against more popular doctrines, and was too deeply occupied with other enquiries to enter on their defence. Several years after, during a visit to Berlin, taking a morning walk with Mitscherlich, I asked what explanation he adopted of the magnetic rotations of Arago. He instantly replied, 'There can be no doubt that yours is the true one.'

It will be a curious circumstance in the history of science, if an erroneous explanation of new and singular experiments in one department should have led to the prevision of another similar set of facts in a different department, and even to the explanation of new facts at first apparently contradicting it.

Mechanical Notation
This also has been described in a former chapter. I look upon it as one of the most important additions I have made to human knowledge. It has placed the construction of machinery in the rank of a demonstrative science. The day will arrive when no school of mechanical drawing will be thought complete without teaching it.

Occulting lights
The great object of all my enquiries has ever been to endeavour to ascertain those laws of thought by which man makes discoveries. It was by following out one of the principles which I had arrived at that I was led to the system of occulting numerical lights for distinguishing lighthouses / and for night signals at sea, which I published about twelve years ago. The principle I allude to is this:

Whenever we meet with any defect in the means we are contriving for the accomplishing a given object, that defect should be noted and reserved for future consideration, and enquiry should be made –

Whether that which is a defect as regards the object in view may

---

[a] 'On electric and magnetic rotation' (1826), *Works of Babbage*, Vol. 4.

not become a source of advantage in some totally different subject.

I had for a long series of years been watching the progress of electric, magnetic, and other lights of that order, with the view of using them for domestic purposes; but their want of uniformity seemed to render them hopeless for that object. Returning from a brilliant exhibition of voltaic light, I thought of applying the above rule. The accidental interruptions might, by breaking the circuit, be made to recur at any required intervals. This remark suggested their adaptation to a system of signals. But it was immediately followed by another, namely: that the interruptions were equally applicable to all lights, and might be effected by simple mechanism.

I then, by means of a small piece of clockwork and an argand lamp, made a *numerical* system of occultation, by which any number might be transmitted to all those within sight of the source of light. Having placed this in a window of my house, I walked down the street to the distance of about 250 yards. On turning round I perceived the number 32 clearly indicated by its occultations. There was, however, a small defect in the apparatus. After each occultation there was a kind of semi-occultation. This arose from the arm which carried the shade rebounding from the stop on which it fell. Aware that this defect could be easily remedied, I / continued my onward course for about 250 yards more, with my back towards the light. On turning round I was much surprised to observe that the signal 32 was repeated distinctly without the slightest trace of any semi-occultation or blink.

I was very much astonished at this change; and on returning towards my house had the light constantly in view. After advancing a short distance I thought I perceived a very faint trace of the blink. At thirty or forty paces nearer it was clearly visible, and at the halfway point it was again perfectly distinct. I knew that the remedy was easy, but I was puzzled as to the cause.

After a little reflection I concluded that it arose from the circumstance that the small hole through which the light passed was just large enough to be visible at five hundred yards, yet that when the same hole was partially covered by the rebound there did not remain sufficient light to be seen at the full distance of five hundred yards.

Thus prepared, I again applied the principle I had commenced with and proceeded to examine whether this defect might not be converted into an advantage.

I soon perceived that a lighthouse, whose number was continually repeated with a blink, obscuring just half its light, would be seen

341

without any blink at all distances beyond half its range; but that at all distances within its half range that fact would be indicated by a blink. Thus with two blinks, properly adjusted, the distance of a vessel from a first-class light would be distinguished at from twenty to thirty miles by occultations indicating its number without any blink; between ten and twenty miles by an occultation with one blink, and within ten miles by an occultation with two blinks.

But another advantage was also suggested by this defect. / If the opaque cylinder which intercepts the light consists of two cylinders, A and B, connected together by rods thus:

If the compound cylinder descend to *a*, and then rise again, there will be a single occultation.

| " | " | " | *b* | " | double occultation. |
| " | " | " | *c* | " | triple occultation. |

Such occultations are very distinct, and are specially applicable to lighthouses.

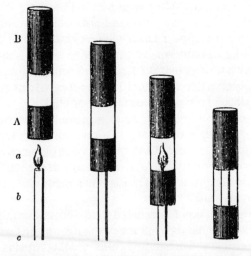

In the year 1851, during the Great Exhibition, the light I have described was exhibited from an upper window of my house in Dorset Street during many weeks. It had not passed unnoticed by foreigners, who frequently reminded me that they had passed my door when I was asleep by writing upon their card the number exhibited by the occulting light and dropping it into my letter-box.

About five or six weeks after its first appearance I received a letter from a friend of mine in the United States, expressing great interest about it, and enquiring whether its construction was a secret. My answer was, that I made no / secret of it, and would prepare and send him a short description of it.

I then prepared a description, of which I had a very few copies printed.[a] I sent twelve of these to the proper authorities of the great maritime countries. Most of them were accompanied by a private note of my own to some person of influence with whom I happened to be acquainted.

One of these was addressed to the present Emperor of the French, then a member of their Representative Chamber. It was dated 30 November, 1852. Three days after I read in the newspapers the account of the *coup* of 2 December, and smiled at the inopportune time at which my letter had accidentally been forwarded. However, three days after I received from M. Mocquard the prettiest note, saying that he was commanded by the Prince President to thank me for the communication, and to assure me that the Prince was as much attached as ever to science, and should always continue to promote its cultivation.

The letter which was sent to the United States was placed in the hands of the Coast Survey. The plan was highly approved, and Congress made a grant of 5000 dollars, in order to try it experimentally. After a long series of experiments, in which its merits were severely tested, a report was made to Congress strongly recommending its adoption. I then received a very pressing invitation to visit the United States, for the purpose of assisting to put it in action. It was conveyed to me by an amiable and highly cultivated person, the late Mr Reed, Professor of English Literature at Philadelphia, who, on his arrival in London, proposed that I should accompany him on his return in October, the best season for the voyage, and in the finest vessel of their mercantile navy. I had long had a great wish to visit the American continent, but I did / not think it worth crossing the Atlantic, unless I could have spent a twelvemonth in America. Finding this impossible under the then circumstances, about a month before the time arrived I resigned with great reluctance the pleasure of accompanying my friend to his own country.

It was most fortunate that I was thus prevented from embarking on board the Arctic, a steamer of the largest class.

---

[a] *Notes respecting lighthouses* (1852), *Works of Babbage*, Vol. 5.

Steaming at the rate of thirteen knots an hour over the banks of Newfoundland during a dense fog, the Arctic was run into by a steamer of about half its size, moving at the rate of seven knots. The concussion was in this instance fatal to the larger vessel.

This sad catastrophe was thus described by the brother of my lost friend:

On the 20th of September, 1854, Mr Reed, with his sister, embarked at Liverpool for New York, in the United States steamship Arctic. Seven days afterwards, at noon, on the 27th, when almost in sight of his native land, a fatal collision occurred, and before sundown every human being left upon the ship had sunk under the waves of the ocean. The only survivor who was personally acquainted with my brother, saw him about two o'clock, P.M., after the collision, and not very long before the ship sank, sitting with his sister in the small passage aft of the dining-saloon. They were tranquil and silent, though their faces wore the look of painful anxiety. They probably afterwards left this position, and repaired to the promenade deck. For a selfish struggle for life, with a helpless companion dependent upon him, with a physical frame unsuited for such a strife, and above all, with a sentiment of religious resignation which taught him in that hour of agony, even with the memory of his wife and children thronging in his mind, to bow his head in submission / to the will of God, – for such a struggle he was wholly unsuited; and his is the praise, that he perished with the women and children.

In 1853 I spent some weeks at Brussels. During my residence in that city a congress of naval officers from all the maritime nations assembled to discuss and agree upon certain rules and observations to be arranged for the common benefit of all. One evening I had the great pleasure of receiving the whole party at my house for the purpose of witnessing my occulting lights.

The portable occulting light which I had brought with me was placed in the verandah on the first floor, and we then went along the Boulevards to see its effect at different distances and with various numerical signals. On our return several papers relating to the subject were lying upon the table. The Russian representative, M.——, took up one of the original printed descriptions and was much interested in it. On taking leave he asked, with some hesitation, whether I would lend it to him for a few hours. I told him at once that if I possesed another copy I would willingly give it to him; but that not being the case I could only offer to lend it. M.—— therefore took it home with him, and when I sat down to breakfast the next morning I found it upon my table. In the course of the day I met my Russian friend in the park. I expressed my hope that he had been interested by the little tract he had so speedily returned. He replied that it had interested him so much that he had sat up all night, had copied the whole of it, and that his transcript and a despatch upon the subject was now on its way by the post to his own government.

Several years after I was informed that *occulting solar / lights* were used by the Russians during the siege of Sebastopol.

Night signals

The system of occulting light applies with remarkable facility to night signals, either on shore or at sea. If it is used numerically, it applies to all the great dictionaries of the various maritime nations. I may here remark, that there exist means by which all such signals may, if necessary, be communicated in cipher.

Sun signals

The distance at which such signals can be rendered visible exceeds that of any other class of signals by means of light. During the Irish Trigonometrical Survey, a mountain in Scotland was observed, with an angular instrument from a station in Ireland, at the distance of 108 miles. This was accomplished by stationing a party on the summit of the mountain in Scotland with a looking-glass of about a foot square, directing the sun's image to the opposite station. No occultations were used; but if the mirror had been larger, and occultation employed, messages might have been sent, and the time of residence upon the mountain considerably diminished. When I was occupied with occulting signals, I made this widely known. I afterwards communicated the plan, during a visit to Paris, to many of my friends in that capital, and, by request, to the Minister of Marine.

I have observed in the 'Comptes Rendus'[a] that the system has to a certain extent been since used in the south of Algeria, where, during eight months of the year, the sun is generally unobscured by clouds as long as it is above the horizon. I have not, however, noticed in those communications to the Institute any reference to my own previous publication. /

Zenith-light signals

Another form of signal, although not capable of use at very great distances, may, however, be employed with considerable advantage,

---

[a] 'On the statistics of lighthouses' (1853), *Works of Babbage*, Vol. 5.

under certain circumstances. Universality and economy are its great advantages. It consists of a looking-glass, making an angle of 45° with the horizon, placed just behind an opening in a vertical board. This being stuck into the earth, the light of the sky in the zenith, which is usually the brightest, will be projected horizontally through the opening, in whatever direction the person to be communicated with may be placed. The person who makes the signals must stand on one side in front of the instrument; and, by passing his hat slowly before the aperture any number of times, may thus express each unit's figure of his signal.

He must then, leaving the light visible, pause whilst he deliberately counts to himself ten.

He must then with his hat make a number of occultations equal to the tens figure he wishes to express.

This must be continued for each figure in the number of the signal, always pausing between each during the time of counting ten.

When the end of the signal is terminated, he must count sixty in the same manner; and if the signal he gave has not been acknowledged, he should repeat it until it has been observed.

The same simple telegraph may be used in a dark night, by substituting a lantern for the looking-glass. The whole apparatus is simple and cheap, and can be easily carried even by a small boy.

I was led to this contrivance many years ago by reading an account of a vessel stranded within thirty yards of the shore. / Its crew consisted of thirteen people, ten of whom got into the boat, leaving the master, who thought himself safer in the ship, with two others of the crew.

The boat put off from the ship, keeping as much out of the breakers as it could, and looking out for a favourable place for landing. The people on shore followed the boat for several miles, urging them not to attempt landing. But not a single word was audible by the boat's crew, who, after rowing several miles, resolved to take advantage of the first favourable lull. They did so – the boat was knocked to pieces, and the whole crew were drowned. If the people on the shore could at that moment have communicated with the boat's crew, they could have informed them that, by continuing their course for half a mile further, they might turn into a cove, and land almost dry.

I was much impressed by the want of easy communication between stranded vessels and those on shore who might rescue them.

I can even now scarcely believe it credible that the very simple means I am about to mention has not been adopted years ago. A list of about a hundred questions, relating to directions and enquiries required to be communicated between the crew of a stranded ship and those on shore who wish to aid it, would, I am told, be amply sufficient for such purposes. Now, if such a list of enquiries were prepared and printed by competent authority, any system of signals by which a number of two places of figures can be expressed might be used. This list of enquiries and answers ought to be printed on cards, and nailed up on several parts of every vessel. It would be still better, by conference with other maritime nations, to adopt the same system of signs, and to have them printed in each language. A looking-glass, a board with a hole in it, and a / lantern would be all the apparatus required. The lantern might be used for night, and the looking-glass for day signals.

These simple and inexpensive signals might be occasionally found useful for various social purposes.

Two neighbours in the country whose houses, though reciprocally visible, are separated by an interval of several miles, might occasionally telegraph to each other.

If the looking-glass were of large size, its light and its occultation might be seen perhaps from six to ten miles, and thus become by daylight a cheap guiding light through channels and into harbours.

It may also become a question whether it might not in some cases save the expense of buoying certain channels.

For railway signals during daylight it might in some cases be of great advantage, by saving the erection of very lofty poles carrying dark frames through which the light of the sky is admitted.

Amongst my early experiments, I made an occulting hand-lantern, with a shade for occulting by the pressure of the thumb, and with two other shades of red and of green glass. This might be made available for military purposes, or for the police.

Greenwich time signals

It has been thought very desirable that a signal to indicate Greenwich time should be placed on the Start Point, the last spot which ships going down the Channel on distant voyages usually sight.

The advantage of such an arrangement arises from this – that chronometers having had their rates ascertained on shore, may have them somewhat altered by the motions to / which they are submitted at sea. If, therefore, after a run of above two hundred miles, they can be informed of the exact Greenwich time, the sea rate of their chronometers will be obtained.

Of course no other difficulty than that of expense occurs in transmitting Greenwich time by electricity to any points on our coast. The real difficulty is to convey it to the passing vessels. The firing of a cannon at certain fixed hours has been proposed, but this plan is encumbered by requiring the knowledge of the distance of the vessel from the gun, and also from the variation of the velocity of the transmission of sound under various circumstances.

During the night the flash arising from ignited gunpowder might be employed. But this, in case of rain or other atmospheric circumstances, might be impeded. The best plan for night signals would be to have an occulting light, which might be that of the lighthouse itself, or another specially reserved for the purpose.

During the day, and when the sun is shining, the time might be transmitted by the occultations of reflected solar light, which would be seen at any distance the curvature of the earth admitted.

The application of my zenith light might perhaps fulfil all the required conditions during daylight.

I have found that, even in the atmosphere of London, an opening only five inches square can be distinctly seen, and its occultations counted by the naked eye at the distance of a quarter of a mile. If the side of the opening were double the former, then the light transmitted to the eye would be four times as great, and the occultations might be observed at the distance of one mile.

The looking-glass employed must have its side nearly in / the proportion of three to two, so that one of five feet by seven and a half ought to be seen at the distance of about eight or nine miles.

Geological theory of isothermal surfaces

During one portion of my residence at Naples my attention was concentrated upon what in my opinion is the most remarkable building upon the face of the earth, the Temple of Serapis, at Puzzuoli.[*][a]

It was obviously built at or above the level of the Mediterranean in

---

[*] In this enquiry I profited by the assistance of Mr Head, now the Right Hon. Sir Edmund Head, Bart, K.C.B., late Governor-General of Canada. An abstract of my own observations was printed in the 'Abstracts of Proceedings' of the Geological Society, vol. ii, p. 72. My friend's historical views were printed in the 'Transactions' of the Antiquarian Society.

[a] *Abstract of a paper entitled 'Observations on the Temple of Serapis at Pozzuoli'* (1834) and *Observations on the Temple of Serapis at Pozzuoli, near Naples* (1847), *Works of Babbage*, Vol. 5.

order to profit by a hot spring which supplied its numerous baths. There is unmistakable evidence that it has subsided below the present level of sea, at least twenty-five feet; that it must have remained there during many years; that it then rose gradually up, probably to its former level, and that during the last twenty years it has been again slowly subsiding.

The results of this survey led me in the following year to explain the various elevations and depressions of portions of the earth's surface, at different periods of time, by a theory which I have called the theory of the earth's isothermal surfaces.

I do not think the importance of that theory has been well understood by geologists, who are not always sufficiently acquainted with physical science. The late Sir Henry De la Beche perceived at an early period the great light those sciences might throw upon his own favourite pursuit, and / was himself always anxious to bring them to bear upon geology.

I am still more confirmed in my opinion of the importance of the 'Theory of Isothermal Surfaces in Geology' from the fact that a few years afterwards my friend Sir John Herschel arrived independently at precisely the same theory. I have stated this at length in the notes to the 'Ninth Bridgewater Treatise'.

Games of skill

A considerable time after the translation of Menabrea's memoir had been published, and after I had made many drawings of the Analytical Engine and all its parts, I began to meditate upon the intellectual means by which I had reached to such advanced and even to such unexpected results. I reviewed in my mind the various principles which I had touched upon in my published and unpublished papers, and dwelt with satisfaction upon the power which I possessed over mechanism through the aid of the Mechanical Notation. I felt, however, that it would be more satisfactory to the minds of others, and even in some measure to my own, that I should try the power of such principles as I had laid down, by assuming some question of an entirely new kind, and endeavouring to solve it by the aid of those principles which had so successfully guided me in other cases.

After much consideration I selected for my test the contrivance of a machine that should be able to play a game of purely intellectual skill successfully; such as tit-tat-to, drafts, chess, etc.

I endeavoured to ascertain the opinions of persons in every class of

349

life and of all ages, whether they thought it required human reason to play games of skill. The almost constant / answer was in the affirmative. Some supported this view of the case by observing, that if it were otherwise, then an automaton could play such games. A few of those who had considerable acquaintance with mathematical science allowed the possibility of machinery being capable of such work; but they most stoutly denied the possibility of contriving such machinery on account of the myriads of combinations which even the simplest games included.

On the first part of my enquiry I soon arrived at a demonstration that every game of skill is susceptible of being played by an automaton.

Further consideration showed that if *any position* of the men upon the board were assumed (whether that position were possible or impossible), then if the automaton could make the first move rightly, he must be able to win the game, always supposing that, under the given position of the men, that conclusion were possible.

Whatever move the automaton made, another move would be made by his adversary. Now this altered state of the board is *one* amongst the *many positions* of the men in which, by the previous paragraph, the automaton was supposed capable of acting.

Hence the question is reduced to that of making the best move under any possible combinations of positions of the men.

Now the several questions the automaton has to consider are of this nature:

1. Is the position of the men, as placed before him on the board, a possible position? that is, one which is consistent with the rules of the game?

2. If so, has automaton himself already lost the game?

3. If not, then has automaton won the game? /

4. If not, can he win it at the next move? If so, make that move.

5. If not, could his adversary, if he had the move, win the game.

6. If so, automaton must prevent him if possible.

7. If his adversary cannot win the game at his next move, automaton must examine whether he can make such a move that, if he were allowed to have two moves in succession, he could at the second move have *two* different ways of winning the game;

and each of these cases failing, automaton must look forward to three or more successive moves.

Now I have already stated that in the Analytical Engine I had devised mechanical means equivalent to memory, also that I had

350

provided each other means equivalent to foresight, and that the engine itself could act on this foresight.

In consequence of this the whole question of making an automaton play any game depended upon the possibility of the machine being able to represent all the myriads of combinations relationg to it. Allowing one hundred moves on each side for the longest game at chess, I found that the combinations involved in the Analytical Engine enormously surpassed any required, even by the game of chess.

As soon as I had arrived at this conclusion I commenced an examination of a game called 'tit-tat-to', usually played by little children. It is the simplest game with which I am acquainted. Each player has five counters, one set marked with a +, the other set with an O. The board consists of a square divided into nine smaller squares, and the object of each player is to get three of his own men in a straight / line. One man is put on the board by each player alternately. In practice no board is used, but the children draw upon a bit of paper, or on their slate, a figure like any of the following.

The successive moves of the two players may be represented as follows:

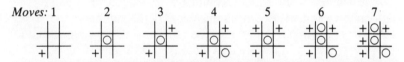

Moves: 1 2 3 4 5 6 7

In this case + wins at the seventh move.

The next step I made was to ascertain what number of combinations were required for all the possible variety of moves and situations. I found this to be comparatively insignificant.

I therefore easily sketched out mechanism by which such an automaton might be guided. Hitherto I had considered only the philosophical view of the subject, but a new idea now entered my head which seemed to offer some chance of enabling me to acquire the funds necessary to complete the Analytical Engine.

It occurred to me that if an automaton were made to play this game, it might be surrounded with such attractive circumstances that a very popular and profitable exhibition might be produced. I imagined that the machine might consist of the figures of two children playing against each other, accompanied by a lamb and a cock. That the child who won the game might clap his hands whilst the cock was

351

crowing, after which, that the child who was beaten might cry and wring his hands whilst the lamb began bleating.

I then proceeded to sketch various mechanical means by which every action could be produced. These, when compared with those I had employed for the Analytical Engine, / were remarkably simple. A difficulty, however, arose of a novel kind. It will have been observed, in the explanation I gave of the Analytical Engine, that cases arose in which it became necessary, on the occurrence of certain conditions, that the machine itself should select one out of two or more distinct modes of calculation. The particular one to be adopted could only be known when those calculations on which the selection depended had been already made.

The new difficulty consisted in this, that when the automaton had to move, it might occur that there were two different moves, each equally conducive to his winning the game. In this case no reason existed within the machine to direct his choice: unless, also, some provision were made, the machine would attempt two contradictory motions.

The first remedy I devised for this defect was to make the machine keep a record of the number of games it had won from the commencement of its existence. Whenever two moves, which we may call A and B, were equally conducive to winning the game, the automaton was made to consult the record of the number of the games he had won. If that number happened to be even, he was directed to take the course A; if it were odd, he was to take the course B.

If there were three moves equally possible, the automaton was directed to divide the number of games he had won by three. In this case the numbers 0, 1, or 2 might be the remainder, and the machine was directed to take the course A, B, or C accordingly.

It is obvious that any number of conditions might be thus provided for. An enquiring spectator, who observed the games played by the automaton, might watch a long time before he discovered the principle upon which it acted. It is also worthy of remark how admirably this illustrates / the best definitions of chance by the philosopher and the poet:

Chance is but the expression of man's ignorance. – Laplace
All chance, design ill understood. – Pope

Having fully satisfied myself of the power of making such an automaton, the next step was to ascertain whether there was any probability, if it were exhibited to the public, of its producing, in a moderate time, such a sum of money as would enable me to construct the Analytical Engine. A friend, to whom I had at an early period communicated the idea, entertained great hopes of its pecuniary success. When it became known that an automaton could beat not merely children but even papa and mamma at a child's game, it seemed not unreasonable to expect that every child who heard of it would ask mamma to see it. On the other hand, every mamma, and some few papas, who heard of it would doubtless take their children to so singular and interesting a sight. I resolved, on my return to London, to make enquiries as to the relative productiveness of the various exhibitions of recent years, and also to obtain some rough estimate of the probable time it would take to construct the automaton, as well as some approximation to the expense.

It occurred to me that if half a dozen were made, they might be exhibited in three different places at the same time. Each exhibitor might then have an automaton in reserve in case of accidental injury. On my return to town I made the enquiries I alluded to, and found that the English machine for making Latin verses, the German talking-machine, as well as several others, were entire failures in a pecuniary point of view. I also found that the most profitable exhibition which had occurred for many years was that of the little dwarf, General Tom Thumb. /

On considering the whole question, I arrived at the conclusion, that to conduct the affair to a successful issue it would occupy so much of my own time to contrive and execute the machinery, and then to superintend the working out of the plan, that even if successful in point of pecuniary profit, it would be too late to avail myself of the money thus acquired to complete the Analytical Engine.

Problem of the three magnetic bodies

The problem of the three bodies, which has cost such unwearied labour to so many of the highest intellects of this and the past age, is simple compared with another which is opening upon us. We now possess a very extensive series of well-recorded observations of the positions of the magnetic needle, in various parts of our globe, during about thirty years.

Certain periods of changes of about ten or eleven years are said to be indicated as connected with changes in the amount of solar spots; but the inductive evidence scarcely rests upon three periods, and it seems more probable that these effects arise from some common cause.

353

1. It has been long known that the earth has at least two if not more magnetic poles.

2. It is probable, therefore, that the sun and moon also have several magnetic poles.

3. In 1826[a] I proved that when a magnet is brought into proximity to a piece of matter capable of becoming magnetic, the magnetism communicated by it requires *time* for its full development in the body magnetized. Also that when the influence of the magnet is removed, the magnetized body requires *time* to regain its former state. /

This being the case, it is required, having assumed certain positions for the poles of these various magnetic bodies, to calculate their reciprocal influences in changing the positions of those poles on the other bodies. The development of the equations representing these forces will indicate cycles which really belong to the nature of the subject. The comparisons of a long series of observations with recorded facts will ultimately enable us to determine both the number and position of those poles upon each body.

Electricity possesses an analogous property with respect to time being required for its full action. If the bodies of our system influence each other electrically, other developments will be required and other cycles discovered.

When the equations resulting from the actions of these causes are formed, and means of developing them arranged, the whole of the rest of the work comes under the domain of machinery. /

---

[a] 'On electric and magnetic rotation' (1826), *Works of Babbage*, Vol. 4.

CHAPTER XXXV

RESULTS OF SCIENCE

Board of Longitude – Professorship of Mathematics at the East India
College – Professorship of Mathematics at Edinburgh – Secretaryship of the
Royal Society – Master of the Mint – Ditto – Ditto – Registrar-General of
Births, Deaths, and Marriages – Ditto – Commissioner of Railways – Ditto –
Ditto abolished

At the commencement of life I had hoped that, whilst I indulged in
the pursuits of science, I might derive from it some advantages for my
family, or at least, that it might enable me to replace a small portion
of the large expenditure, without which one of my most important
discoveries could not be practically worked out.

I shall now mention briefly several of those appointments for which
I had the vanity to suppose myself qualified, and the simplicity to
believe that fitness for the office was of the slightest use without
interest to get the appointment.

1. In the early part of 1816 the Professorship of Mathematics at the
East India College at Haileybury became vacant. The salary, I
believe, was £500 a year. I became a candidate, and had strong
recommendations from Ivory and Playfair. I was informed that it was
usual for the candidates to call on the directors. I did so. One of them
was an honest man, for he was kind enough to tell me the truth. He
said, 'If you have interest, you will get it; if not, you will not
succeed.' /

2. In 1819 the Professorship of Mathematics at Edinburgh became
vacant by the death of Playfair, and the succession of Professor Leslie
to his chair. I immediately became a candidate, and received
testimony of my fitness from Lacroix, Biot, and Laplace.

These communications, though gratifying to myself, were useless
for the object. Not being a Scot, I was rejected at Edinburgh. That
visit, however, led to a very agreeable incident. I spent a delightful
week at Kinneil with Dugald Stewart. The second volume of his
'Philosophy of the Human Mind' had fortunately fallen into my hands

at an early period during my residence at Cambridge, and I had derived much instruction from that valuable work.

3. About this time, in a conversation with Sir Joseph Banks, I mentioned my wish to have a seat at the Board of Longitude – an office to which a salary of £100 a year was attached. Although not then appointed, hopes were held out by Sir Joseph that at some future occasion I might be more successful. In 1820 another vacancy occurred in the Board of Longitude. I called on Sir Joseph Banks to ask his influence with the Admiralty; this he declined, alleging as a reason for withholding it – the part I had taken in the institution of the Astronomical Society.

I was one of its founders, had been one of its first honorary secretaries, and had taken an active part in that committee, by which the 'Nautical Almanac' was remodelled.

4. In 1824 an opportunity unexpectedly presented itself. I was invited to take the entire organization and management of an office for the assurance of lives, then about to be established.

It is sufficient to state that amongst our officers were the late Marquis of Lansdowne, the late Lord Abercrombie, the / present Master of the Rolls, and the present Judge of the Admiralty Court; and that our direction included some of the first merchants in the City, two or three directors of the Bank of England, and about an equal number of India directors.

The proposition made to me was that I should have the entire management of the concern as director and actuary, with a salary of £1500 a year, and apartments in the establishment, with liberty to practise as an actuary.

On consulting my friend the late Francis Baily, F.R.S., who had himself practised as an actuary, he strongly advised me to accept the office. He assured me that the profit arising from private practice could scarcely be less than £1000 a year, and would probably be much more.

Under these circumstances, I accepted the proposition. On examining the materials which existed for a table of the value of lives, I found in one of the addresses of Mr Morgan, the actuary of the Equitable, materials with which to construct, by the aid of various calculations, a very tolerable table of the actual mortality in that society. Upon this basis I calculated the tables of our new institution. After three months' labour, when the whole of the arrangements had been completed, and the day for our opening had been fixed, circumstances occurred which induced us to give up the plan. After the experience I had now had of the amount of time occupied by such an office, I was unwilling to renew the engagement with other parties. I hoped by great exertions to complete the Difference Engine after the lapse of a few years, and that I should not be allowed to become a serious loser by that course.

The institution was therefore given up, and we each contributed about £100 to discharge the expenses incurred.

Within the subsequent twelvemonth, an application to take / the management of another life assurance society was made to me, which I declined. That office is still in existence.

The information and experience I had thus gained led me to think that the public were not sufficiently informed respecting the nature of assurances on lives, and that a small popular work on the subject might be useful. I prepared such a work as intervals of leisure admitted, and early in 1826 published it under the title of 'A Comparative View of the various Institutions for the Assurance of Lives'.[a] This little volume was soon translated into German, and became the groundwork upon which the Great Life Assurance Society of Gotha was founded. Every year since that event I have received a copy of the report of the state of the institution – a gratifying attention which I am happy to have this opportunity of acknowledging.

The wish expressed by my translator, in his preface,* has also been fulfilled by the establishment of many other excellent life assurance offices, founded on similar principles.

In Germany alone there were, in 1860, twenty-four life assurance companies, in which about 260,000 persons were assured to the amount of upwards of forty millions sterling. The oldest and most successful of these institutions have adopted my table of the Equitable experience, and I am informed that it agrees very well with the results of their own experience up to about the fifty-seventh year. After this the deaths are rather more frequent than those of the Equitable.

Another still more gratifying result arose. My father, whose acquaintance with mercantile affairs was very extensive, / was so

---

* May this book soon give rise to many flourishing life assurance companies in our beloved fatherland, by which proportionate wealth and happiness may be promoted amongst us, and at the same time prepare for the decline of lotteries.' *German translation of Babbage on Life Assurance.*

[a] *Works of Babbage*, Vol. 6

pleased with the little book that, during the two last years of his life, he read it through three times.

5. In 1846 the Mastership of the Mint became vacant. In former days it was held by Newton. I had pointed it out in 'The Decline of Science' as one of those offices to which men of science might reasonably aspire. A complete acquaintance with the most advanced state of mechanical science, which the demands of my own machinery had compelled me to improve, added to a knowledge of the internal economy of manufactories, appeared to me to constitute fair claims to that office.

In the event of my succeeding, I had proposed to let the whole of my salary accumulate, so that at the end of ten or twelve years I might retire from the office, and be enabled, with the £20,000 thus earned, to construct the Analytical Engine.

I wrote to Lord Melbourne on the subject, but I did not mention that circumstance even to my most intimate friends. It came, however, to the knowledge of one of them, who took a very warm interest in my success; and I believe that at first I had a very fair chance. The appointment remained for a short time in abeyance; but it was found necessary to detach Sheil from O'Connell, and the appointment was therefore given to Sheil.

Some years after, when Sheil was appointed our Minister at the court of Tuscany, he asked me to give him a letter of introduction to the Grand Duke Leopold II. Of course I treated the application as a joke; but Sheil assured me that he was quite serious, and that he knew it would be of use to him. I therefore gave him a letter of introduction to a sovereign from whom both before and subsequently I have been honoured by many gratifying attentions. /

6. In 1849, on the promotion of Sheil, the Mastership of the Mint again became vacant. I thought my own claims sufficiently known to the public; but I had no political interest. My friend Sir John Herschel was more fortunate, and he received the appointment.

7. After a few years, the office again became vacant by the resignation of Sir John Herschel. The Government had now for the third time an opportunity of partially repairing its former neglect. I had, however, no political party to support me, and the present Master of the Mint, Mr Graham, then received the appointment.

Registrar-General of Births, Deaths, etc.

8. In 1835 a new office was created, that of Registrar-General of

Births, Deaths, and Marriages. Mr Francis Baily and others of my friends suggested to me that, being known to the public as qualified for this situation by my previous publications, I had a fair claim to the appointment. Having made enquiries on this subject, I found that it would be useless to make any application, as the place was intended for the brother-in-law of a Secretary of State.

9. On the death of Mr Lister, a few years after, the same office again became vacant, when other friends then made a similar suggestion.

On making preliminary enquiries, I found, as before, that all applications would be useless, as the appointment was intended for a military officer, Major Graham, the brother of another Secretary of State.

Commissioners of Railways

10. Some years ago, the alarm created by accidents occurring upon railways, induced the Government to consider / about the appointment of a commission to examine into their causes, and to lay down rules for the guidance of the companies in the prevention of those dangers.

In 1846 an Act of Parliament was passed appointing commissioners for the supervision of railways. Having myself thought much upon the subject, and having had personally some experience on railways, I had the vanity to think that the mechanical knowledge of the author of 'The Economy of Manufactures' would justify his appointment as one of those commissioners.

Applying, under such circumstances, for a Commissionership of the Railway Board, I expected that I should find few competitors with higher claims. But I had no interest – a military engineer was appointed, who already held a civil appointment, and who died in less than two years after.

11. On the occurrence of this vacancy another military officer was appointed. I was again passed over, under circumstances which at the time I thought must have caused deep regret in the mind of the minister who made the appointment.

After an existence of a few years, public opinion was so strongly expressed against the Railway Commission that it was dissolved.

I am satisfied that in each of these cases, the appointment was entirely due to family or political influence.

I have, in the course of my experience, frequently heard of appointments made in the most flattering and unexpected manner; of titles offered, in fact, in such a way, that it was impossible to decline them. Having myself seen a good deal behind the scenes of the drama of life, I have repeatedly found that these unsolicited honours have been obtained by the most persevering applications, and by the most servile / flattery. Indeed, to the great scandal of public life, success has in some instances been attained by a man condescending for a time to oppose his own party, and, as some observer has wittily remarked, 'of attempting to break into the shop for the purpose of serving behind the counter'.

It cannot be doubted that patronage entrusted to the disposition of a minister often proves an onerous and ungrateful trust, demanding powers of discrimination and forbearance not always found in public men; whilst a careful observation of the manner in which patronage is usually dispensed does not lead to the conclusion that its exercise is always free from the influence of corrupt motives. Even in the cases in which such impure motives *seem* absent, it too frequently happens that other influences beside a just and honest discrimination appear to have taken a part in regulating the distribution of public favour. It would be invidious to speculate on the motives or discuss the merits of the appointments to which I have had occasion to refer: with their propriety or otherwise I have individually no concern: of the positive motives which induced them I have no knowledge, at least not sufficient to justify me in condemning them on that score. But I cannot help thinking that such appointments have not always been made without some degree of pain or misgiving, and perhaps a conscientious scruple on the part of the minister; indeed I have sometimes indulged a suspicion that a little firmness to resist external pressure would occasionally secure more fairness to candidates for public employment, and tend to retain the services of more efficient agents of the public weal.

Although mankind may differ amongst one another individually *ad infinitum*, they possess certain moral elements which are common to the race. Such belong to the animal, / and are never obliterated, though they may occasionally be concealed by the ermine of office or the robe of state. Self-interest is the great lever of society; and though the patriot profess to sacrifice it for the public good, or the cynic affect to despise its influence as opposed to his philosophy, both these may claim our respect, but neither should be permitted to deceive us.

A minister who professes to cast off the attributes of humanity is either a victim of delusion who has succeeded in deceiving himself, or a knave who is bent upon deceiving others. He may spurn the temptation of a bribe, because his wants do not lie in that direction; and, notwithstanding his generous pretensions, he will never discern merit unless accompanied by popular suffrage or political influence: in *his* balance one grain of *nepotism* will weigh down all the *honesty* he has at his disposal. /

CHAPTER XXXVI

AGREEABLE RECOLLECTIONS

In the course of this volume I have mentioned, under other heads, many agreeable circumstances, and many others remain unwritten. I shall now confine myself to two.

On one occasion when I was engaged in my workshop in arranging some machinery for experiments on a difficult part of the Analytical Engine, as intimate friend called, and I went into the library to see him. An unopened letter lying on the table, he asked whether I usually treated my letters in that way. I looked at the letter, which appeared to be a printed one. When my friend had left me, I opened it, and found that it professed to be from the Institute of France, announcing my nomination as a corresponding member of that distinguished body. On looking at the conclusion for the well-known signature of my friend Arago, I found another name which I could not read. I therefore concluded that some wag had played me a trick. I however doubted whether the joke was intended to hit me or the Academy of Sciences.

Having left the paper on my table, I returned to my experiments. After dinner I took up the neglected document, and then for the first time perceived that it professed to be from the Academy of Moral Sciences. On re-examining the signature, I found it to be that of its eminent secretary, / M. Mignet, and that it was the official announcement of my election as a Corresponding Member of that Academy.

Now the first impression on my own mind was one of sincere regret. I felt for a moment that the Academy might have thus honoured me not solely for my labours in their own, but in other departments of science. This painful feeling was, however, only momentary. It then occurred to me that I had written the 'Economy of Manufactures', which related to political economy, one section; and the 'Ninth Bridgewater Treatise', which related to philosophy, another section of the Academy of Moral Sciences. I now felt a real pleasure, which amply compensated me for the transitory regret; and I am sure no member of the many academies who have honoured me by enrolling my name on their list will reproach me for stating the fact – that no other nomination ever gave me greater satisfaction than the one to which I have now adverted.

Some years ago my eldest son, Mr B. Herschel Babbage, was employed by the Government of South Australia to explore and survey part of the north-western portion of that colony. After an absence of about six months, a considerable portion of which time he spent in a desert, he reached a small station at the head of Spencer's Gulf, intending to wait there until the arrival of a steamer from Adelaide, which was expected in about a week to carry back the wool of the distant and scattered colonists.

It so happened that, a few days before, a Swedish merchant-vessel, commanded by Captain Orling, a part-owner of the ship, had also arrived in search of a freight of wool. Captain Orling on going ashore heard of the arrival at the settlement of a stranger from the interior, and on enquiry found that he bore my name. /

He immediately went in search of my son, and having found him, said, 'I am not personally acquainted with your father, but I am well acquainted with his name: he has shown such kindness to a countryman of mine* that every Swede would be proud of an opportunity of acknowledging it. The steamer for which you are waiting cannot arrive until a week hence. There are no accommodations in this station, not even a public-house; I entreat you to come on board my ship and be my guest until the steamer arrives and is ready to take you to Adelaide.'

My son, who during the six previous months had slept under no canopy but that of heaven, accepted this delightful invitation, and enjoyed, during a week, the society of a very agreeable and highly-informed gentleman.

I have received many marks of attention of various kinds from natives of Sweden – paragraphs translated from Swedish newspapers which were peculiarly interesting to me, engravings, and printed volumes. I have been honoured with these attentions by persons in

---

* It had been my good fortune to have an opportunity of rendering justice to the merits of Mr Scheutz, the inventor of the Swedish Difference Engine.

various classes of society up to the highest, and I am confident that the enlightened and accomplished prince to whom I allude will not think me ungrateful when I avow that the most gratifying of all these attentions to a father, whose name in his own country has been useless to himself and to his children, was to hear from England's antipodes of a grateful Swede welcoming and giving hospitality on the part of his countrymen to my son for the sake of the name he bore. /

Conclusion

I will now conclude, as I began, by invoking the attention of my reader to a subject which, if he is young, may be of importance to him in after-life. He may reasonably ask what peculiarities of mind enabled me to accomplish what even the most instructed in their own sciences deemed impossible.

I have always carefully watched the exercise of my own faculties, and I have also endeavoured to collect from the light reflected by other minds some explanation of the question.

I think one of the most important guiding principles has been this: that every moment of my waking hours has always been occupied by *some train of enquiry*. In far the largest number of instances the subject might be simple or even trivial, but still work of enquiry, of some kind or other, was always going on.

The difficulty consisted in adapting the work to the state of the body. The necessary training was difficult. Whenever at night I found myself sleepless, and wished to sleep, I took a subject for examination that required little mental effort, and which also had little influence on worldly affairs by its success or failure.

On the other hand, when I wanted to concentrate my whole mind upon an important subject, I studied during the day all the minor accessories, and after two o'clock in the morning I found that repose which the nuisances of the London streets only allow from that hour until six in the morning.

At first I had many a sleepless night before I could thus train myself.

I believe my early perception of the immense power of signs in aiding the reasoning faculty contributed much to / whatever success I may have had. Probably a still more important element was the intimate conviction I possessed that the highest object a reasonable being could pursue was to endeavour to discover those laws of

364

mind by which man's intellect passes from the known to the discovery of the unknown.

This feeling was ever present to my own mind, and I endeavoured to trace its principle in the minds of all around me, as well as in the works of my predecessors. /

APPENDIX

Note (A), page 293

It has always occurred to my mind that many difficulties touching miracles might be reconciled, if men would only take the trouble to agree upon the nature of the phenomenon which they call 'miracle'. That writers do not always mean the same thing when treating of miracles is perfectly clear; because what may appear a miracle to the unlearned is to the better instructed only an effect produced by some unknown law hitherto unobserved. So that the idea of miracle is in some respect dependent upon the opinion of man. Much of this confusion has arisen from the definition of miracle given in Hume's celebrated essay,[a] namely, that it is the 'violation of a law of Nature'.

Now a miracle is not necessarily a violation of any law of Nature, and it involves no physical absurdity.

As Brown well observes, 'the laws of Nature surely are not violated when a new antecedent is followed by a new consequent; they are violated only when the antecedent, being exactly the same, a different consequent is the result'; so that a miracle has nothing in its nature inconsistent with our belief of the uniformity of Nature. All that we see in a miracle is an effect which is new to our observation, and whose cause is concealed.

The cause may be beyond the sphere of our observation, and would be thus beyond the familiar sphere of Nature; but this does not make the event a violation of any law of Nature. The limits of man's observation lie within very narrow boundaries, / and it would be arrogance to suppose that the reach of man's power is to form the limits of the natural world. The universe offers daily proof of the

---

[a] David Hume, 'An essay on miracles' in *Philosophical essays concerning human understanding* (1748, etc.).

existence of power of which we know nothing, but whose mighty agency nevertheless manifestly appears in the most familiar works of creation. And shall we deny the existence of this mighty energy simply because it manifests itself in delegated and feeble subordination to God's omnipotence?

There is nothing in the nature of a miracle that should render it incredible: its credibility depends upon the nature of the evidence by which it is supported. An event of extreme probability will not necessarily command our belief unless upon a sufficiency of proof; and so an event which we may regard as highly improbable may command our belief if it is sustained by sufficient evidence. So that the credibility or incredibility of an event does not rest upon the nature of the event itself, but depends upon the nature and sufficiency of the proof which sustains it.

Mill, in speaking of Hume's celebrated principle, 'that nothing is credible which is contradictory to experience, or at variance with the laws of Nature', calls it a very plain and harmless proposition, being, in effect, nothing more than that whatever is contradictory to a complete induction is incredible.

Admit the existence of a Deity, and the possibility of a miracle is the natural consequence. No doubt our examination of the evidence which sustains an unusual phenomenon should be most carefully conducted; but we must not measure the credibility or incredibility of an event by the narrow sphere of our own experience, nor forget that there is a Divine energy which overrides what we familiarly call the laws of Nature.

If a miracle is not a suspension or a violation of the laws of Nature, it may fairly be asked, What is it?

If we define a miracle as an effect of which the cause is unknown to us, then we make our ignorance the source of miracles! and the universe itself would be a standing miracle. / A miracle might be perhaps defined more exactly as an effect which is not the consequence or effect of any known laws of Nature. Dr Clarke defines a miracle as a singular event produced contrary to the ordinary laws of Nature by the intervention of an intelligent Being superior to man. The Abbé Houteville defines a miracle as the result of the general order of the mechanism of the universe. 'It is,' he says, 'a result of the harmony of the general laws which God has decreed for the working out of the system of the universe.' Spinosa says, 'As men call that science Divine which surpasses the reach of the human mind, so they detect the hand of God in every phenomenon of which the cause is unknown to them.' And certain it is that men attach more importance to an apparent suspension or violation of the ordinary laws of nature than to the wonderful harmony and uniformity of the laws of the universe; as though it implied a greater degree of power to suspend or interfere with such laws than to establish them and preserve their uniformity in the economy of the universe. Whilst nature follows out her ordinary course, man, familiarized with the movement of the celestial orbs, sees myriads of globes revolve in moving harmony about their spheres with a kind of vacant indifference, nor imagines for a moment that he sees aught to excite his wonder or stimulate his intelligence into enquiry; in fact, he does not see God in His works. But if this harmony and uniformity are interrupted for a moment, man detects the power of God in the interruption, albeit he could not perceive it in the uniformity of natural cause and effect. This singular obtuseness of the human mind I leave to the discussion of theologians and philosophers; for my own part, I confess my utter inability to comprehend it. Whatever truly exists must emanate from the will of God, whether the event falls within what we understand by the uniformity of nature, or whether it is otherwise. A miracle must fall within one of these categories; and in either case it is the effect of the will of God. Such an interruption does not imply any notion of caprice or imperfection in the Deity; but, on the contrary, it / is one of the attributes of His power, and quite consistent with our notions of the liberty of His will, unrestrained by any laws which it may be His pleasure to promulgate for the government of the universe.

'Opera mutat, consilia non mutat,'[a] says St Augustin. Miracles may be, for anything we know to the contrary, phenomena of a higher order of God's laws, superior to, and, under certain conditions, controlling the inferior order known to us as the ordinary laws of Nature.

The great difficulty in the consideration of miracles is, that being in the nature of things incapable of verification, the evidence which would be sufficient to establish the truth of an ordinary event within the sphere of natural phenomena would not be sufficient to command our assent in the case of a miracle. And this does not arise from a miracle being opposed to nature, but on account of the infirmity of

---

[a] *Translation:* He changes His works, He does not change His scheme.

our nature; for we are always liable to be deceived, not only by others, but even by our own senses.

The extraordinary character of an event, although it does not necessarily render the truth of its existence incredible, should, nevertheless, put us upon our guard, and render us particularly cautious in examining the evidence upon which its truth is asserted. We should even examine with care and caution the evidence of phenomena of the most ordinary character before we yield our complete assent to the apparent truth of their manifestation; and *à fortiori* in the examination of the evidence which sustains extraordinary phenomena we should require much stronger evidence, and such as rebuts the possibility of being deceived by other persons, or even by our senses.

But we must be careful to discriminate between our own incapacity to test truth and the necessary improbability of an event. It is plain that from our ignorance of the remote spheres of God's action we cannot judge of His works removed from our experience; but a fact is not necessarily doubtful because it cannot be reached by our ordinary senses. To recapitulate, we may lay down the following propositions: /

1. That there is no real physical distinction between miracles and any other operations of the Divine energy: that we regard them differently is because we are familiar with one order of events and not the other.

2. There is nothing incredible in a miracle, and the credibility of a miraculous event is to be measured only by the evidence which sustains it. And although the extraordinary character of a phenomenon may render the event itself improbable, it does not, therefore, necessarily render it either incredible or untrue.

RELIGION

Note (B), page 300

St Athanasius is not the author of the Creed which bears his name. It did not, in fact, exist within a century after his death. It originally appeared in a Latin text, and consequently in the Western provinces. Gennadius, Patriarch of Constantinople, was less tolerant of its eccentricities, or more sensible to its sublimity even than myself, for he was so amazed at the extraordinary character of its composition that he frankly pronounced it to be the work of a drunken man. See 'Petav. Dogmat. Theologica', tom. II, lvii, c. 8, p. 687; and Gibbon's 'Decline and Fall', vol. iv, p. 335. If we may trust La Bletterie for the character of Athanasius, nothing is more improbable than that he could be the author of the Creed still preserving his name. 'He was,' says La Bletterie, 'the greatest man of his age, and perhaps the greatest that the Church has ever possessed. He was endued with a well-balanced, a lively, and penetrating mind; a generous and disinterested heart; a courage and heroism always equal; a lively faith, and a charity without bounds; a profound humility; a Christianity bold, but simple and noble as the Gospel. His eloquence was natural, distinguished by a rare precision of speech.'

The foundation of all religion is the belief in a God, and that He exists in certain relation with His creatures. Such belief / necessarily leads to the consciousness of some obligation towards the Deity; and this consciousness suggests the duty of worship; and in the selection of the form of this worship originates the various creeds which distinguish and distract mankind. There is a sort of geography of religion; and I regret to think that the majority of mankind take their creed from the clime in which they happen to be born; and that many, and not an inconsiderable portion of mankind, suffer the sacred torch to burn out altogether, in their contact with the world, and then vainly imagine that they can recover the sacred fire by striking a spark out of dogmatic theology!

ADDITION TO THE CHAPTER ON RAILROADS

One of the most important facts which the engine-driver ought to know is the exact time since the preceding train has passed the point of railroad on which his own engine is.

This may be done by placing signals, about to be described, by the side of or across the road at all places where such knowledge is most important.

The principle to be employed is, that at the passage of those places the engine itself should, in its transit, wind up a weight or spring. That this weight should act upon an arm standing perpendicularly, which would immediately commence moving slowly to the horizontal position. This it should attain by an equable motion at the end of three, five, or any desirable number of minutes.

370

The means of raising the weight may be derived either from a projection below the engine or by one above it. The latter, which seems preferable, might be attached to a light beam traversing the road to which the apparatus should be fixed. /

LIST OF MR. BABBAGE'S PRINTED PAPERS.

Many applications having been made to the Author and to his Publishers, for detached Papers which he has from time to time printed, he takes this opportunity of giving a list of those Papers, with references to the Works in which they may be found.

1. The Preface; jointly with Sir John Herschel.

2. On Continued Products.

Memoirs of the Analytical Society. 4to. Cambridge, 1813.

3. An Essay towards the Calculus of Functions.—*Phil. Trans.* 1815.

4. An Essay towards the Calculus of Functions, Part. 2.—*Phil. Trans.* 1816. P. 179.

5. Demonstrations of some of Dr. Matthew Stewart's General Theorems, to which is added an Account of some New Properties of the Circle.—*Roy. Inst. Jour.* 1816. Vol. i. p. 6.

6. Observations on the Analogy which subsists between the Calculus of Functions and other branches of Analysis.—*Phil. Trans.* 1817. P. 179.

7. Solution of some Problems by means of the Calculus of Functions.—*Roy. Inst. Jour.* 1817. P. 371.

8. Note respecting Elimination.—*Roy. Inst. Jour.* 1817. P. 355.

9. An Account of Euler's Method of Solving a Problem relating to the Knight's Move at Chess.—*Roy. Inst. Jour.* 1817. P. 72.

10. On some new Methods of Investigating the Sums of several Classes of Infinite Series.—*Phil. Trans.* 1819. P. 245.

11. Demonstration of a Theorem relating to Prime Numbers.—*Edin. Phil. Jour.* 1819. P. 46.

12. An Examination of some Questions connected with Games of Chance. —*Trans. of Roy. Soc. of Edin.* 1820. Vol. ix. p. 153.

13. Observations on the Notation employed in the Calculus of Functions.— *Trans. of Cam. Phil. Soc.* 1820. Vol. i. p. 63.

14. On the Application of Analysis, &c. to the Discovery of Local Theorems and Porisms.—*Trans. of Roy. Soc. of Edin.* Vol. ix. p. 337. 1820.

15. Translation of the Differential and Integral Calculus of La Croix, 1 vol. 1816.

16. Examples to the Differential and Integral Calculus. 2 vols. 8vo. 1820.

These two works were executed in conjunction with the Rev. G. Peacock (Dean of Ely) and Sir John Herschel, Bart.

17. Examples of the Solution of Functional Equations. Extracted from the preceding. 8vo. 1820.

18. Note respecting the Application of Machinery to the Calculation of Mathematical Tables.—*Memoirs of the Astron. Soc.* June, 1822. Vol. i. p. 309.

19. A Letter to Sir H. Davy, P.R.S., on the Application of Machinery to the purpose of calculating and printing Mathematical Tables. 4to. July, 1822.

20. On the Theoretical Principles of the Machinery for calculating Tables. —*Brewster's Edin. Jour. of Science.* Vol. viii. p. 122. 1822.

21. Observations on the application of Machinery to the Computations of Mathematical Tables, Dec. 1822.—*Memoirs of Astron. Soc.* 1824. Vol. i. p. 311.

22. On the Determination of the General Term of a new Class of Infinite Series.—*Trans. Cam. Phil. Soc.* 1824. Vol. ii. p. 218.

23. Observations on the Measurement of Heights by the Barometer.—*Brewster's Edin. Jour. of Science*, 1824. P. 85.

24. On a New Zenith Micrometer.—*Mem. Astro. Soc.* March, 1825.

25. Account of the repetition of M. Arago's Experiments on the Magnetism manifested by various substances during Rotation. By C. Babbage, Esq. and Sir John Herschel.—*Phil. Trans.* 1825. P. 467.

26. On the Diving Bell.—*Ency. Metrop.* 4to. 1826.

27. On Electric and Magnetic Rotation.—*Phil. Trans.* 1826. Vol. ii. p. 494

28. On a method of expressing by Signs the Action of Machinery.—*Phil. Trans.* 1826. Vol. ii. p. 250.

29. On the Influence of Signs in Mathematical Reasoning.—*Trans. Cam. Phil. Soc.* 1826. Vol. ii. p. 218.

30. A Comparative View of the different Institutions for the Assurance of Life. 1 vol. 8vo. 1826. German Translation. Weimar, 1827.

31. On Notation.—*Edinburgh Encyclopedia.* 4to.

32. On Porisms.—*Edinburgh Encyclopedia.* 4to.

33. A Table of the Logarithms of the Natural Numbers, from 1 to 108,000. Stereotyped. 1 vol. 8vo. 1826.

34. Three editions on coloured paper, with the Preface and Instructions translated into German and Hungarian, by Mr. Chas. Nagy, have been published at Pesth and Vienna. 1834.

35. Notice respecting some Errors common to many Tables of Logarithms. —*Mem. Astron. Soc.* 4to. 1827. Vol. iii. p. 65.

Evidence on Savings-Banks, before a Committee of the House of Commons, 1827.

36. Essay on the general Principles which regulate the Application of Machinery.—*Ency. Metrop.* 4to. 1829.

37. Letter to T. P. Courtenay on the Proportion of Births of the two Sexes amongst Legitimate and Illegitimate Children.—*Brewster's Edin. Jour. of Science.* Vol. ii. p. 85. 1829. This letter was translated into French and published by M. Villermé, Member of the Institute of France.

38. Account of the great Congress of Philosophers at Berlin, on 18 Sept. 1828.—Communicated by a Correspondent [C. B.]. *Edin. Journ. of Science by David Brewster.* Vol. x. p. 225. 1829.

39. Note on the Description of Mammalia.—*Edin. Jour. of Science*, 1829. Vol. i. p. 187. *Ferussac Bull*, vol. xxv. p. 296.

40. Reflections on the Decline of Science in England, and on some of its Causes. 4to. and 8vo. 1830.

41. Sketch of the Philosophical Characters of Dr. Wollaston and Sir H. Davy. Extracted from the *Decline of Science*. 1830.

42. On the Proportion of Letters occurring in Various Languages, in a letter to M. Quételet.—*Correspondence Mathematique et Physique.* Tom. vi. p. 136.

43. Specimen of Logarithmic Tables, printed with different coloured inks and on variously-coloured papers, in twenty-one volumes 8vo. London. 1831.

The object of this Work, of which *one single copy only* was printed, is to ascertain by experiment the tints of the paper and colours of the inks least fatiguing to the eye.

One hundred and fifty-one variously-coloured papers were chosen, and the same two pages of my stereotype Table of Logarithms were printed upon them in inks of the following colours: light blue, dark blue, light green, dark green, olive, yellow, light red, dark red, purple, and black.

Each of these twenty volumes contains papers of the same colour, numbered in the same order, and there are two volumes printed with each kind of ink.

The twenty-first volume contains metallic printing of the same specimen in gold, silver, and copper, upon vellum and on variously-coloured papers.

For the same purpose, about thirty-five copies of the complete table of logarithms were printed on thick drawing paper of various tints.

An account of this work may be found in the *Edin. Journ. of Science* (*Brewster's*), 1832. Vol. vi. p. 144.

44. Economy of Manufactures and Machinery. 8vo. 1832.

There are many editions and also American reprints, and several Translations of this Work into German, French, Italian, Spanish, &c.

45. Letter to Sir David Brewster, on the Advantage of a Collection of the Constants of Nature and Art.—*Brewster's Edin. Jour. of Science.* 1832. Vol. vi. p. 334. Reprinted by order of the British Association for the Promotion of Science. Cambridge, 1833. See also pp. 484, 490, Report of the Third Meeting of the British Association. Reprinted in Compte Rendu des Travaux du Congres Général de Statistique, Bruxelles, Sept. 1853.

46. Barometrical Observations, made at the Fall of the Staubbach, by Sir John Herschel, Bart., and C. Babbage, Esq.—*Brewster's Edin. Jour. of Science.* Vol. vi. p. 224. 1832.

47. Abstract of a Paper, entitled Observations on the Temple of Serapis, at Pozzuoli, near Naples ; with an attempt to explain the causes of the frequent elevation and depression of large portions of the earth's surface in remote periods, and to prove that those causes continue in action at the present time. Read at Geological Society, 12 March, 1834. See *Abstract of Proceedings of Geol. Soc.* Vol. ii. p. 72.

This was the first *printed* publication of Mr. Babbage's Geological Theory of the Isothermal Surfaces of the Earth.

48. The Paper itself was published in the *Proceedings of the Geological Soc.* 1846.

49. Reprint of the same, with Supplemental Conjectures on the Physical State of the Surface of the Moon. 1847.

50. Letter from Mr. Abraham Sharpe to Mr. J. Crosthwait, Hoxton, 2 Feb. 1721–22. Deciphered by Mr. Babbage. See *Life of Flamsteed*, by Mr. F. Baily. Appendix, pp. 348, 390. 1835.

51. The Ninth Bridgewater Treatise. 8vo. May, 1837; Second Edition, Jan. 1838.

52. On some Impressions in Sandstone.—*Proceedings of Geological Society.* Vol. ii. p. 439. Ditto, *Phil. Mag.* Ser. 3. Vol. x. p. 474. 1837.

52*. Short account of a method by which Engraving on Wood may be rendered more useful for the Illustration and Description of Machinery.—*Report of Meeting of British Association at Newcastle.* 1838. P. 154.

53. Letter to the Members of the British Association. 8vo. 1839.

54. General Plan, No. 25, of Mr. Babbage's Great Calculating or Analytical Engine, lithographed at Paris. 24 by 36 inches. 1840.

55. Statement of the circumstances respecting Mr. Babbage's Calculating Engines. 8vo. 1843.

56. Note on the Boracic Acid Works in Tuscany.—*Murray's Handbook of Central Italy.* First Edition, p. 178. 1843.

57. On the Principles of Tools for Turning and Planing Metals, by Charles Babbage. Printed in the Appendix of Vol. ii. Holtzapffel Turning and Mechanical Manipulation. 1846.

58. On the Planet Neptune.—*The Times*, 15th March, 1847.

59. Thoughts on the Principles of Taxation, with reference to a Property Tax and its Exceptions. 8vo. 1848. Second Edition, 1851. Third Edition, 1852.

An Italian translation of the first edition, with notes, was published at Turin, in 1851.

60. Note respecting the pink projections from the Sun's disc observed during the total solar eclipse in 1851.—*Proceedings of the Astron. Soc.*, vol. xii., No. 7.

61. Laws of Mechanical Notation, with Lithographic Plate. Privately printed for distribution. 4to. July, 1851.

62. Note respecting Lighthouses (Occulting Lights). 8vo. Nov. 1851. Communicated to the Trinity House, 30 Nov. 1851.
Reprinted in the Appendix to the Report on Lighthouses presented to the Senate of the United States, Feb. 1852.
Reprinted in the *Mechanics' Magazine*, and in various other periodicals and newspapers. 1852–3.
It was reprinted in various parts of the Report of Commissioners appointed to examine into the state of Lighthouses. Parliamentary Paper. 1861.

63. The Exposition of 1851 ; or, Views of the Industry, the Science, and the Government of England. *6s. 6d.* Second Edition, 1851.

64. On the Statistics of Light-houses. Compte Rendu des Traveaux du Congres Général, Bruxelles, Sept. 1853.

65. A short description of Mr. Babbage's Ophthalmoscope is contained in the Report on the Ophthalmoscope by T. Wharton Jones, F.R.S.—*British and Foreign Medical Review.* Oct. 1854. Vol. xiv. p. 551.

66. On Secret or Cipher Writing. Mr. T.'s Cipher Deciphered by C.—*Jour. Soc. Arts*, July, 1854, p. 707.

67. On Mr. T.'s Second Inscrutable Cipher Deciphered by C.—*Jour. Soc. Arts*, p. 777, Aug. 1854.

68. On Submarine Navigation.—*Illustrated News*, 23rd June, 1855.

69. Letter to the Editor of the *Times*, on Occulting Lights for Lighthouses and Night Signals. Flashing Lights at Sebastopol. 16th July, 1855.

70. On a Method of Laying Guns in a Battery without exposing the men to the shot of the enemy. *The Times*, 8 Aug., 1855.

71. Sur la Machine Suédoise de M. Scheutz pour Calculer les Tables Mathématiques. 4to. *Comptes Rendus et l'Académie des Sciences.* Paris, Oct. 8, 1855.

72. On the Action of Ocean-currents in the Formation of the Strata of the Earth. —*Quarterly Journal Geological Society*, Nov. 1856.

73. Observations by Charles Babbage, on the Mechanical Notation of Scheutz's Difference Engine, prepared and drawn up by his Son, Major Henry Prevost Babbage, addressed to the Institution of Civil Engineers. *Minutes of Proceedings*, vol. xv. 1856.

74. Statistics of the Clearing-House. Reprinted from *Trans. of Statistical Soc.* 8vo. 1856.

75. Observations on Peerage for Life. July, 1833. Reprinted, 1856.

76. Observations addressed to the President and Fellows of the Royal Society on the Award of their Medals for 1856. 8vo.

77. Table of the Relative Frequency of Occurrence of the Causes of Breaking Plate-glass Windows.—*Mech. Mag.* 24th Jan. 1857.

78. On Remains of Human Art, mixed with the Bones of Extinct Races of Animals. *Proceedings of Roy. Soc.* 26th May, 1859.

79. Passages from the Life of a Philosopher. 8vo. 1864.

80. [In the press]. History of the Analytical Engine. 4to. It will contain Chapters V., VI., VII., and VIII., of the present Volume. Reprint of The Translation of General Menabrea's Sketch of the Analytical Engine invented by Charles Babbage. From the *Bibliothèque Universelle de Genève*, No. 82, Oct. 1842. Translated by the late Countess of Lovelace, with extensive Notes by the Translator.

INDEX

378

379

King's College, London 72n, 112, 114, 125

labour, division of 327–8
Lacroix, S. F. (1765–1843), French mathematician 28, 355
Differential and integral calculus 19, 20
Lagrange, J. L. (1736–1813), French mathematician *Theorie des fonctions* 19
Lamb, William, Viscount Melbourne (1779–1848), statesman 66, 68, 70, 71, 358
Langdale, Lord *see* Bickersteth, Henry
languages 18
Lansdowne, marquis of *see* Petty-Fitzmaurice, Henry
Laplace, P. S. de (1749–1827), French physicist 103, 145, 355
Lardner, D. (1793–1859), scientific popularist 34–5, 103, 117, 242, 244
Lawrence, Thomas (1769–1830), painter 158
Lax, William (1761–1836), astronomer 24
Le Verrier, U. J. J. (1811–77), French astronomer 103, 277
Leibniz, G. W. (1646–1716), German philosopher notation of fluxions 19, 20, 27
Lemon, Charles 325
Leopold II, grand duke of Tuscany 323–4, 356
Leslie, Hon (1766–1832), mathematician and natural philosopher 355
life assurance, CB's work trans. into German 357
life assurance companies 356–8
light, occulting 340–2
lighthouses 245, 341
Lister, Thomas Henry (1800–42), novelist 359
Liverpool 225
  Manchester–L. railway 234–5
Lloyd, Humphrey (1800–81), provost of Trinity College, Dublin and man of science 290
locks and keys 173–4
London
  beggars 180–6
  earthquake 165–6

street musicians 253–71
Lovelace, Lady *see* King, Ada Augusta
Lunn, Francis (1795–1839), chemist 22
Lyndhurst, Lord *see* Copley, John Singleton

MacCullagh, James (1809–47), mathematician 90–1, 98
Maclaurin, C. (1698–1746), Scottish mathematician 19
Maclean, Revd, Dean of Trinity College, Dublin 294, 295
Mahon, Viscount (Lord Standhope) 116
Malthus, Thomas (1766–1834), political economist 290, 325
Manchester
  statue of Dalton 219–20
manufactures
  gold chains 280–1
  needles 328
manufacturing processes and mechanical operations
  glass cutting 282–6
  ice making 335–6
Marryat, Frederick (1792–1848), naval captain and novelist 14, 15
mathematical science
  calculus of functions 327
  Cambridge curriculum 19
  notation of fluxions 19–21
  triangular numbers 37–42
mathematical tables
  method of differences 35–42
  triangular numbers 39
  printing of 32–4
Maule, Frederick 21
Mechanical Notation 79, 86, 105, 107–10, 117
Melbourne, Lord *see* Lamb, William
Menabrea, L. F. (1809–96), Italian general and statesman 77, 98, 101–2
Mensdorf, Count 126–8
Mill, John Stuart (1806–73), philosopher 367
Minchin, James, barrister 197–9
mines, Wales 166–8
Mitscherlich, E. (1794–1863), Prussian chemist 340
Moll, G. (1785–1838), Dutch scientist 167, 168
Monk, James Henry (1784–1856),

381

bishop of Gloucester and Bristol 221

monopolies 331

Morgan, William (1750–1833), actuary 356

Morland, Samuel (1625–95), mathematician 116

Mosotti, O. F., Italian physicist 98, 99

Murray, John (1778–1843), bookseller and publisher 138–40

Napier, Charles James (1782–1853) conqueror of Scinde 129–30, 131

National Art Gallery, London 250n

Nautical Almanac 104

Nicolas, Sir Harris (1799–1848), antiquary 53

observatories
Dudley, Albany, NY 35

Oken, L. (1799–1851), German philosopher 324

Orling, Captain, Swedish merchant 361

Oxford University 220

Palmerston, viscount *see* Temple, Henry John

Parsons, William (Lord Oxmantown, 3rd earl of Rosse) (1800–67), president of the Royal Society 75–83 *passim*

patronage 358–9

Peacock, George (1791–1858), mathematician and dean of Ely Cathedral 21, 23, 25, 28–9

Peel, Robert (1788–1850), statesman 71–3

Petty-Fitzmaurice, Henry, 3rd marquis of Lansdowne, politician 326, 329

Plana, G. (1781–1864), Italian mathematician 97, 98, 105

Plantamour, E., Italian scientist 98

Playfair, John (1748–1818), political economist 355

Plymouth, Devon, CB tries the diving bell 154

Poisson, S. D. (1781–1840), French mathematician 146

political economy 325–31

Pontéculant, G. de, French astronomer 105

postal services 336–8

prices
retail 328
verification 337–8

proteus anguineus 291

Prussia, Congress of Philosophers (1828) 148–9, 324

Quetelet, L. A. J. (1796–1874), Belgian statistician 325–7

railways
CB's broad gauge experiments 239–40
CB's safety devices 237–8, 245–8, 370–1
commissioners 359
monopolize best draughtsmen 86
opening of Liverpool–Manchester 234–6

Registrar General 114, 358–9

religion 297–304

Robinson, Frederick James, viscount Goderich and earl of Ripon (1782–1859), politician 54, 56–7

Robison, John (1778–1855), inventor 324

Rogers, Samuel (1763–1855), poet 2, 86, 141–3

Rogers, Miss 141

Rosse, earl of *see* Parsons, William

Royal Astronomical Society 109

Royal Mint 358

Royal Society of London
Difference Engine 54, 57, 76–83, 113
CB not elected secretary 138–40

Rue, Warren de la (1815–99), inventor 191n

Russian
interest in CB's mechanical notation 116n

Ryan, Edward (1792–1875), judge 21, 127

St Leu, comte de 151

Scheutz, P. G. Swedish printer and inventor 35, 82, 113–15, 117, 120

science, miracles and 290–3, 331, 366–9

scientific discoveries and observations
air shot 159
fire damp 167–8

scientific equipment and inventions
barometer 161–2
chronometer 347

382